Rude & Barbarous Kingdom

RUDE & BARBAROUS KINGDOM

Russia in the Accounts of Sixteenth-Century English Voyagers

Edited by Lloyd E. Berry and Robert O. Crummey

The University of Wisconsin Press
Madison, Milwaukee, and London, 1968

Published by
The University of Wisconsin Press
Box 1379, Madison, Wisconsin 53701
The University of Wisconsin Press, Ltd.
27–29 Whitfield Street, London, W.1

Printed in the United States of America by the
George Banta Company, Inc., Menasha, Wisconsin
Library of Congress Catalog Card Number 68–16059

Contents

v

Illustrations

General Introduction

When the Elizabethan era came to a close, Muscovy had a secure place in the ordinary Englishman's view of the world. Crowds in London gathered to gape when the arrival of a Russian ambassador and his suite provided a show of oriental splendor.[1] In hours of leisure, men read paeans of praise to the mariners who braved the Arctic storms to sail to Muscovy and the travelers' own stories of their adventures at sea and descriptions of the strange sights that greeted them in the domains of the tsar.[2]

Yet in spite of the intensity of Englishmen's interest in Russia and the remarkable quantity of literature that appeared in the second half of the sixteenth century to satisfy their curiosity, Muscovy remained, in English minds, as exotic as the lands of the Far East or the New World. It is perhaps significant that the best-known allusion to Rus-

1. See, for example, the references to the appearance of Muscovite ambassadors in N. E. McClure (ed.), *The Letters of John Chamberlain*, Vol. XII of *Memoirs of the American Philosophical Society* (1939).
2. On the treatment of Russia in sixteenth-century English literature, see Karl Heinz Ruffmann, *Das Russlandbild im England Shakespeares* (Göttingen, 1952), esp. pp. 145–73.

sians in Elizabethan literature, the "masque of the Muscovites" in Shakespeare's *Love's Labour's Lost,* concerns the romantic ploy of gentlemen of Navarre who disguised themselves in the strange costumes of Russians and could as conveniently have wooed their ladies as barbarous Turks or heathen Chinee.[3] Shakespeare's scene betrays the same superficial view of Russian customs as Henry VIII's similar masquerade in 1510, many years before the voyages that laid the foundation for close contact between the two nations.[4]

That Englishmen found Muscovy mysterious after half a century of diplomatic and commercial contact is scarcely surprising considering the differences of language, religion, political and social structure, and style of life that separated the two countries; Muscovite diplomats at Elizabeth's court found England just as strange.[5] The blend of comfortable familiarity and incredulity in Englishmen's reaction to Russian ways is also, in part, the result of the limited nature of their contacts with the Muscovite state.

England and Muscovy met in the market place. Impelled by the desire to find new markets for English goods and the gnawing awareness that the Spanish and Portuguese were far ahead in the race to exploit the riches of the New World and the Far East, a group of London merchants sponsored a venture that sent three ships out in 1553 to find a sea route along the northern coasts of Europe and Asia to China. The poignant story of the expedition is well-known: unaccustomed to the rigors of the northern climate, Sir Hugh Willoughby, the commander, and the crews of two of his ships perished when autumn storms forced them to winter on the barren Arctic coast. The third vessel, under the command of Richard Chancellor, took refuge in the White Sea and unwittingly landed in the domains of Ivan IV, the tsar of Muscovy. Ivan and his unexpected guest quickly recognized that their fortuitous encounter offered advantages to both. Ivan, buoyed up by his recent conquest of the khanate of Kazan', welcomed the chance to establish ties with a western European power; Chancellor was in search of opportunities for trade and Muscovy, although a far cry from the fabled

3. William Shakespeare, *Love's Labour's Lost,* V, ii, 79–265.

4. Raphael Holinshed, *The Chronicles of England, Scotland, and Ireland* (London, 1587), III, 805; Ruffman, *Das Russlandbild im England Shakespeares,* pp. 171–72.

5. For the reactions of Russian ambassadors to English life and customs, see the official reports of F. A. Pisemskii (1582–83) ond G. I. Mikulin (1600–1601) in D. S. Likhachev, Ia. S. Lur'e, and R. B. Miuller (eds.), *Puteshestviia russkikh poslov XVI–XVII vv.* (Moscow-Leningrad, 1954), pp. 100–205.

lands of the East, offered rewards of its own and the hope that its
roads and waterways would bring English traders into the heart of
Asia. When he sailed home after a lavish welcome, Chancellor carried
the tsar's charter granting English merchants full freedom to trade in
his domains. It was the beginning of almost a century of Anglo-Russian
entente.

England's relations with Russia in the second half of the sixteenth
century were less an *entente cordiale* than a contest of adroitness and
strength of will between two master diplomats—Queen Elizabeth, cautious and hard-headed, and Ivan IV, mercurial and melodramatic.
From Elizabeth's point of view, Muscovy presented a limited but valuable opportunity for trade. Of particular importance was the fact that
her merchants found Russia an ideal source of naval stores, since the
price of rope and tar was lower than in Danzig and the northern sea
route, in spite of its hazards, was less vulnerable to blockade by a hostile power than the Baltic.[6] The queen's goals in her dealings with Ivan
and his successors were clear and she never lost sight of them: each of
her ambassadors had orders to win for English traders as generous
trading rights and tax concessions as possible, to make sure that the
Russia Company, which had been chartered in 1554 to exploit the opportunities opened up by Chancellor's voyage, enjoyed a monopoly
over English trade with Russia, and, if possible, to secure for her subjects a monopoly over Muscovy's overseas trade that would exclude
traders from other maritime powers of western Europe.

Ivan's goals were more complex and shifted with his changes of
mood and the ebb and flow of his fortunes in the war for control of the
Baltic littoral. Trade with England was important for its own sake. Besides England's principal export, cloth, the Russia Company's merchants brought to Russia metal products and chemicals such as saltpeter and sulphur for the manufacture of munitions.[7] The English traders
were useful, moreover, because their expeditions across Russia to Persia did business on Ivan's behalf as well as their own.[8] Looking beyond
the clear economic and strategic advantages of the trade, the tsar at

6. The best study of Anglo-Russian trade in the sixteenth century is T. S.
Willan, *The Early History of the Russia Company, 1553–1603* (Manchester, 1956).

7. The regime of Tsar Fedor took particular pains to ensure that the Company
provided sufficient quantities of these strategic materials. See *Sbornik Imperatorskago russkago istoricheskago obshchestva* (St. Petersburg, 1867–1916), XXXVIII,
203; Lloyd E. Berry (ed.), *The English Works of Giles Fletcher, the Elder* (Madison, 1964), p. 374.

8. Willan, *Early History*, p. 58.

times seemed to see the indistinct shape of even greater benefits in his ties with England. The island kingdom, far beyond the barrier that the Polish-Lithuanian commonwealth and Sweden built along Muscovy's western frontier, was often the focus of his hopes and fantasies. On occasion Ivan went to great lengths to ensure that, should his subjects rise and overthrow him, he could take refuge in England. In such moods his greatest disappointment was Elizabeth's refusal to address to him a similar request for sanctuary. On two occasions, between 1568 and 1572 and again between 1579 and 1584 when he suffered devastating defeats in the struggle for Livonia, the tsar tried to cajole the queen into entering a full military alliance. In retrospect, it is difficult to imagine how a military alliance with England, predominantly a naval power, could have helped him stave off defeat in a land war in northeastern Europe. Yet, in the face of a military disaster, it was reasonable to canvass every possible source of support, no matter how unpromising.

Throughout the changing winds of Ivan's diplomacy, Elizabeth adamantly pursued her clear and limited objectives. When Ivan sharpened his requests for an alliance with threats that he would cancel the Russia Company's trading privileges, her ambassadors did not yield and, after many stormy scenes, the tsar, more actor than madman, recognized the futility of his dreams and settled for continuation of limited but profitable commercial ties.[9]

After Ivan's death in 1584, the roles were reversed: Elizabeth became the suitor and the new Muscovite government, with Ivan's son Fedor on the throne and Boris Godunov at the helm, the object of her courting. Godunov regarded England as a valuable trading partner but saw no reason why he should not do business with the Dutch traders who frequented Russia's northern ports. For a time the queen protested that since her subjects had been first to make extensive use of the northern sea route, they deserved a full monopoly over Muscovy's northern commerce. Once she had tested the determination of the new regime, however, she retreated gracefully and contented herself with

9. On Anglo-Russian relations in the sixteenth century, see Willan, *Early History;* I. Liubimenko, *Les relations commerciales et politiques de l'Angleterre avec la Russie avant Pierre le Grand* (Paris, 1933), pp. 19–78; and Ia. S. Lur'e's brilliant article "Russko-angliiskie otnosheniia i mezhdunarodnaia politika vtoroi poloviny XVI v.," *Mezhdunarodnye sviazi Rossii do XVII v.* (Moscow, 1961), pp. 419–43.

concessions that left the Russia Company with the most advantageous position in the newly-opened competition for control of Russia's overseas trade.[10]

The Russia Company's privileged position served as a gateway through which many Englishmen came to Russia in the latter half of the sixteenth century. English mariners probed the northern coast of Russia in search of the northeast passage to the Orient, traders and apprentices manned the Company's factories within the tsar's domains, and the queen's ambassadors visited his court to negotiate on the Company's behalf. By the end of the century, Elizabeth's subjects had accumulated a store of experience of Muscovite life and customs far richer than that of any other European nation.

Muscovy was the first distant and exotic land open to the scrutiny of Englishmen. Many who served there were fascinated by what they saw and, in an age when their countrymen were ravenously eager for travel literature, could not resist the urge to share their experiences with the reading public. Their writings were numerous and vary in scope from brief travel diaries to Giles Fletcher's celebrated analysis of Muscovite institutions and society. For this volume we have selected the principal works of six men—Richard Chancellor,[11] Anthony Jenkinson,[12] Thomas Randolph, George Turberville, Fletcher, and Jerome Horsey. The texts record observations made over a period of nearly four decades, from Chancellor's fortuitous landfall until Horsey's expulsion in 1591, by men of differing origins and tastes—Chancellor and Jenkinson, sea captains and explorers, Randolph, a seasoned diplomat, Turberville, poet and man of fashion, Fletcher, a scholar in public life, and Horsey, an adventurer in business and diplomacy. Together they present the most

---

10. In the first half of the seventeenth century, the Dutch gradually ousted the English traders from their preeminent position and, by 1649 when Tsar Alexis revoked the special privileges of the Russia Company and placed severe restrictions on its operations in a gesture of retaliation for the execution of Charles I, Anglo-Russian trade had all but come to a halt (Liubimenko, *Les relations commerciales et politiques*, p. 198. See also Miss Liubimenko's article "The Struggle of the Dutch with the English for the Russian Market in the Seventeenth Century," *Transactions of the Royal Historical Society*, Series IV, Vol. VII, 27–51).

11. We have chosen the expanded version of Chancellor's account, that related to Clement Adams, because it combines Chancellor's observations with an account of the formation of the Russia Company.

12. Jenkinson travelled to Russia on four separate occasions. We have decided to include the account of his first voyage because it gives his first and most extensive observations on Russia.

thorough and diversified foreign picture of the landscape, institutions, and customs of Muscovy in the late sixteenth century.

Their testimony is of particular significance because it supplements the relatively laconic Russian sources on the reigns of Ivan IV and Fedor. Since the great general histories of Russia by Karamzin and Solov'ev, most scholars have found it impossible to deal with the politics, economics, and social life of the period without placing considerable reliance on the information provided by European travelers and diplomats of several nationalities. To do so is a treacherous, although necessary, undertaking. Perceptive foreign writings on any society are usually prized for the acuity and freshness of their comments on its institutions and personalities and for their attention to the details of topography and daily life that, because of their very familiarity, might well escape the notice of native commentators. By the same token, native sources ought to be more reliable guides to the structure and function of the government and society. Yet, because of scarcity of Russian documents, especially for the last two decades of Ivan's reign, historians have been forced to rely on the foreign accounts of the period even for the kinds of information that native sources ought logically to provide. The writings in this volume, for example, present unique testimony on subjects ranging from the tsar's relations with the church and the operations of his council to the details of his wardrobe.

The works of the English travelers throw light of varying quality and intensity on each period of Muscovite history from the early years of Ivan's majority until the Time of Troubles at the beginning of the seventeenth century. If a single person dominates their collected writings, it is the figure of Ivan IV. His portrait evolves from the shadowy, yet dignified and confident, prince of Chancellor's and Jenkinson's accounts through the enigmatic diplomat whom Randolph met to the overpowering personality who usurped the center stage in the works of Fletcher and Horsey, written in the time of his successors. Their contrasting assessments of his policies are a just measure of the complexity of a historical figure who remains fascinating and still refuses to submit to the interpretative categories in which historians have attempted to capture him.[13]

13. The most useful biography of Ivan IV in English is still the somewhat dated work of K. Waliszewski, *Ivan the Terrible* (London, 1904; new printing, Hamden, Conn., 1966). The recent study of B. Nørretranders, *The Shaping of Czar-*

Ivan's politics receive uneven treatment in the works of the English visitors to his court. His greatest achievements of the 1550's, the conquest of Kazan' and Astrakhan' and the reforms of the army, the judicial system, and the conduct of local administration, are barely mentioned in the collection. As the first Englishmen to visit Muscovy, Chancellor and Jenkinson gave their attention to the features of landscape, trade, judicial practice, military operations, and court ceremony that first caught their eye; they make no mention at all of the tsar's domestic policies and, if they were aware of his reforms, they probably lacked the knowledge of Muscovy's history needed to appreciate their significance.[14]

The *oprichnina* occupies a more important place in the English picture of Muscovy. In 1565, in a gesture that confused Ivan's contemporaries as much as it puzzles historians, the tsar divided the Muscovite state into two parts, took one of them as his private domain, and manned it with a special military force in whose members he had complete confidence.[15] From his new stronghold, he launched a campaign of terror against those of his subjects whom he suspected of treason. Oddly enough the English descriptions of the oprichnina are not the work of Randolph and Turberville, the writers who visited Moscow at the time of its operations. Its impact on Muscovite society was so profound, however, that Fletcher and Horsey described its functions at some length because it was the inescapable precursor of the events of which they were themselves witnesses. And their descriptions are significant precisely as a measure of that impact rather than as a source of detailed information about the tsar's experiment.[16] Fletcher and Horsey likewise give an account of a somewhat similar episode, the strange

---

dom under Ivan Groznyj (Copenhagen, 1964), presents a subtle analysis of Ivan's political philosophy and a provocative interpretation of the tsar's personality and policies. Ivan's letters to Prince Kurbskii, the most revealing of his writings, are available in J. L. I. Fennell's excellent translation in *The Correspondence between Prince A. M. Kurbsky and Tsar Ivan IV of Russia, 1564–1579* (Cambridge, 1955).

14. On the reform period of Ivan's reign, see A. A. Zimin, *Reformy Ivana Groznogo* (Moscow, 1960).

15. On the oprichnina, see S. B. Veselovskii's brilliant collection of essays, *Issledovaniia po istorii oprichniny* (Moscow, 1963) and Zimin's *Oprichnina Ivana Groznogo* (Moscow, 1964).

16. The best contemporary account of the oprichnina is contained in the work of the German adventurer, Heinrich von Staden, *Aufzeichnungen über den Moskauer Staat*, ed. F. T. Epstein (Hamburg, 1964). The English translation is the work of Thomas Esper, *The Land and Government of Muscovy* (Stanford, 1967).

reign of Simeon Bekbulatovich, a converted Tatar whom Ivan placed on
the throne in his stead in the fall of 1575 and removed slightly less
than a year later. Once again their opinions have greater historical interest than their data, although, in this instance, most scholars are inclined to doubt their assessment of Ivan's motives in staging the cha-
rade.

The works of Fletcher and Horsey excel in their treatment of the
reign of Fedor.[17] Horsey's colorful story of Ivan's death and his son's
accession captures, with particular vividness, the mood of uncertainty
that gripped courtiers who had just lost a powerful master and were
not sure how to deal with his weak successor. His *Travels* continue by
recording the courtiers' struggle for influence which resulted in the victory of Boris Godunov. Fletcher's study of Muscovite institutions com-
pletes the picture by providing an unsurpassed description of the state
of the court and administration after Godunov had consolidated his position. In *Of the Russe Commonwealth*, there are insights into the characters of Fedor and Boris and precise information on Godunov's private wealth and role in public life. After 1589, however, the quality of
the English record of Russia declines precipitously. Even though Horsey continued his narrative up to the election of Mikhail Romanov as
tsar in 1613, his account of the events of the 1590's and after is neither
trustworthy nor particularly interesting.

As one might expect, the English writers were most successful in de-
picting the surface of Muscovite life. Their works are full of sharp and
vivid observations on a multitude of subjects—topography, trade, government and judicial system, court life, popular customs, and even
prevalent political gossip. Their diligence and perceptiveness as tourists overcame all obstacles except the geographical limits placed upon
them by the nature of their business in Russia and the feeling of
strangeness in a country whose customs were so unlike those of England. As diplomats and agents of the Russia Company, their commissions took them to northern Russia and Moscow and, as a consequence,
their general observations on the state of the Muscovite economy and
the style of life of the people should perhaps be viewed as comments

17. The classic study of the reigns of Fedor and Boris Godunov is S. F. Platonov,
Boris Godunov (Petrograd, 1921; French translation, Paris, 1929). See also
Platonov's *Ocherki po istorii smuty v moskovskom gosudarstve XVI–XVII vv.*
(St. Petersburg, 1910).

on the north rather than on the country as a whole. Even Fletcher, a voracious collector of facts and figures, learned a good deal more about the central and northern regions than the southern borderlands. And Fletcher, drawing on nearly forty years of English experience in Russia, shared with all of the others both the sense of wonder at the magnificence of the tsar's court and the distaste for a way of life that seemed to them crude, inhuman, and uncomfortable. Throughout the sixteenth century, Muscovy remained, in English eyes, a strange and barbaric realm.

Of the English travelers to Russia, only Fletcher attempted to analyse the institutional framework and social structure in order to explain the phenomena that all of them noticed. His *Of the Russe Commonwealth* is a systematic description and interpretation of the Muscovite system of government that is remarkably thorough and precise, especially considering the brevity of his stay in Russia. The strength of his treatment lies in his presentation of the skeleton of the constitutional machinery. When he tried to set the machine into motion, however, he seems to have exaggerated the ruthlessness and efficiency of the system by assuming that the wheels of government meshed as neatly in practice as in a diagram of the constitutional structure. A number of his comments on the workings of the administration seem to be the product of logical deduction rather than of observation, for his analysis neglects the ritualistic aspects of Muscovite practice that made the tsars' government somewhat less "totalitarian" in effect than Fletcher believed it to be. *Of the Russe Commonwealth* and the other English writings devote comparatively little space to the social structure of Muscovy, a subject on which it must have been particularly difficult to gather information. Besides the remarks on Russian manners common to all of the texts in this collection, however, Fletcher's work provides comments on the changing condition of the nobility and the common people that are highly significant even though they are probably somewhat too categorical.

Oddly enough, the chief English writings on Russia in the sixteenth century are weakest in their treatment of Anglo-Russian diplomacy, even though every one of the writers took part in the negotiations between the two nations. Jenkinson and Randolph both provide a laconic record of their reception at Ivan's court, but Horsey's *Travels*, the memoirs of a diplomat of sorts, is, for the most part, positively misleading in its description of its author's diplomatic activities. When compared with other sources of the period, Horsey's work seems trustworthy in inverse proportion to the extent of his participation in the events he describes and his stake in them.

England's contacts with Muscovy in the reign of Elizabeth did not extend beyond the limits of a small but strategically important commercial venture. One can scarcely speak of Russian influence on Elizabethan England and, outside the realms of trade and diplomacy, the impact of England on Muscovy was limited to the services of a very small number of expert technicians, sent by the queen at the tsar's request. Yet these limited contacts gave a number of Englishmen a unique opportunity to visit Russia and record their impressions so that, by the end of the century, those of their countrymen who were so inclined could gather from Richard Hakluyt's collection of travel literature a far better understanding of Muscovy than that displayed by Shakespeare's masquers. For later generations, the writings of English visitors have preserved a priceless record of sixteenth-century Russia.

We would like to express our sincere gratitude to the Research Board of the University of Illinois for its generous support of this project with funds for photostats of original materials and for research assistants. And we indeed appreciate the diligent work of our research assistants, Mr. John Via and Mr. Henry L. Eaton, who have aided considerably in making this book more accurate in detail.

The grant of a fellowship by the Folger Shakespeare Library to Mr. Berry and the grant of a Summer Faculty Fellowship by the University of Illinois to Mr. Crummey greatly expedited the progress of this edition.

We are deeply grateful as well to Mr. Sergei Pushkarev who made many valuable comments on the notes concerning Russia and to Professor Michael Cherniavsky who read an earlier version of the introductory material.

In the illustrations section, the portrait of Ivan the Terrible (Pl. 1) is reproduced by courtesy of the National Museum, Copenhagen, Denmark, and Plates 2 and 3 are reproduced from D. S. Likhachev and Ia. S. Lur'e (eds.), *Poslaniia Ivana Groznogo* (Moscow-Leningrad, 1951). Plates 4–7 are reproduced by courtesy of the Beinecke Rare Book and Manuscript Library, Yale University. Plate 4 comes from Hessel Gerritsz (ed.), *Descriptio ac delineatio geographica detectionis freti* . . . (Amsterdam, 1613); Plates 5–7 are taken from Sigismund von Herberstein, *Comentarii della Moscovia* . . . (Venice, 1550). Plates 8–10 are reproduced from *Portrety, gerby i pechati Bol'shoi Gosudarstvennoi Knigi 1672 g.* (St. Petersburg, 1903).

In a collaborative effort, the work is, of course, parceled out; and in this edition the introductory essays are primarily the work of Mr. Crummey; the texts, that of Mr. Berry; and the notes, the joint work of both. However, we have read and criticized each other's work and stand jointly responsible for the finished product.

LLOYD E. BERRY

ROBERT O. CRUMMEY

Urbana, Illinois
New Haven, Connecticut
August 1, 1967

Note on the Text

The present edition presents a modernized text of the accounts of Russia by Richard Chancellor, Anthony Jenkinson, George Turberville, Sir Thomas Randolph, Giles Fletcher, and Sir Jerome Horsey. The principles that have governed the preparation of the texts are as follows. The spelling has been brought into conformity with modern usage. The punctuation and capitalization have been modernized; but since no attempt has been made to modernize the syntax, it has been difficult to achieve complete consistency. Geographical place names follow, where possible, the form and spelling in the *Columbia Lippincott Gazetteer of the World*. Russian words and names are transliterated according to System II in J. Thomas Shaw's, *The Transliteration of Modern Russian for English-Language Publications* (Madison: University of Wisconsin Press, 1967). Those place and personal names which could not be identified are left as they were in the original, with a comment in the notes. Substantive variants in the early texts of the accounts of Chancellor, Jenkinson, Randolph, and Turberville are recorded in the notes as this information is not elsewhere available. The reader is referred to the textual notes of Mr. Berry's edition *Of the*

Russe Commonwealth in *The English Works of Giles Fletcher, the Elder.* Any substantive emendation of any of the texts is recorded in the notes. The side notes in the various printed texts have been ignored.

The text of the accounts of Chancellor, Jenkinson, and Randolph is based on the 1589 edition of Richard Hakluyt's *Principal Navigations* and collated with the 1598 edition of the work.

The text of Turberville's account is based on that in *Tragicall Tales* (London, 1587), which has been collated with both the 1589 and 1598 editions of Hakluyt's *Principal Navigations*. This is the first time the text of the *Tragicall Tales* has been used, and a collation of the text with that of Hakluyt's reveals that in the "Letter to Dancie" Hakluyt omitted six lines of scathing attack on the personal morals of Russian men.

The text of Fletcher's *Of the Russe Commonwealth* is based on that in Mr. Berry's *The English Works of Giles Fletcher, the Elder.* Only departures from this text are recorded in the notes.

The text of Horsey's *Travels* is based on the manuscript in the British Museum (Harleian MS 1813), as there was no edition of this work until 1856.

The titles that precede the first four voyages and the section divisions in Horsey's *Travels* have been added by the editors.

The dating of events recorded in Russian sources has been preserved except for year-numbers which we have given in modern form. The process of modernizing Muscovite dates is complicated by the fact that in the calendar then in use in Russia the year began with September 1. Therefore, when the sources assign an event to the year 7098, for example, but do not indicate the precise month in which it took place, it is impossible to be sure whether the correct modern form of the year is 1589 or 1590. Accordingly, in such cases, we have given the year as 1589/90, meaning the year beginning on September 1, 1589 and ending on August 31, 1590.

ABBREVIATIONS AND SHORT TITLES

Berry   Lloyd E. Berry (ed.), *The English Works of Giles Fletcher, The Elder* (Madison, 1964)

Bond   Edward A. Bond (ed.), *Russia at the Close of the Sixteenth Century* (London, 1856)

DNB   *Dictionary of National Biography*

DRV   N. I. Novikov (ed.), *Drevniaia rossiiskaia vivliofika,* 20 vols. (Moscow, 1788–91)

Hakluyt   Richard Hakluyt, *The Principal Navigations, Voyages, Traffiques & Discoveries of the English Nation . . . ,* 12 vols. (Glasgow, 1903–5)

Hamel, *England   J. Hamel, *England and Russia,* trans. by John and Russia*   Studdy Leigh (London, 1854). Also published in 1857 with the title, *Early English Voyages to Northern Russia.*

Herberstein   R. H. Major (trans.), *Notes Upon Russia: being a translation of the earliest account of that country, entitled* Rerum moscoviticarum commentarii *by the Baron Sigismund von Herberstein,* 2 vols. (London, 1851–52)

Kobrin   V. B. Kobrin, "Sostav oprichnogo dvora Ivana Groznogo," *Arkheograficheskii ezhegodnik za 1959 god* (Moscow, 1960), pp. 16–91

Materialy, II   O. A. Iakovleva (ed.), "Piskarevskii letopisets," *Materialy po istorii SSSR,* Vol. II (Moscow, 1955), 5–210

Morgan and   E. Delmar Morgan and C. H. Coote (eds.), *Early Coote*   Voyages and Travels to Russia and Persia . . . ,* 2 vols. (London, 1886)

NL   *Novgorodskiia letopisi* (St. Petersburg, 1879)

PDS   *Pamiatniki diplomaticheskikh snoshenii drevnei Rossii s derzhavami inostrannymi . . . ,* 10 vols. (St. Petersburg, 1851–71)

PRP   *Pamiatniki russkogo prava* (Moscow, 1952–)

PSRL   *Polnoe sobranie russkikh letopisei* (St. Petersburg, 1841–Moscow–)

RBS	*Russkii biograficheskii slovar'*, 25 vols. (St. Petersburg, 1896–1918)
RK	V. I. Buganov (ed.), *Razriadnaia kniga 1475–1598 gg.* (Moscow, 1966)
Sbornik IRIO	*Sbornik Imperatorskago russkago istoricheskago obshchestva,* 148 vols. (St. Petersburg, 1867–1916)
Seredonin	S. M. Seredonin, *Sochinenie Dzhil'sa Fletchera* "Of the Russe common wealth," *kak istoricheskii istochnik* (St. Petersburg, 1891)
Tikhomirov	M. N. Tikhomirov, *Rossiia v XVI stoletii* (Moscow, 1962)
Tolstoy	George Tolstoy (ed.), *The First Forty Years of Intercourse Between England and Russia, 1553–1593* (St. Petersburg, 1875)
Veselovskii, *Feodal'noe zemlevladenie*	S. B. Veselovskii, *Feodal'noe zemlevladenie v Severo-Vostochnoi Rusi,* Vol. I (Moscow-Leningrad, 1947)
Veselovskii, *Issledovaniia*	S. B. Veselovskii, *Issledovaniia po istorii oprichniny* (Moscow, 1963)
Willan, *Early History*	T. S. Willan, *The Early History of the Russia Company, 1553–1603* (Manchester, 1956)
Willan, *Muscovy Merchants*	T. S. Willan, *The Muscovy Merchants of 1555* (Manchester, 1953)
Zimin, *Oprichnina*	A. A. Zimin, *Oprichnina Ivana Groznogo* (Moscow, 1964)
Zimin, *Reformy*	A. A. Zimin, *Reformy Ivana Groznogo* (Moscow, 1960)
Zimin, "Sostav boiarskoi dumy,"	A. A. Zimin, "Sostav boiarskoi dumy v XV–XVI vekakh," *Arkheograficheskii ezhegodnik za 1957 god* (Moscow, 1958), pp. 41–87

Two Early Voyages

The discovery of Russia by the northern ocean, made first, of any nation that we know, by English men, might have seemed an enterprise almost heroic; if any higher end than the excessive love of gain and traffic, had animated the design. Nevertheless that in regard that many things not unprofitable to the knowledge of nature, and other observations are hereby come to light, as good events ofttimes arise from evil occasions, it will not be the worst labor to relate briefly the beginning, and prosecution of this adventurous voyage; until it became at last a familiar passage.

John Milton, *A Brief History of Moscovia*

Richard Chancellor

Introduction

V ery little is known of the life of Chancellor, and what is known, by and large, comes from his own writings. According to his statements in this account of his voyage, he was reared by Sir Henry Sidney, but he must have meant William Sidney, Sir Henry's father, as Sir Henry was only twenty-four when the first Russian voyage took place in 1553.

A few other details of Chancellor's career are known. In 1551, he accompanied Roger Bodenham on a voyage to Chios and Candia. We learn further from his own brief account of the Russian expedition that he probably traveled to France at one time: "I have seen the king's majesty's of England and the French king's pavilions, which are fair, yet not like unto his."[1]

In the present account, Chancellor states that he has "two little sons." According to Hamel he took one of them with him to Russia, to show him the city of the tsar.[2] The other son, named Nicholas, later became a member of the Russia Company (see below, p. 15).

1. Hakluyt II, 229.
2. *England and Russia*, p. 24.

Chancellor made a second voyage to Russia in the summer of 1555, and began his return voyage to England on July 25, 1556. The ship was wrecked off Pitsligo on the coast of Aberdeenshire in November, and Chancellor and the greater part of his crew perished with her.[3]

The account of Chancellor's voyage of 1553 is a fitting monument to an extraordinary venture. Into a few pages, Chancellor and his literary collaborator compressed all of the themes of that daring enterprise, the sober calculation that led to the founding of the trading company, the bumbling heroism and stark tragedy of the voyage, and the sense of wonder at the strange land in which the survivors took refuge.

The version of the work in this collection is the creation of two men, Chancellor and Clement Adams. To this collaboration the returned traveler contributed the information and Adams the literary artistry. The core of their work is Chancellor's own written account of his experiences in Muscovy. Adams, who was never in Russia as far as is known, rearranged and polished Chancellor's work and added the introductory sections on the founding of the company and the course of the expedition until the hero's arrival in Russia.

The only section of the work that is entirely Adams' creation is the story of the founding of the company and the plans for its initial venture. Adams tells the story in a formalized, pseudo-classical style, including the long set speech in praise of Chancellor that is reminiscent of Thucydides. Stripped of its embellishments, however, the narrative probably gives an accurate record of the motives that led the shareholders to form the company and the way in which they pooled their resources to float their first venture. Adams' reconstruction of the members' reasoning is particularly interesting: the London merchant community was disturbed by the loss of markets in western Europe and decided that, like the Spaniards and Portuguese, they could revive their fortunes by opening up trade with territories overseas.

The product of these calculations was the expedition of 1553. Adams' description of the departure and the voyage to Russia is surely based on the reminiscences of Chancellor or one of his men. Although his treatment of the journey is impressionistic, it effectively records the impact of the elements on the sailors and their changing moods in reaction to the events of the trip, especially the loss of Willoughby and his ships.

3. *DNB* and Hamel, *England and Russia,* pp. 22–25.

Yet it is Chancellor's notes on Muscovy that form the most remarkable and valuable part of the account. If he had left no trace on history apart from this work, he would still be remembered as an exceptional figure. When he set sail from London, Chancellor had no idea that he would land in Muscovy and knew nothing about conditions there. Nevertheless, during the few months of his stay in Russia, he gained a rather accurate picture of the country and its people and achieved a remarkable understanding of the forces shaping the society.

As he described the geography of Russia, Chancellor paid particular attention to the economic significance of the main towns of the realm. His observations are recorded with the precision one would expect in the agent of a trading company and are of great value to historians both in themselves and for the impression they project of the general state of the Muscovite economy in the mid-sixteenth century. In Chancellor's time, Muscovy thrived. Each region produced its own specialties: Novgorod grew flax, Iaroslavl' grain, the north contributed furs, salt, and fish, and all engaged in lively trade with the other regions of Russia or with foreign countries. Chancellor's portrait of prosperity stands in stark contrast to Fletcher's gloomy observations recorded during the depression at the end of the century.

As the capital and chief trading center, Moscow lay at the heart of Chancellor's interests. The city impressed him "as in bigness . . . as great as the city of London," but it fell far short of its English counterpart in organization and grandeur. Despite his reservations, Moscow emerges from his account as a haphazard mass of wooden houses and crooked alleys teeming with life. Over it loomed the Kremlin, the core of its defenses and the focus of its political and religous life.

In his dealings with the Muscovite government, Chancellor was accorded the full ceremonial honors customarily accorded foreign ambassadors but apparently had no opportunity to probe the power relations behind the pomp. His account of his reception is a lavish description of the appearance of the tsar and his court and of the rituals they performed. Ivan IV plays the central role in the pageant with impressive dignity but does not take life as an independent personality. Chancellor offers no answers to the tantalizing questions about Ivan's early adult years—the nature of the young tsar's character and of his relations with his closest advisers such as Adashev and Viskovatyi, both of whom appear beside the tsar in the tableau.

The army, one of the bases of the tsar's power, attracted Chancellor's keen interest. In describing the Muscovite armed forces, he conveys a vivid impression of life in the ranks. He marveled particularly at the toughness of the troops, who survived cold and hunger without complaint. At the same time, Chancellor, like other foreign commentators, exaggerates the extent to which the Muscovite army was an undisciplined mass of humanity. The army was much smaller than he thought and was organized on every campaign into five corps consisting of a number of units of one hundred men each.

He was aware that the core of the army consisted of service nobles who were granted estates in reward for their service. These *pomest'e* grants, as Chancellor rightly noted, carried with them the condition that the recipient continue to perform service proportionate to the size of his estate until his retirement. If a service noble was killed in the line of duty, his estate reverted to the crown except for a small section that was granted to his widow as a form of pension. In the latter half of the sixteenth century, the Muscovite government took a number of steps in the direction of extending the same service conditions to the hereditary (*votchina*) estates of the nobility. Chancellor displayed remarkable acuity in noticing a line of policy that became pronounced only in later decades. All the same, he badly exaggerated the extent to which the government attempted to regulate the rights and duties of the hereditary landowners. Only under exceptional circumstances did the tsar confiscate votchina estates in the manner he describes.

Chancellor's remarks on the Muscovite legal system are also very perceptive. He noted with admiration that trials were simple in form, allowing the plaintiff and defendant to represent themselves in court. Muscovite justice, as Chancellor saw it, was also rough and ready. In outlining trial procedure, he indicated that when the accused was arrested, he was publicly beaten until he or his friends posted bond. The observation is at odds with the specifications of the legislation of the period that prescribed public beating (*pravezh*) for non-payment of debts or failure to pay the fine levied by a judge as sentence on the guilty party in a dispute. The discrepancy may be simply a reflection of the difference between legislation and its application in practice. Chancellor likewise took note of the survival of the judicial duel as the last resort in a case in which the clashing testimony of the parties could not be resolved by less drastic means. His description is very similar to the stipulations of contemporary legislation and remains the best surviving picture of how a duel may actually have been conducted.

Despite its admirable simplicity and the good intentions of the tsar, who stood at the pinnacle of the system as final court of appeal, Muscovite legal practice had some unfortunate characteristics. One practice that drew Chancellor's condemnation made chronic debtors the bondsmen of their creditors. The author noted as well that what was basically a device for guaranteeing the rights of creditors was being turned into a form of servitude by which the impoverished would borrow money specifically for the purpose of becoming bondslaves of the lender and thus escaping from taxation and other forms of service. The observation is remarkable because the practice of bondage by loan contract did not reach its full development until the economic collapse at the end of the century and the civil wars that followed.

Chancellor paid relatively little attention to the details of the average man's life. His notes on Russian houses and clothing are very brief and his commentary on Muscovite morals is limited to the tried and true observation that drunkenness was the national vice. What drove the Russians to drink he did not explain.

The author's reactions to the Orthodox church are rather complicated. His treatment, although critical, is still mild in comparison to the protocols of the Stoglav church council of 1551. Like the other English travelers, he was repelled by the Orthodox emphasis on ritual but gave the monks and the laity alike credit for a genuine determination to observe the celebrations and fasts of their church to the letter. On the subject of the tsar's attitude toward the church, he made the curious observation that when the abbot of an important monastery died, the tsar would impound its treasure and force the new abbot to redeem it for a considerable ransom. Usually not even Ivan the Terrible interfered with the monasteries so blatantly.

Chancellor's account of Russia is almost purely descriptive, but his description is of a very high order. For he not only portrayed many important features of Muscovite life in his own time but took note as well of dynamic features of the society that were to shape its future development.

Chancellor's account of his voyage was first published in Richard Hakluyt, *Principal Navigations* (3 vols.; London, 1589), I, Sigs. Ddl^v–Eel^v. It also appeared in subsequent editions of Hakluyt: *Principal Navigations* (3 vols.; London, 1598–1600), I, Sigs. X2^r–Y2^r; and *Principal Navigations* (12 vols.; Glasgow, 1903–5), II, 239–70. His account was also included in Samuel Purchas, *Purchas His Pilgrimes* (4 vols.; London, 1625), III, VI^v–V3^r and in the modern edition, *Purchas His Pilgrimes* (20 vols.; Glasgow, 1905–7), XI, 615–21.

Chancellor's account has also been translated into Russian: "Pervoe puteshestvie anglichan v Rossiiu, opisannoe Klimentom Adamom, drugom Chanselera, kapitana sei ekspeditsii i posviashchennoe Filippu, koroliu angliiskomu," *Otechestvennyia zapiski*, XXVII (1826), 368–95; XXVIII (1827), 83–103, 177–88; and I. Tarnava-Borichevskii (trans.), "Pervoe puteshestvie anglichan v Rossiiu, v 1553 godu," *Zhurnal Ministerstva narodnago prosveshcheniia*, XX (1838), 35–64, based on a somewhat abridged Latin variant of Adams' version of the account. Iu. V. Got'e (trans.), *Angliiskie puteshestvenniki v moskovskom gosudarstve v XVI veke* (Leningrad, 1937), combines Adams' version of the formation of the Russia Company and Chancellor's voyage to Russia (pp. 47–55) with Chancellor's own account of his experiences in Russia (pp. 55–66).

Richard Chancellor

The First Voyage to Russia

At what time our merchants perceived the commodities and wares of England to be in small request with the countries and people about us and near unto us, and that those merchandises which strangers in the time and memory of our ancestors did earnestly seek and desire were now neglected and the price thereof abated although by us carried to their own ports, and all foreign merchandises in great account and their prices wonderfully raised, certain grave citizens of London, and men of great wisdom and careful of the good of their country, began to think with themselves how this mischief might be remedied. Neither was a remedy (as it then appeared) wanting to their desires for the avoiding of so great an inconvenience, for seeing that the wealth of the Spaniards and Portuguese by the discovery and search of new trades and countries was marvelously increased, supposing the same to be a course and mean for them also to obtain the like, they thereupon resolved upon a new and strange navigation.[1] And

1. The only Russian account of Chancellor's visit to Moscow is contained in the Dvina Chronicle, a compilation of sources dating from the eighteenth century. According to this story, Chancellor reached the mouth of the Dvina on August 24,

whereas at the same time one Sebastian Cabot,[2] a man in those days
very renowned, happened to be in London, they began first of all to
deal and consult diligently with him; and after much speech and conference together, it was at last concluded that three ships should be
prepared and furnished out for the search and discovery of the northern part of the world, to open a way and passage to our men for travel
to new and unknown kingdoms.

And whereas many things seemed necessary to be regarded in this so
hard and difficult a matter, they first make choice of certain grave and
wise persons in manner of a senate or company which should lay their
heads together and give their judgments and provide things requisite
and profitable for all occasions. By this company it was thought expe-
dient that a certain sum of money should publicly be collected to serve
for the furnishing of so many ships. And lest any private man should be
too much oppressed and charged, a course was taken that every man
willing to be of the society should disburse the portion of twenty and
five pounds apiece, so that in short time by this means the sum of six
thousand pounds being gathered, the three ships were bought, the
most part whereof they provided to be newly built and trimmed. But
in this action I wot not whether I may more admire the care of the
merchants or the diligence of the shipwrights: for the merchants, they
get very strong and well seasoned planks for the building; the shipwrights, they with daily travail and their greatest skill do fit them for
the dispatch of the ships; they calk them, pitch them, and among the
rest they make one most stanch and firm by an excellent and ingenious
invention. For they had heard that in certain parts of the ocean a kind

---

1553, and continued on to Kholmogory by small boat. When he explained his
mission to the authorities there, the elected officials (*vybornye golovy*), Filipp
Rodionov and Feofan Makarov, sent news of his arrival to Moscow. On November
25, Chancellor set off for the capital. When he was received by the tsar he requested that the English be allowed to trade in Russia and his request was granted.
On March 15, the tsar formally dismissed him and he returned to the north coast.
When navigation opened, he set sail for home (A. A. Titov [ed.], *Letopis'
dvinskaia* [Moscow, 1889], pp. 10–11).

2. Cabot (1474–1557), famous as the discoverer of Nova Scotia, a sea captain
and pilot with many years' experience in voyages of exploration, suggested the
formation of the Company of Merchants Adventurers of London in 1551 to seek
a northeast passage to China. He supervised the northeast expedition to Russia
in 1553 and 1556, and was named governor of the Russia Company in 1555. See
DNB.

of worms is bred which many times pierceth and eateth through the strongest oak that is; and therefore that the mariners and the rest to be employed in this voyage might be free and safe from this danger, they cover a piece of the keel of the ship with thin sheets of lead. And having thus built the ships and furnished them with armor and artillery, then followed a second care no less troublesome and necessary than the former, namely, the provision of victuals, which was to be made according to the time and length of the voyage. And whereas they afore determined to have the east part of the world sailed unto, and yet that the sea towards the same was not open except they kept the northern tract, where as yet it was doubtful whether there were any passage yea or no, they resolved to victual the ships for eighteen months, which they did for this reason: for our men being to pass that huge and cold part of the world, they, wisely foreseeing it, allow them six months' victual to sail to the place, so much more to remain there if the extremity of the winter hindered their return, and so much more also for the time of their coming home.

Now this provision being made and carried aboard with armor and munition of all sorts, sufficient captains and governors of so great an enterprise were as yet wanting; to which office and place although many men (and some void of experience) offered themselves, yet one Sir Hugh Willoughby,[3] a most valiant gentleman and wellborn, very earnestly requested to have that care and charge committed unto him. Of whom before all others both by reason of his goodly personage (for he was of a tall stature) as also for his singular skill in the services of war, the company of the merchants made greatest account, so that at the last they concluded and made choice of him for the general of this voyage and appointed to him the admiral with authority and command over all the rest. And for the government of the other ships, although divers men seemed willing and made offers of themselves thereunto, yet by a common consent one Richard Chancellor, a man of great estimation for many good parts of wit in him, was elected, in whom alone great hope for the performance of this business rested. This man was

3. Sir Hugh was the youngest son of Sir Henry Willoughby of Middleton. He served in the expedition to Scotland in 1544, and was knighted by the earl of Hertford (afterwards duke of Somerset) at Leith on May 11, 1544. He afterwards had a commission on the border, and was captain of Lowther Castle in 1548–49, but the downfall of Somerset altered his position. Chancellor's voyage accounts for the rest of his life story (*DNB*).

brought up by one Master Henry Sidney,[4] a noble young gentleman and very much beloved of King Edward, who at this time coming to the place where the merchants were gathered together began a very eloquent speech or oration and spake to them after this manner following:

"My very worshipful friends, I cannot but greatly commend your present godly and virtuous intention in the serious enterprising (for the singular love you bear to your country) a matter which I hope will prove profitable for this nation and honorable to this our land. Which intention of yours, we also of the nobility are ready to our power to help and further; neither do we hold anything so dear and precious unto us which we will not willingly forgo and lay out in so commendable a cause. But principally I rejoice in myself, that I have nourished and maintained that wit which is like by some means and in some measure to profit and stead you in this worthy action. But yet I would not have you ignorant of this one thing, that I do now part with Chancellor not because I make little reckoning of the man or that his maintenance is burdensome and chargeable unto me, but that you might conceive and understand my goodwill and promptitude for the furtherance of this business, and that the authority and estimation which he deserveth may be given him. You know the man by report, I by experience, you by words, I by deeds, you by speech and company, but I by the daily trial of his life have a full and perfect knowledge of him. And you are also to remember into how many perils for your sakes and his country's love he is now to run, whereof it is requisite that we be not unmindful if it please God to send him good success. We commit a little money to the chance and hazard of fortune; he commits his life—a thing to a man of all things most dear—to the raging sea and the uncertainties of many dangers. We shall here live and rest at home quietly with our friends and acquaintance; but he in the meantime laboring to keep the ignorant and unruly mariners in good order and obedience, with how many cares shall he trouble and vex himself, with how many troubles shall he break himself, and how many disquietings shall he be forced to sustain? We shall keep our own coasts and country. He shall seek strange and unknown kingdoms. He shall commit his

---

4. Actually Sir Henry's father, Sir William Sidney (see above, p. 3), who was one of the four gentlemen of the privy chamber of Edward VI. Sir Henry (1529–86) was three times lord deputy of Ireland and was president of the Welsh Marches from 1559 until his death (*DNB*).

safety to barbarous and cruel people and shall hazard his life amongst the monstrous and terrible beasts of the sea. Wherefore in respect of the greatness of the dangers and the excellency of his charge, you are to favor and love the man thus departing from us; and if it fall so happily out that he return again, it is your part and duty, also, liberally to reward him."

After that this noble young gentleman had delivered this or some such like speech, much more eloquently than I can possibly report it, the company then present began one to look upon another, one to question and confer with another; and some (to whom the virtue and sufficiency of the man was known) began secretly to rejoice with themselves and to conceive a special hope that the man would prove in time very rare and excellent, and that his virtues already appearing and shining to the world would grow to the great honor and advancement of this kingdom.

After all this, the company growing to some silence, it seemed good to them that were of greatest gravity amongst them to inquire, search, and seek what might be learned and known concerning the easterly part or tract of the world. For which cause two Tatars which were then of the king's stable were sent for and an interpreter was gotten to be present, by whom they were demanded touching their country and the manners of their nation. But they were able to answer nothing to the purpose, being indeed more acquainted (as one there merrily and openly said) to toss pots than to learn the states and dispositions of people. But after much ado and many things passed about this matter, they grew at last to this issue, to set down and appoint a time for the departure of the ships, because divers were of opinion that a great part of the best time of the year was already spent, and if the delay grew longer the way would be stopped and barred by the force of the ice and the cold climate. And therefore it was thought best by the opinion of them all, that by the twentieth day of May[5] the captains and mariners should take shipping and depart from Ratliffe upon the ebb, if it so pleased God. They, having saluted their acquaintance, one his wife, another his children, another his kinsfolk, and another his friends dearer than his kinsfolk, were present and ready at the day appointed; and having weighed anchor, they departed with the turning of the water and sailing easily came first to Greenwich. The greater ships

5. Willoughby (Hakluyt II, 217) states the date of sailing was May 10, 1553, which is probably correct as Willoughby's account is in the form of a log.

were towed down with boats and oars, and the mariners, being all apparelled in watchet or sky-colored cloth, towed amain and made way with diligence. And being come near to Greenwich (where the court then lay), presently upon the news thereof the courtiers came running out and the common people flocked together, standing very thick upon the shore; the Privy Council they looked out at the windows of the court, and the rest ran up to the tops of the towers. The ships hereupon discharge their ordnance and shoot off their pieces after the manner of war and of the sea, insomuch that the tops of the hills sounded therewith, the valleys and the waters gave an echo, and the mariners they shouted in such sort that the sky rang again with the noise thereof. One stood in the poop of the ship and by his gesture bids farewell to his friends in the best manner he could; another walks upon the hatches; another climbs the shrouds; another stands upon the main yard and another in the top of the ship. To be short, it was a very triumph (after a sort) in all respects to the beholders. But, alas, the good King Edward, in respect of whom principally all this was prepared, he only by reason of his sickness was absent from this show; and not long after the departure of these ships, the lamentable and most sorrowful accident of his death followed.[6] But to proceed in the matter.

The ships going down with the tide came at last to Woolwich, where they stayed and cast anchor with purpose to depart there hence again as soon as the turning of the water and a better wind should draw them to set sail. After this they departed and came to Harwich, in which port they stayed long, not without great loss and consuming of time; yet at the last with a good wind they hoisted up sail and committed themselves to the sea, giving their last adieu to their native country, which they knew not whether they should ever return to see again or not. Many of them looked oftentimes back and could not refrain from tears, considering into what hazards they were to fall and what uncertainties of the sea they were to make trial of.

Amongst the rest Richard Chancellor, the captain of the "Edward Bonaventure," was not a little grieved with the fear of wanting victuals, part whereof was found to be corrupt and putrefied at Harwich, and the hogsheads of wine also leaked and were not stanch. His natural and fatherly affection also somewhat troubled him, for he left behind him his two little sons, which were in the case of orphans if he

6. King Edward died on July 6, 1553.

sped not well.[7] The estate also of his company moved him to care, being in the former respects after a sort unhappy, and were to abide with himself every good or bad accident. But in the meantime, while his mind was thus tormented with the multiplicity of sorrows and cares, after many days sailing they kenned land afar off, whereunto the pilots directed the ships; and being come to it they land and find it to be Rost Island, where they stayed certain days and afterwards set sail again; and proceeding towards the north, they espied certain other islands which were called the Cross of Islands.[8] From which places when they were a little departed, Master[9] Willoughby, the general, a man of good foresight and providence in all his actions, erected and set out his flag, by which he called together the chiefest men of the other ships, that by the help and assistance of their counsels the order of the government and conduction of the ships in the whole voyage might be the better; who being come together accordingly, they conclude and agree that if any great tempest should arise at any time and happen to disperse and scatter them, every ship should endeavor his best to go to Vardo,[10] a haven or castle of some name in the kingdom of Norway, and that they that arrived there first in safety should stay and expect the coming of the rest.

The very same day in the afternoon, about four of the clock, so great a tempest suddenly arose and the seas were so outrageous that the ships could not keep their intended course, but some were perforce driven one way and some another way to their great peril and hazard. The general with his loudest voice cried out to Richard Chancellor and earnestly requested him not to go far from him; but he neither would nor could keep company with him if he sailed still so fast, for the admiral was of better sail than his ship. But the said admiral (I know not by what means), bearing all his sails, was carried away with so great

7. See above, p. 3. In a letter of 1560, written by the Russia Company to its agents in Russia (Hakluyt II, 409) we note: "Also we send you Nicholas Chancellor to remain there, who is our apprentice for years; our mind is he should be set about such business as he is most fit for; he hath been kept at writing school long; he hath his Algorism, and hath understanding of keeping of books of reckonings." Eight years later he was one of the Company's servants accused of private trade, but in 1580 he was appointed as merchant for the Company's expedition to discover the northeast passage (Willan, *Early History*, p. 39).

8. Probably located in or near the Lofoten Islands.

9. *Master*. Sir Hugh 1599.

10. Wardhouse 1589, 1599.

force and swiftness that not long after he was quite out of sight; and the third ship also with the same storm and like rage was dispersed and lost us.

The ship boat of the admiral, striking against the ship, was overwhelmed in the sight and view of the mariners of the "Bonaventure"; and as for them that are already returned and arrived, they know nothing of the rest of the ships what was become of them.[11]

But if it be so, that any miserable mishap have overtaken them, if the rage and fury of the sea have devoured those good men, or if as yet they live and wander up and down in strange countries, I must needs say they were men worthy of better fortune; and if they be living, let us wish them safety and a good return; but if the cruelty of death hath taken hold of them, God send them a Christian grave and sepulcher.

Now Richard Chancellor with his ship and company being thus left alone and become very pensive, heavy, and sorrowful by this dispersion of the fleet, he (according to the order before taken) shapeth his course for Vardo in Norway, there to expect and abide the arrival of the rest of the ships. And being come thither, and having stayed there the space of seven days and looked in vain for their coming, he deter-

---

11. It is evident that Willoughby and his ships, the "Bona Speranza" and the "Confidentia," had passed Vardo and were wandering along the coasts of Russian Lapland. Willoughby's journal continues with its entries until the end of September. According to the account in Hakluyt (II, 224), a will found in the "Speranza" indicates "that Sir Hugh Willoughby and most of the company were alive in January 1554." The fate of Willoughby and his crew remained unknown to the Englishmen until their second voyage to Russia in 1555. The two ships, found by Russian fishermen on the Arzina River near Kegor, were returned to Chancellor by Ivan during his second trip. The best account of the episode is in a letter of Giovanni Michiel, Venetian ambassador in England, to the Doge and Senate of Venice (*Calendar of State Papers, Venetian,* 1555–56, p. 240). It is dated November 4, 1555. The account reads: "The vessels which departed hence some months ago [May 1555] bound for Cathay, either from inability or lack of daring, not having got beyond Muscovy and Russia, whither the others went in like manner last year, have returned safe, bringing with them the two vessels of the first voyage, having found them on the Muscovite coast, with the men on board all frozen; and the mariners now returned from the second voyage narrate strange things about the mode in which they were frozen, having found some of them seated in the act of writing, pen still in hand, and the paper before them; others at table, platter in hand and spoon in mouth; others opening a locker, and others in various postures, like statues, as if they had been adjusted and placed in those attitudes. They say that some dogs on board the ships displayed the some phenomena. They found the effects and merchandise all intact in the hands of the natives, and brought them back hither with the vessels."

mined at length to proceed alone in the purposed voyage. And as he was preparing himself to depart, it happened that he fell in company and speech with certain Scottishmen who, having understanding of his intention and wishing well to his actions, began earnestly to dissuade him from the further prosecution of the discovery by amplifying the dangers which he was to fall into and omitted no reason that might serve to that purpose. But he, holding nothing so ignominious and reproachful as inconstancy and levity of mind, and persuading himself that a man of valor could not commit a more dishonorable part than for fear of danger to avoid and shun great attempts, was nothing at all changed or discouraged with the speeches and words of the Scots, remaining steadfast and immutable in his first resolution, determining either to bring that to pass which was intended or else to die the death.

And as for them which were with Master Chancellor in his ship, although they had great cause of discomfort by the loss of their company whom the foresaid tempest had separated from them and were not a little troubled with cogitations and perturbations of mind in respect of their doubtful course, yet, notwithstanding, they were of such consent and agreement of mind with Master Chancellor that they were resolute and prepared under his direction and government to make proof and trial of all adventures without all fear or mistrust of future dangers. Which constancy of mind in all the company did exceedingly increase their captain's carefulness, for he, being swallowed up with like good will and love towards them, feared lest through any error of his the safety of the company should be endangered. To conclude, when they saw their desire and hope of the arrival of the rest of the ships to be every day more and more frustrated, they provided to sea again, and Master Chancellor held on his course towards that unknown part of the world and sailed so far that he came at last to the place where he found no night at all, but a continual light and brightness of the sun shining clearly upon the huge and mighty sea. And having the benefit of this perpetual light for certain days, at the length it pleased God to bring them into a certain great bay, which was of one hundred miles or thereabouts over.[12] Whereinto they entered and somewhat far within it cast anchor; and looking every way about them, it happened that they espied afar off a certain fisher boat which Master Chancellor, accompanied with a few of his men, went towards to common[13] with the fisher-

12. The White Sea.
13. Communicate.

men that were in it and to know of them what country it was, and
what people, and of what manner of living they were. But they, being
amazed with the strange greatness of his ship (for in those parts before
that time they had never seen the like), began presently to avoid and
to flee; but he still following them at last overtook them, and being
come to them they, being in great fear as men half dead, prostrated
themselves before him, offering to kiss his feet. But he, according to his
great and singular courtesy, looked pleasantly upon them, comforting
them by signs and gestures, refusing those duties and reverences of
theirs, and taking them up in all loving sort from the ground. And it is
strange to consider how much favor afterwards in that place this humanity of his did purchase to himself; for they, being dismissed, spread
by and by a report abroad of the arrival of a strange nation of a singular gentleness and courtesy. Whereupon the common people came together, offering to these new-come guests victuals freely and not refusing to traffic with them, except they had been bound by a certain religious use and custom not to buy any foreign commodities without the
knowledge and consent of the king.

By this time our men had learned that this country was called Russia
or Muscovy, and that Ivan Vasil'evich, which was at that time their
king's name, ruled and governed far and wide in those places. And the
barbarous Russes asked likewise of our men whence they were and
what they came for. Whereunto answer was made that they were Englishmen sent into those coasts from the most excellent King Edward the
Sixth, having from him in commandment certain things to deliver to
their king, and seeking nothing else but his amity and friendship and
traffic with his people, whereby they doubted not but that great commodity and profit would grow to the subjects of both kingdoms.

The barbarians heard these things very gladly and promised their
aid and furtherance to acquaint their king out of hand with so honest
and reasonable a request.

In the meantime Master Chancellor entreated victuals for his money
of the governor of that place, who together with others came aboard
him, and required hostages of them likewise for the more assurance of
safety to himself and his company. To whom the governors answered
that they knew not in that case the will of their king, but yet were willing in such things as they might lawfully do to pleasure him, which
was as then to afford him the benefit of victuals.

Now whiles these things were a-doing, they secretly sent a messenger unto the emperor to certify him of the arrival of a strange nation and withal to know his pleasure concerning them, which message was very welcome unto him, insomuch that voluntarily he invited them to come to his court. But if by reason of the tediousness of so long a journey they thought it not best so to do, then he granted liberty to his subjects to bargain and to traffic with them, and further promised that, if it would please them to come to him, he himself would bear the whole charges of post horses. In the meantime the governors of the place deferred the matter from day to day, pretending divers excuses, and saying one while that the consent of all the governors, and another while that the great and weighty affairs of the kingdom, compelled them to defer their answer; and this they did of purpose so long to protract the time until the messenger sent before to the king did return with relation of his will and pleasure.

But Master Chancellor, seeing himself held in this suspense with long and vain expectation, and thinking that of intention to delude him they posted the matter off so often, was very instant with them to perform their promise, which if they would not do, he told them that he would depart and proceed in his voyage. So that the Muscovites, although as yet they knew not the mind of their king, yet fearing the departure indeed of our men who had such wares and commodities as they greatly desired, they at last resolved to furnish our people with all things necessary and to conduct them by land to the presence of their king. And so Master Chancellor began his journey, which was very long and most troublesome, wherein he had the use of certain sleds, which in that country are very common; for they are carried themselves upon sleds, and all their carriages are in the same sort, the people almost not knowing any other manner of carriage, the cause whereof is the exceeding hardness of the ground, congealed in the wintertime by the force of the cold, which in those places is very extreme and horrible, whereof hereafter we will say something.

But now they, having passed the greater part of their journey, met at last with the sledman, of whom I spake before, sent to the king secretly from the justices or governors, who by some ill hap had lost his way and had gone to the seaside which is near to the country of the Tatars, thinking there to have found our ship. But having long erred and wandered out of his way, at the last in his direct return he met (as he was coming) our captain on the way. To whom he by and by delivered the emperor's letters, which were written to him with all courtesy and in

Map 1. Russia in the sixteenth century. Map by the University of
Wisconsin Cartographic Laboratory

the most loving manner that could be, wherein express commandment was given that post horses should be gotten for him and the rest of his company without any money. Which thing was of all the Russes in the rest of their journey so willingly done that they began to quarrel, yea, and to fight also in striving and contending which of them should put their post horses to the sled; so that after much ado and great pains taken in this long and weary journey (for they had traveled very near fifteen hundred miles), Master Chancellor came at last to Moscow, the chief city of the kingdom and the seat of the king, of which city, and of the emperor himself, and of the principal cities of Muscovy, we will speak immediately more at large in this discourse.

Of Muscovy, which is also called Russia

M uscovy, which hath the name also of Russia the white, is a very large and spacious country, every way bounded with divers nations. Towards the south and the east it is compassed with Tatary; the northern side of it stretcheth to the Scythian Ocean; upon the west part border the Lapps, a rude and savage nation living in woods, whose language is not known to any other people. Next unto these, more towards the south, is Sweden, then Finland, then Livonia, and last of all Lithuania. This country of Muscovy hath also very many and great rivers in it and is marish ground in many places; and as for the rivers, the greatest and most famous amongst all the rest is that which the Russes in their own tongue call Volga, but others know it by the name of Rha. Next unto it in fame is Tanaïs, which they call Don, and the third Borysthenes, which at this day they call Dnieper. Two of these, to wit, Rha and Borysthenes, issuing both out of one fountain,[14] run very far through the land. Rha, receiving many other pleasant rivers into it and running from the very head or spring of it towards the east, after many crooked turnings and windings dischargeth itself and all the other waters and rivers that falls into it, by divers passages,

14. The Volga and the Dnieper do not have a common source. Both have their source in the Valdai Hills area and at one point near Rzhev the Volga flows about 50 kilometers from the source of the Dnieper.

into the Caspian Sea. Tanaïs, springing from a fountain of great name in those parts and growing great near to his head, spreads itself at length very largely and makes a great lake, and then growing narrow again doth so run for certain miles until it fall into another lake which they call Ivan,[15] and there hence, fetching a very crooked course, comes very near to the river Volga, but disdaining as it were the company of any other river doth there turn itself again from Volga and runs toward the south and falls at last into the Lake of *Maeotis*.[16] Borysthenes, which comes from the same head that Rha doth (as we said before), carrieth both itself and other waters that are near unto it towards the south, not refusing the mixture of other small rivers, and, running by many great and large countries, falls at last into *Pontus Euxinus*.[17] Besides these rivers are also in Muscovy certain lakes and pools. The lakes breed fish by the celestial influence. And amongst them all, the chiefest and most principal is called Beloe Ozero, which is very famous by reason of a very strong tower built in it, wherein the kings of Muscovy reserve and repose their treasure in all time of war and danger.

Touching the Riphean mountains,[18] whereupon the snow lieth continually and where hence in times past it was thought that Tanaïs the river did spring and that the rest of the wonders of nature which the Grecians feigned and invented of old were there to be seen, our men which lately came from thence neither saw them nor yet have brought home any perfect relation of them, although they remained there for the space of three months and had gotten in that time some intelligence of the language of Muscovy. The whole country is plain and champion,[19] and few hills in it; and towards the north it hath very large and spacious woods wherein is great store of fir trees, a wood very necessary and fit for the building of houses. There are also wild beasts bred in those woods, as buffs,[20] bears, and black wolves, and another

---

15. The Don has its source in a small lake called Ivan Ozero but there are no large lakes anywhere on its course. In his famous map of 1562, Jenkinson made the same error as Chancellor and gave the "lakes" on the Don the names Riazan' Ozero, Ploga Ozero, and Ivan Ozero.
16. Sea of Azov.
17. Black Sea.
18. The Urals.
19. Level, open country.
20. Buffalo.

kind of beast unknown to us but called by them *rosomakha;* and the nature of the same is very rare and wonderful, for when it is great with young and ready to bring forth, it seeketh out some narrow place between two stakes and so going through them presseth itself, and by that means is eased of her burden, which otherwise could not be done. They hunt their buffs for the most part a-horseback, but their bears afoot with wooden forks. The north parts of the country are reported to be so cold that the very ice or water which distilleth out of the moist wood which they lay upon the fire is presently congealed and frozen, the diversity growing suddenly to be so great, that in one and the self-same firebrand a man shall see both fire and ice. When the winter doth once begin there, it doth still more and more increase by a perpetuity of cold; neither doth that cold slake until the force of the sunbeams doth dissolve the cold and make glad the earth returning to it again. Our mariners which we left in the ship in the meantime to keep it, in their going up only from their cabins to the hatches had their breath oftentimes so suddenly taken away that they eftsoons fell down as men very near dead, so great is the sharpness of that cold climate; but as for the south parts of the country, they are somewhat more temperate.

Of Moscow, the chief city of the kingdom, and of the emperor thereof

It remaineth that a larger discourse be made of Moscow, the principal city of that country, and of the prince also as before we have promised. The empire and government of the king is very large and his wealth at this time exceeding great. And because the city of Moscow is the chiefest of all the rest, it seemeth of itself to challenge the first place in this discourse. Our men say that in bigness it is as great as the city of London with the suburbs thereof. There are many and great buildings in it, but for beauty and fairness nothing comparable to ours. There are many towns and villages also, but built out of order and with no handsomeness: their streets and ways are not paved with stone as ours are, the walls of their houses are of wood, the roofs for the most part are covered with shingle boards. There is hard by the city a very fair castle, strong and furnished with artillery, whereunto the city is joined directly towards the north with a brick wall; the walls also of the castle are built with brick and are in breadth or thickness eighteen foot. This castle hath on the one side a dry ditch, on the other side the river Volga,[21] whereby it is made almost inexpugnable. The same Volga trending towards the east doth admit into it the company of the river Oka.

In the castle aforesaid there are in number nine churches or chapels, not altogether unhandsome, which are used and kept by certain religious men, over whom there is after a sort a patriarch, or governor, and with him other reverend fathers, all which for the greater part dwell within the castle. As for the king's court and palace, it is not of the neatest, only in form it is foursquare and of low building, much surpassed and excelled by the beauty and elegancy of the houses of the kings of England. The windows are very narrowly built, and some of them by glass, some other by lattices, admit the light; and whereas the palaces of our princes are decked and adorned with hangings of cloth of gold, there is none such there; they build and join to all their walls benches, and that not only in the court of the emperor but in all private men's houses.

Now after that they had remained about twelve days in the city, there was then a messenger sent unto them to bring them to the king's house, and they, being after a sort wearied with their long stay, were very ready and willing so to do; and being entered within the gates of the court, there sat a very honorable company of courtiers to the number of one hundred, all appareled in cloth of gold down to their ankles. And there hence being conducted into the chamber of presence, our men began to wonder at the majesty of the emperor. His seat was aloft in a very royal throne, having on his head a diadem or crown of gold, appareled with a robe all of goldsmith's work, and in his hand he held a scepter garnished and beset with precious stones; and besides all other notes and appearances of honor, there was a majesty in his countenance proportionable with the excellency of his estate. On the one side of him stood his chief secretary,[22] on the other side the great

21. The Moscow Kremlin is situated on the bank of the Moskva, a tributary of the Oka.

22. Probably Ivan Mikhailovich Viskovatyi. A man of humble origins, Viskovatyi was a specialist in diplomacy. In 1549 he was made secretary in charge of the office of foreign affairs (*Posol'skii prikaz*). From that time until his death he played a leading part in the conduct of foreign policy. In 1561 he was promoted

commander of silence, both of them arrayed also in cloth of gold; and then there sat the council, of one hundred and fifty in number, all in like sort arrayed and of great state. This so honorable an assembly, so great a majesty of the emperor and of the place, might very well have amazed our men and have dashed them out of countenance; but, notwithstanding, Master Chancellor, being therewithal nothing dismayed, saluted and did his duty to the emperor after the manner of England and withal delivered unto him the letters[23] of our[24] King Edward the Sixth. The emperor, having taken and read the letters, began a little to question with them and to ask them of the welfare of our king; whereunto our men answered him directly and in few words; hereupon our men presented something to the emperor, by the chief secretary, which at the delivery of it put off his hat, being before all the time covered. And so the emperor, having invited them to dinner, dismissed them from his presence, and going into the chamber of him that was master of the requests[25] to the emperor, and having stayed there the space of two hours, at the last the messenger cometh and calleth them to dinner. They go, and being conducted into the golden court (for so they call it although not very fair), they find the emperor sitting upon a

---

to the office of *pechatnik* (keeper of the privy seal) and in the following year was sent to Denmark as an ambassador. In 1570 he suddenly fell from grace, was accused of treason and tortured to death. (Veselovskii, *Issledovaniia*, pp. 366–67; *Novoe izvestie o Rossii vremeni Ivana Groznogo. "Skazanie" Al'berta Shlikhtinga* [hereafter Schlichting] [Leningrad, 1934], pp. 46–47. See also N. Andreev, "Interpolations in the 16th-Century Muscovite Chronicles," *Slavonic and East European Review*, XXXV (1956), 100–5).

23. The letter is printed in Hakluyt (II, 206–7) and an English translation follows (II, 209–11). The letter is also found in *Calendar of State Papers, Domestic, Elizabeth, 1601–3, Addenda, 1547–63*, pp. 422–43.

24. *our.* their 1589.

25. Probably Aleksei Fedorovich Adashev. Adashev was one of the tsar's most influential advisers from the late 1540's until 1560. Throughout his career, his influence exceeded his formal rank. He began his service career in the office of *spal'nik* (groom of the bedchamber) and in 1550 he became court treasurer (*kaznachei*). Three years later he became a member of the boiar duma with the rank of *okol'nichii*, the second highest in the council (I. I. Smirnov, *Ocherki politicheskoi istorii russkogo gosudarstva 30–50kh godov XVI veka* [Moscow-Leningrad, 1958], pp. 212, 218; *RK*, pp. 12–13). In 1560 he suddenly fell into disgrace and was sent to serve in Livonia. It is usually assumed that he died in Dorpat in the same year (Veselovskii, *Issledovaniia*, p. 354). Recently discovered evidence suggests, however, that he may have died sometime after September, 1561 (Zimin, "Sostav boiarskoi dumy," p. 66).

high and stately seat, appareled with a robe of silver and with another diadem on his head; our men, being placed over against him, sit down. In the midst of the room stood a mighty cupboard upon a square foot, whereupon stood also a round board in manner of a diamond, broad beneath and towards the top narrow, and every step rose up more narrow than another. Upon this cupboard was placed the emperor's plate, which was so much that the very cupboard itself was scant able to sustain the weight of it; the better part of all the vessels and goblets was made of very fine gold. And amongst the rest there were four pots of very large bigness which did adorn the rest of the plate in great measure, for they were so high that they thought them at the least five foot long. There were also upon this cupboard certain silver casks, not much differing from the quantity of our firkins, wherein was reserved the emperor's drink. On each side of the hall stood four tables, each of them laid and covered with very clean tablecloths, whereunto the company ascended by three steps or degrees, all which were filled with the assembly present. The guests were all appareled with linen without and with rich skins within and so did notably set out this royal feast. The emperor, when he takes any bread or knife into his hand, doth first of all cross himself upon his forehead. They that are in special favor with the emperor sit upon the same bench with him, but somewhat far from him; and before the coming in of the meat, the emperor himself, according to an ancient custom of the kings of Muscovy, doth first bestow a piece of bread upon every one of his guests with a loud pronunciation of his title and honor in this manner: "The great duke of Muscovy and chief emperor of Russia, Ivan Vasil'evich (and then the officer nameth the guest), doth give thee bread." Whereupon all the guests rise up and by and by sit down again. This done, the gentleman usher of the hall comes in, with a notable company of servants carrying the dishes, and having done his reverence to the emperor, puts a young swan in a golden platter upon the table and immediately takes it thence again, delivering it to the carver and seven other of his fellows to be cut up; which being performed, the meat is then distributed to the guests with the like pomp and ceremonies. In the meantime the gentleman usher receives his bread and tasteth to the emperor; and afterward, having done his reverence, he departeth. Touching the rest of the dishes, because they were brought in out of order, our men can report no certainty; but this is true, that all the furniture of dishes and drinking vessels which were then for the use of a hundred guests was all of pure gold, and the tables were so laden with vessels of gold that there was no room for some to stand upon them.

We may not forget that there were one hundred and forty servitors arrayed in cloth of gold that in the dinner time changed thrice their habit and apparel, which servitors are in like sort served with bread from the emperor as the rest of the guests. Last of all, dinner being ended and candles brought in (for by this time night was come), the emperor calleth all his guests and noblemen by their names, in such sort that it seems miraculous that a prince, otherwise occupied in great matters of estate, should so well remember so many and sundry particular names. The Russes told our men that the reason thereof, as also of the bestowing of bread in that manner, was to the end that the emperor might keep the knowledge of his own household, and withal, that such as are under his displeasure might by this means be known.

Of the discipline of war amongst the Russes

Whensoever the injuries of their neighbors do call the king forth to battle, he never armeth a less number against the enemy than three hundred thousand soldiers, one hundred thousand whereof he carrieth out into the field with him, and leaveth the rest in garrison in some fit places for the better safety of his empire.[26] He presseth no husbandmen nor merchant, for the country is so populous that, these being left at home, the youth of the realm is sufficient for all his wars. As many as go out to warfare do provide all things of their own cost.[27]

26. Chancellor exaggerates the size of the Russian army. Seredonin (pp. 335–46) estimates that late in the sixteenth century there were about 110,000 men in various branches of the army. Zimin suggests that the Russian army had a strength of about 150,000 men in Chancellor's time (Zimin, Reformy, pp. 447–48).

27. Chancellor's statements are not entirely accurate. It is true that the Muscovite army of the sixteenth century consisted largely of cavalry made up of members of the service nobility. Nevertheless, certain groups of townsmen and peasants served in the infantry (V. O. Kliuchevskii, Skazaniia inostrantsev o moskovskom gosudarstve [Moscow, 1916], p. 83). The military reforms enacted by Ivan IV in 1555–56 increased the total size of the army and the proportion of commoners in it (A.V. Chernov, Vooruzhennye sily russkogo gosudarstva v XV–XVII vv. [Moscow, 1954], pp. 27–29, 94–95).

They fight not on foot but altogether on horseback. Their armor is a coat of mail and a helmet; the coat of mail without is gilded or else adorned with silk, although it pertain to a common soldier; they have a great pride in showing their wealth. They use bows and arrows as the Turks do; they carry lances also into the field. They ride with a short stirrup after the manner of the Turks; they are a kind of people most sparing in diet and most patient in extremity of cold above all others. For when the ground is covered with snow and is grown terrible and hard with the frost, this Russe hangs up his mantle, or soldier's coat, against that part from whence the wind and snow drives, and so, making a little fire, lieth down with his back towards the weather; this mantle of his serves him for his bed, wall, house, and all. His drink is the cold water of the river mingled with oatmeal, and this is all his good cheer, and he thinketh himself well and daintily fed therewith and so sitteth down by his fire and upon the hard ground roasteth as it were his weary sides thus daintily stuffed. The hard ground is his featherbed and some block or stone his pillow; and as for his horse, he is as it were a chamber-fellow with his master, faring both alike. How justly may this barbarous and rude Russe condemn the daintiness and niceness of our captains, who, living in a soil and air much more temperate, yet commonly use furred boots and cloaks! But thus much of the furniture of their common soldiers. But those that are of higher degrees come into the field a little better provided. As for the furniture of the emperor himself, it is then above all other times most notable. The coverings of his tent for the most part are all of gold, adorned with stones of great price and with the curious workmanship of plumasiers. As often as they are to skirmish with the enemy, they go forth without any order at all; they make no wings nor military divisions of their men as we do,[28] but lying for the most part in ambush do suddenly set upon the enemy. Their horses can well abstain two whole days from any meat. They feed upon the barks of trees and the most tender branches in all the time of war. And this scant and miserable manner of living both the horse and his master can well endure sometimes for the space of two months, lusty and in good state of body. If any man behave himself valiantly in the field to the contentation of the emperor, he bestoweth upon him in recompense of his service some farm or so much ground as he and his may live upon, which notwithstanding after his death returneth again to the emperor if he die without a male issue. For although

28. The Russian army was divided into five units or corps for a campaign.

his daughters be never so many, yet no part of that inheritance comes to them, except peradventure the emperor of his goodness give some portion of the land amongst them to bestow them withal.[29] As for the man, whosoever he be, that is in this sort rewarded by the emperor's liberality, he is bound in a great sum to maintain so many soldiers for the war, when need shall require, as that land in the opinion of the emperor is able to maintain.[30] And all those to whom any land falls by inheritance are in no better condition, for if they die without any male issue all their lands falls into the hands of the emperor.[31] And, moreover, if there be any rich man amongst them who in his own person is unfit for the wars and yet hath such wealth that thereby many noblemen and warriors might be maintained, if any of the courtiers present his name to the emperor, the unhappy man is by and by sent for and in that instant deprived of all his riches which with great pains and travail all his lifetime he had gotten together, except perhaps some small portion thereof be left him to maintain his wife, children, and family. But all this is done of all the people so willingly at the emperor's commandment that a man would think they rather make restitution of

29. Chancellor gives a good general description of the conditions of service land holding (pomest'e). Usually the widow or daughter of a service noble without male heirs received a portion of the estate for her support (na prozhitok) and the remainder of the land reverted to the crown. In 1644, a century after Chancellor's visit, for example, the widow usually received 20 per cent of her husband's lands and a daughter 10 per cent (PRP, V, 481).

30. At the time of Chancellor's visit, the holders of pomest'e estates were obliged to appear at muster with a number of armed fighting men and servants in proportion to the size of their estates. The surviving sources do not, however, make clear precisely how many men the service noble had to provide per unit of land (Chernov, Vooruzhennye sily, p. 26). In 1556 Ivan IV issued a precise definition of the obligations of the pomeshchiki. They were to supply one cavalryman in full armor for every 100 chetverti of good land (PSRL, XIII, i, 268–69; Chernov, Vooruzhennye sily, pp. 58–59).

31. In the sixteenth century the rulers of Muscovy were attempting to force the owners of votchina (hereditary) estates to perform service for the state in the same fashion as the holders of pomest'e (Veselovskii, Feodal'noe zemlevladenie, pp. 88–89). According to the decrees of 1562 and 1572, close male relatives other than sons could inherit a votchina estate but the widow of the former owner or a sister or daughter could not receive the land in full inheritance although she might be granted a holding to support her for the rest of her life. When there was no male heir, the votchina ultimately reverted to the crown (PRP, IV, 529–32). It is not clear if the decrees were enforced. Veselovskii suggests that they probably were not, at least during the time of the oprichnina (Feodal'noe zemlevladenie, p. 50).

other men's goods than give that which is their own to other men.[32] Now the emperor, having taken these goods into his hands, bestoweth them among his courtiers according to their deserts; and the oftener that a man is sent to the wars, the more favor he thinketh is borne to him by the emperor, although he go upon his own charge, as I said before. So great is the obedience of all men generally to their prince.

Of the ambassadors of the emperor of Muscovy

The Muscovite, with no less pomp and magnificence than that which we have spoken of, sends his ambassadors to foreign princes in the affairs of estate. For while our men were abiding in the city of Moscow, there were two ambassadors sent to the king of Poland accompanied with five hundred notable horse. And the greater part of the men were arrayed in cloth of gold and of silk, and the worst apparel was of garments of a blue color, to speak nothing of the trappings of the horses, which were adorned with gold and silver and very curiously embroidered. They had also with them one hundred white and fair spare horses to use them at such times as any weariness came upon them.[33] But now the time requireth me to speak briefly of other cities of the Muscovites and of the wares and commodities that the country yieldeth.

Novgorod

Next unto Moscow, the city of Novgorod is reputed the chiefest of Russia; for although it be in majesty inferior to it, yet in greatness it goeth beyond it. It is the chiefest and greatest mart town

32. Under normal circumstances, the rulers of Muscovy did not confiscate votchina estates in the manner Chancellor describes.

33. In 1553/54, Ivan sent an embassy to Poland-Lithuania to conclude a truce; its members were the boiar Vasilii Mikhailovich Iur'ev, the treasurer (kaznachei) Fedor Ivanovich Sukin, and the secretary (d'iak) Ishuk Bukharin (PSRL, XIII, i, 235).

of all Muscovy;[34] and albeit the emperor's seat is not there but at Moscow, yet the commodiousness of the river, falling into that gulf which is called *Sinus Finnicus*,[35] whereby it is well frequented by merchants, makes it more famous than Moscow itself. This town excels all the rest in the commodities of flax and hemp; it yields also hides, honey, and wax. The Flemings there sometimes had a house of merchandise, but by reason that they used the like ill dealing there which they did with us, they lost their privileges, a restitution whereof they earnestly sued for at the time that our men were there.[36] But those Flemings, hearing of the arrival of our men in those parts, wrote their letters to the emperor against them, accusing them for pirates and rovers, wishing him to detain and imprison them. Which things when they were known of our men, they conceived fear that they should never have returned home. But the emperor, believing rather the king's letters which our men brought than the lying and false suggestions of the Flemings, used no ill entreaty towards them.

Iaroslavl'

I aroslavl' also is a town of some good fame for the commodities of hides, tallow, and corn which it yields in great abundance. Cakes of wax are there also to be sold, although other places have greater store. This Iaroslavl' is distant from Moscow about two hundred miles,

34. Chancellor's opinion was widely held in Europe in the sixteenth century. Although Moscow may have surpassed Novgorod as a commercial center by mid-century, the former city-state was still the focal point of Russia's trade with western Europe through the Baltic. See A. P. Pronshtein, *Velikii Novgorod v XVI veke* (Khar'kov, 1957), pp. 131–34.

35. Gulf of Finland.

36. Scheltma points out that after the capture of Novgorod by Ivan III, the monopoly of the Hansa over the Baltic trade with Russia was effectively broken. Thus in the first half of the sixteenth century, German and Dutch merchants competed for trading rights in the Novgorod area. He accepts Chancellor's account of the protests by the Dutch merchants of Novgorod but gives no further information about their identity or activities (Jakov Scheltma, *Rusland en de Nederlanden* [Amsterdam, 1817], I, 18–19, 37). On Muscovite trade with Western Europe through the Baltic, see T. Esper, "Russia and the Baltic, 1494–1558," *Slavic Review*, XXV (1966), 458–74.

and betwixt them are many populous villages. Their fields yield such store of corn that in conveying it towards Moscow sometimes in a forenoon a man shall see seven hundred or eight hundred sleds, going and coming, laden with corn and salt fish. The people come a thousand miles to Moscow to buy that corn and then carry it away upon sleds; and these are those people that dwell in the north parts where the cold is so terrible that no corn doth growth there, or if it spring up it never comes to ripeness. The commodities that they bring with them are salt fish, skins, and hides.

Vologda

Vologda, being from Moscow five hundred and fifty miles,[37] yields the commodities of hemp and flax also, although the greatest store of flax is sold at Novgorod.

Pskov

The town of Pskov is frequented of merchants for the good store of honey and wax that it yieldeth.

Kholmogory

The north parts of Russia yield very rare and previous skins, and amongst the rest those principally which we call sables, worn about the necks of our noblewomen and ladies. It hath also martens' skins; white, black, and red fox skins; skins of hares and ermines and others, which they call and term barbarously as beavers, minks, and minivers. The sea adjoining breeds a certain beast which they call the

---

37. The distance between Vologda and Moscow is 420 versts or about 283 miles (V. A. Petrov, "Geograficheskie spravochniki XVII v.," *Istoricheskii arkhiv*, V [1950], 106).

morzh, which seeketh his food upon the rocks, climbing up with the help of his teeth. The Russes use to take them for the great virtue that is in their teeth, whereof they make as great account as we do of the elephant's tooth. These commodities they carry upon deer's backs to the town of Lampozhnia,[38] and from thence to Kholmogory, and there in the winter time are kept great fairs for the sale of them. This city of Kholmogory serves all the country about it with salt and salt fish. The Russes also of the north parts send thither oil, which they call train, which they make in a river called Una, although it be also made elsewhere; and here they use to bottle the water of the sea, whereof they make very great store of salt.

Of controversies in law and how they are ended

Having hitherto spoken so much of the chiefest cities of Russia as the matter required, it remaineth that we speak somewhat of the laws that the Muscovites do use, as far forth as the same are come to our knowledge. If any controversy arise among them they first make their landlords judges in the matter, and if they cannot end it, then they prefer it to the magistrate. The plaintiff craveth of the said magistrate that he may have leave to enter law against his adversary, and, having obtained it, the officer fetcheth the defendant and beateth him on the legs till he bring forth a surety for him. But if he be not of such credit as to procure a surety, then are his hands by an officer tied to his neck, and he is beaten all the way till he come before the judge. The judge then asketh him, as for example in the matter of debt, whether he oweth anything to the plaintiff. If he denies it then saith the judge, "How canst thou deny it?" The defendant answereth, "By an oath." Thereupon the officer is commanded to cease from beating of him until the matter be further tried. They have no lawyers, but every man is his own advocate, and both the complaint of the accuser and the answer of the defendant are in manner of petition delivered to the emperor entreating justice at his hands. The emperor himself heareth every great controversy and, upon the hearing of it, giveth judgment, and

38. Lampas 1589, 1599

that with great equity, which I take to be a thing worthy of special commendation in the majesty of a prince. But although he do this with a good purpose of mind, yet the corrupt magistrates do wonderfully pervert the same; but if the emperor take them in any fault, he doth punish them most severely. Now at the last when each party hath defended his cause with his best reasons, the judge demandeth of the accuser whether he hath any more to say for himself; he answereth that he will try the matter in fight by his champion, or else entreateth that in fight betwixt themselves the matter may be ended, which being granted, they both fight it out; or if both of them, or either of them, seem unfit for that kind of trial, then they have public champions to be hired which live by ending of quarrels. These champions are armed with iron axes and spears and fight on foot, and he whose champion is overcome is by and by taken and imprisoned and terribly handled until he agree with his adversary. But if either of them be of any good calling and degree and do challenge one another to fight, the judge grateth it, in which case they may not use public champions. And he that is of any good birth doth condemn the other if he be basely born and will not fight with him.[39] If a poor man happen to grow in debt, his creditor takes him and maketh him pay the debt in working either to himself or to some other man, whose wages he taketh up.[40] And there are some among them that use willingly to make themselves, their wives, and children bondslaves unto rich men to have a little money at the first into their hands, and so forever after content themselves with meat and drink, so little account do they make of liberty.[41]

39. The judicial duel was a regular part of Russian trial procedure up to the end of the sixteenth century. Chancellor's description of the duel is in basic accord with the provisions of the *Sudebnik* (Legal Code) of 1550. The *Sudebnik*, however, specifies that the combatants should be equally capable of fighting but does not stipulate that they had to belong to the same social class (*PRP*, IV, 236; see also H. W. Dewey, "Trial by Combat in Muscovite Russia," *Oxford Slavonic Papers*, IX [1960], 21–31).

40. A debtor who could not fulfill his obligations was normally given in servitude to his creditor in order to work off his debt (*PRP*, IV, 360). It is most unlikely that a debtor could be given in servitude to a third party.

41. Bondage by means of a loan contract (*kabal'noe kholopstvo*) was a common form of servitude in the sixteenth century. The *Sudebnik* of 1550 placed certain limits on those entering bondage. They could not contract a debt of more than 15 rubles and a father could not sell into bondage a son born while the father was still free. Members of the lesser nobility (*deti boiarskie*) were forbidden to sell themselves into debt servitude (*PRP*, IV, 254–56).

Of punishments upon thieves

I f any man be taken upon committing of theft, he is imprisoned and often beaten, but not hanged for the first offense as the manner is with us, and this they call the law of mercy. He that offendeth the second time hath his nose cut off and is burnt in the forehead with a hot iron. The third time he is hanged. There are many cutpurses among them, and if the rigor of the prince did not cut them off they could not be avoided.[42]

Of their religion

T hey maintain the opinions of the Greek church. They suffer no graven images of saints in their churches, but their pictures painted in tables they have in great abundance, which they do adore and offer unto, and burn wax candles before them and cast holy water upon them, without other honor. They say that our images, which are set up in churches and carved, have no divinity in them. In their private houses they have images for their household saints, and for the most part they are put in the darkest place of the house; he that comes into his neighbor's house doth first salute his saints, although he see them not. If any form or stool stand in his way, he oftentimes beateth his brow upon the same and, often ducking down with his head and body, worshipeth the chief image. The habit and attire of the priests and of the laymen doth nothing at all differ. As for marriage, it is forbidden to no man; only this is received and held amongst them for a rule and custom, that if a priest's wife do die he may not marry again nor take a second wife; and therefore they of secular priests, as they call them, are made monks to whom then chastity forever is commanded.[43] Their divine service is all done and said in their own

42. The district judicial ordinance (*gubnoi nakaz*) issued to the district of Medyn' in 1555 established the same penalties for theft that Chancellor describes. The sole difference lies in the punishment of the second offense for which the Medyn' statute prescribed beating the offender and cutting off his hand (*PRP*, IV, 184).

43. See D. E. Kozhanchikov (ed.), *Stoglav* (St. Petersburg, 1863), pp. 234–35.

language that every man may understand it. They receive the Lord's Supper with leavened bread, and after the consecration they carry it about the church in a saucer and prohibit no man from receiving and taking of it that is willing so to do.[44] They use both the Old and the New Testament and read both in their own language, but so confusedly that they themselves that do read understand not what themselves do say; and while any part of either Testament is read, there is liberty given by custom to prattle, talk, and make a noise, but in the time of the rest of the service they use very great silence and reverence, and behave themselves very modestly and in good sort.[45] As touching the Lord's Prayer, the tenth man amongst them knows it not; and for the articles of our faith and the Ten Commandments, no man, or at the least very few of them, do either know them or can say them. Their opinion is that such secret and holy things as they are should not rashly and imprudently be communicated with the common people.[46] They hold for a maxim amongst them that the Old Law and the Commandments also are all[47] abolished by the death and blood of Christ. All studies and letters of humanity they utterly refuse; concerning the Latin, Greek, and Hebrew tongues, they are altogether ignorant in them.[48]

Every year they celebrate four several fasts, which they call according to the names of the saints: the first begins with them at the time that our Lent begins; the second is called amongst them the fast of Saint Peter; the third is taken from the day of the Virgin Mary; and the fourth and last begins upon Saint Philip's day.[49] But as we begin our Lent upon Wednesday, so they begin theirs upon the Sunday. Upon the Saturday they eat flesh. Whensoever any of those fasting feasts do

44. Adams did not repeat Chancellor's observation that the Russians take the sacrament in both kinds.

45. A much sharper denunciation of disorder in the church is presented in the *Stoglav*, pp 51–52.

46. In Chancellor's own account, he makes the same observation but explains that the Russians would not repeat the Creed outside a church "for they say it should not be spoken of, but in the churches" (Hakluyt II, 236).

47. *all. om.* 1599.

48. By the standards of sixteenth-century England, the classical languages were little known in Russia. Nevertheless there were exceptional figures who knew Latin.

49. The four fasts are Lent, the fast of St. Peter and St. Paul (the second Monday after Pentecost through June 28), the fast of the Assumption of Our Lady (August 1–14), and the fast of St. Philip (November 15 through December 24).

draw near, look what week doth immediately go before them; the same week they live altogether upon white meats, and in their common language they call those weeks the fast of butter.

In the time of their fasts the neighbors everywhere go from one to another and visit one another and kiss one another with kisses of peace in token of their mutual love and Christian concord, and then also they do more often than at any other time go to the Holy Communion.[50] When seven days are past from the beginning of the fast, then they often do[51] either go to their churches or keep themselves at home and use often prayer, and for that sevennights[52] they eat nothing but herbs; but after that sevennight[53] fast is once past, then they return to their old intemperancy of drinking, for they are notable tosspots. As for the keeping of their fasting days, they do it very straitly; neither do they eat anything besides herbs and salt fish as long as those fasting days do endure, but upon every Wednesday and Friday in every week throughout the year they fast.

There are very many monasteries of the order of Saint Benedict amongst them to which many great livings for their maintenance do belong, for the friars and the monks do at the least possess the third part of the livings throughout the whole Muscovite empire. To those monks that are of this order there is amongst them a perpetual prohibition that they may eat no flesh, and, therefore, their meat is only salt fish, milk, and butter. Neither is it permitted them by the laws and customs of their religion to eat any fresh fish at all;[54] and at those four fasting times whereof we spake before, they eat no fish at all; only they live with herbs and cucumbers, which they do continually for that purpose cause and take order to grow and spring for their use and diet.

As for their drink, it is very weak and small. For the discharge of their office they do every day say service, and that early in the mornings before day, and they do in such sort and with such observation begin their service that they will be sure to make an end of it before day; and about nine of the clock in the morning they celebrate the Communion. When they have so done they go to dinner, and after din-

50. Adams, in retelling Chancellor's story, took details referring to Holy Week and applied them to all four fasting periods. Cf. Hakluyt II, 237.
51. *often do.* doo often 1599.
52. *sevennights.* sevennight 1599.
53. *sevennight.* sevennights 1599.
54. The dietary rules of the Russian church do not distinguish between fresh and salt fish.

ner they go again to service (and the like also after supper), and in the meantime while they are at dinner there is some exposition or interpretation of the Gospel used.

Whensoever any abbot of any monastery dieth, the emperor taketh all his household stuff, beasts, flocks of sheep, gold, silver, and all that he hath, or else he that is to succeed him in his place and dignity doth redeem all those things and buyeth them of the emperor for money.[55]

Their churches are built of timber, and the towers of their churches for the most part are covered with shingle boards. At the doors of their churches they usually build some entrance or porch as we do, and in their churchyards they erect a certain house of wood wherein they set up their bells, wherein sometimes they have but one, in some two, and in some also three.

There is one use and custom amongst them which is strange and rare, but yet it is very ridiculous, and that is this: when any man dieth amongst them, they take the dead body and put it in a coffin or chest; and in the hand of the corpse they put a little scroll, and in the same there are these words written, that the same man died a Russe of Russes, having received the faith and died in the same. This writing or letter they say they send to Saint Peter, who, receiving it as they affirm, reads it and by and by admits him into heaven, and that his glory and place is higher and greater than the glory of the Christians of the Latin church, reputing themselves to be followers of a more sincere faith and religion than they;[56] they hold opinion that we are but half Christians and themselves only to be the true and perfect church. These are the foolish and childish dotages of such ignorant barbarians.

Of the Muscovites that are idolaters, dwelling near to Tartaria

There is a certain part of Muscovy bordering upon the countries of the Tatars wherein those Muscovites that dwell are very great idolaters. They have one famous idol amongst them which they

55. This passage is extremely dubious since it is inconsistent with the relative independence of the great monasteries in the sixteenth century.
56. Several other foreign travellers report the same custom. See, for example,

call the Golden Old Wife;[57] and they have a custom that whensoever
any plague or any calamity doth afflict the country, as hunger, war, or
such like, then they go by and by[58] to consult with their idol, which
they do after this manner: they fall down prostrate before the idol, and
pray unto it, and put in the presence of the same a cymbal, and about
the same certain persons stand which are chosen amongst them by lot;
upon their cymbal they place a silver toad and sound the cymbal, and
to whomsoever of those lotted persons that toad goeth, he is taken and
by and by slain; and immediately, I know not by what illusions of the
devil or idol, he is again restored to life and then doth reveal and deliver the causes of the present calamity. And by this means knowing
how to pacify the idol, they are delivered from the imminent danger.

Of the form of their private houses, and of the apparel of the people

The common houses of the country are everywhere built of beams
of fir tree. The lower beams do so receive the round hollowness
of the uppermost that, by the means of the building thereupon, they
resist and expel all winds that blow; and where the timber is joined
together, there they stop the chinks with moss. The form and fashion of
their houses in all places is foursquare with straight and narrow windows, whereby with a transparent casement made or covered with skin
like to parchment they receive the light. The roofs of their houses are
made of boards covered without with the bark of trees. Within their
houses they have benches or greces,[59] hard by their walls, which com-

---

Samuel Collins, *The Present State of Russia* (London, 1671), p. 21, and A.
Mayerberg, *Iter in Moschoviam* (n.p. 1680), p. 55. See also Fletcher's account,
p. 235 below.

57. Many of the early voyagers mention this myth. Herberstein II, 41, 42
records the story: ". . . this idol of the Golden Old Woman is a statue, representing an old woman holding her son in her lap, and that recently another
infant has been seen, which is said to be her grandson . . . ." But he does not
say what magical powers she is supposed to have. In all probability, Adams
took the story directly from Herberstein's book since it is not mentioned by
Chancellor. Characteristically, Adams oversimplifies the issue. Herberstein related the story as a legend to be treated skeptically but Adams gives it as fact.

58. *by and by. om.* 1599.

59. Steps.

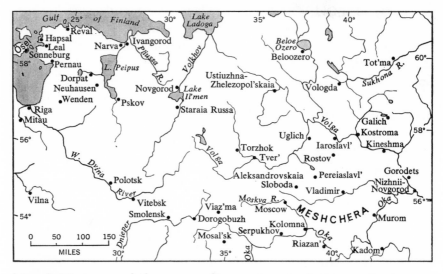

Map 2. Moscow and the surrounding regions in the sixteenth century.
Map by the University of Wisconsin Cartographic Laboratory

monly they sleep upon, for the common people know not the use of
beds. They have floors wherein in the morning they make a fire, and the
same fire doth either moderately warm or make very hot the whole
house.

The apparel of the people for the most part is made of wool. Their
caps are peaked like unto a rick or diamond, broad beneath and sharp
upward, in the manner of making whereof there is a sign and representation of nobility; for the loftier or higher their caps are, the greater is
their birth supposed to be, and the greater reverence is given them by
the common people.

The conclusion to Queen Mary

These are the things, most excellent queen, which your subjects
newly returned from Russia have brought home concerning the

state of that country.[60] Wherefore if your majesty shall be favorable and grant a continuance of the travel, there is no doubt but that the honor and renown of your name will be spread amongst those nations, whereunto three only noble personages from the very creation have had access, to whom no man hath been comparable.

60. The date of Chancellor's return cannot be precisely determined as records of the return voyage do not exist. Tsar Ivan's letter to King Edward (of whose death, of course, he had no knowledge) was dated "February 1554" and was sent to England "by the hands of Richard Chancellor" (Hakluyt II, 271–72).

Anthony Jenkinson

Introduction

Anthony Jenkinson, while still a youth, was sent in 1546 into the Levant as training for a mercantile career, and during the following years he seems to have traveled to most of the countries bordering on the Mediterranean. In 1555 he was admitted a member of the Mercers' Company, and in 1557 was appointed by the Russia Company captain-general of the fleet sailing for Russia, and their agent there for three years. He traveled to Russia on three subsequent occasions and continued in the service of the Russia Company until 1572.

Jenkinson married Judith, daughter of John Mersh, governor of the Merchants Adventurers. About 1578 he moved to Sywell, which he had bought from his father-in-law, and lived there for the next twenty years or more. Sometime about 1600 he moved to Ashton in Northamptonshire. He died in 1611 and was buried in Teigh in Rutland. Jenkinson had one son and five daughters, all of whom married and had issue; two other daughters and two sons died in childhood.[1]

An attractive character and good fortune provided Jenkinson with a better opportunity than any other Englishman to gain a thorough

1. Morgan and Coote, I, lxxxvii–cvii.

knowledge of Russian life during the first years of the Anglo-Muscovite entente. In the course of his career, he won and retained the respect of Ivan IV and was therefore able to visit the court as an honored guest and travel freely through the country. It is, in a sense, unfortunate that his most detailed description of Russia is contained in his account of his first voyage in 1557–58. Yet even on that first journey, Jenkinson saw and recorded many things of interest alike to his contemporaries and to future readers.

The account of the Russian part of Jenkinson's first voyage is divided into two sections. The first of these is a detailed and meticulously accurate description of his route from England to the mouth of the Dvina, interspersed with a few comments about the sights along the way. As a veteran captain, Jenkinson was well prepared to record his journey and an amateur geographer retracing his path can only wonder at his skill.

The second part of the work consists of a group of well-composed vignettes of Muscovy and its citizens. These descriptive passages, usually presented without interpretative comment, are distinguished by the same precision that marks the author's record of his voyage. In describing the route from the White Sea coast to Vologda, for example, Jenkinson succeeds in a few words in presenting a vivid impression of the landscape, a pithy description of the river trade and an account of the appearance and economic significance of Vologda, the main entrepôt of the north.

In his capacity as ambassador, Jenkinson had the chance to observe the ceremonies of the court. Although many foreign visitors to Muscovy recorded their impressions of the formal reception of ambassadors in the Moscow Kremlin and the ritual of the blessing of the waters at Epiphany, Jenkinson's description of these observances is among the most effective in all of the foreign literature on the Muscovite state. Likewise his picture of Moscow is an invaluable record of the city's appearance before the Tatar invaders destroyed much of it in 1571.

Nowhere in his work does Jenkinson theorize on the nature of the Muscovite state and society or the factors underlying their evolution. The chain of visual images is broken only by a few capsule comments on the government, the church, and the mores of the subjects. Most of the statements are not controversial: in discussing the nature of the Muscovite government, Jenkinson remarks simply that the tsar had great power over his subjects and in legal matters acted as the final court of appeal. The only aspect of governmental activity which attracted his detailed attention was the administration of the taverns, of which he left a description unique in the literature of the mid-sixteenth century.

The taverns also occupied a central position in his brief comments on Muscovite manners. Jenkinson's remarks were much gentler than those of most of his countrymen. He regarded drunkenness as the chief Russian vice and like Fletcher presented a Hogarthian sketch of the baleful effects of the public houses on the fortunes and morals of their customers.

Jenkinson's work ends on a characteristically vivid note with an evocative description of the scene that for many writers has symbolized Russia: a sleigh moving across the snow of a winter landscape.

Jenkinson's account was included in Richard Hakluyt, *Principal Navigations* (3 vols.; London 1589), I, Hh4^r–Hh6^v; (3 vols.; London, 1598–1600), I, Cc5^v–Ddl^v; (12 vols.; Glasgow, 1903–5), II, 413–25. It was subsequently included in Samuel Purchas, *Purchas, His Pilgrimes* (4 vols.; London, 1625), III, V3^v–V5^v; (20 vols.; Glasgow, 1905–7), XI, 623–35. All of Jenkinson's works are included in Morgan and Coote.

Jenkinson's account has been translated twice into Russian: V. N. Berkh (trans.), "Puteshestvie angliiskago kuptsa Antona Dzhenkinsona iz Londona v Moskvu v 1557 godu," *Syn otechestva*, LXXVIII (1822), 103–29; and Iu. V. Got'e (trans.), *Angliiskie puteshestvenniki v moskovskom gosudarstve v XVI veke* (Leningrad, 1937), pp. 71–80. S. M. Seredonin, "Izvestiia anglichan o Rossii vo vtoroi polovine XVI veka," *Chteniia v Imperatorskom obshchestve istorii i drevnostei rossiiskikh pri Moskovskom universitete* (Moscow, 1884), Book IV, Part III, pp. 30–36, is a translation of the last part of Jenkinson's account, beginning with the narrator's arrival in Russia.

Anthony Jenkinson

A Voyage to Russia in 1557

First, by the grace of God, the day and year above mentioned,[1] I departed from the said city, and the same day at Gravesend embarked myself in a good ship named the "Primrose," being appointed, although unworthy, chief captain of the same and also of the other three good ships, to say, the "John Evangelist," the "Anne," and the "Trinity," having also the conduct of the emperor of Russia his ambassador, named Osip Grigor'evich Nepea, who passed with his company in the said "Primrose."[2] And thus our four tall ships being well appointed, as well for men and[3] victuals as other necessary furniture, the

1. The headnote to the voyage reads: "The first voyage made by Master Anthony Jenkinson, from the City of London, toward the land of Russia, begun the twelfth day of May, in the year 1557."

2. The ambassador who went to England with Chancellor in 1556 and returned with Jenkinson in the following year. He is usually referred to as governor (*namestnik*) of Vologda (Tolstoy, p. 9) but the title was probably purely honorary, granted, according to the practice of the period, in order to give the ambassador greater personal authority while carrying out his mission. The Russian chronicle which mentions his journey describes him simply as a "Vologdan" (*PSRL*, XIII, i, 270).

3. *and.* as 1599.

said twelfth day of the month of May we weighed our anchors and departed from the said Gravesend in the afternoon. And plying down the Thames, the wind being easterly and fair weather, the thirteenth day we came aground with the "Primrose" upon a sand called the Blacktail,[4] where we sat fast until the fourteenth day in the morning; and then, God be praised, she came off, and that day we plied down as far as Our Lady of Holland[5] and there came to an anchor, the wind being easterly, and there remained until the twentieth day. Then we weighed and went out at Goldmer Gat,[6] and from thence in at Balsey Slade,[7] and so into Orwell Wands where we came to an anchor. But as we came out at the said Goldmer Gat, the "Trinity" came on ground on certain rocks that lie to the northward of the said gat and was like to be bilged and lost. But by the aid of God at the last she came off again, being very leaky;[8] and the twenty-first day, the "Primrose" remaining at an anchor in the wands, the other three ships bore into Orwell Haven, where I caused the said "Trinity" to be grounded, searched, and repaired. So we remained in the said haven until the twenty-eighth day; and then, the wind being westerly, the three ships that were in the haven weighed and came forth, and in coming forth the "John Evangelist" came on ground upon a sand called the Andros,[9] where she remained one tide, and the next full sea she came off again without any great hurt, God be praised.

The twenty-ninth day in the morning all four ships weighed in the wands and that tide went as far as Orfordness, where we came to an anchor because the wind was northerly. And about six of the clock at night the wind veered to the southwest, and we weighed anchor and bore clear of the ness and then set our course northeast and by north until midnight, being then clear of Yarmouth sands. Then we winded north and by west and north-northwest until the first of June at noon; then it waxed calm and continued so until the second day at noon. Then the wind came at northwest with a tempest and much rain; and we lay close by and caped north-northeast, and northeast and by north

4. The Blacktail spit is on the Maplin sands, just beyond Shoeburyness.
5. 1599; Lady Holland 1589. The place was so named after the church dedicated to the Virgin, now in ruins. It is a promontory on the coast of Essex, known now as Little Holland.
6. A sandbar.
7. Marked "the Sledway" on old maps.
8. *leaky.* leake 1589, 1599.
9. It is possible that this is Andrew's shoal, near to Orfordness.

as the wind shifted, and so continued until the third day at noon. Then the wind veered westerly again, and we went north, our right course, and so continued our way until the fourth day at three of the clock in the afternoon, at which time the wind veered to the northwest again and blew a fresh gale and so continued until the seventh day in the morning, we lying with all our ships close by and caping to the north-wards. And then, the wind veering more northerly, we were forced to put roomer[10] with the coast of England again and fell overthwart New-castle, but went not into the haven and so plied upon the coast the eighth day and the ninth.

The tenth day the wind came to the north-northwest, and we forced to bear roomer with Flamborough Head, where we came to an anchor and there remained until the seventeenth day. Then the wind came fair, and we weighed and set our course north and by east and so con-tinued the same with a merry wind until the twenty-first at noon, at which time we took the sun and had the latitude in 60 degrees. Then we shifted our course and went north-northeast, and northeast and by north until the twenty-fifth day. Then we discovered certain islands, called the Heilick Islands,[11] lying from us northeast, being in the lati-tude of 66 degrees, 40 minutes. Then we went north and by west be-cause we would not come too nigh the land, and running that course four hours we discovered and had sight of Rost Islands, joining to the mainland of Finnmark. Here the sun continueth in sight above the hori-zon almost two months together, day and night.[12] Thus continuing our course along the coast of Norway and Finland, the twenty-seventh day we took the sun, being as far shot as Lofoten, and had the latitude in 69 degrees. And the same day in the afternoon appeared over our heads a rainbow like a semicircle with both ends upward. Note that there is between the said Rost Islands and Lofoten a whirlpool called Maelstrom, which from half-ebb until half-flood maketh such a terrible noise that it shaketh the rings in the doors of the inhabitants' houses of the said islands ten miles off.[13] Also, if there cometh any whale within the current of the same, they make a pitiful cry. Moreover, if great

10. Run at large.

11. Jenkinson was probably referring to the Traenen Islands which are located at the latitude mentioned. The name may have been derived from Helgeland, the name of the nearest part of the Norwegian mainland.

12. *Here . . . night. om.* 1599.

13. The Maelstrom or Moskenstrom is the current running through a narrow passage between two of the southernmost islands of the Lofoten group. Under certain conditions it forms a whirlpool.

trees be carried into it by force of streams and after with the ebb be cast out again, the ends and boughs of them have been so beaten that they are like the stalks of hemp that is bruised. Note that all the coast of Finnmark is high mountains and hills, being covered all the year with snow. And hard aboard the shore of this coast there is one hundred or one hundred and fifty fathoms of water in depth. Thus proceeding and sailing forward, we fell with an island called Senja, being in the latitude of 70 degrees. About this island we saw many whales, very monstrous, about our ships, some by estimation of sixty foot long; and being the engendering time they roared and cried terribly. From thence we fell with an island called Kettelwike.[14] This coast from Rost unto Lofoten lieth north and south, and from Lofoten to Senja, northeast and southwest, and from Senja to Kettelwike, east-northeast and west-southwest. From the said Kettelwike we sailed east and by north ten leagues and fell with a land called Ingöy Sound, where we fished, being becalmed, and took great plenty of cods. Thus plying along the coast, we fell with a cape called the North Cape, which is the northernmost land that we pass in our voyage to Saint Nicholas, and is in the latitude of 71 degrees and 10 minutes, and is from Ingöy Sound east and to the northwards fifteen leagues. And being at this North Cape the second day of July we had the sun at north four degrees above the horizon. The third day we came to Vardo,[15] having such mists that we could not see the land. This Vardo is a castle standing in an island two miles from the main of Finland, subject to the king of Denmark and the easternmost land that he hath. There are two other islands near adjoining unto that whereon the castle of Vardo standeth. The inhabitants of those three islands live only by fishing and make much stockfish, which they dry with frost. Their most feeding is fish; bread and drink they have none but such as is brought them from other places. They have small store of cattle, which are also fed with fish. From Vardo we sailed south-southeast ten leagues and fell with a cape of land called Kegor, the northernmost part of the land of Lapland. And between Vardo and the said cape is a great bay called Domes half,[16] in the south part whereof is a monastery of monks of the Russes' religion

14. In all probability, the name refers not to an island but to a promontory on the island of Soroy. In his account of his voyage through the same waters, Stephen Burrough used the name "Kedilwike" to refer to a chapel on a headland he passed on his way to North Cape (Hakluyt II, 325).
15. Wardhouse 1589, 1599.
16. Varanger Fjord.

called Pechenga. Thus proceeding forward, and sailing along the coast of the said land of Lapland winding southeast, the fourth day, through great mists and darkness, we lost the company of the other three ships and met not with them again until the seventh day when we fell with a cape or headland called Sviatoi Nos,[17] which is the entering into the Bay of Saint Nicholas.[18] At this cape lieth a great stone, to the which the barks that passed thereby were wont to make offerings of butter, meal, and other victuals, thinking that unless they did so their barks or vessels should there perish, as it hath been oftentimes seen; and there it is very dark and misty. Note that the sixth day we passed by the place where Sir Hugh Willoughby with all his company perished, which is called Arzina *reka,* that is to say, the river Arzina. The land of Lapland is an high land, having snow lying on it commonly all the year. The people of the country are half gentiles. They live in the summertime near the seaside and use to take fish of the which they make bread; and in the winter they remove up into the country into the woods where they use hunting and kill deer, bears, wolves, foxes, and other beasts, with whose flesh they be nourished and with their skins appareled in such strange fashion that there is nothing seen of them bare but their eyes. They have none other habitation but only in tents, removing from place to place according to the season of the year. They know no art nor faculty but only shooting, which they exercise daily, as well men as women, and kill such beasts as serve them for their food. Thus proceeding along the coast from Sviatoi Nos aforesaid, the ninth day of July we came to Cape Grace, being in the latitude of 66 degrees and 45 minutes and is at the entering in of the Bay of Saint Nicholas.[19] Aboard this land there is twenty or thirty fathoms water and sundry grounds good to anchor in. The current at this cape runneth southwest and northeast. From this cape we proceeded along until we came to Cross Island,[20] which is seven leagues from the said cape southwest, and from this island we set over to the other side of the bay and went south-southwest and fell with an headland called Foxenose,[21] which is

17. Suetinose 1589, 1599.
18. The White Sea.
19. At the latitude of 66° 45′ the coastline of the Kola Peninsula is comparatively regular. It is difficult to identify the precise point of land that Jenkinson had in mind.
20. Identified by Morgan and Coote as Sosnovets Island (Morgan and Coote, I, map facing p. 40).
21. Probably Cape Kerets.

from the said island twenty-five leagues. The entering of this bay from Cross Island to the nearest land on the other side is seven leagues over. From Foxenose proceeding forward, the twelfth day of the said month of July all our four ships arrived in safety at the road of Saint Nicholas, in the land of Russia, where we anchored, and had sailed from London unto the said road seven hundred and fifty leagues. The Russian ambassador and his company with great joy got to shore; and our ships here forthwith discharged themselves and, being laden again and having a fair wind, departed toward England the first of August. The third of the said month I with other of my company came unto the city of Kholmogory, being an hundred versts from the Bay of Saint Nicholas and in the latitude of 64 degrees, 25 minutes. I tarried at the said Kholmogory until the fifteenth day, and then I departed in a little boat up the great river of Dvina, which runneth very swiftly, and the self same day passed by the mouth of a river called Pinega, leaving it on our left hand fifteen versts from Kholmogory. On both sides of the mouth of this river Pinega is high land, great rocks of alabaster, great woods, and pineapple trees lying along within the ground, which by report have lain there since Noah's flood. And thus proceeding forward the nineteenth day in the morning, I came into a town called Emets,[22] an hundred versts from Kholmogory. All this way along they make much tar, pitch, and ashes of aspen trees. From thence I came to a place called Velikii[23] Ustiug, an ancient city, the last day of August. At this city meet two rivers, the one called Iug, and the other Sukhona, both which fall into the aforesaid river of Dvina. The river of Iug[24] hath his spring in the land of the Tatars called Cheremiss, joining to the country of Perm'; and Sukhona hath his head from a lake not far from the city of Vologda. Thus departing from Velikii[25] Ustiug and passing up[26] the river Sukhona we came to a town called Tot'ma. About this place the water is very shallow and stony and troublesome for barks and boats of that country, which they call *nasady* and *doshchaniki*, to pass that way, wherein merchandise are transported from the aforesaid Kholmogory to the city of Vologda. These vessels called nasady are very long builded, broad made, and close above, flat bottomed, and

22. Yemps 1589, 1599. The "pineapple trees" referred to above are conifers.
23. *Velikii. om.* 1589, 1599.
24. *of Iug.* Yug 1599.
25. *Velikii. om.* 1589, 1599.
26. *up. of* 1599.

draw not above four foot water, and will carry two hundred tons; they have none iron appertaining to them but all of timber. And when the wind serveth they are made to sail; otherwise they have many men, some to haul and draw by the necks with long small ropes made fast to the said boats and some set with long poles. There are many of these barks upon the river of Dvina. And the most part of them belongeth unto the city of Vologda, for there dwell many merchants, and they occupy the said boats with carrying of salt from the seaside unto the said Vologda.[27] The twentieth of September I came unto Vologda, which is a great city, and the river passeth through the midst of the same. The houses are builded with wood of fir trees, joined one within another and round without. The houses are foursquare without any iron or stonework, covered with birch barks and wood over the same. Their churches are all of wood, two for every parish, one to be heated for winter and the other for summer.

On the tops of their houses they lay much earth for fear of burning, for they are sore plagued with fire. This Vologda is in 59 degrees, 11 minutes, and is from Kholmogory one thousand versts.

All the way I never came in house but lodged in the wilderness by the river's side and carried provision for the way. And he that will travel those ways must carry with him an hatchet, a tinderbox, and a kettle, to make fire and seethe meat when he hath it; for there is small succor in those parts unless it be in towns.

The first day of December I departed from Vologda in post in a sled, as the manner is in winter. And the way to Moscow is as followeth: from Vologda to Commelski, twenty-seven versts; so to Olmor, twenty-five versts; so to Teloytske, twenty versts; so to Ure, thirty versts; so to Voshansko, thirty versts; then to Iaroslavl', thirty versts, which standeth upon the great river Volga; so to Rostov, fifty versts; then to Rogarin, thirty versts; so to Pereiaslavl', ten versts, which is a great town standing hard by a fair lake; from thence to Dowbnaye, thirty versts; so to Godoroke, thirty versts; so to Owchay, thirty versts; and last to the Moscow, twenty-five versts, where I arrived the sixth day of December.[28]

27. In the sixteenth century, Vologda was a major center of the salt trade. Both the Solovetskii Monastery and the St. Kirill Monastery of Beloozero maintained trading bases there (Tikhomirov, pp. 231–32, 243–44).

28. Several of these post stations on the road from Vologda to Moscow are no longer in existence. It is impossible in these cases to discover the original Rus-

There are fourteen posts, called *iamy*, between Vologda and Moscow, which are accounted five hundred versts asunder.

The tenth day of December I was sent for to the emperor's castle by the said emperor and delivered my letters[29] unto the secretary, who talked with me of divers matters by the commandment of the emperor. And after that my letters were translated, I was answered that I was welcome and that the emperor would give me that I desired.

The twenty-fifth day, being the day of the Nativity, I came into the emperor's presence and kissed his hand, who sat aloft in a goodly chair of estate, having on his head a crown most richly decked and a staff of gold in his hand, all appareled with gold and garnished with precious stones.

There sat distant from him about two yards his brother[30] and next unto him a boy of twelve years of age who was inheritor to the emperor of Kazan',[31] conquered by this emperor eight years past. Then sat his nobility round about him richly appareled with gold and stone. And after I had done obeisance to the emperor, he with his own mouth, calling me by my name, bade me to dinner; and so I departed to my

---

sian form of the names and indicate their precise locations. Iaroslavl', Rostov, and Pereiaslavl' are still significant centers. In three cases, Olmor (Obnora), Dowbnaye (Dubna), and Owchay (Ucha), the post houses were probably named after small rivers on which they were located. Teloytske probably refers to Teliatskii Iam (Petrov, "Geograficheskie spravochniki," p. 107). Commelski, Godoroke, Ure, Rogarin, and Voshansko could not be identified.

29. The letter is in the Public Record Office (*Calendar of State Papers, Foreign,* 1553–58, no. 595). It is printed in Tolstoy, pp. 13–15.

30. Prince Iurii Vasil'evich was born on October 30, 1532, and died on November 24, 1563 (*PSRL*, XIII, i, 66; ii, 372). He was mentally retarded and, although he was accorded the honors traditionally associated with his position, he played no role in political or military affairs. For example, he was left behind in Moscow during the last attack on Kazan' in 1552. In 1553, when Ivan seemed to be dying, no one apparently consided the possibility that Iurii might be his successor.

31. Utemysh Girey. He was the son of Safa Girey, the prince of the Crimean house who was khan of Kazan'. When his father died in 1549, he was apparently about two years old. For the next two years, the pro-Crimean party maintained control of the Kazan' government, but in 1551 a rival faction made an agreement to accept the Muscovite candidate, Shah-Ali, as khan, and to hand Utemysh Girey and his mother over to Ivan. When Utemysh was brought to Moscow, he lived at the tsar's court and on January 8, 1553, was christened and given the name Aleksandr (*PSRL*, XIII, i, 229; ii, 459, 468–69; *Prodolzhenie Drevnei rossiiskoi vivliofiki,* VIII, 310–11; IX, 134).

lodging till dinner time, which was at six of the clock by candlelight.

The emperor dined in a fair great hall, in the midst whereof was a pillar foursquare very artificially made, about which were divers tables set; and at the uppermost part of the hall sat the emperor himself, and at his table sat his brother, his uncle's son,[32] the metropolitan,[33] the young emperor of Kazan', and divers of his noblemen, all of one side. There were divers ambassadors and other strangers, as well Christians as heathens, diversely appareled, to the number of six hundred men, which dined in the said hall, besides two thousand Tatars, men of war, which were newly come to render themselves to the emperor and were appointed to serve him in his wars against the Livonians,[34] but they dined in other halls. I was set at a little table, having no stranger with me, directly before the emperor's face. Being thus set and placed, the emperor sent me divers bowls of wine, and mead, and many dishes of meat from his own hand, which were brought me by a duke. And my table served all in gold and silver, and so likewise on other tables there were set bowls of gold set with stone, worth by estimation four hundred pounds sterling one cup, besides the plate which served the tables.

There was also a cupboard of plate, most sumptuous and rich, which was not used, among the which was a piece of gold of two yards long, wrought in the top with towers and dragons' heads, also divers barrels of gold and silver with castles on the bungs, richly and artificially made. The emperor and all the hall throughout was served with dukes;[35] and when dinner was ended, the emperor called me by name

32. Prince Vladimir Andreevich of Staritsa, son of one of the younger brothers of Vasilii III. He was the candidate of those boiars who, during Ivan's illness in 1553, would not at first recognize the tsar's infant son, Dmitrii, as his successor. Since he was the potential focus of boiar opposition, Vladimir Andreevich was deeply distrusted by the tsar. In 1569 he was poisoned on Ivan's orders.

33. Makarii was metropolitan from 1542 to 1563. He was one of the exceptional figures of his generation. As head of the church, he administered its affairs energetically and defended vigorously its doctrines and practices and its possessions. He was, at the same time, a spokesman for the imperial pretensions of the rulers of Muscovy; it was Makarii who was primarily responsible for staging the coronation of Ivan IV as tsar in 1547.

34. A number of Tatar detachments took part in the initial attack on Livonia in January 1558 (PSRL, XIII, i, 287). It is unclear to which of them Jenkinson refers. Livonians: Lyfflanders 1589, 1599.

35. Stol'niki, court functionaries, one of whose duties was to serve at banquets held on high state occasions. The stol'niki, originally court waiters, eventually became a numerous category of Moscow service men.

and gave me drink with his own hand, and so I departed to my lodging.

Note that when the emperor drinketh all the company stand up, and at everytime he drinketh or tasteth of a dish of meat he blesseth himself. Many other things I saw that day not here noted.

The fourth of January, which was Twelfthtide with them, the emperor, with his brother and all his nobles all most richly appareled with gold, pearls, precious stones, and costly furs, with a crown upon his head of the Tatarian fashion, went to the church in procession with the metropolitan, and divers bishops and priests. That day I was before the emperor again in Russe apparel, and the emperor asked if that were not I, and his chancellor answered, yea. Then he bade me to dinner. Then came he out of the church and went with the procession upon the river, being all frozen; and there standing bareheaded with all his nobles, there was a hole made in the ice, and the metropolitan hallowed the water with great solemnity and service and did cast of the said water upon the emperor's son and the nobility. That done, the people with great thronging filled pots of the said water to carry home to their houses, and divers children were thrown in, and sick people, and plucked out quickly again, and divers Tatars christened, all which the emperor beheld. Also there were brought the emperor's best horses to drink at the said hallowed water. All this being ended, he returned to his palace again and went to dinner by candlelight and sat in a wooden house very fairly gilded.[36] There dined in the place above three hundred strangers, and I sat alone as I did before directly before the emperor, and had my meat, bread, and drink sent me from the emperor.

The city of Moscow is great, the houses for the most part of wood and some of stone, with windows of iron which serve for summertime. There are many fair churches of stone, but more of wood, which are made hot in the wintertime. The emperor's lodging is in a fair and large castle, walled foursquare of brick high and thick, situated upon a hill two miles about, and the river on the southwest side of it, and it hath sixteen gates in the walls and as many bulwarks. His palace is separated from the rest of the castle by a long wall going north and south to the riverside. In his palace are churches, some of stone and some of wood, with round towers fairly gilded. In the church doors

36. *gilded.* gilt 1589, 1599.

and within the churches are images of gold. The chief markets for all things are within the said castle, and for sundry things, sundry markets, and every science by itself. Also[37] in the winter there is a great market without the castle upon the river, being frozen, and there is sold corn, earthen pots, tubs, sleds, etc. The castle is in circuit 2,900 paces.

The country is full of marish ground and plain, in woods and rivers abundant, but it bringeth forth good plenty of corn. This emperor is of great power, for he hath conquered much as well of the Livonians, Poles, Latvians,[38] and Swedes, as also of the Tatars, and gentiles called Samoyeds, having thereby much enlarged his dominions.[39] He keepeth his people in great subjection; all matters pass his judgment be they never so small. The law is sharp for all offenders.

The metropolitan dealeth in matters of religion as himself listeth, whom the emperor greatly honoreth. They use the ceremonies and orders of the Greek church. They worship many images painted on tables, and specially the image of Saint Nicholas. Their priests be married, but their wives being dead they may not marry the second time and so become monks, whereof are a great number in the land.

They have four Lents in the year, and the week before Shrovetide they call the Butter Week, etc.[40]

They have many sorts of meats and drinks when they banquet and delight in eating of gross meats and stinking fish. Before they drink they use to blow in the cup; their greatest friendship is in drinking. They are great talkers and liars, without any faith or trust in their words, flatterers and dissemblers. The women be there very obedient to their husbands and are kept straitly from going abroad but at some seasons.

At my being there I heard of men and women that drunk away their

37. *Also.* And 1599
38. Lettos 1589, 1599.
39. It is unclear whether Jenkinson refers to the past rulers of Muscovy in general or Ivan IV in particular. If the passage is supposed to be a list of Ivan's conquests, it exaggerates the extent of his triumphs. His great military achievements were the conquest of Kazan' in 1552 and Astrakhan' in 1556. During his minority, the regency conducted a war with Poland-Lithuania which resulted in a loss of territory. Between 1554 and 1557, there was a war with Sweden which consisted of a series of small-scale skirmishes along the border. The peace settlement brought a return to the status quo (*PSRL,* XIII, i, 259–61, 279–80).
40. See Chancellor, p. 36 above, and note.

children and all their goods at the emperor's tavern; and not being able
to pay, having impawned himself, the taverner bringeth him out to the
highway and beats him upon the legs. Then they that pass by, knowing
the cause and having peradventure compassion upon him, giveth the
money, and so he is ransomed.

In every good town there is a drunken tavern called a *korchma*,
which the emperor sometime letteth out to farm and sometimes bestoweth for a year or two on some duke or gentleman in recompense of
his service; and for that time he is lord of all the town, robbing and
spoiling and doing what pleaseth him. And then he, being grown rich,
is taken by the emperor and sent to the wars again, where he shall
spend all that which he hath gotten by ill means so that the emperor in
his wars is little charged, but all the burden lieth upon the poor people.

They use saddles made of wood and sinews with the tree gilded
with damask work and the seat covered with cloth, sometimes of gold
and the rest saffian leather,[41] well stitched. They use little drums at
their saddle bows, by the sound whereof their horses use to run more
swiftly.

The Russe is appareled in this manner: his upper garment is of cloth
of gold, silk, or cloth, long, down to the foot, and buttoned with great
buttons of silver or else laces of silk set on with brooches, the sleeves
thereof very long, which he weareth on his arm ruffed up; under that
he hath another long garment buttoned with silk buttons, with a high
collar standing up of some color, and that garment is made straight;
then his shirt is very fine and wrought with red silk or some gold, with
a collar of pearl; under his shirt he hath linen breeches; upon his legs a
pair of hose without feet and his boots of red or yellow leather; on his
head he weareth a white *kolpak* with buttons of silver, gold, pearl, or
stone, and under it a black fox cap turned up very broad.

When he rideth on horseback to the wars or any journey, he hath a
sword of the Turkish fashion and his bow and arrows of the same manner. In the town he weareth no weapon but only two or three pair of
knives having the hafts of the tooth of a fish called the morzh.

In the wintertime the people travel with sleds in town and country,
the way being hard and smooth with snow; the waters and rivers are

41. A fine soft leather, usually goatskin or sheepskin.

all frozen, and one horse with a sled will draw a man upon it four hundred miles in three days; but in the summertime the way is deep with mire and traveling is very ill.

The Russe, if he be a man of any ability, never goeth out of his house in the winter but upon his sled and in summer upon his horse; and in his sled he sits upon a carpet or a white bear's skin. The sled is drawn with a horse well decked with many foxes and wolves' tails at his neck and is conducted by a little boy upon his back; his servants stand upon the tail of the sled, etc.

A Diplomatic Mission

Sir Thomas Randolph

Introduction

S ir Thomas, son of Avery Randolph, was born in Badlesmere, Kent, in 1523. He entered Christ Church, Oxford, at the time of its foundation and graduated B.A. in October, 1545, and B.C.L. in 1548. In 1549 he was made principal of Broadgates Hall (now Pembroke College), Oxford. He continued there until 1553, when the Protestant persecutions under Queen Mary compelled him to resign and retire to France.

Soon after the accession of Elizabeth, in 1558, Randolph was acting as an agent in Germany, and in 1559 began the first of several important missions to Scotland for the queen. Besides his mission to Russia in 1568, he served the queen in France in 1573 and in 1576. He was also the principal negotiator with King James of Scotland in the important negotiations of the early 1580's.

He married Anne Walsingham, sister of Sir Francis Walsingham, in 1571, and by her had three children, two sons and a daughter. He held the joint offices of Chancellor of the Exchequer and Postmaster-General until his death, on June 8, 1590.[1]

1. See *DNB* and Conyers Read, *Mr. Secretary Walsingham and the Policy of Queen Elizabeth* (Oxford, 1925).

Randolph's account of his journey to Russia in 1568 and 1569 is the laconic report of a professional diplomat. The ambassador narrates in skeleton form the main events of his voyage and reception in Moscow, stopping only occasionally to describe what he saw or comment on his experiences. The terseness and precision of his work is likely to inspire two reactions in the modern reader. If Randolph can be judged by his writing on Russia, he was a careful observer who strove to record his experiences with complete accuracy. For this very reason, his work is also frustrating because it describes so little and is silent on so many issues on which Randolph could probably have made valuable comments.

The core of the work is Randolph's description of his embassy to Moscow. The record of his mission resembles the Russian diplomatic reports of the same period in that the ambassador reports in considerable detail on the ceremonial form of his reception and gives very little information about the content of the negotiations he conducted. Like many other foreign ambassadors to Muscovy, Randolph was deeply impressed and at the same time profoundly depressed by the treatment he received. His 1568 letter to Lord Burghley makes clear that while he was still in northern Russia he had already heard of the reign of terror brought on by the institution of the oprichnina. He was understandably fearful and expressed the desire to finish his mission as quickly as possible and get out of Russia. His apprehension increased when he was subjected to the solicitous but stifling care of the officials assigned to accompany and provide for him according to the usual Muscovite practice when receiving foreign dignitaries. When he reached Moscow and discovered that he would have to wait indefinitely in isolation before meeting the tsar, he jumped to the conclusion that "some evil had been intended upon us."

On the basis of Randolph's narrative, it is difficult to tell whether he received the treatment usually accorded to foreign ambassadors or was received with unusual discourtesy. The latter alternative is possible since Ivan IV had expected Queen Elizabeth to send Jenkinson as ambassador and was annoyed when a stranger appeared in his place. The operations of the oprichnina might also have prompted the authorities in Moscow to apply unusual restrictions to the ambassador's freedom of action. One can only guess, since Randolph makes no attempt to explain what motivated the unpleasant features of his reception.

The manner in which he was received at court made a much more favorable impression upon him. Once he was allowed to carry out his mission, the elaborate ceremony that had previously annoyed him seemed awesome and a little confusing. After his formal reception, according to his description of the mission, he met Ivan and completed his task without further complications. Once again, however, Randolph is silent on the most interesting aspects of his negotiations with the tsar. Other sources suggest that he and Ivan engaged in hard bargaining and only through skill and patience did he succeed in winning fresh concessions for the Russia Company although he offered the tsar nothing in return for his generosity.

Around his central theme, Randolph added glimpses of Russian life outside the reception chamber. His brief descriptions of the towns and countryside of northern and central Russia are interesting because they portray the area as rich in natural resources and prosperous. Despite its paucity of detail, his picture is in sharp contrast with the reports of travellers who covered the same route from the mouth of the Dvina to Moscow two decades later. The discrepancy is eloquent testimony to the disastrous consequences of the economic collapse that Russia suffered in the last years of the sixteenth century.

On Muscovite faith and morals, Randolph's comments are very similar to those of the other English travellers. With his usual economy of words, he simply states as axioms that Orthodoxy is a superstitious, ceremony-ridden religion akin to Catholicism and that Russians indulge in all kinds of "abominable vices." His comments are, in fact, rather restrained considering the depth of his personal convictions, as it will be remembered that he was exiled during the reign of Queen Mary. Randolph makes no attempt to explain the causes of the phenomena he observed; unlike Fletcher, he did not argue that the Muscovites' loose morals were the result of their corrupt religion.

Randolph's work is remarkable, above all, for the subjects he did not discuss. His treatment of Ivan IV is a case in point. The "terrible" tsar who dominates the pages of other works on Russia appears as a manikin without distinguishing features of physique or character. He is simply present as the figure to whom Randolph addressed his greetings and from whom he received the concessions he had sought. Yet the author makes clear that he had long interviews both in Moscow and in the Aleksandrovskaia Sloboda, the center of the oprichnina. Since Randolph must surely have formed a clear picture of the tsar, his reticence is deeply disappointing.

His silence on the oprichnina is even more puzzling. Although the period of his stay in Moscow apparently coincided with a temporary lull in the campaign of executions of the tsar's suspected enemies, his previous fears for his own head must surely have aroused his curiosity about the tsar's experiment in government, if only to find out how he should act in order to get out of the country alive. Moreover, even if he was in Moscow at a comparatively peaceful time, he probably made contact with the representatives of the Russia Company after his initial quarantine. The Company's policy during the period of the oprichnina indicates that its employees in Russia had a good understanding of the political situation which they would surely have explained to a newly arrived ambassador. Whatever the reason for his silence, Randolph probably took with him to the grave insights on the composition and workings of the oprichnina that would provide a corrective to the sensational tales of the Germans and Livonians who served in it.

Randolph's account of Russia, then, is important for its terse revelations, but, above all, tantalizing in its silence.

Randolph's account is included in Richard Hakluyt, *Principal Navigations* (3 vols.; London, 1589), I, Ool^r–Oo2^v; (3 vols.; London, 1598–1600), I, Ii2^v–Ii3^v; and (12 vols.; Glasgow, 1903–5), III, 102–8. His account has also been edited by Morgan and Coote, II, 243–50.

Randolph's account has been translated into Russian by S. M. Seredonin, "Izvestiia anglichan o Rossii vo vtoroi polovine XVI veka," *Chteniia v Imperatorskom obshchestve istorii i drevnostei rossiiskikh pri Moskovskom universitete* (Moscow, 1884), Book IV, Part III, 91–95.

Sir Thomas Randolph

A Mission to Muscovy

The twenty-second day of June in the year of our Lord 1568, I
went aboard the "Harry," lying in the road at Harwich, with my
company being to the number of forty persons or thereabouts, of which
the one half were gentlemen desirous to see the world.

Within one day's sailing we were out of the sight of all land and,
following our course directly north till we came to the North Cape, we
sailed for the space of twelve days with a prosperous wind without
tempest or outrage of sea. Having compassed the North Cape, we directed our course flat southeast, having upon our right hand Norway,
Vardo,[1] and[2] Lapland, all out of sight till we came to Cape Gallant.[3]
And so sailing between two bays, the two and thirtieth day after our
departure from Harwich, we cast anchor at Saint Nicholas road. In all
the time of our voyage, more than the great number of whales engendering together, which we might plainly behold, and the *spermaceti*,
which we might see swimming upon the sea, there was no great thing
to be wondered at. Sometimes we had calms, wherein our mariners

---

1. Wardhouse 1589, 1599.
2. *and. om.* 1589, 1599.
3. Sviatoi Nos (Morgan and Coote, Vol. I, map facing p. 40).

fished and took good store of divers sorts. At Saint Nicholas we landed the twenty-third of July, where there standeth an abbey of monks (to the number of twenty) built all of wood. The apparel of the monks is superstitious, in black hoods as ours have been. Their church is fair but full of painted images, tapers, and candles. Their own houses are low and small rooms. They lie apart; they eat together and are much given to drunkenness; unlearned, write they can; preach they do never, ceremonious in their church, and long in their prayers.

At my first arrival I was presented from their prior with two great rye loaves; fish, both salt and fresh, of divers sorts, both sea fish and fresh water; one sheep alive, black with a white face, to be the more grateful unto me; and so with many solemn words inviting me to see their house, they took their leave.

Town or habitation at Saint Nicholas there is none more than about four houses near the abbey and another built by the English company for their own use.

This part of the country is most part wood saving here and there pasture and arable ground, many rivers, and divers islands uninhabited, as the most part of the country is for the coldness in winter.

Saint Nicholas standeth northeast, the elevation of the pole 64 degrees. The river that runneth there into the sea is called Dvina, very large but shallow. This river taketh his beginning about seven hundred miles within the country; and upon this river standeth Kholmogory and many pretty villages, well situated for pasture, arable land, wood, and water. The river pleasant between high hills of either side inwardly inhabited, and in a manner a wilderness of high fir trees and other wood.

At Kholmogory, being one hundred versts, which we account for three quarters of a mile every verst, we tarried three weeks, not being suffered to depart before the emperor had word of our coming, who sent to meet us a gentleman of his house to convey us and to see us furnished of victuals and all things needful upon his own charge.

The allowance of meat and drink was for every day two rubles, besides the charge of boats by water, and four score post horses by land, with above one hundred carts to carry my wines and other carriage.

Kholmogory is a great town builded all of wood, not walled but scattered house from house. The people are rude in manners and in apparel homely, saving upon their festival and marriage days.

The people of this town, finding commodity by the Englishmen's traffic with them, are much at their commandment, given much to drunkenness and all other kind of abominable vices.

In this town the Englishmen have lands of their own given them by the emperor and fair houses with offices for their commodity very many.

Of other towns until I come to Vologda I write not because they are much like to this and the inhabitants not differing from them.

I was five whole weeks upon the river of Dvina till I came to Vologda, being drawn with men against the stream, for other passage there is none.

Vologda standeth upon the river of Vologda, which cometh into Dvina. The town is great and long, built all of wood as all their towns are.

In this town the emperor hath built a castle environed with a wall of stone and brick, the walls fair and high about. Here (as in all other their towns) are many churches, some built of brick, the rest of wood, many monks and nuns in it—a town also of great traffic and many rich merchants there dwelling.

From hence we passed by land towards Moscow in post, being five hundred versts great, which are equal with our miles.[4] In their towns we baited or lay, being post towns.

The country is very fair, plain, and pleasant; well inhabited; corn, pasture, meadows enough; rivers and woods, fair and goodly.

At Iaroslavl' we passed the river of Volga, more than a mile over. This river taketh his beginning at Beloe Ozero[5] and descendeth into *Mare Caspium*, portable through of very great vessels with flat bottoms, which far pass any that our country useth.

To sail by this river into Mare Caspium, the English company caused a bark to be built of twenty-seven tons,[6] which there was never seen before. This bark, built and ready rigged to the sea with her whole furniture, cost not the company above one hundred marks there.

To Moscow we came about the end of September, received by no man; not so much as our own countrymen suffered to meet us, which bred suspicion in me of some other course intended than we had hitherto found.

We were brought to a house built of purpose by the emperor for ambassadors, fair and large after the fashion of that country.

Two gentlemen were appointed to attend upon me—the one to see

4. The verst equals 0.68 mile.
5. The notion that the Volga originates in Beloe Ozero was probably derived from Jenkinson's map of 1562 which contains the same mistake.
6. *tons.* tunne 1589.

us furnished of victuals and that we lacked nothing of the emperor's allowance, the other to see that we should not go out of the house nor suffer any man to come unto us—in which they left nothing undone that belonged to their charge. But specially he that looked to our persons so straitly handled us that we had no small cause to doubt that some evil had been intended unto us. No supplication, suit, or request could take place for our liberty nor yet to come to his presence.

Having passed over seventeen weeks in this sort, the emperor sendeth word that we should be ready against Tuesday, the twentieth of February, at eight a clock in the morning.

The hour being come that I should go the court, the two gentlemen, *pristavy* as they call them, came unto me appareled more princely than before I had ever seen them. They press us to depart and mounted upon their own horses and the ambassador upon such a one as he had borrowed, his men marching on foot to their great grief.

The ambassador (being myself) was conveyed into an office where one of the chancellors doth use to sit, being there accompanied with the two foresaid gentlemen. I tarried two long hours before I was sent for to the emperor. In the end, message being brought that the emperor was set, I was conveyed by my gentlemen up a pair of stairs through a large room where sat by my estimation three hundred persons, all in rich attire taken out of the emperor's wardrobe for that day, upon three ranks of benches set round about the place, rather to present a majesty than that they were either of quality or honor.

At the first entry into the chamber, I with my cap gave them the reverence such as I judged their stately sitting, grave countenances, and sumptuous apparel required; and seeing that it was not answered again of any of them, I covered my head; and so passing to a chamber where the emperor was, there received me at the door from my two gentlemen or governors two of the emperor's counselors, and showed me to the emperor and brought me to the middle of the chamber where I was willed to stand still and to say that which I had to say. I, by my interpreter, opened my message as I received it from the queen my mistress,[7] from whom I came, at whose name the emperor stood up and demanded divers questions of her health and state; whereunto

7. The instructions of the queen to Randolph are preserved in a draft dated June 16, 1568 (*Calendar of State Papers, Foreign,* 1566–68, no. 2272). The document is printed in Morgan and Coote, II, 240–43.

answer being made, he gave me his hand in token of my welcome and caused me to sit down and further asked me divers questions.

This done, I delivered her majesty's present, which was a notable great cup of silver curiously wrought, with verses graven in it expressing the histories workmanly set out in the same.[8]

All being said and done (as appeared) to his contentment, he licensed me and my whole company to depart, who were all in his presence and were saluted by him with a nod of his head, and said unto me: "I dine not this day openly, for great affairs I have; but I will send thee my dinner, and give leave to thee and thine to go at liberty, and augment our allowance to thee in token of our love and favor to our sister the queen of England."

I with reverence took my leave, being conveyed by two other of greater calling than those that brought me to the emperor's sight, who delivered me to the two first gentlemen, who conducted me to the office where I first was, where came unto me one called the "long duke"[9] with whom I conferred a while, and so returned to my lodging.

Within one hour after, in comes to my lodging a duke richly appareled accompanied with fifty persons, each of them carrying a silver dish with meat and covered with silver. The duke first delivered twenty loaves of bread of the emperor's own eating, having tasted the same, and delivereth every dish into my hands and tasted of every kind of drink that he brought.

This being done, the duke and his company sat down with me and

8. In the instructions of the queen to Randolph, Elizabeth gives specific directions for presenting this gift: "We have ordained that you shall present him from us with a rich standing cup of the weight of [blank] ounces, containing in it great numbers of pieces of plate artifically wrought, which when you shall present, you shall recommend it for the rarity of the fashion, assuring him that we do send him the same rather for the newness of the device than for the value, it being the first that ever was made in these parts of that manner. And so as you see cause to set forth the gift, as indeed the work of itself doth well deserve" (Tolstoy, pp. 45–46).

9. Probably Afanasii Ivanovich Viazemskii. In his letter of June 20, 1569, to Queen Elizabeth, Ivan mentioned that Viazemskii was his chief agent in conducting negotiations with Randolph (Morgan and Coote, II, 281–82). Viazemskii was a member of an old but impoverished family who rose rapidly to become one of Ivan's closest companions in the years of the oprichnina. He was accused of treason and disgraced in 1570. It is uncertain when and how he died (Kobrin, pp. 31–33).

took part of the emperor's meat and filled themselves well of all sorts and went not away from me unrewarded.

Within few nights after, the emperor had will to speak secretly with me and sent for me in the night by the "long duke." The place was far off, and the night cold; and I, having changed my apparel into such as the Russes do wear, found great incommodity thereby.

Having talked with him above three hours, towards the morning I was dismissed and so came home to my lodging, where I remained above six weeks after before I heard again from the emperor, who went the next day to Sloboda, the house of his solace.[10] After the end of which six weeks, which was about the beginning of April, the emperor returned from Sloboda aforesaid and sent for me again to make repair unto him. And being come, I dealt effectually with him in the behalf of our English merchants and found him so graciously inclined towards them that I obtained at his hands my whole demands for large privileges in general, together with all the rest my particular requests.[11]

And then he commended to my conduct into England a nobleman of his called Andrei Sovin as his ambassador for the better confirmation of his privileges granted and other negotiations with her majesty.[12] And thus being dispatched with full contentment, the said ambassador and myself departed and embarked at Saint Nicholas about the end of July and arrived safely at London in the month of September following.

10. The Aleksandrovskaia Sloboda, located northeast of Moscow. It was the tsar's headquarters during the time of the oprichnina.

11. On June 20, 1569, Ivan IV gave Randolph a charter of privileges granted to the Russia Company. The Company received a monopoly of overseas trade with Russia through the White Sea. Its members were also recognized as the only Englishmen who had the right to trade in the tsar's ports on the Baltic. In accordance with the queen's requests, Ivan cancelled the privileges he had previously granted to a rival group of English traders who were trying to make inroads into the trade with Russia. The Company's agents were exempted from customs duties and were granted many special favors. In particular, their Moscow base was incorporated into the oprichnina, that part of the Muscovite state that the tsar had carved out as his private principality. Inclusion in the oprichnina put the Company's agents at the center of power under the direct protection of the tsar. The charter also spelled out a number of detailed concessions—the right to hire Russian domestic help, to establish posts in a number of provincial towns, and to mine iron ore in a certain district (Morgan and Coote, II, 265–75).

12. Andrei Grigor'evich Sovin was in England as Ivan's ambassador from 1569 to 1570. Sovin had instructions to present Queen Elizabeth with a draft of a treaty of alliance. He was under orders to insist that she accept the document without any changes. Since the queen had no desire to enter a binding alliance with Russia, Sovin could not but fail in his mission (Tolstoy, p. 85).

George Turberville

Introduction

L ittle is known about Turberville's life. He was the son of Henry Turberville, and he had a brother named Nicholas who is incorrectly credited by Anthony à Wood with being George's father.[1] According to Wood, he was a graduate of New College and attended one of the inns of court, but there is no evidence to support this claim. In his "Farewell to a mother cousin, at his going towards Muscovy," Turberville states that he is making the voyage in an attempt to improve his fortunes, which were evidently in none too flourishing a condition, since he had all his years "in studies fond applied." Before his trip he had published four books, three volumes translated from the Latin of Ovid, Mantuan, and Mancinus respectively, and a volume of his own poems entitled *Epitaphes, Epigrams, Songs and Sonets.* This volume, and the Mancinus, were dedicated to the Countess of Warwick. After his voyage to Russia, he wrote three more books: *Tragicall Tales* (the only surviving edition is that of 1587), *The Booke of Faulconrie or Hauking* (1575), and *The Noble Arte of Venerie or Hunting* (1575).

1. *Athenae Oxonienses,* ed. Philip Bliss (London, 1813–20), I, 627.

The date of his death is unknown, although 1597 has been suggested as probable.[2]

Turberville, Randolph's secretary on the mission of 1568–69, set down his impressions of Russia in three chatty letters to friends in England. These letters are extraordinary in both form and content. They were written in poulters measure (an obsolete form consisting of alternate lines of twelve and fourteen syllables respectively) and abound in precious turns of phrase. Their content is the usual subject matter of tourists' postcards except that the message is the exact reverse of the usual travellers' cliches. Turberville described the landscape of Muscovy and the quaint native customs that caught his eye but was emphatic that he was having anything but a wonderful time. If his friends were wise, he insisted, they would stay in England where they were well off, and he would rejoin them as quickly as possible.

In fairness to Turberville, it should be noted that the circumstances of his visit were not likely to give him a favorable picture of Russia. What we know of him would suggest that he had no intrinsic interest in Russia and no professional stake in the success of Randolph's mission. His journey was an interruption of his activity as a writer, an annoyance to which he submitted only because he hoped to make enough money from the venture to pay his debts. It was, moreover, a singularly nerve-wracking method of straightening out his finances. For after the hazardous northern voyage, Randolph and his staff had to face the strains of a stay in Russia during the oprichnina. If the ambassador who had been hardened in the in-fighting of Scottish politics was unnerved at the prospect, it is easy to imagine the impact of the atmosphere in Russia on Turberville, who had no previous experience of the rigors of a diplomat's life.

The image of Russia in Turberville's letters is one of barbarity, ignorance, and squalor. Yet, stripped of the pious moralisms in which the work abounds, the descriptions of Muscovite customs are clear and, on the whole, in close agreement with the observations of other foreign travellers of the same period. His pictures of Russian clothing, styles of building, and military tactics are very similar to Fletcher's treatment of the same themes.

2. The best accounts of Turberville are found in John Erskine Hankins, *The Life and Works of George Turberville* (Lawrence, Kansas, 1940), and Hyder E. Rollins, "New Facts about George Turbervile," *Modern Philology*, XV (1918), 513–38.

The main weakness of Turberville's descriptive passages is a lack of precision in defining the context in which the observations are to be set. In his portrayal of life in the countryside, for example, he conveys a vivid impression of the endless struggle of the peasants to wrest a living from a harsh and forbidding environment. These comments are an interesting contrast to the picture of prosperity presented in Randolph's account. But their value is limited because we do not know at what time in his journey he recorded them. It is impossible to discover whether Turberville intended to describe conditions in a particular area of northern Russia or in the country as a whole.

Turberville's comments on the morals and manners of the Muscovites were, to say the least, unflattering. He charged them with an impressive catalogue of vices—drunkenness, deceit, adultery, and sodomy. Their extraordinary moral confusion was illustrated, he felt, by the treatment of their women, who were encouraged to paint themselves like whores, then kept in confinement for fear that they should act the part. Turberville did not, however, attempt to develop a systematic explanation of the reasons for their extraordinary immorality. In summing up his impressions, he remarked that morality and good order cannot exist among a people "that neither love nor stand in awe of his [God's] assured rod." The statement is an embryonic version of Fletcher's argument that bad morals are the direct result of a false religion. Certainly Turberville shared Fletcher's unsympathetic attitude toward Orthodoxy, which he regarded as idolatrous and riddled with superstitious ceremonies.

The Muscovite system of government also attracted Turberville's ire. He viewed it as a tyrannical state in which the ruler had arbitrary power over every detail of his subjects' lives. Neither law nor custom inhibited the prince into whose hands was gathered all the revenue of the country. Even the "best estates" had no guarantee of their safety nor of their right to pass on their titles or property to their children. Turberville's comments lose much of their possible significance because the author has not made clear what he is describing. His remarks are so general that it is impossible to know whether he intended to describe the peculiar qualities of the rule of Ivan IV or the traditional prerogatives of all rulers of Muscovy. If he intended to describe the tsar's policies during the exceptional period of the oprichnina, his sweeping statements are appropriate. It is certainly extraordinary that a visitor to Moscow in 1568–69 should never explicitly mention the oprichnina in his writings, and it would be inconceivable that his general view of Russia would not be shaped by his knowledge of the tsar's experiment in government. If, on the other hand, Turberville intended to describe normal Muscovite practice, he exaggerated the powers of the tsar and underestimated the strength of both the hereditary and the service nobles who had "assurance good of lands" and a virtual monopoly over the important offices at court and in government.

Turberville's poems combine the descriptions of an intelligent observer and the judgments of a consummate snob. The Muscovites' morals were corrupt and their government tyrannical, but ultimately their worst failing was their lack of *bon ton*. In the final analysis, his message was a simple one: Muscovy was no place for a gentleman.

Turberville's poems were first published in *Tragicall Tales* (London, 1587), Sigs. Z7ᵛ–Bb1ᵛ. They were also printed in the various editions of Richard Hakluyt's collection of voyages: *Principal Navigations* (3 vols.; London, 1589), I, Sigs. Oo5ᵛ–Pp2ʳ; *Principal Navigations* (3 vols.; London, 1598–1600), I, Sigs. Ii6ᵛ–Kk3ʳ; and *Principal Navigations* (12 vols.; Glasgow, 1903–05), III, 124–35. The poems were also included in R. H. Major's translation of Sigismund von Herberstein's *Rerum Moscoviticarum commentarii* (2 vols.; London, 1851–52), I, cxlix–clvi.

George Turberville

Verse
Letters from Russia

To Dancie

My Dancie[1] dear: when I recount within my breast
My London friends and wonted mates, and thee above the
rest,
I feel a thousand fits of deep and deadly woe
To think that I from land to sea,[2] from bliss to bale did go.
I left my native soil, full like a reckless man,
And unacquainted of the coast among the Russies ran:
A people passing rude, to vices vile inclin'd,
Folk fit to be of Bacchus' train so quaffing is their kind.
Drink is their whole desire, the pot is all their pride;
The sob'rest head doth once a day stand needful of a guide.
If he to banquet bid his friends, he will not shrink
On them at dinner to bestow a dozen kinds of drink,
Such liquor as they have and as the country gives,
But chiefly two: one called *kvas*, whereby the *muzhik* lives,

1. Edward Dancie. We have been unable to identify this person. Several of
the poems in *Tragicall Tales* are addressed to him.
2. *land to sea*. sea to land *Trag. Tales.*

75

Small-ware and waterlike but somewhat tart in taste;
The rest is mead of honey made, wherewith their lips they baste.
And if he go unto his neighbor as a guest,
He cares for little meat if so his drink be of the best.
Perhaps the muzhik hath a gay and gallant wife
To serve his beastly lust, yet he will lead a bugger's life.
The monster more desires a boy within his bed
Than any wench, such filthy sin ensues a drunken head.
The woman to repay her drowsy husband's debts
From stinking stove unto her mate to bawdy banquet gets.[3]
No wonder though they use such vile and beastly trade,
Sith with the hatchet and the hand their chiefest gods be made.
Their idols have their hearts; on God they never call,
Unless it be Nicholas Bough[4] that hangs against the wall.
The house that hath no god or painted saint within
Is not to be resorted to—that roof is full of sin.
Besides their private gods, in open places stand
Their crosses unto which they crouch and bless themselves with hand.
Devoutly down they duck with forehead to the ground;
Was never more deceit in rags and greasy garments found.
Almost the meanest man in all the country rides;
The woman eke against our use her trotting horse bestrides.
In sundry colors they both, men and women, go
In buskins, all that money have on buskins to bestow.
Each woman hanging hath a ring within her ear,
Which all of ancient use, and some of very pride do wear.
Their gait is very grave,[5] their countenance wise and sad,
And yet they follow fleshly lusts, their trade of living bad.
It is no shame at all accounted to defile
Another's bed; they make no care their follies to conceal.
Is not the meanest man in all the land but he,
To buy her painted colors, doth allow his wife a fee,

3. *Perhaps . . . gets.* om. 1589, 1599.
4. St. Nicholas of Bari, who was one of the most popular saints of the Russian church. The only certain information about his life is the fact that he was Bishop of Myra in Asia Minor at some time in the first half of the fourth century. His life has been the subject of many legends throughout Europe. In 1087 his relics were taken to Bari, Italy, and since that time his cult has had its center there.
5. *grave.* brave 1589, 1599.

Wherewith she decks herself and dyes her tawny skin.
She pranks and paints her smoky face, both brow, lip, cheek, and chin.
Yea, those that honest are, if any such there be
Within the land, do use the like; a man may plainly see
Upon some women's cheeks the painting how it lies
In plaster sort; for that too thick, her face the harlot dyes.
But such as skillful are and cunning dames indeed
By daily practice do it well; yea, sure they do exceed.
They lay their colors so, as he that is full wise
May easily be deceiv'd therein if he do trust his eyes.
I not a little muse what madness makes them paint
Their faces, weighing how they keep the stove by mere constraint,
For seldom when, unless on church or marriage day,
A man shall see the dames abroad that are of best array.
The Russie means to reap the profit of her pride,
And so he mews her to be sure she lie by no man's side.
Thus much friend Dancie I did mean to write to thee,
To let thee weet in Russia land what men and women be.
Hereafter I perhaps of other things will write
To thee and other of my friends which I shall see with sight,
And other stuff besides which true report shall tell.
Meanwhile I end my loving lines and bid thee now farewell.

To Spencer

If I should now forget or not remember thee,
Thou, Spencer,[6] mightest a foul rebuke and shame impute to me.
For I to open show did love thee passing well,
And thou wert he at parture, whom I loath'd to bid farewell.

6. Anthony à Wood (*Athenae Oxonienses*, ed. Bliss, I, 627) suggests the poet Edmund Spenser, as do J. P. Collier (*A Bibliographical and Critical Account of the Rarest Books* . . . [4 vols.; New York, n.d.], III, 86–87, IV, 178), and Emil Koeppel ("George Turberviles Verhältniss zur italienischen Litteratur," *Anglia*, XIII [1891], 42–71). John Hankins in his biography of Turberville takes no position on the matter. Hyder Rollins, in *Modern Philology*, XV (1918), 149–51, suggests that "Thomas Spencer, or another of his family, was the person addressed."

And as I went thy friend, so I continue still;
No better proof thou can'st desire than this[7] of true good will.
I do remember well when needs I should away
And that the post would license us no longer time to stay,
Thou wrung'st me by the fist, and holding fast my hand
Didst crave of me to send thee news and how I liked the land.
It is a sandy soil, no very fruitful vein,
More waste and woody grounds there are than closes fit for grain.
Yet grain there growing is, which they untimely take
And cut, or ere the corn be ripe they mow[8] it on a stake,[9]
And laying sheaf by sheaf, their harvest so they dry.
They make the greater haste for fear the frost the corn destroy,
For in the wintertime, so glary is the ground
As neither grass nor other grain in pastures may be found.
In comes the cattle then, the sheep, the colt, the cow;
Fast by his bed the muzhik, then, a lodging doth allow
Whom he with fodder feeds and holds as dear as life:
And thus they wear the winter with the muzhik and his wife.
Seven months the winter dures; the glare it is so great
As it is May before he turn his ground to sow his wheat.
The bodies eke that die unburied lie till[10] then,
Laid up in coffins made of fir, as well the poorest men
As those of greater state; the cause is lightly found,
For that in wintertime they cannot come to break the ground.
And wood so plenteous is quite throughout all the land,
As rich and poor at time of death assur'd of coffins stand.
Perhaps thou musest much how this may stand with reason,
That bodies dead can uncorrupt abide so long a season.
Take this for certain truth, as soon as heat is gone
The force of cold the body binds as hard as any stone,
Without offense at all to any living thing;
And so they lie in perfect state till next return of spring.
Their beasts be like to ours as far as I can see
For shape and show, but somewhat less of bulk and bone they be,
Of wat'rish taste, the flesh not firm like English beef,

7. *can'st . . . this.* canst then this desire 1589, 1599.
8. Pile, heap
9. *stake.* stacke *Trag. Tales,* 1599.
10. *till.* they 1589, 1599.

And yet it serves them very well and is a good relief.
Their sheep are very small, sharp singled,[11] handful long.
Great store of fowl on sea and land, the moorish reeds among;
The greatness of the store doth make the prices less.
Besides in all the land they know not how good meat to dress.
They use neither broach nor spit; but when the stove they heat,
They put their victuals in a pan and so they bake their meat.
No pewter to be had, no dishes but of wood,
No use of trenchers, cups cut out of birch are very good.
They use but wooden spoons which, hanging in a case,
Each muzhik at his girdle ties and thinks it no disgrace.
With whittles two or three, the better man the moe,
The chiefest Russies in the land with spoon and knives do go.
Their houses are not huge of building, but they say
They plant them in the loftiest ground to shift the snow away,
Which in the winter time each where full thick doth[12] lie,
Which makes them have the more desire to set their houses high.
No stonework is in use; their roofs of rafters be
One linked in another fast; their walls are all of tree,
Of masts both long and large with moss put in between.
To keep the force of weather out, I never erst have seen
A gross device so good; and on the roof they lay
The burden bark to rid the rain and sudden showers away.
In every room a stove to serve the winter turn;
Of wood they have sufficient store, as much as they can burn.
They have no English glass; of slices of a rock
Hight *sliuda* they their windows make, that English glass doth mock.
They cut it very thin and sew it with a thread
In pretty order, like to panes, to serve their present need.
No other glass, good faith, doth give a better light,
And sure the rock is nothing rich, the cost is very slight.
The chiefest place is that where hangs the god by it.
The owner of the house himself doth never use to[13] sit
Unless his better come, to whom he yields the seat;
The stranger bending to the god, the ground with brow must beat.
And in that very place which they most sacred deem

11. Closely shaven.
12. *doth.* they 1589, 1599.
13. *use to.* om. 1589, 1599.

The stranger lies, a token that his guest he doth esteem,
Where he is wont to have a bear's skin for his bed,
And must instead of pillow clap a saddle to his head.
In Russia other shift there is not to be had,
For where the bedding is not good, the bolsters are but bad.
I mused very much what made them so to lie,
Sith in their country down is rife and feathers out of cry,
Unless it be because the country is so hard,
They fear by niceness of a bed their bodies would be marr'd.
I wish't thee oft with us, save that I stood in fear
Thou would'st have loathed to have laid thy limbs upon a bear,
As I and Stafford[14] did, that was my mate in bed;
And yet (we thank the God of heaven) we both right well have sped.
Lo, thus I make an end; none other news to thee,
But that the country is too cold, the people beastly be.
I write not all I know, I touch but here and there,
For if I should, my pen would pinch and eke offend, I fear.
Who so shall read this verse, conjecture of the rest,
And think by reason of our trade that I do think the best.
But if no traffic were, then could I boldly pen
The hardness of the soil and eke the manners of the men.
They say the lion's paw gives judgment of the beast;
And so may you deem of the great by reading of the least.

To Parker

My Parker[15]: paper, pen, and ink were made to write,
And idle hands that little do have leisure to indite;
Wherefore, respecting these and thine assured love,
If I would write no news to thee, thou might'st my pen reprove.

14. "Master Richard Stafford, minister" is mentioned among the names of "the twelve Counsellors" of the voyage of Willoughby and Chancellor (Hakluyt II, 206). However, in a listing of the persons aboard Chancellor's ship, the "Bona Esperanza," the name given is John Stafford (Hakluyt II, 213). This is the only Stafford associated with the Russia Company; and, of course, he may not be the Stafford alluded to.

15. We have been unable to identify this person.

And sithence fortune thus hath shov'd my ship from[16] shore
And made me seek another realm unseen of me before,
The manners of the men I purpose to declare,
And other private points besides which strange and geason[17] are.
The Russie men are round of bodies, fully fac'd,[18]
The greatest part with bellies big that overhang the waist,
Flat-headed for the most, with faces nothing fair
But brown by reason of the stove and closeness of the air.
It is their common use to shave or else to shear
Their heads. For none in all the land long lolling locks doth wear,
Unless perhaps he have his sovereign prince displeas'd;
For then he never cuts his hair until he be appeas'd.
A certain sign to know who in displeasure be,
For every man that views his head will say, "Lo, this is he;"
And during all the time he lets his locks to grow,
Dares no man for his life to him a face of friendship show.
Their garments be not gay nor handsome to the eye:
A cap aloft their heads they have that standeth very high,
Which kolpak they do term. They wear no ruffs at all.
The best have collars set with pearl, *rubashka* they do call.[19]
Their shirts in Russie long, they work them down before,
And on the sleeves with colored silks two inches good or[20] more.
Aloft their shirts they wear a garment jacketwise
Hight *odnoriadka;* and about his burly waist he ties
His *portki,* which instead of better breeches be;
Of linen cloth that garment is, no codpiece is to see.
A pair of yarnen socks, to keep the cold away,
Within his boots the Russie wears; the heels they underlay
With clouting clamps of steel, sharp pointed at the toes.
And over all a *shuba* furr'd, and thus the Russies goes.
Well button'd is the shuba, according to his state;
Some silk, of silver other some, but those of poorest rate
Do wear no shuba at all, but grosser gowns to sight
That reacheth down beneath the calf, and that *armiak* hight—

16. *from.* on 1589, 1599.
17. Rare, uncommon.
18. *fac'd.* faste *Trag. Tales,* 1589
19. *rubashka . . . call.* which they *rubashka* call 1589, 1599.
20. *or.* and 1589, 1599.

These are the Russies' robes. The richest use to ride
From place to place; his servant runs and follows by his side.
The Cossack bears his felt to force away the rain;
Their bridles are not very brave; their saddles are but plain.
No bits but snaffles all, of birch their saddles be,
Much fashioned like the Scottish seats, broad flacks to keep the knee
From sweating of the horse; the panels larger far
And broader be than ours; they use short stirrups for the war.
For when the Russie is pursued by cruel foe
He rides away, and suddenly betakes him to his bow
And bends me but about in saddle as he sits,
And therewithal amids his race his following foe he hits.
Their bows are very short, like Turkish bows outright,
Of sinews made with birchen bark in cunning manner dight.
Small arrows, cruel heads, that fell and forked be,
Which being shot from out those bows a cruel way will flee.
They seldom shoe their horse unless they use to ride[21]
In post upon the frozen floods, then cause they shall not slide
He sets a slender calk,[22] and so he rides his way.
The horses of the country go good four score versts a day
And all without the spur. Once prick them and they skip.
But go not forward on their way, the Russie hath his whip
To rap him on the ribs, for though all booted be,
Yet shall you not a pair of spurs in all the country see.
The common game is chess: almost the simplest will
Both give a check and eke a mate; by practice comes their skill.
Again they[23] dice as fast: the poorest rogues of all
Will sit them down in open field and there to gaming fall.
Their dice are very small (in fashion like to those
Which we do use); he takes them up, and over thumb he throws,
Not shaking them a whit; they cast suspiciously,
And yet I deem them void of art that dicing most apply.
At play when silver lacks, goes saddle, horse, and all,
And each thing else worth silver walks, although the price be small.
Because thou lovest to play, friend Parker, other while,

21. *shoe . . . ride.* use to shoe their horse unless they ride 1589, 1599.
22. A pointed piece of iron on a horseshoe to prevent slipping.
23. *they.* the *Trag. Tales,* 1589, 1599.

I wish thee there the weary day with dicing to beguile.
But thou wert better far at home, I wist it well,
And would'st be loath among such louts[24] so long a time to dwell.
Then judge of us thy friends what kind of life we had,
That near the frozen pole to waste our weary days were glad,
In such a savage soil where laws do bear no sway,
But all is at the king his will to save or else to slay,
And that sans cause, God wot, if so his mind be such.
But what mean I with kings to deal? We ought no saints[25] to touch.
Conceive the rest yourself, and deem what lives they lead
Where lust is law, and subjects live continually in dread,
And where the best estates have none assurance good
Of lands, of lives, nor nothing falls unto the next of blood;
But all of custom doth unto the prince redound,
And all the whole revenue comes unto the king his crown.
Good faith, I see thee muse at what I tell thee now,
But true it is; no choice, but all at prince's pleasure bow.
So Tarquin ruled Rome, as thou rememb'rest well,
And what his fortune was at last I know thyself canst tell.[26]
Where will in commonweal doth bear the only sway
And lust is law, the prince and realm must needs in time decay.
The strangeness of the place is such, for sundry things I see,
As if I would, I cannot write each private point to thee:
The cold is rare, the people rude, the prince so full of pride,
The realm so stored with monks and nuns, and priests on every side,
The manners are so Turkish like, the men so full of guile,
The women wanton, temples stuft with idols that defile
The seats that sacred ought to be, the customs are so quaint,
As if I would describe the whole, I fear my pen would faint.
In sum, I say I never saw a prince that so did reign,
Nor people so beset with saints, yet all but vile and vain.

24. *louts.* lows 1599.
25. *saints.* faults 1589, 1599.
26. L. Tarquinius Superbus, after murdering Servius Tullius, commenced his reign without any of the forms of elections, and became a byword for cruelty and tyranny. He abolished the rights which had been conferred upon the plebians by Servius, and put to death or drove into exile the senators and patricians whom he mistrusted, or whose wealth he coveted. Tarquin reigned twenty-four years and was banished in 510 B.C.

Wild Irish are as civil as the Russies in their kind;
Hard choice which is the best of both, each bloody, rude, and blind.
If thou be wise, as wise thou art, and wilt be rul'd by me,
Live still at home and covet not those barbarous coasts to see.
No good befalls a man that seeks and finds no better place,
No civil customs to be learn'd where God bestows no grace.
And truly ill they do deserve to be belov'd of God
That neither love nor stand in awe of his assured rod,
Which though be long, yet plagues at last the vile and beastly sort
Of sinful wights that all in vice do place their chiefest sport.

    Adieu, friend Parker, if thou list to know the Russes well,
To Sigismundus' book repair, who all the truth can tell.[27]
For he long erst in message went unto that savage king,
Sent by the Pole, and true report in each respect did bring.
To him I recommend myself to ease my pen of pain,
And now at last do wish thee well and bid farewell again.

27. Sigismund von Herberstein (1486–1566) was a diplomat in the service of the Hapsburgs. On two occasions he visited Moscow. In 1517 Emperor Maximilian I sent him to mediate between Poland and Muscovy and to persuade both powers to join the Empire in an alliance against the Turks. In 1526 he carried out a similar mission and helped to arrange an extension of the existing truce between Poland and Russia. He recorded his observations of Russia in *Rerum Moscoviticarum commentarii* which was first published in 1549 and went through a number of editions in the course of the sixteenth century. The work was the best eyewitness account of Russia available to western and central Europeans in the middle decades of the century. The best known English translation is the work of R. H. Major, *Notes upon Russia* (2 vols.; London, 1851–52).

Giles Fletcher

Of the Russe Commonwealth

Giles Fletcher

Introduction

Giles Fletcher's *Of the Russe Commonwealth* is, in many ways, the summary of the English experience in Muscovy. It is unquestionably the most important English work on Russia before the reign of Peter the Great, and presents a more thorough and systematic analysis of Muscovite institutions than any other foreign work of the period.

Fletcher's achievement is all the more remarkable when one considers that he spent very little time in Russia. As Queen Elizabeth's ambassador, he reached northern Russia late in the summer of 1588 and sailed for home less than a year later. Moreover, because of his official status, he was accorded the stiflingly formal reception with which the Muscovite government honored foreign dignitaries, and had far less chance to see the country than did the tradesmen who worked for the Russia Company.

By inclination and by training, Fletcher was a scholar. Born in Watford, Hertfordshire, in 1546, he studied at Eton and at King's College, Cambridge, of which he became a fellow in 1568, and where he remained until 1581 in various scholarly and administrative capacities. Academically, the most significant post Fletcher held was that of lecturer in Greek, a position that apparently required him to deliver a daily oration in the Greek language. In 1581, however, personal considerations abruptly put an end to his academic career: early in that year he married Joan Sheafe, and soon resigned from the college since custom dictated that no married man could retain a fellowship. Once the university was closed to him, he looked to public service for a livelihood. His election to parliament in 1584 proved to be the decisive steppingstone: during the session of 1584–85 he seems to have attracted the patronage of Sir Francis Walsingham and Sir Thomas Randolph, and it was probably through their sponsorship that he received several diplomatic appointments, including his mission to the court of Tsar Fedor. He was moreover appointed Remembrancer of the City of London in 1585, at Queen Elizabeth's request, and from 1597 to 1611, the year of his death, he was treasurer of St. Paul's.

In 1590 both Walsingham and Randolph died. Fletcher then sought the patronage of Lord Burghley, but was rebuffed and subsequently turned to the earl of Essex, whose political and religious inclinations were, it appears, congenial with his own. Essex's rebellion in 1601 caused Fletcher to be held under house arrest, but he was evidently exonerated of any implication in the plot as none of his public offices were taken from him.[1]

If one may judge the man by his writings, Fletcher lost none of the qualities of a scholar while in official service. A facility with languages, sharpened by his training in classics, allowed him to learn a remarkable amount of Russian in a very short time: while it is impossible to be sure how well he knew the language at the end of his mission, *Of the Russe Commonwealth* does indicate that he had accurate command of at least a considerable number of terms and phrases. Since he had the services of an interpreter[2] and probably received assistance as well from other English residents of Moscow, it may be assumed that linguistic barriers did not hinder seriously his study of Muscovite life and institutions.

The diplomatic difficulties that he encountered were much more serious. In the late 1580's a flurry of diplomatic activity signalled a basic change in the nature of Anglo-Russian relations. For many years the

---

1. On Fletcher's biography see Berry, pp. 3–49. Besides *Of the Russe Commonwealth*, he wrote numerous Latin poems, the sonnet sequence *Licia*, and the curious prose tract *The Tartars or the Ten Tribes*.

2. Berry, p. 367; Bond, p. 343; Tolstoy, p. 397.

Russia Company controlled Russia's foreign trade over the northern sea route, and in 1569 it was officially granted a monopoly of the northern trade and exemption from all customs duties. After the death of Ivan IV in 1584, however, the new regime with Boris Godunov at the helm had to deal with fundamentally different conditions. In the early 1580's Dutch traders began to use the northern route and provided a welcome means of diversifying Russia's trade with western Europe. Moreover, the conclusion of the Livonian War provided the Muscovite government with new challenges and new opportunities; the loss of Narva forced the Russians to funnel as much of their foreign trade as possible through the northern Dvina ports and the end of the military emergency gave the new government freedom to be particular about the conditions under which it would enter alliances and make trade agreements. From the Russian point of view, the Russia Company's monopoly was obsolete since it interfered with the expansion of the northern trade, and Godunov's regime ignored it. At first, however, the directors of the Company refused to recognize the loss of their favored status and fought a rearguard action to save as many as possible of their old privileges.[3]

The central theme of the diplomatic exchanges between Godunov and Queen Elizabeth at the time of Fletcher's embassy was the basic discrepancy in their views on the rights of the Company's agents in Russia. Elizabeth, as always, supported its claims, and, although in 1589 she reluctantly recognized that "the strangers who will go for trade with your subjects shall not be hindered," she continued to insist that the Company's agents should be the only Englishmen permitted to trade in the tsar's domains.[4]

In their correspondence, however, the two courts devoted less attention to this fundamental question than to several less important but more inflammatory issues that were symptomatic of their increasing estrangement. Late in the 1580's the tsar's government expressed its indignation at the conduct of several English traders in Russia. The charges, probably inspired by Andrei Shchelkalov, the Anglophobe director of the foreign office, alleged that Robert Peacock and John Chappell had carried on treasonous correspondence with enemies of

3. On Anglo-Russian relations in the 1580's, see Willan, *Early History*, pp. 163–79; I. Liubimenko, *Les relations commerciales et politiques de l'Angleterre avec la Russie avant Pierre le Grand* (Paris, 1933), pp. 50–53, 65–71.

4. Tolstoy, pp. 308–9.

Muscovy and that Peacock and Jerome Horsey were planning to inter-
cept the ships of other nations which should approach Russian ports.[5]
Even more embarrassing to the queen was the case of Anthony Marsh.
In setting up his own trading operations, Marsh accumulated stagger-
ing debts to the Muscovite treasury and a number of private citizens,
then slipped back to England leaving his creditors furious.[6] In response
to their protests, Godunov made the Russia Company responsible for
the debts on the grounds that Marsh had been able to float the loans
only because he was known as one of its employees.[7] As if to make its
displeasure unmistakable, the Muscovite government also demanded
that the officials of the Company pay arrears of customs duties and
rent on their headquarters in Moscow.[8]

The queen sent Fletcher to Moscow on essentially the same assignment as earlier ambassadors—to do battle for the Company. Her chief
concerns were to free its members from responsibility for Marsh's debts
and to secure for them new privileges stipulating that no other Englishmen could trade in Russia.[9] At the same time, Fletcher was some-
how to combine militancy on the Company's behalf with the tact
needed to reassure Godunov of the good faith of the queen and her
subjects.

When he reached Russia, Fletcher quickly found out how deeply his
hosts were annoyed with the English. He also learned to his dismay
that the Muscovite government was negotiating with envoys from the
emperor, who urged the Russians to join the Hapsburg coalition that,
in western Europe, was aimed primarily at England. From the beginning, everything went wrong. When he reached Moscow, no official
welcomed him and he had to wait almost a month for an audience with
the tsar. When it was finally granted, it was marred by a bout of diplomatic fencing: Fletcher refused to address Tsar Fedor with his full
title, feigning forgetfulness but actually out of determination to defend
the honor of Queen Elizabeth, whose "style" was considerably shorter.
He gave in at last after Andrei Shchelkalov threatened to terminate the

5. *Ibid,* p. 298.

6. *Sbornik IRIO,* XXXVIII, pp. 191–92, 198–99, 205–10; Tolstoy, pp. 298–99,
356–57.

7. Tolstoy, p. 299.

8. Berry, p. 374; Bond, p. 349.

9. Tolstoy, p. 295; "Stateinyi spisok priezda i prebyvaniia v Rossii angliiskago
posla Elizara Fletchera," *Vremennik Imperatorskago moskovskago obshchestva
istorii i drevnostei rossiiskikh,* Book VIII (1850), iii, 5.

audience unless Fletcher adhered to the letter of court ceremonial. His embarrassment was compounded when the gifts which Elizabeth had sent Fedor were brought to his quarters and dumped at his feet in a blunt demonstration that the queen had, not for the first time, taken her celebrated parsimony too far. He spent many days thereafter in discomfort and anxiety since Shchelkalov kept him isolated in "unwholesome" quarters on an inadequate living allowance while the government entertained visitors whose presence it valued more highly.[10]

The emperor's ambassador was not Fletcher's only rival for the government's attention. In 1588 the patriarch of Constantinople, Jeremiah, came to Russia for alms and, after tortuous negotiations, Boris Godunov persuaded him to establish the new office of patriarch of Moscow and so provide institutional recognition of the long-established fact that the Russian church was a fully independent member of the Orthodox community. Finally Fletcher's patience was rewarded. He found the tsar's officials more cooperative once the new patriarch was installed, and the allure of a Hapsburg alliance faded after he circulated Sir Francis Drake's letters announcing England's victory over the Spanish Armada.[11]

In the end, he carried out his assignment with remarkable success. By the time of his farewell audience with the tsar on April 22, 1589, he had reassured his hosts of the queen's good will and won for the Russia Company a new grant of privileges which transferred its affairs from the jurisdiction of Shchelkalov to Godunov's supervision.[12] He can scarcely be blamed for his failure to achieve Elizabeth's broader objectives: in his answer to the queen's requests, Tsar Fedor stated plainly that it was not in his country's interest to turn away any honest trader. Thereafter Elizabeth could expect no help from the Muscovite government for her campaign to keep English interlopers out of the Russian trade.[13] Fedor also decreed that, in spite of its protests, the Company would have to pay half of the customs dues which other foreigners paid;[14] before long, however, Godunov intervened privately and restored the traditional full exemption.[15]

Even as he prepared to leave Moscow, Fletcher's troubles were not

10. Berry, pp. 367–71; Bond, pp. 342–47.
11. Berry, p. 371; Bond, p. 347.
12. Berry, p. 375; Bond, p. 350.
13. Tolstoy, pp. 348–49, 352–53.
14. Tolstoy, pp. 349, 352.
15. Willan, *Early History*, p. 176.

over, for he had not been able to settle the question of Marsh's debts.
When new instructions arrived from England on April 27, he requested
another audience but was refused and had to bear the annoyance of
conducting the remaining negotiations by letter.[16] On May 6, he left
for the northern town of Vologda but, on the tsar's orders, was forced
to wait there for the outcome of the government's deliberations.[17] At
last, when Marsh appeared in Moscow to plead his own case, the tsar
issued his decision.[18] The final compromise is a tribute to Fletcher's
skill and doggedness: the Russia Company was held responsible for a
sum of 7800 rubles, a relatively small proportion of the total debt.[19]
Fletcher was finally free to set sail for England.

In view of the delicacy of his mission and the delays and harass-
ments from which he suffered, it is hardly surprising that he was relieved to return in safety to England. To a friend, he is said to have
"expressed his thankfulness to God for his safe return from so great a
danger; for the poets cannot fancy Ulysses more glad to be come out of
the den of Polyphemus, than he was to be rid out of the power of such
a barbarous prince."[20] It is easy to imagine how his experiences might
have given him an unfavorable impression of Muscovy and its government.

Whatever his feelings, he realized the significance of what he had
seen and heard. Soon after he returned to England, he completed a
draft of a treatise on Russia and presented it to the queen. Over the
course of the next two years he revised and expanded the work, adding
principally the chapter on the cities of Russia, the sections on the ruling house of Muscovy and the coronation of the tsars, and many details
and anecdotes taken from the writings of historians and cosmographers. He published the manuscript in 1591 with the title *Of the Russe
Commonwealth*.[21]

In its aims and its scope, Fletcher's work far surpasses the other English writings on Muscovite Russia. Its author attempted to fulfill two
complementary goals, "to note things for mine own experience, of more

16. "Stateinyi spisok" (n. 9 above), pp. 48, 58.
17. *Ibid.*, pp. 72–73.
18. *Ibid.*, pp. 73–74.
19. *Ibid.*, p. 89; Berry, p. 373; Bond, p. 349; Tolstoy, p. 357.
20. Thomas Fuller, *The Worthies of England,* ed. John Freeman (London,
1952), p. 279.
21. For a discussion of the process of composition and revision of the work, see
Berry, pp. 135–44.

importance than delight, and rather true than strange" and to analyse the workings of the government and society of Muscovy in order to provide a systematic explanation of what he had observed.

He was remarkably successful in carrying out his first task. Even though his visit to Russia was short and his diplomatic responsibilities must have occupied much of his attention, he managed to gather an astonishing store of facts and impressions. To supplement his own observations in northern Russia and in Moscow, he used every opportunity to question the Russians he met on issues that aroused his curiosity. He also had at his disposal the collective experience of the English residents of Moscow, some of whom had travelled in regions of the country which he did not visit and witnessed customs which he did not see.

The Muscovite government which had caused him so much grief unwittingly made an important contribution to his work when it expelled Jerome Horsey.[22] On the long journey back to England Fletcher travelled with Horsey and had an opportunity to question him about his experiences during his sixteen years of residence in Russia. How much he learned from Horsey is not clear. In his own memoirs Horsey described Fletcher's work and left no doubt about his view of his role in its composition; *Of the Russe Commonwealth* dealt with "the original nature and disposition of the Russe people, the laws, languages, government, discipline for their church and commonwealth, revenues, commodities, climate and situation, whereof it most consist, and with whom they have most league and commerce—with all which I did furnish him."[23] While Horsey's appraisal is undoubtedly a gross exaggeration, he probably told Fletcher a good deal about recent Russian history and may well have supplied him with details on the politics and ceremonies of the Muscovite court. Whatever his contribution, there is good reason to be grateful to him for assisting a writer whose independence of judgment and literary skill far surpassed his own.

Fletcher's diligence made *Of the Russe Commonwealth* a small encyclopedia of Muscovite life. Into its pages he packed a great deal of information that, on the whole, seems remarkably accurate when compared with the testimony of other sources of the period. The sections of the work are, to be sure, varied in quality and in importance but, apart

22. Bond, p. 337; Tolstoy, p. 353.
23. See below, p. 360.

from the historical and philological material which is admittedly deriv-
ative, every section offers the reader something of value, whether it be
precise data, stimulating opinions, or revealing misconceptions.

Three parts of the book that stand somewhat outside the central
structure of the argument serve as illustrations. As was fitting for the
author of a systematic treatise on a foreign land, Fletcher began the
work with a section entitled "Cosmography" in which he described the
natural setting of Muscovy, its soil and climate, its products, and its
chief towns. For the most part, this is one of the less interesting sections of his book since much of the material is derived from the writings of other authors, classical and modern.[24] What gives it distinction
is the detailed list of the main products of the Muscovite state and
their region of origin. In compiling it, Fletcher probably recorded what
he learned from the agents of the Russia Company: business was the
reason for their presence in Russia and knowledge of the country's economic prospects was one of the keys to success in their endeavors.

Despite his evident fascination with the peoples who lived around
the borders of Muscovy, his descriptions of their customs seem to be a
mixture of literary tradition, popular legend, and hearsay. It could
hardly be otherwise since he did not visit the regions where they lived.
Yet even the hearsay has a certain interest. In vivid terms Fletcher recorded the Muscovites' picture of the Tatars and the other peoples of
the borderlands. From his description one can easily understand why
the Russians feared the ruthless and ingenious raiders from the steppes
and took elaborate measures to defend the frontier against their sorties.

Fletcher's gifts as a reporter are most evident in the passages describing the daily life and customs of Tsar Fedor and his subjects. The
description of the tsar's appearance and daily routine is full, finely-
drawn, and completely convincing: it is unique in the literature of the
sixteenth century. His description of the life of the common people is
somewhat less striking, if only because other foreign visitors to Russia
recorded much the same impressions. This is not to demean his efforts.
His picture is a rich and clear one and his judgments, although very
harsh, are no more severe than the comments of other foreign writers
and of many Muscovites as well.

In spite of the high quality of these descriptive passages, they are a
secondary element in his work. The core of the *Russe Commonwealth*

---

24. On Fletcher's literary sources, see Berry, pp. 144–46; Seredonin, pp. 45–56.

is a dissection and interpretation of the "manner of government by the Russe emperor." Such an analysis must necessarily rest on the author's general assumptions about the nature of good and bad government. In Fletcher's case, however, the attempt to discover the axioms that lie beneath his specific remarks on Russia is a treacherous undertaking.

Of the Russe Commonwealth itself provides few unambiguous indications of its author's political philosophy. For the most part, Fletcher adhered strictly to his primary purpose and limited his general comments to the state of Russia in his own time. On that subject his opinions are clear from the very first page of the book, the dedication to Queen Elizabeth in which he promised to describe "a true and strange face of a tyrannical state (most unlike to your own) without true knowledge of God, without written law, without common justice." The implication, and the only one that Fletcher could be expected to draw, is that the queen's government is good government. He did not specify, however, which elements or qualities of the English system of government made it the best of all possible regimes; his only direct comment on England was the routine compliment that Elizabeth was a "prince of subjects, not of slaves, that are kept within duty by love, not by fear."

His other writings provide no clearer answers. The only other work that inspired reflections on a political theme was his poem, *The Rising to the Crown of Richard the Third,* written a few years before his comments on Russia.[25] The literary form which Fletcher chose to describe Richard's notorious career was that of *A Mirror for Magistrates,* the celebrated collection of verse monologues in which characters from recent English history tell their stories from beyond the grave and give the reader instruction on how to avoid the fate that befell them.[26] In Fletcher's poem, too, Richard speaks but his message is ambivalent; greed and ambition had led him to commit many crimes, including murder, to gain the throne and, in the end, divine retribution had fallen upon him, but Richard nevertheless refused to repent since he had, after all, "bought a crown so cheap."[27] When the king suggested that amoral political behavior has its own rewards, was he also speaking for his author? One cannot be sure.

---

25. Berry, pp. 123–32. In his introduction to the poem, Berry suggests that it was composed "sometime between 1577 and 1586" (p. 65).
26. Lily B. Campbell (ed.), *A Mirror for Magistrates* (Cambridge, 1938).
27. Berry, p. 132.

Fletcher's career likewise gives few clear indications of his position on the constitutional, legal, and religious issues that divided his countrymen. During his years in public life, for example, he served at various times as a member of parliament, as a diplomat appointed by the crown, and as an officer of the city of London. The most consistent pattern in his career was his frequent association with zealously Protestant patrons such as Walsingham. Only once did such ties prove dangerous, when in 1601 he fell under suspicion of complicity in the rebellion of his patron, the earl of Essex. Otherwise he lived cautiously and avoided troublesome commitments.

Of the Russe Commonwealth, to be sure, leaves no doubt of Fletcher's attitudes on certain broad political and cultural issues. No one who reads his work can miss his patriotism and his staunch Protestantism. He made his religious commitment one of the central elements in his interpretation of the Muscovite system of government, arguing that Orthodoxy butressed the absolute power of the tsar because, by its very nature, it kept the people of Russia ignorant and submissive. His views on the Russian government also make clear that he believed that parliament should play an important part in the government of a country, that every state should have a comprehensive code of laws and an independent judiciary to enforce it, and that the estates of the realm should have the right to maintain their traditional privileges. These general attitudes he shared with a large number of his countrymen. If his political philosophy included views more precise or more original than these common assumptions, his surviving writings show no trace of them.

What is remarkable about Fletcher's work on Russia is the sharpness of his observation and the acuity of his judgments on the Muscovite government and society. His portrayal of the "tyrannical" government of Russia is an original interpretation which differs in many respects from the other descriptions of tyranny in Elizabethan political literature.[28] Yet, in spite of its unusual qualities, one of its intercon-

---

28. Richard Pipes has recently made the interesting suggestion that Sir Thomas Smith's work, *De republica Anglorum,* may have inspired Fletcher's work on Russia (Richard Pipes and John V. A. Fine [eds.], *Giles Fletcher, Of the Russe Commonwealth* [Cambridge, Mass., 1966], pp. 26–29). It is entirely possible, although by no means certain, that Fletcher may have shared some of Smith's views on the English constitution. It is most unlikely, however, that Smith's work influenced Fletcher's analysis of the government of Russia. According to Smith, tyranny very rarely existed in a pure form but was usually mixed with

nected elements draws on a well-established literary tradition. A number of Fletcher's comments, especially those concerning the policies of Ivan IV and their consequences for Russia, reflect the values of the Elizabethan chronicles and the *Mirror for Magistrates*. To the writers of these earlier works, a tyrant was a ruler who, through ambition and self-indulgence, offended against the moral order of the universe and brought down God's punishment either upon himself or on his country in the form of a succession crisis, party strife, or popular revolt. Fletcher's oft-quoted prediction that civil war would break out in Russia, for example, lies in the mainstream of this tradition.

In Fletcher's picture of the Muscovite government, the tsar occupied the central position. Like all foreign visitors of the sixteenth and seventeenth centuries, Fletcher was amazed at the extent of the tsar's powers. As he rightly observed, the emperor legislated, appointed the chief officers of the realm, declared war and made peace, and acted as the final court of law. His presentation likewise captures the elaborate ceremonies of respect that surrounded the tsar and includes a very precise description of the coronation of Fedor, which took place four years before his journey to Russia.

Fletcher was well aware of the ironic contrast between the tsar's sweeping powers and the personal weakness of the successors of Ivan IV—Fedor, a ruler dominated by powerful courtiers, and his younger half-brother, Dmitrii, a small child exiled from the court. When he told the stories of Dmitrii's sadistic games and of the attempt to poison him, he probably did no more than immortalize choice bits of Moscow gossip. Yet, whatever the basis of fact behind the rumors, their very existence indicated widespread uneasiness about the succession to the throne and the future welfare of the country.

The central administrative and consultative body in Muscovy was the boiar duma. Indeed, if one may cast Muscovite practice in western phrases, sovereignty theoretically resided in the tsar-in-council. Fletcher's treatment of the duma is remarkably successful. A check of his list of duma members reveals that he knew the identity of most of them and their approximate position in the ceremonial ranking system:

---

aristocratic and democratic elements. Like any other form, tyranny would in time give way to a form in which one of the other elements predominated. On the other hand, Fletcher pictured the Russian regime as a pure tyranny which showed no trace of mutability short of cataclysmic upheaval. For Smith's general remarks on tyranny, see Sir Thomas Smith, *De republica Anglorum: A Discourse on the Commonwealth of England*, ed. L. Alston (Cambridge, 1906), pp. 11–16.

his description is misleading only in that it somewhat underestimates their number. His brief account of the times at which the council met and the means by which it was summoned is of exceptional interest since it is the only such record dating from the sixteenth century and is completely plausible in view of later practice.[29]

According to Fletcher, the Muscovite administration was ruthlessly centralized. The emperor appointed all officials who governed the provinces of the realm and made them responsible only to himself and the duma. The courts were simply another branch of the tsar's administration since the governors of the provinces were also the judges and appeals went directly to the tsar and his councillors. In the vital area of state finance, everything likewise depended on the tsar and "both nobility and commons" were "but storers for the prince, all running in the end into the emperor's coffers." There were neither elected officers nor was there a full code of laws that could protect the people from the arbitrary acts of the sovereign and his officials.

This neat and consistent picture has considerable merit and Fletcher offers an impressive array of telling illustrations to support his contentions. In comparison with the England of Elizabeth, the Muscovite state after the reign of Ivan IV was indeed highly centralized. The Muscovite nobleman derived whatever status and influence he possessed from his service in the army or the central administration, not from his wealth in land or his leadership in his home district. In the sixteenth century, moreover, the tsars were engaged in building a professional bureaucracy, formed, as Fletcher indicated, chiefly of talented men of comparatively humble origin. Yet, in spite of the rough justice of his presentation, a number of reservations should be made.

Understandably enough, the details of Fletcher's account of the Muscovite administration are not always accurate. Sometimes his determination to present a complete picture of the workings of Muscovite institutions forced him to deal with subjects about which it must have been impossible to obtain precise information. His discussion of the structure of the bureaucracy, for example, is confused by his failure to distinguish between the functions of the chetverti and the *prikazy*. The distinction, admittedly, is one that may also have escaped most Muscovites. The prikazy or ministries managed the main sectors of the gov-

29. V. O. Kliuchevskii, *Boiarskaia duma drevnei Rusi* (Moscow, 1909), pp. 406–9.

ernment's activity—foreign affairs, the gentry levies that made up most of the army, the special branches of the military, and the collection of most state revenues: the chetverti, a somewhat later innovation, were agencies which supervised the collection of a variety of revenues from particular districts of the country. To complete the confusion, one official was often at the same time the director both of a major prikaz and a chetvert'. Fletcher can scarcely be blamed for running the two together.

His detailed discussion of the finances of the state is open to criticism for much the same reasons. Since the condition of a nation's finances is a delicate matter, it is unlikely that Fletcher received his information from official sources. Where he gathered his material is not clear and there is likewise no sure means of testing the accuracy of his figures nor of verifying the anecdotes with which he illustrates the government's ingenious methods of increasing its revenue. What we can discover suggests that his account is to be treated cautiously. Seredonin, Fletcher's nineteenth-century critic, advanced elaborate and, on the whole, convincing arguments to prove that he greatly exaggerated the total income of the Muscovite treasury.[30]

More serious than errors of fact is Fletcher's failure to appreciate those features of the Muscovite administration which ran counter to the prevailing currents of absolutism and centralization. These omissions are responsible, in part, for the excessive simplification that gives his remarks a rather dogmatic tone. Both the treatment of local government and the fine description of Muscovite legal practice, for example, are incomplete because they do not give an adequate account of the local fiscal officers and judges, the *zemskie* and *gubnye starosty*, who, contrary to his statements, were elected by the local population from the ranks of the gentry. It would, of course, be easy to go too far and replace Fletcher's misconception with an equally serious one. The district elders derived their authority from the tsars' recognition that leading citizens of the localities concerned could deal with certain issues of local importance more effectively than appointees of the central administration. The central government was careful not to give the elders too much rein; their powers were sharply limited and their decisions subject to the close scrutiny of the appropriate branches of the central bureaucracy. They do, however, represent a small measure of local

30. Seredonin, pp. 307–35.

autonomy in a system that was, on the whole, highly centralized. By
failing to give them their due, Fletcher made his scheme of interpretation too neat.

His description of the legislative process in Muscovy is also somewhat confused. In his search for the body that, like the English parliament, joined the sovereign in establishing the laws of the land, he came
upon an institution which he called the *sobor*. His description indicates clearly that he had in mind a *dumnyi sobor*, a joint meeting of
the boiar duma and the leaders of the church hierarchy that met on
occasion to advise the tsar. In his treatment of the dumnyi sobor, the
only feature that raises doubt is his insistence that it was entirely su-
pine and, indeed, existed primarily to give the people the false impression that the tsar really consulted with their representatives. While the
dumnyi sobor was a far cry from the English parliament, its members
did occasionally express opposition to the tsar's policies.[31]

Oddly enough, he made no mention at all of the *zemskii sobor*, the
one body in the Muscovite system that even vaguely resembled parliament. The oversight is understandable. The zemskii sobor, an institution similar to the estates-general of France, met infrequently in the
sixteenth century when summoned by the tsar to lend its support to the
government's policy on such vital matters as the succession to the
throne or the conclusion of an important treaty. In the years before
Fletcher's visit, the sobor last met in 1584 to confirm the succession of
Fedor, and its most recent large and well-documented meeting had
taken place even earlier, in 1566.

His oversight, however, had an important role in shaping his interpretation of the essential characteristics of the Muscovite system of
government and of its future prospects. In his discussion of the constitutional structure of the state he emphasized "how hard a matter it were
to alter the state of the Russe government, as it now standeth." In 1589
Muscovite institutions seemed to him static and unshakeable, in part
because he did not notice the zemskii sobor, an embryonic representative element in the apparently monolithic Muscovite autocracy. With
the help of hindsight, we know that the social upheaval of the Time
of Troubles caused the collapse of the imperial administration and created the conditions in which the sobor on two occasions was a decisive
force in Russian political life.

31. Kliuchevskii, *Boiarskaia duma*, pp. 522–23; Seredonin, pp. 236–38.

When he described Muscovite society, Fletcher cast his views in characteristic Elizabethan terminology. As in any country, the laity in Russia formed two estates, the nobility and the commons, and it was his task to describe the situation of each, their mutual relationship, and their relations with the crown. From what he saw and heard, he concluded that the tsar dominated society as completely as he controlled the administration of the country. If any estate possessed guaranteed liberties and an independent role in politics, it would reasonably be the nobility. Nevertheless, according to Fletcher, the princes of Moscow had so thoroughly dominated the old noble families that their members had accepted the humiliating custom of referring to themselves as the tsar's bondslaves.

To give a more detailed explanation of the methods through which the tsars had subjugated the nobility, Fletcher turned his attention to the policies of Ivan IV and Boris Godunov. Mention of Ivan IV inevitably raised the question of the oprichnina. In an interpretation that lies very close to the explanations of Ivan himself and the views of a number of historians of our own time, Fletcher argued that the tsar's aim in dividing his realm and creating his own private military force was to punish those of his subjects whom he suspected of treasonous relations with the Poles and the Crimean Tatars. The experiment was not directed against the nobility as such and the oprichnina army included those nobles who remained in the tsar's favor. The effect, however, was to destroy many nobles who happened to fall suspect and to sow ineradicable fear among the mass of Muscovite citizens.

What Ivan did to destroy the power of the nobility as a class was less spectacular but more effective. According to Fletcher, both he and Boris Godunov destroyed the economic independence of the great nobles by confiscating their patrimonial estates and replacing them with lands granted on pomest'e by which tenure depended on the performance of regular service to the tsar. If individual grandees seemed too powerful, the rulers sent them on assignment to distant provinces or forced them to take monastic vows. By such small steps, they weakened the most illustrious families so much that they were left with nothing but ceremonial recognition and were in grave danger of dying out within a generation or two.

How accurate is Fletcher's analysis? The evidence that he presented indicates, at least, that he managed to find out a great deal about the chief noble clans. He knew which families were the descendents of the

rulers of independent principalities, how many sons each had to carry
on their tradition, and, on the whole, was correct in predicting which
ones would soon die out altogether. One cannot be sure, however, that,
in spite of his precision in dealing with particular cases, Fletcher may
not have gone too far in building a general theory around them. There
were, to be sure, many instances of disgrace, imprisonment, and execution that tend to support his contentions. If Ivan and Boris had intended to destroy the high nobility as such, however, how is one to explain the continued prominence of some of their number such as the
Shuiskiis and the Odoevskiis?

From the state of the nobility it is a short step to the condition of
the Muscovite army in which most of them served. Fletcher treated the
armed forces briefly but with the thoroughness and sharpness of ex-
pression that marks his best work. Like the earlier English commentators, he paid particular attention to the special tactics that the Russians
had adopted for warfare in the steppe and praised their toughness and
doggedness, particularly in defensive operations. But if the army was
so large and the individual soldiers so tough, why had the Muscovite
army not made a better showing, especially against the forces of the
country's western neighbors?

In answer, Fletcher pointed primarily to the incompetence of the
majority of the generals in recent campaigns. In his opinion, the weakness of the high command was another undesirable consequence of a
despotic system of government. The tsar usually chose, as commander
of each of the main divisions of the army, a member of one of the highest noble families, "but so chosen otherwise as that he is of small valor
or practice in martial matters." "For in this point they are very wary,
that these two, to wit, nobility and power, meet not both in one."
Really competent commanders were assigned to subordinate posts in
which they would make up for the weaknesses of their superior officers
but not achieve the renown that might make them a threat to the tsar's
power.

In all probability less sinister considerations guided the tsar in
choosing the commanders of his armies. Although his power to make
appointments was subject to no constitutional limits, he was trapped in
a cobweb of traditional practices, above all the *mestnichestvo* system,
according to which each member of the Muscovite nobility was ranked
by the eminence of his ancestors and the time and position in which they

had served the princes of Moscow.[32] Traditionally each man in this lad-
der-like arrangement could be sure at least that no one of lower rank
could hold a position in government service more prestigious than he
or a more honored place at court ceremonies. In practice, the system
tied the tsar's hands less tightly than an outline of its workings might
suggest, for a determined ruler could stretch it to suit his purposes or
break through its threads altogether. In some respects, indeed, mestnichestvo actually strengthened the tsar's authority. As Fletcher pointed
out in his chapter on the nobility, the great families of the realm were
so busy quarreling with one another over their respective right to offices and ceremonial positions that they could not unite to resist the
tsar's growing power.[33]

Even though the system did not ultimately limit the tsar's authority, its workings left their imprint on the day-to-day business of the administration, including the management of the army. In theory the
army lay outside of the system since in 1550 Ivan IV had decreed that
its operations were suspended and no appeals from disgruntled commanders were to be entertained while the forces were actually in the
field.[34] It was extremely difficult in practice, however, to make the
officers give up their traditional pattern of behavior; even at the time
of Fletcher's visit, thirty-eight years after the decree had been issued,
the tsar still received many complaints from officers who believed that,
by lineage and family tradition of service, they deserved a higher posting than one of their superiors.[35]

The continuing influence of mestnichestvo may explain why many of
the chief commanders of the Muscovite forces were men of distinguished ancestry and little aptitude for command. If the tsar had attempted to put a gifted officer like Dmitrii Ivanovich Khvorostinin in

32. On the mestnichestvo system and its impact on the Muscovite system of
government, see S. O. Shmidt's stimulating article, "Mestnichestvo i absoliutizm
(postanovka voprosa)," *Absoliutizm v Rossii (XVII–XVIII vv.). Sbornik statei k
semidesiatiletiiu so dnia rozhdeniia i sorokapiatiletiiu nauchnoi i pedagogicheskoi
deiatel'nosti B. B. Kafengauza* (Moscow, 1964), pp. 168–205. See also Marc
Raeff, *Origins of the Russian Intelligentsia: The Eighteenth-Century Nobility*
(New York, 1966), pp. 19–22.

33. Shmidt, "Mestnichestvo i absoliutizm," p. 189.

34. Zimin, *Reformy*, pp. 342–45.

35. The most extensive military service lists covering the year of Fletcher's
visit (7097 by the Muscovite system) record 19 distinct protests against the
government's alleged violation of mestnichestvo ranking (*RK*, pp. 400–12).

charge of one of the main divisions of the army, he would have met a
wave of protests from those who had a higher ranking on the mestnichestvo ladder.[36] Rather than fight traditional prejudices, it was easier,
especially for an insecure regime like that of Fedor and Boris Godunov, to follow custom and appoint to the highest commands men of the
highest mestnichestvo standing regardless of their military capacities.

If the Muscovite nobility was subservient to the crown, the fate of
the common man was, in Fletcher's opinion, worse still, since the ordinary Russian suffered from the exactions of the nobles as well as of the
tsar. Since they had no representation in a parliament, the common
people had no defense against crushing taxation and the caprice of officials who could extract far more even than the law allowed. It was
Fletcher's conviction that the government's policy of exacting as much
as possible from its subjects was disastrously shortsighted for two reasons. In the first place, Fletcher reported seeing about fifty villages on
the road from Vologda to Moscow which were deserted because their
inhabitants could bear their burdens no longer. As he rightly observed,
peasant flight was a very widespread phenomenon in the late sixteenth
century and indeed remained a millstone weighing down the Russian
government for many generations. The government's oppressive policies had the second effect of destroying the economic initiative of the
ordinary citizen. If success in business would serve only to attract the
avaricious attention of the treasury, why bother to make an effort at
all? Fletcher believed that such an attitude had a deleterious effect on
the welfare of the state and the morals of its citizens, for in spite of its
abundant natural resources, the Muscovite state conducted little foreign trade, and its people whiled away their time "in idleness and
drinking." Whatever the merits of his argument as a whole, he weakened his case by pointing to the Stroganov family as an example of
how a highhanded government could destroy a flourishing enterprise.
Although the Stroganovs had to pay a high price in money and service
for their privileges, their enterprises continued to thrive long after his
visit to Russia.[37]

One reason why the Russian people bore such severe oppression was
the fact that they lived without "true knowledge of God." In Fletcher's

36. Three of the 19 protests complained specifically about Khvorostinin's assignment (*RK*, pp. 408–9).
37. On the Stroganovs, see A. A. Vvedenskii, *Dom Stroganovykh v XVI–XVII
vekakh* (Moscow, 1962).

opinion, the Muscovite church was an important link in the chain of despotic government that tied them down: the ecclesiastical leaders of Russia gave the tsars their unqualified support in return for "extraordinary favors and immunities to the bishop's sees, abbeys, and friaries" and performed an even greater service by maintaining a "superstitious and false religion" that best agreed "with a tyrannical state" because it produced ignorant and subservient subjects. His critique of the practices of the church employs all of the motifs that one would expect in the work of a writer of strongly Protestant, perhaps even Puritan, sympathies. He joined the other English writers of the period in condemning the emphasis on liturgical observances, which seemed to him idolatry, the large numbers and low morals of the monks, who were a drain on the economy and a bad example for the faithful, and the church's neglect of education. His portrayal is not entirely somber since it is relieved by excellent descriptions of ceremonies such as the Blessing of the Waters at Epiphany and an ordinary marriage. The dominant note of his discussion, nevertheless, is a nagging insistence that the readers should be aware of all of "their chiefest errors in matter of faith" and practice.

Fletcher's strange treatment of the creation of the Patriarchate of Moscow suggests one reason for his strong antipathy toward Orthodoxy. He assumed that the visit to Moscow of Patriarch Jeremiah of Constantinople was part of a plan to convert Russia to Roman Catholicism and win her participation in the Hapsburg coalition against the Protestant powers. In reality, the creation of the patriarchal dignity increased the prestige of the Muscovite church and of the state, whose leaders were as hostile to Catholicism as Fletcher. His misunderstanding of events that took place under his nose seems to indicate that, in the year of the Spanish Armada, he was obsessed with the menace of Catholicism—in a sense the chief enemy both of his religion and of his country. Russian Orthodoxy, whose dogmas and rites seemed so similar to those of the Roman church, had to share the burden of his anti-Catholic sentiments.

What did the future hold for Russia? The tsar's government, secure in the support of the church, the army, and the bureaucracy, seemed unshakeable. Yet the Muscovite state faced one ominous prospect that might shake its foundations. Ironically it was Ivan IV, the ruler who perfected Muscovite despotism and whose shadow fell across the whole of the *Russe Commonwealth,* who sowed the seeds of the system's destruction. Fletcher closed his description of the oprichnina with the words, "And this wicked policy and tyrannous practice . . . hath so troubled that country and filled it so full of grudge and mortal hatred ever since, that it will not be quenched . . . till it burn again into a civil flame."

Historians have often seized upon this arresting prediction as proof that, at the time of Fletcher's visit, Russian society was already irrevocably bound for the civil war and rebellions that broke out fifteen years later. Two considerations should, however, raise questions about the real significance of his observation. In the first place, the statement stands in striking contradiction to Fletcher's principal thesis that the Muscovite government was so effectively tyrannical that nothing, not even popular unrest, could shake it. It was, moreover, a commonplace of Elizabethan political literature that tyrannical rulers might force their subjects to rise in revolt against themselves or their successors. The author of the *Mirror for Magistrates*, for example, makes a very similar remark about the fall of Richard III:

First they [Richard and his advisers] should have known what the people misliked and grudged at, . . . and so might have found means, either by amendment . . . or by some other policy to have stayed the people's grudge; the forerunner commonly of rulers' destructions. *Vox populi, vox dei*, in this case is not so famous a proverb as true: The experience of all times doth approve it.[38]

Fletcher's remark, then, appears to be a conventional moral judgment rather than a political forecast. From his point of view, civil strife probably seemed inevitable for moral, not sociological, reasons: since Ivan IV had not suffered sufficient punishment for the horrors of the oprichnina, his successors had necessarily to taste the bitter fruit of retribution.

Ever since Fletcher finished writing it, *Of the Russe Commonwealth* has provoked strong reactions in its readers. Its obvious merits led many Russian historians of the nineteenth century to rely heavily on it for information on Muscovite politics, constitutional practice, and social life. Since the appearance in 1891 of S. M. Seredonin's extremely critical analysis of the work, scholars have proceeded more cautiously,

---

38. *A Mirror for Magistrates*, p. 359; see also the remarks on Richard's fall in Edward Hall's *Chronicle* (London, 1809), pp. 381–420.

especially in their use of Fletcher's account of the fiscal policy of the tsars. Yet *Of the Russe Commonwealth* has come through the fire of its serious critics and stands as a historical source of the highest importance.

Scholarly critics have been the least of Fletcher's adversaries. On at least two occasions published editions of his work have suffered confiscation for political reasons. When the first edition appeared, the governors of the Russia Company complained to Lord Burghley that if the tsar's government found out about the book, "the revenge thereof will light on their [the Company's] people, and goods remaining in Russia, and utterly overthrow the trade forever."[39] The Company's directors objected to the unflattering tone of the work and a number of specific criticisms which Fletcher directed against the despotic characteristics of the Russian regime and the loose morals of the people. His value judgments were not all that frightened the Company. They were afraid that even the mention of widely-known facts such as Tsar Fedor's unheroic physique or Ivan IV's murder of his eldest son might provoke the tsar's government to cancel the Company's remaining trading privileges.[40] The Company's petition met with success and Fletcher's book was suppressed.[41]

Over 250 years later, in September, 1848, Nicholas I of Russia supervised the confiscation of the first Russian translation of the work and meted out severe punishment to the officials of the Imperial Moscow Society of Russian History and Antiquities in whose *Proceedings* it had appeared.[42] The episode, however, is a more accurate reflection of the mood and methods of Nicholas' regime than of Fletcher's qualities as a reporter.

It is odd that Fletcher, so cautious a citizen, proved so controversial an author. Perhaps we are at last dispassionate enough to read his work without idealizing him or condemning him out of hand. His work certainly bears the marks of his qualities of mind and character—intelli-

39. Berry, pp. 150–51.
40. Berry, pp. 150–53; Bond, pp. 352–55.
41. Berry, pp. 153–54.
42. See S. A. Belokurov, " 'Delo Fletchera,' 1848–1864 gg.," *Chteniia v Imperatorskom obshchestve istorii i drevnostei rossiiskikh pri Moskovskom universitete* (1910), III, ii, 1–39; A. A. Titov, "Istoriia pervago perevoda sochineniia Fletchera," in *O gosudarstve russkom-sochinenie Fletchera* (St. Petersburg, 1906), pp. vii–xiv. For a discussion of the "Fletcher affair" in English, see Pipes and Fine, *Giles Fletcher, Of the Russe Commonwealth*, pp. 38–41.

gence, perceptiveness, diligence, and obstinacy in the defense of his convictions. For all of the personal touches, it is a priceless record of a society that was soon overwhelmed by civil war and foreign invasion and, in spite of the loving efforts of seventeenth-century statesmen to revive it, was never quite the same again.

The Russe Commonwealth was first published in 1591 and reprinted in 1643. Another issue of the 1643 edition appeared in 1657. Richard Hakluyt included *The Russe Commonwealth,* with almost every unfavorable comment on the Russian government excised, in the second edition of the *Principal Navigations* (3 vols.; London, 1598–1600), I, Rr3ʳ–Tt3ʳ, and also in the modern reprint of the *Principal Navigations* (12 vols.; Glasgow, 1903–5), III, 252–405. The work also appeared in Samuel Purchas, *Purchas His Pilgrimes* (4 vols.; London, 1625), III, Nn3ʳ–Rr2ʳ, and in the modern reprint of *Purchas His Pilgrimes* (20 vols.; Glasgow, 1905–7), XII, 499–633. Edward A. Bond reprinted the 1591 edition in *Russia at the Close of the Sixteenth Century* (London, 1856), pp. 1–152; and Lloyd E. Berry published a critical edition of the work in *The English Works of Giles Fletcher, the Elder* (Madison, 1964), pp. 169–306. Most recently Richard Pipes and J. V. A. Fine have published a photographic reprint of the 1591 edition (Cambridge, Mass., 1966); and Albert J. Schmidt has published a modernized text, *Of the Rus Commonwealth,* for the Folger Shakespeare Library (Ithaca, N.Y.: Cornell University Press, 1966).

Fletcher's *The Russe Commonwealth* has been translated into Russian. The suppressed 1848 edition translated by D. I. Gippius and edited by N. V. Kachalov first appeared in an emigré edition in 1867 with the title, *O gosudarstve russkom, ili obraz pravleniia russkago tsaria.* The first version of the text to be published inside Russia was an abridgement in A. Burtsev, *Opisanie redkikh russkikh knig,* Vol. III (St. Petersburg, 1897), pp. 185–293, with an introduction by K. M. Obolenskii. The full text of the Gippius-Kachalov edition was published in St. Petersburg in 1905 and was reissued later in the same year and again in 1906. A final Russian edition appeared in 1911. Charles du Bouzet translated *The Russe Commonwealth* into French, *La Russie au XVIe Siècle par Giles Fletcher* (Leipzig and Paris, 1864).

Giles Fletcher

Of the Russe Commonwealth

Preface

Most gracious sovereign: being employed in your majesty's service to the emperor of Russia, I observed the state and manners of that country. And having reduced the same into some order by the way as I returned, I have presumed to offer it in this small book to your most excellent majesty. My meaning was to note things for mine own experience, of more importance than delight, and rather true than strange. In their manner of government your highness may see both; a true and strange face of a tyrannical state (most unlike to your own) without true knowledge of God, without written law, without common justice, save that which proceedeth from their "speaking law," to wit, the magistrate who hath most need of a law to restrain his own injustice. The practice hereof as it is heavy and grievous to the poor oppressed people that live within those countries, so it may give just cause to myself and other your majesty's faithful subjects to acknowledge our happiness on this behalf and to give God thanks for your majesty's most prince-like and gracious government, as also to your highness more joy and contentment in your royal estate, in that you are a prince of subjects, not of slaves, that are kept within duty by love, not

109

by fear. The Almighty still bless your highness with a most long and happy reign in this life, and with Christ Jesus in the life to come.

Your majesty's most humble

subject and servant,

G. Fletcher

Chapter 1. The description of the country of Russia with the breadth, length, and names of the shires

The country of Russia was sometimes called Sarmatia. It changed the name (as some do suppose) for that it was parted into divers small and yet absolute governments, not depending nor being subject the one to the other. For "Russe" in that tongue doth signify as much as to "part" or "divide." The Russe reporteth that four brethren, Truvor, Riurik, Sineus, and Variuus, divided among them the north parts of the country. Likewise that the south parts were possessed by four other, Kii, Shchek, Khoriv, and their sister, Lybed', each calling his territory after his own name. Of this partition it was called Russia about the year from Christ 860.[1] As for the conjecture which I find in some cosmographers that the Russe nation borrowed the name of the people called Roxolani[2] and were the very same nation with them, it is without all good probability, both in respect of the etymology of the word (which is very far set) and especially for the seat and dwelling of that people, which was betwixt the two rivers of Tanaïs and Borysthenes (as Strabo reporteth), quite another way from the country of Russia.[3]

1. The whole first paragraph is probably based on Martin Cromer's *De origine et rebus gestis Polonorum* (Basel, 1568), pp. 16–19. The ultimate source of the legends about the four brethren is probably one of the versions of the *Russian Primary Chronicle*. The variant of the story given by Cromer and Fletcher differs from the Russian source only by the addition of Riurik's third brother, Variuus. This change may have resulted from careless reading of the chronicle entry for the years 860–62 which lists the names of Riurik, Truvor, and Sineus and early in the next sentence uses the word *variag*, the genitive plural off the word for a Varangian or Viking (D. S. Likhachev [ed.], *Povest' vremennykh let* [Moscow-Leningrad, 1950], I, 18).
2. A branch of the Sarmatians.
3. Strabo, *Geography* (London: Loeb Classical Library, 1918–32), III. 223.

When it bare the name of Sarmatia it was divided into two chief parts, the White and the Black. The White Sarmatia was all that part that lieth towards the north and on the side of Livonia—as the provinces now called Dvina, Vaga, [Velikii] Ustiug, Vologda, Kargopol', Novgorod, etc.—whereof Novgorod Velikii was the metropolis or chief city. Black Sarmatia was all that country that lieth southward towards the Euxine or Black Sea—as the dukedom of Vladimir, of Moscow, Riazan', etc. Some have thought that the name of Sarmatia was first taken from one Sarmates, whom Moses and Josephus call Hazarmaveth, son to Joktan and nephew to Eber, of the posterity of Shem. But this seemeth to be nothing but a conjecture taken out of the likeness of the name Hazarmaveth. For the dwelling of all Joktan's posterity is described by Moses to have been betwixt Mesha or Masius (an hill of the Ammonites) and Sephar (near to the river Euphrates), which maketh it very unlikely that Hazarmaveth should plant any colonies so far off in the north and northwest countries. It is bounded northward by the Lapps and the North Ocean, on the south side by the Tatars, called Krym. Eastward they have the Nogaian Tatar, that possesseth all the country on the east side of Volga towards the Caspian Sea. On the west and southwest border lieth Lithuania, Livonia, and Poland.

The whole country, being now reduced under the government of one, containeth these chief provinces or shires: Vladimir, which beareth the first place in the emperor's style because their house came of the dukes of that country; Moscow; Nizhnii-Novgorod; Pskov; Smolensk; Novgorod Velikii, or Novgorod of the low country;[4] Rostov; Iaroslavl'; Beloozero; Riazan'; Dvina; Kargopol'; Meshchera; Vaga; Ustiug; [and] Galich. These are the natural shires pertaining to Russia, but far greater and larger than the shires of England though not so well peopled. The other countries or provinces which the Russe emperors have gotten perforce added of late to their other dominion are these which follow: Tver'; Yougoria;[5] Perm'; Viatka; Bulgaria; Chernigov;

---

4. Fletcher confused Novgorod Velikii (Great Novgorod) with Nizhnii-Novgorod (Lower Novgorod).

5. A very vague term which many map-makers confused with Udoriia and therefore located in the Mezen' valley on the Arctic coast of European Russia. Somewhat more convincing is the suggestion that the term Yougoria is related to the name of the Iugorskii Shar, the narrow strait separating Vaigach Island from the coast of the mainland almost directly north of the Urals. Yougoria might then refer to a large area of the Arctic coast from Vaigach to the mouth of the Taz river in western Siberia (P. Semenov, Slovar' rossiiskoi imperii [St. Petersburg, 1863–85], V, 892).

Oudoria;[6] Obdoria;[7] Condora;[8] with a great part of Siberia, where the
people, though they be not natural Russes, yet obey the emperor of
Russia and are ruled by the laws of his country, paying customs and
taxes as his own people do.[9] Besides these he hath under him the kingdoms of Kazan' and Astrakhan', gotten by conquest not long since.[10] As
for all his possession in Lithuania (to the number of thirty great towns
and more), with Narva and Dorpat in Livonia, they are quite gone,
being surprised of late years by the kings of Poland and Sweden.[11]
These shires and provinces are reduced all into four jurisdictions which
they call chetverti, that is, tetrarchies or fourthparts, whereof we are to
speak in the title or chapter concerning the provinces and their manner
of government.

The whole country is of great length and breadth. From the north to
the south, if you measure from Kola to Astrakhan', which bendeth
somewhat eastward, it reacheth in length about 4,260 verst or miles.[12]
Notwithstanding, the emperor of Russia hath more territory northward
—far beyond Kola unto the river of Tromschua,[13] that runneth a 1,000
verst, wellnigh beyond Pechenga near to Vardo—but not entire nor
clearly limited, by reason of the kings of Sweden and Denmark, that
have divers towns there as well as the Russe, plotted together the one

6. *Udorskaia zemlia,* probably the Mezen' valley, since one of the main tributaries of that river, the Vazhka, was formerly called the Udora. (See, for example, J. N. De l'Isle, [ed.], *Russischer atlas welcher in einer General-Charte
und neunzehen Special Charten das gesamte Russische Reich und dessen angränt-
zende Länder* . . . [St. Petersburg, 1745], map 6).

7. *Obdorskaia zemlia,* the lower Ob valley in northwestern Siberia (Semenov,
Slovar' rossiiskoi imperii, III, 577).

8. *Kondinskaia zemlia,* another term that frequently confused the early map-
makers. It probably refers to the valley of the Konda river, a tributary of the
Irtysh, in northwestern Siberia (Semenov, *Slovar' rossiiskoi imperii,* II, 704–5).

9. Fletcher, writing between 1589 and 1591, reflected the Muscovite government's claims to control over Siberia rather that the actual situation in the area.
The "shires" and provinces that Fletcher mentions were not administrative
units in the sixteenth century. Seredonin suggests that Fletcher may have taken
the names of these districts from the tsar's formal title in which they are all
mentioned along with other territories not named in this passage (pp. 128–29).

10. Ivan IV captured the khanate of Kazan' in 1552 and Astrakhan' in 1556.

11. Narva was lost to Sweden in 1581 and Dorpat (now called Tartu) to
Poland in 1582.

12. It is perhaps not a coincidence that the total distance from Archangel to
Moscow and then by water to Astrakhan' was exactly 4260 versts (V. A. Petrov,
"Geograficheskie spravochniki XVII v.," *Istoricheskii arkhiv,* V [1950], 110, 122).

13. Fletcher may have derived the name from the island and settlement of
Tromso in Norway.

with the other, every one of them claiming the whole of those north parts as his own right. The breadth (if you go from that part of his territory that lieth farthest westward on the Narva side to the parts of Siberia eastward where the emperor hath his garrisons) is 4,400 verst or thereabouts.[14] A verst (by their reckoning) is a thousand paces, yet less by one quarter than an English mile. If the whole dominion of the Russe emperor were all habitable and peopled in all places, as it is in some, he would either hardly hold it all within one regiment or be overmighty for all his neighbor princes.

Chapter 2. Of the soil and climate

The soil of the country for the most part is of a slight sandy mold, yet very much different one place from another, for the yield of such things as grow out of the earth. The country northwards towards the parts of Saint Nicholas and Kola and northeast towards Siberia is all very barren and full of desert woods by reason of the climate and extremity of the cold in wintertime. So likewise along the river Volga betwixt the countries of Kazan' and Astrakhan', where, notwithstanding the soil is very fruitful, it is all uninhabited, saving that upon the river Volga on the west side the emperor hath some few castles with garrisons in them. This happeneth by means of the Krym Tatar, that will neither himself plant towns to dwell there, living a wild and vagrant life, nor suffer the Russe, that is far off with the strength of his country, to people those parts. From Vologda[1] (which lieth almost 1,700 verst from the port of Saint Nicholas) down towards Moscow and so towards the south part that bordereth upon the Krym (which containeth the like space of 1,700 verst or thereabouts)[2] is a very fruitful and pleasant country yielding pasture and corn, with woods and

14. The distance from Narva to Tobol'sk, the last Muscovite outpost in Siberia in Fletcher's time, was about 3,290 versts (Petrov, "Geograficheskie spravochniki," pp. 112, 146; K. N. Serbina [ed.], *Kniga Bol'shomu Chertezhu* [Moscow-Leningrad, 1950], p. 153).

1. The route from Archangel to Vologda was 1080 versts (Petrov, "Geograficheskie spravochniki," pp. 106, 110).

2. The distance from Vologda to Moscow was 420 versts and from there to the southern frontier roughly 450 or 500 versts (*ibid.*, pp. 106, 130).

waters in very great plenty. The like is betwixt Riazan' (that lieth southeast from Moscow) to Novgorod and Pskov[3] that reach farthest towards the northwest. So betwixt Moscow and Smolensk (that lieth southwest towards Lithuania) is a very fruitful and pleasant soil.

The whole country differeth very much from itself by reason of the year, so that a man would marvel to see the great alteration and difference betwixt the winter and summer in[4] Russia. The whole country in the winter lieth under snow, which falleth continually and is sometime of a yard or two thick but greater towards the north. The rivers and other waters are all frozen up a yard or more thick, how swift or broad soever they be. And this continueth commonly five months, viz., from the beginning of November till towards the end of March, what time the snow beginneth to melt, so that it would breed a frost in a man to look abroad at that time and see the winter face of that country. The sharpness of the air you may judge of by this, for that water dropped down or cast up into the air congealeth into ice before it come to the ground. In the extremity of winter, if you hold a pewter dish or pot in your hand or any other metal (except in some chamber where their warm stoves be), your fingers will freeze fast unto it and draw off the skin at the parting. When you pass out of a warm room into a cold you shall sensibly feel your breath to wax stark and even stifling with the cold as you draw it in and out. Divers, not only that travel abroad, but in the very markets and streets of their towns, are mortally pinched and killed withal, so that you shall see many drop down in the streets, many travelers brought into the towns sitting dead and stiff in their sleds. Divers lose their noses, the tips of their ears, and the balls of their cheeks, their toes, feet, etc. Many times when the winter is very hard and extreme, the bears and wolves issue by troops out of the woods, driven by hunger, and enter the villages, tearing and ravening all they can find, so that the inhabitants are fain to fly for safeguard of their lives. And yet in the summertime you shall see such a new hue and face of a country, the woods (for the most part which are all of fir and birch) so fresh and so sweet, the pastures and meadows so green and well grown (and that upon the sudden), such variety of flowers, such noise of birds (specially of nightingales that seem to be more loud and of a more variable note than in other countries), that a man shall not lightly travel in a more pleasant country.

3. Vobsko in the original text.
4. *summer in.* summer in the original text.

And this fresh and speedy growth of the spring there seemeth to proceed from the benefit of the snow which, all the wintertime being spread over the whole country as a white robe and keeping it warm from the rigor of the frost, in the springtime (when the sun waxeth warm and dissolveth it into water) doth so thoroughly drench and soak the ground, that is somewhat of a slight and sandy mold, and then shineth so hotly upon it again, that it draweth the herbs and plants forth in great plenty and variety in a very short time. As the winter exceedeth in cold, so the summer inclineth to overmuch heat, specially in the months of June, July, and August, being much warmer than the summer air in England.

The country throughout is very well watered with springs, rivers, and *ozera* or lakes. Wherein the providence of God is to be noted, for that much of the country being so far inland as that some part lieth a thousand miles and more every way from any sea, yet it is served with fair rivers, and that in very great number, that, emptying themselves one into another, run all into the sea. Their lakes are many and large, some of sixty, eighty, one hundred, and two hundred miles long with breadth proportionate.

The chief rivers are these: The first, Volga, that hath his head or spring at the root of an alder tree about two hundred verst above Iaroslavl', and groweth so big by the increase of other rivers by that time it cometh thither that it is broad an English mile and more, and so runneth into the Caspian Sea, about 2,800 verst or miles of length.[5]

The next is Borysthenes (now called Dnieper) that divideth the country from Lithuania and falleth into the Euxine Sea.

The third, Tanaïs or Don, the ancient bounder betwixt Europe and Asia, that taketh his head out of Riazan' Ozero,[6] and so running through the country of the Krym Tatar falleth into the great sea lake or mere called Maeotis by the city of Azov. By this river (as the Russe reporteth) you may pass from their city Moscow to Constantinople, and so into all those parts of the world by water, drawing your boat (as their manner is) over a little isthmus or narrow slip of land a few versts overthwart, which was proved not long since by an ambassador sent to Constantinople, who passed the river of Moskva and so into another called Oka, whence he drew his boat over into Tanaïs and thence passed the whole way by water.

5. The Volga is 3,694 kilometers or about 2,300 miles long.
6. Fletcher apparently got this information from Jenkinson's map of Russia. The Don has its source in a small lake called Ivan Ozero.

The fourth is called Dvina, many hundred miles long, that falleth northward into the Bay of Saint Nicholas and hath great alabaster rocks on the banks towards the seaside.

The fifth, Dvina, that emptieth into the Baltic Sea by the town Riga.

The sixth, Onega, that falleth into the Bay at Solovetskii, ninety verst from the port of Saint Nicholas. This river below the town Kargopol' meeteth with the river Volock that falleth into the Finland Sea by the town Iam, so that from the port of Saint Nicholas into the Finland Sea and so into the sound you may pass all by water, as hath been tried by the Russe.[7]

The seventh, Sukhona, that floweth into Dvina and so into the North Sea.

The eighth, Oka, that fetcheth his head from the borders of the Krym and streameth into Volga.

The ninth, Moskva, that runneth through the city Moscow and giveth it the name.

There is Vychegda, also a very large and long river, that riseth out of Perm' and falleth into Volga.[8]

All these are rivers of very large streams, the least to be compared to the Thames in bigness and in length far more, besides diverse other. The pole at Moscow is 55 degrees, 10 minutes;[9] at the port of Saint Nicholas towards the north 63 degrees and 50 minutes.[10]

Chapter 3. The native commodities of the country

For kinds of fruits they have apples; pears; plums; cherries, red and black (but the black, wild); a *dynia* like a muskmelon but more sweet and pleasant; cucumbers and gourds (which they call

---

7. The Russian word *volok* means portage. There is no river connecting the Onega with the Gulf of Finland. It has been suggested, however, that in the sixteenth century there may have been a trade route from the Onega by land to the headwaters of the Vytegra River and thence by water to Lake Onega and the Gulf of Finland (Seredonin, p. 115).

8. The Vychegda flows into the northern Dvina.

9. 55°1'.

10. About 64°40'.

arbuz); rasps; strawberries; and hurtleberries, with many other berries in great quantity in every wood and hedge. Their kinds of grain are wheat, rye, barley, oats, pease, buckway, [and] *pshenitsa,* that in taste is somewhat like to rice. Of all these grains the country yieldeth very sufficient with an overplus quantity, so that wheat is sold sometime for two *altyny* or ten pence sterling the chetvert', which maketh almost three English bushels.[1]

Their rye is sowed before the winter, all their other grain in the springtime, and for the most part in May. The Permians and some other that dwell far north and in desert places are served from the parts that lie more southward and are forced to make bread sometimes of a kind of root (called *vaghnoy*)[2] and of the middle ring of the fir tree. If there be any dearth (as they accounted this last year, anno 1588, wheat and rye being at thirteen *altyny* or five shillings, five pence sterling the chetvert'),[3] the fault is rather in the practice of their nobility that use to engross it than in the country itself.

The native commodities of the country, wherewith they serve both their own turns and send much abroad to the great enriching of the emperor and his people, are many and substantial. First, furs of all sorts, wherein the providence of God is to be noted that provideth a natural remedy for them to help the natural inconvenience of their country by the cold of the climate.[4] Their chief furs are these: black fox, sables, lynx, dun fox, martens, *gornostae* or ermines, lassets or miniver, beaver, wolverines, the skin of a great water rat that smelleth naturally like musk, calaber or gray squirrel, red squirrel, red and white fox. Besides the great quantity spent within the country (the people

1. *Buckway* is modern buckwheat. Fletcher's figure of 12 *den'gi* per chetvert is much lower than any grain prices recorded in Russian sources for the last four decades of the century with the exception of one commodity: oats frequently cost even less than 12 den'gi (A. G. Man'kov, *Le mouvement des prix dans l'état russe du XVIe siècle* [Paris, 1957], pp. 131–38). The altyn was a monetary unit equal to 6 den'gi (200 den'gi = 1 ruble). The chetvert' was a dry measure which, in the late sixteenth century, was equal to about 4 puds or 144 pounds of rye (E. I. Kamentseva and N. V. Ustiugov, *Russkaia metrologiia* [Moscow, 1965], p. 91).

2. This word could not be identified.

3. Fletcher's statement that wheat cost 13 altyny or 78 den'gi per chetvert' in Moscow in 1588 is in harmony with the other figures for that year. Wheat sold for 89 den'gi per chetvert' in Vologda and 100 den'gi in Kholmogory (Man'kov, *Le mouvement des prix,* pp. 135–36).

4. On the Russian fur trade, see R. H. Fisher, *The Russian Fur Trade, 1550–1700* (Berkeley, Cal., 1943).

being clad all in furs the whole winter), there are transported out of the country some years by the merchants of Turkey, Persia, Bulgaria,[5] Georgia, Armenia, and some other of Christendom, to the value of four or five hundred thousand rubles[6] as I have heard of the merchants. The best sable fur groweth in the country of Pechora, Momgosorskoy, and Obdorskoy, the worser sort in Siberia, Perm', and other places.[7] The black fox and red come out of Siberia, white and dun from Pechora, whence also come the white wolf and white bear skin, the best wolverine also thence and from Perm'. The best martens are from Siberia, Kadom, Murom, Perm', and Kazan'. Lynx, miniver, and ermines, the best are out of Galich and Uglich, many from Novgorod and Perm'. The beaver of the best sort breedeth in Murmansk by Kola. Other common furs and most of these kinds grow in many, and some in all, parts of the country.

The second commodity is of wax, whereof hath been shipped into foreign countries (as I have heard it reported by those that best know it) the sum of 50,000 *pud* yearly, every pud containing forty pound, but now about 10,000 pud a year.[8]

The third is their honey, whereof, besides an exceeding great quantity spent in their ordinary drinks (which is mead of all sorts) and their other uses, some good quantity is carried out of the country. The chief increase of honey is in Mordva[9] and Kadom near to the Cheremiss Tatar,[10] much out of Severskii,[11] Riazan', Murom, Kazan', Dorogobuzh, and Viaz'ma.

Fourthly, of tallow they afford a great weight for transportation, not only for that their country hath very much good ground apt for pasturage of cattle, but also by reason of their many lents and other fasts and partly because their greater men use much wax for their lights; the poorer and meaner sort, birch dried in their stoves and cut into long

5. Probably the former domain of the Bulgars on the middle Volga.

6. Fisher questions this figure as being somewhat high and suggests that "an amount half as large as that appears more consistent with the facts as we understand them." (*The Russian Fur Trade*, p. 230n.)

7. Momgosorskoy could not be identified. Obdorskoy is probably a reference to the same region identified earlier (p. 112) as "Obdoria."

8. 1 pud = 36 American pounds.

9. The region inhabited by the Mordvinians, south and west of the great bend in the Volga near Kazan'.

10. Also known as the Mari. The Cheremiss speak a language of the Ugro-Finnic group and live in the middle Volga valley and the surrounding districts.

11. Novgorod-Severskii.

shivers which they call *luchiny*. Of tallow there hath been shipped out of the realm a few years since about a 100,000 pud yearly, now not past 30,000 or thereabouts. The best yield of tallow is in the parts and territories of Smolensk, Iaroslavl', Uglich, Novgorod, and Vologda, Tver', and Gorodets.

Another principal commodity is their *los'* and cow hide. Their los' or buff hide is very fair and large. Their bull and cow hide (for oxen they make none, neither yet wether) is of a small size. There hath been transported by merchants strangers some years a 100,000 hides; now it is decreased to a 30,000 or thereabouts, besides great store of goats' skins, whereof great numbers are shipped out of the country. The largest kind of los' or buff breedeth about Rostov, Vychegda, Novgorod, Murom, and Perm', the lesser sort within the kingdom of Kazan'.

Another very great and principal commodity is their train oil drawn out of the seal fish, where it will not be impertinent to show the manner of their hunting the seal which they make this oil of, which is in this sort. Towards the end of summer (before the frost begin) they go down with their boats into the Bay of Saint Nicholas to a cape called Cusconesse or Foxnose where they leave their boats till the next springtide.[12] When the sun waxeth warm toward the spring, and yet the ice not melted within the bay, they return thither again. Then drawing their boats over the sea ice, they use them for houses to rest and lodge in. There are commonly about seventeen or eighteen fleet of them, of great large boats which divide themselves into divers companies, five or six boats in a consort.

They that first find the haunt fire a beacon which they carry with them for the nonce. Which being espied by the other companies by such among them as are appointed of purpose, they come altogether and compass the seals round about in a ring that lie sunning themselves together upon the ice, commonly four or five thousand in a shoal, and so they invade them every man with his club in his hand. If they hit them on the nose they are soon killed. If on the sides or back they bear out the blow and many times so catch and hold down the club with their teeth by main force that the party is forced to call for help to his fellows.

---

12. On William Borough's map of the northern coast of Europe, Cusconess (probably Kuiskii Nos in Russian) is a small headland on the east shore of the Gulf of Archangel, roughly halfway between Cape Kerets or Foxnose and the Dvina estuary (Morgan and Coote, II, inset facing p. 254).

The manner of the seals is, when they see themselves beset, to gather all close together in a throng or plump to sway down the ice, and to break it (if they can), which so bendeth the ice that many times it taketh the sea water upon it and maketh the hunters to wade a foot or more deep. After the slaughter, when they have killed what they can, they fall to sharing every boat his part in equal portions; and so they flay them, taking from the body, the skin and the lard or fat withal that cleaveth to the skin. This they take with them, leaving the bodies behind, and so go to shore where they dig pits in the ground of a fathom and an half deep or thereabout. And so taking the fat or lard off from the skin, they throw it into the pit and cast in among it hot burning stones to melt it withal. The uppermost and purest is sold and used to oil wool for cloth; the grosser (that is of a red color) they sell to make soap.

Likewise of *ikra* or caviar, a great quantity is made upon the river of Volga out of the fish called *beluga,* the sturgeon, the *sevriuga,* and the sterlet, whereof the most part is shipped by French and Netherlandish merchants for Italy and Spain, some by English merchants.

The next is of flax and hemp, whereof there hath been shipped (as I have heard merchants say) at the port of Narva a great part of a hundred ships small and great yearly, now not past five.[13] The reason of this abating and decrease of this and other commodities that were wont to be transported in a greater quantity is the shutting up of the port of the Narva, towards the Finland Sea, which now is in the hands and possession of the Swedes; likewise the stopping of the passage overland by the way of Smolensk and Polotsk by reason of their wars with the Poles, which causeth the people to be less provident in maintaining and gathering these and like commodities for that they lack sales. Partly also for that the merchants and muzhiki (for so they call the common sort of people) are very much discouraged by many heavy and intolerable exactions that of late time have been imposed upon them, no man accounting that which he hath to be sure his own, and therefore regard not to lay up anything or to have it beforehand for that it causeth them many times to be fleeced and spoiled not only of their goods but also of their lives. For the growth of flax the province of Pskov and the country about is the chief and only place, for hemp Smolensk, Dorogobuzh, and Viaz'ma.

13. See Willan, *Early History,* pp. 141–43.

The country besides maketh great store of salt. Their best salt is made at Staraia Rusa in very great quantity, where they have great store of salt wells about 250 verst from the sea. At Astrakhan' salt is made naturally by the sea water that casteth it up into great hills, and so it is digged down and carried away by the merchants and other that will fetch it from thence. They pay to the emperor for acknowledgment or custom three pence Russe upon every hundredweight. Besides these two, they make salt in many other places of the realm, as in Perm', Vychegda, Tot'ma, Kineshma, Solovetskii, Ocona, Bombasey, and Nenoksa,[14] all out of salt pits save at Solovetskii which lieth near to the sea.

Likewise of tar they make a great quantity out of their fir trees in the country of Dvina and Smolensk, whereof much is sent abroad. Besides these, which are all good and substantial commodities, they have divers other of smaller account that are natural and proper to that country, as the fish tooth (which they call *ribazuba*)[15] which is used both among themselves and the Persians and Bulgarians that fetch it from thence for beads, knives, and sword hafts of noblemen and gentlemen, and for divers other uses. Some use the powder of it against poison, as the unicorn's horn. The fish that weareth it is called a morzh and is caught about Pechora. These fish teeth, some of them, are almost two foot of length and weigh eleven or twelve pound apiece.

In the province of Karelia and about the river Dvina towards the North Sea there groweth a soft rock which they call sliuda. This they cut into pieces and so tear it into thin flakes, which naturally it is apt for, and so use it for glass lanterns and such like. It giveth both inwards and outwards a clearer light than glass, and for this respect is better than either glass or horn, for that it neither breaketh like glass nor yet will burn like the lantern. Saltpeter they make in many places, as at Uglich, Iaroslavl' and Ustiug, and some small store of brimstone upon the river Volga, but want skill to refine it. Their iron is somewhat brittle, but a great weight of it is made in Karelia, Kargopol', and Ustiuzhna-Zhelezopol'skaia. Other mine they have none growing within the realm.

Their beasts of strange kinds are the los', the *olen'*, the wild horse, the bear, the wolverine or wood dog, the lynx, the beaver, the sable, the marten, the black and dun fox, the white bear towards the

14. These names refer perhaps to the salt works on the Una and Nenoksa rivers (Seredonin, p. 127). Bombasey and Ocona could not be identified.
15. Presumably walrus tusks.

seacoast of Pechora, the gornostai, the lasset or miniver. They have a kind of squirrel that hath growing on the pinion of the shoulder bone a long tuft of hair, much like unto feathers, with a far broader tail than have any other squirrels which they move and shake as they leap from tree to tree, much like unto a wing. They skice[16] a large space and seem for to fly withal, and therefore they call them *letach vechshe,* that is, the flying squirrels.[17] Their hares and squirrels in summer are of the same color with ours; in winter the hare changeth her coat into milk white, the squirrel into gray, whereof cometh the calaber.

They have fallow deer, the roebuck, and goats, very great store. Their horses are but small, but very swift and hard. They travel them unshod both winter and summer without all regard of pace. Their sheep are but small and bear coarse and harsh wool. Of fowl they have divers of the principal kinds: first, great store of hawks, the eagle, the gerfalcon, the slightfalcon, the goshawk, the tercel, the sparhawk, etc. But the principal hawk that breedeth in the country is counted the gerfalcon.

Of other fowls their principal kinds are the swan, tame and wild (whereof they have great store), the stork, the crane, the tedder, of the color of a pheasant but far bigger and liveth in the fir woods. Of pheasant and partridge they have very great plenty. An owl there is of a very great bigness, more ugly to behold than the owls of this country, with a broad face and ears much like unto a man.

For fresh water fish besides the common sorts (as carp, pikes, perch, tench, roach, etc.) they have divers kinds very good and delicate, as the beluga or bellougina, of four or five ells long, the *osetrina* or sturgeon, the sevriuga, and sterlet, somewhat in fashion and taste like to the sturgeon but not so thick nor long. These four kinds of fish breed in the Volga and are catched in great plenty and served thence into the whole realm for a great food. Of the roes of these four kinds they make very great store of ikra or caviar as was said before.

They have, besides these that breed in the Volga, a fish called the *ryba belaia* or white salmon, which they account more delicate than they do the red salmon, whereof also they have exceeding great plenty in the rivers northward, as in Dvina, the river of Kola, etc. In the *ozero* or lake near a town called Pereiaslavl', not far from the Moscow, they have a small fish which they call the fresh herring, of the fashion and

16. Skip or frisk about.
17. Perhaps *letuchaia veksha,* meaning flying squirrel.

somewhat of the taste of a sea herring. Their chief towns for fish are Iaroslavl', Beloozero, Novgorod, Astrakhan', and Kazan', which all yield a large custom to the emperor every year for their trades of fishing which they practice in summer, but send it frozen in the wintertime into all parts of the realm.

Chapter 4. The chief cities of Russia

The chief cities of Russia are Moscow, Novgorod, Rostov, Vladimir, Pskov, Smolensk, Iaroslavl', Pereiaslavl', Nizhnii-Novgorod, Vologda, Ustiug, Kholmogory, Kazan', Astrakhan', Kargopol', Kolomna.

The city of Moscow is supposed to be of great antiquity though the first founder be unknown to the Russe.[1] It seemeth to have taken the name from the river that runneth on the one side of the town. Berosus the Chaldean in his fifth book telleth that Nimrod (whom other profane stories call Saturn) sent Assyrius, Medus, Moscus, and Magog into Asia to plant colonies there, and that Moscus planted both in Asia and Europe,[2] which may make some probability that the city, or rather the river whereon it is built, took the denomination from this Moscus, the rather because of the climate or situation which is in the very farthest part and list of Europe bordering upon Asia. The city was much enlarged by one Ivan, or John,[3] son to Daniel, that first changed his title of duke into king, though that honor continued not to his posterity, the rather because he was invested into it by the Pope's legate, who at that time was Innocentius the Fourth, about the year 1246,[4] which was very

1. The first mention of Moscow is in 1147, when Iurii Dolgorukii, prince of Suzdal', met Sviatoslav of Seversk and his allies.
2. Berosus, *Chaldaei Sacerdotis* (2 vols.; Lyons, 1554), I, sig. K3ʳ: "Eadem tempestate Saturnus rex Babyloniae misit principes coloniarum Assyrium, Medum, Moscum et Magogum: qui regna condiderunt Assyrium, Medum et Magogum in Asia, Moscos vero et in Asia simul et Europa."
3. Ivan I (d. 1341) transformed the Moscow Kremlin. During his reign, he finished the first stone church in Moscow and added four more stone churches, a monastery, and a bell tower (I. Zabelin, *Istoriia goroda Moskvy* [Moscow, 1902], I, 75–84).
4. Ivan I did not change his title from "duke" to "king." To his title of "grand duke of Vladimir" he added the words "and of all Russia." Semen the Proud, Ivan's son and successor, continued the new usage. Fletcher apparently

much misliked by the Russe people, being then a part of the Eastern or
Greek church. Since that time the name of this city hath grown more
famous and better known to the world, insomuch that not only the
province but the whole country of Russia is termed by some by the
name of Muscovy the metropolitan city. The form of this city is in a
manner round with three strong walls circling the one within the other
and streets lying between, whereof the inmost wall and the buildings
closed within it (lying safest as the heart within the body, fenced and
watered with the river Moskva that runneth close by it) is all accounted the emperor's castle. The number of houses (as I have heard)
through the whole city (being reckoned by the emperor a little before
it was fired by the Krym) was 41,500 in all.[5] Since the Tatar besieged
and fired the town (which was in the year 1571) there lieth waste of it
a great breadth of ground which before was well set and planted with
buildings, specially that part on the south side of Moskva built not
long before by Vasilii the emperor for his garrison of soldiers to whom
he gave privilege to drink mead and beer at the dry or prohibited
times when other Russes may drink nothing but water, and for that
cause called this new city by the name of Naloi, that is "skink" or "pour
in," so that now the city of Moscow is not much bigger than the city of
London.[6] The next in greatness, and in a manner as large, is the city
Novgorod, where was committed (as the Russe saith) the memorable
war so much spoke of in stories of the Scythian servants that took arms
against their masters, which they report in this sort, viz., that the boiars
or gentlemen of Novgorod and the territory about (which only are soldiers after the discipline of those countries) had war with the Tatars,
which being well performed and ended by them, they returned home-
wards, where they understood by the way that their *kholopy* or bondslaves, whom they left at home, had in their absence possessed their
towns, lands, houses, wives, and all. At which news being somewhat
amazed and yet disdaining the villainy of their servants, they made the

---

confused Daniil of Moscow with Daniil of Galicia who agreed to prevail on his
subjects to recognize the Pope as head of the church in return for military aid
against the Mongols. He was crowned king in 1253 with the blessing of Pope
Innocent IV (George Vernadsky, *The Mongols and Russia* [New Haven, 1953],
pp. 146–47).

5. Fletcher's figure for the number of houses in Moscow is exactly the same as
the one given by Herberstein (II, 5).

6. Herberstein (II, 4) made almost identical comments about the district south
of the Moskva River which he called Nali. *Skink:* serve drink.

more speed home and so not far from Novgorod met them in warlike manner marching against them. Whereupon advising what was best to be done, they agreed all to set upon them with no other show of weapon but with their horsewhips (which as their manner is every man rideth withal) to put them in remembrance of their servile condition, thereby to terrify them and abate their courage. And so marching on and lashing altogether with their whips in their hands they gave the onset, which seemed so terrible in the ears of their villeins and struck such a sense into them of the smart of the whip which they had felt before, that they fled altogether like sheep before the drivers. In memory of this victory the Novgorodians ever since have stamped their coin (which they call a *den'ga novgorodskaia,* current through all Russia) with the figure of a horseman shaking a whip aloft in his hand. These two cities exceed the rest in greatness.[7] For strength their chief towns are Pskov, Smolensk, Kazan', and Astrakhan', as lying upon the borders. But for situation Iaroslavl' far exceedeth the rest; for besides the commodities that the soil yieldeth of pasture and corn, it lieth upon the famous river Volga and looketh over it from a high bank, very fair and stately to behold, whereof the town taketh the name, for Iaroslavl' in that tongue signifieth as much as a "fair" or "famous bank." In this town (as may be guessed by the name) dwelt the Russe king Vladimir, surnamed Iaroslav, that married the daughter of Harold, king of England, by mediation of Sueno the Dane, as is noted in the Danish story, about the year 1067.[8]

The other towns have nothing that is greatly memorable save many ruins within their walls, which showeth the decrease of the Russe people under this government. The streets of their cities and towns instead of paving are planked with fir trees, planed and laid even, close the one to the other. Their houses are of wood without any lime or stone, built very close and warm with fir trees planed and piled one upon another. They are fastened together with dents or notches at every corner and so clasped fast together. Betwixt the trees or timber they thrust in

7. Herodotus IV. 1–4 is the ultimate source for the story (London: Loeb Classical Library, 1921–24), II, 201, 203. Seredonin (p. 52) points out that the Novgorodians never made such a coin as Fletcher describes.

8. Vladimir Monomakh married Gyda, daughter of Harold II of England. Vladimir's patronymic was actually Vsevolodovich; Iaroslav the Wise was his grandfather. It is possible that Fletcher actually knew this story in Saxo Grammaticus' *Historia Danica* (Paris, 1514), sig. O6ᵛ. But Fletcher might have gotten the story from Hakluyt, who included it in his 1589 edition of the *Voyages.*

moss, whereof they gather plenty in their woods, to keep out the air. Every house hath a pair of stairs that lead up into the chambers out of the yard or street after the Scottish manner. This building seemeth far better for their country than that of stone and brick, as being colder and more dampish than their wooden houses, specially of fir that is a dry and warm wood. Whereof the providence of God hath given them such store, as that you may build a fair house for twenty or thirty rubles, or little more where wood is most scant. The greatest inconvenience of their wooden building is the aptness for firing, which happeneth very oft and in very fearful sort by reason of the dryness and fatness of the fir that being once fired burneth like a torch and is hardly quenched till all be burnt up.

Chapter 5. Of the house or stock of the Russe emperors

The surname of the imperial house of Russia is called Bela.[1] It took the original (as is supposed) from the kings of Hungary, which may seem the more probable for that the Hungarian kings many years ago have borne that name, as appeareth by Bonfinius and other stories written of that country. For about the year 1059 mention is made of one Bela, that succeeded his brother Andrew, who reduced the Hungarians to the Christian faith from whence they were fallen by atheism and Turkish persuasion before. The second of that name was called Bela the Blind, after whom succeeded divers of the same name.[2]

That their ancestry came not of the Russe nation Ivan Vasil'evich,

1. The Muscovite ruling house was descended from the Kievan line of Riurik through Daniil, the youngest son of Aleksandr Nevskii. Seredonin suggests that Fletcher's error springs from a misunderstanding of the epithet "white (belii) tsar" which the Muscovite rulers adopted in imitation of the khans of the Golden Horde (p. 55).

2. The source is Antony Bonfinius, *Rerum Vngaricarum decades quatuor cum dimidia* (Hanover, 1606), pp. 203–4. But Bonfinius does not mention the idea that the Russian house of "Bela" came from Hungary.

The conversion of Hungary generally dates from the reign of Stephen I (1000–38). Andrew I ruled from 1047 to 1060, and was succeeded by his brother, Bela I (1060–63). Bela II, the Blind, ruled from 1131 to 1141. See Denis Sinor, *History of Hungary* (London, 1959), pp. 35–52.

father to this emperor, would many times boast, disdaining (as should seem) to have his progeny derived from the Russe blood, as namely to an Englishman, his goldsmith, that had received bullion of him to make certain plate, whom the emperor commanded to look well to his weight. "For my Russes," said he, "are thieves all." Whereat the workman, looking upon the emperor, began to smile. The emperor being of quick conceit charged him to tell him what he smiled at. "If your majesty will pardon me," quoth the goldsmith, "I will tell you. Your highness said that the Russes were all thieves and forgot in the meanwhile that yourself was a Russe." "I thought so," quoth the emperor, "but thou art deceived. For I am no Russe; my ancestors were Germans"; for so they account of the Hungarians to be part of the German nation, though indeed they come of the Huns that invaded those countries and rested in those parts of Pannonia now called Hungary.

How they aspired to the dukedom of Vladimir (which was their first degree and engrafting into Russia), and whether it were by conquest or by marriage or by what other means, I could not learn any certainty among them.[3] That from these beginnings of a small dukedom (that bare, notwithstanding, an absolute government with it, as at that time did also the other shires or provinces of Russia), this house of Bela spread itself forth and aspired by degrees to the monarchy of the whole country is a thing well known and of very late memory. The chief of that house that advanced the stock and enlarged their dominions were the three last that reigned before this emperor, to wit, Ivan Vasil'evich and Ivan, father to the other that reigneth at this time. Whereof the first that took unto him the name and title of emperor was Vasilii, father to Ivan and grandfather to this man, for before that time they were contented to be called great dukes of Moscow.[4] What hath been done by either of these three, and how much they have added to their first estate by conquest or otherwise, may be seen in the chapter of their colonies or purchases perforce. For the continuance of the race this house of Bela at this present is in like case as are many of the greatest houses of Christendom, viz., the whole stock and race con-

---

3. The first prince of Moscow who became grand duke of Vladimir was Iurii, who received the patent of Uzbeg, khan of the Golden Horde, in 1319. He was deprived of the office in 1322. In 1332, however, Uzbeg granted the title to Iurii's brother, Ivan I Kalita, and from that time the princely house of Moscow retained possession of the office with only brief interruptions until Fletcher's time.

4. Ivan IV was the first to be invested formally with the title of tsar.

cluded in one, two, or some few of the blood. For besides the emperor
that now is who hath no child (neither is like ever to have for ought
that may be conjectured by the constitution of his body and the bar-
renness of his wife after so many years' marriage),[5] there is but one
more, viz., a child of six or seven years old in whom resteth all the
hope of the succession and the posterity of that house. As for the other
brother that was eldest of the three[6] and of the best towardness, he
died of a blow given him by his father upon the head in his fury with
his walking staff, or (as some say) of a thrust with the prong of it
driven deep into his head. That he meant him no such mortal harm
when he gave him the blow may appear by his mourning and passion
after his son's death, which never left him till it brought him to the
grave. Wherein may be marked the justice of God that punished his
delight in shedding of blood with this murder of his son by his own
hand, and so ended his days and tyranny together with the murdering
of himself by extreme grief for this his unhappy and unnatural fact.[7]

The emperor's younger brother of six or seven years old (as was said
before) is kept in a remote place[8] from the Moscow under the tuition of
his mother and her kindred of the house of the Nagois, yet not safe (as
I have heard) from attempts of making away by practice of some that
aspire to the succession if this emperor die without any issue. The
nurse that tasted before him of certain meat (as I have heard) died
presently.[9] That he is natural son to Ivan Vasil'evich the Russe people
warrant it by the father's quality that beginneth to appear already in
his tender years. He is delighted (they say) to see sheep and other cattle killed and to look on their throats while they are bleeding (which

5. In May 1592 Fedor's wife, Irina, bore a daughter, Feodosiia, who died at an
early age.

6. By his first wife, Anastasiia, Ivan IV had two sons who survived infancy.
Dmitrii, the "child of six or seven years old," was the son of Ivan's seventh wife,
Mariia Nagaia.

7. Ivan IV fatally wounded his son during a quarrel that took place in November 1581. According to Possevino, the trouble began when the tsar paid a surprise
visit to his son's wife, who was then pregnant. Ivan took exception to the manner
in which she was dressed and, in reproving her, beat her so severely that she had
a miscarriage. Subsequently her enraged husband took up the quarrel with his
father. In the course of the argument, the tsar mortally wounded his son with a
blow of his staff (A. Possevino, *Moscovia* [Antwerp, 1587], pp. 28–30).

8. The town of Uglich, north of Moscow.

9. Whether true or not, this story of an attempt to poison Dimitrii is probably
typical of rumors circulating in Moscow at the time of Fletcher's visit.

commonly children are afraid to behold), and to beat geese and hens with a staff till he see them lie dead.[10] Besides these of the male kind, there is a widow that hath right in the succession, sister to the old emperor and aunt to this man, sometime wife to Magnus Duke of Holstein, brother to the king of Denmark, by whom she had one daughter. This woman since the death of her husband hath been allured again into Russia by some that love the succession better than herself, which appeareth by the sequel. For herself with her daughter so soon as they were returned into Russia were thrust into a nunnery where her daughter died this last year, while I was in the country, of no natural disease as was supposed. The mother remaineth still in the nunnery, where (as I have heard) she bewaileth herself and curseth the time when she returned into Russia, enticed with the hope of marriage and other fair promises in the emperor's name.[11] Thus it standeth with the imperial stock of Russia of the house of Bela, which is like to determine in those that now are and to make a conversion of the Russe estate. If it be into a government of some better temper and milder constitution, it will be happy for the poor people that are now oppressed with intolerable servitude.

Chapter 6. Of the manner of crowning or inauguration of the Russe emperors

The solemnities used at the Russe emperor's coronation are on this manner.[1] In the great church of Precheste (or Our Lady) within the emperor's castle is erected a stage whereon standeth a

10. In his history of Muscovy during the Time of Troubles, Conrad Bussow records similar stories about Dmitrii (Konrad Bussov, *Moskovskaia khronika 1584–1613* [Moscow-Leningrad, 1961], p. 204).

11. The entry in the Piskarevskii Chronicle is identical in outline with Fletcher's account except that it gives no hint that the daughter of Mariia Vladimirovna was the victim of foul play. Mother and daughter returned to Russia in 1585/86 (*Materialy*, II, 78). For Horsey's version of the story, see pp. 315–17, below.

1. On the whole, Fletcher's account of the coronation ceremony is remarkably accurate. It differs from the official version of Fedor's coronation chiefly in the omission of several parts of the service. In describing the first part of the service, Fletcher left out the speeches of the tsar and the metropolitan which preceded

screen that beareth upon it the imperial cape and robe of very rich stuff.[2] When the day of the inauguration is come, there resort thither first the patriarch with the metropolitans, archbishops, bishops, abbots, and priors, all richly clad in their pontificalibus.[3] Then enter the deacons with the choir of singers, who so soon as the emperor setteth foot into the church begin to sing: "Many years may live noble Fedor Ivanovich," etc. Whereunto the patriarch and metropolitan with the rest of the clergy answer with a certain hymn, in form of a prayer, singing it altogether with a great noise. The hymn being ended, the patriarch with the emperor mount up the stage where standeth a seat ready for the emperor. Whereupon the patriarch willeth him to sit down, and then placing himself by him upon another seat provided for that purpose, boweth down his head towards the ground and sayeth this prayer: "Oh, Lord God, King of Kings, Lord of Lords, which by thy prophet Samuel diddest choose thy servant David and anoint him for king over thy people Israel, hear now our prayers and look from thy sanctuary upon this thy servant Fedor, whom thou hast chosen and exalted for king over these thy holy nations; anoint him with the oil of gladness; protect him by thy power; put upon his head a crown of gold and precious stones; give him length of days; place him in the seat of justice; strengthen his arm; make subject unto him all the barbarous nations. Let thy fear be in his whole heart; turn him from an evil faith and from all error and show him the salvation of thy holy and universal church, that he may judge thy people with justice, and protect the children of the poor, and finally attain everlasting life." This prayer he speaketh with a low voice and then pronounceth aloud: "All praise and power to God the Father, the Son, and the Holy Ghost." The prayer being ended, he commandeth certain abbots to reach the imperial robe and cape, which is done very decently and with great solemnity, the patriarch withal pronouncing aloud: "Peace be unto all." And so he be-

---

the metropolitan's prayer. From the latter part of the rite, he omitted the metropolitan's admonition to the tsar, the metropolitan's blessing, the reading of the Gospel, the anointing of the tsar and his receiving of the sacrament. Fletcher's account contains two anomalies. He failed to mention that the tsar was invested with the crown and scepter. Moreover, he used anachronistic terms to describe the church dignitaries taking part in the service. The coronation of Fedor took place in 1584 and the Patriarchate of Moscow was created only in 1589. See *Sobranie gosudarstvennykh gramot i dogovorov khraniashchikhsia v Gosudarstvennoi kollegii inostrannykh del* (Moscow, 1813–28), II, 72–85.

  2. Precheste—the Cathedral of the Assumption of Our Lady in the Kremlin.
  3. Pontificalia, official robes or vestments.

ginneth another prayer to this effect: "Bow yourselves together with us and pray to him that reigneth over all. Preserve him, Oh, Lord, under thy holy protection; keep him that he may do good and holy things; let justice shine forth in his days that we may live quietly without strife and malice." This is pronounced somewhat softly by the patriarch, whereto he addeth again aloud: "Thou art the king of the whole world and the savior of our souls; to thee the Father, Son, and Holy Ghost be all praise forever and ever, amen." Then putting on the robe and the cape he blesseth the emperor with the sign of the cross, saying withal: "In the name of the Father, the Son, and the Holy Ghost." The like is done by the metropolitans, archbishops, and bishops, who all in their order come to the chair and one after another bless the emperor with their two forefingers. Then is said by the patriarch another prayer that beginneth: "O most holy virgin mother of God," etc. After which a deacon pronounceth with an high loud voice: "Many years to noble Fedor, good, honorable, beloved of God, great duke of Vladimir, of Moscow, emperor and monarch of all Russia," etc. Whereto the other priests and deacons that stand somewhat far off by the altar or table answer, singing: "Many years, many years, to the noble Fedor." The same note is taken up by the priests and deacons that are placed at the right and left side of the church; and then altogether they chant and thunder out, singing: "Many years to the noble Fedor, good, honorable, beloved of God, great duke of Vladimir, Moscow, emperor of all Russia," etc. These solemnities being ended, first cometh the patriarch with the metropolitans, archbishops, and bishops, then the nobility and the whole company in their order to do homage to the emperor, bending down their heads and knocking them at his feet to the very ground.

The style wherewith he is invested at his coronation runneth after this manner: "Fedor Ivanovich, by the grace of God, great lord and emperor of all Russia, great duke of Vladimir, Moscow, and Novgorod, king of Kazan', king of Astrakhan', lord of Pskov, and great duke of Smolensk, of Tver', Yougoria, Perm', Viatka, Bulgaria, and others, lord and great duke of Novgorod of the low country, of Chernigov, Riazan', Polotsk, Rostov, Iaroslavl', Beloozero, Livonia, Oudoria, Obdoria, and Kondinskaia [Zemlia],[4] commander of all Siberia and of the north parts, and lord of many other countries," etc.[5]

4. Condensa in the original text.
5. Fletcher gives the tsar's title with complete precision with the exception of one small omission. The opening phrases should read "Fedor Ivanovich, by the

This style containeth in it all the emperor's provinces and setteth forth his greatness. And therefore they have a great delight and pride in it, forcing not only their own people but also strangers (that have any matter to deliver to the emperor by speech or writing) to repeat the whole form from the beginning to the end, which breedeth much cavil and sometimes quarrel betwixt them and the Tatar and Polish ambassadors, who refuse to call him tsar, that is emperor, and to repeat the other parts of his long style. Myself when I had audience of the emperor thought good to salute him only with thus much, viz., "emperor of all Russia, great duke of Vladimir, Moscow, and Novgorod, king of Kazan', king of Astrakhan'." The rest I omitted of purpose, because I knew they gloried to have their style appear to be of a larger volume than the queen's of England. But this was taken in so ill part that the chancellor (when then attended the emperor with the rest of the nobility) with a loud chafing voice called still upon me to say out the rest.[6] Whereto I answered that the emperor's style was very long and could not so well be remembered by strangers, that I had repeated so much of it as might show that I gave honor to the rest, etc. But all would not serve till I commanded my interpreter to say it all out.

Chapter 7. The state or form of their government

The manner of their government is much after the Turkish fashion, which they seem to imitate as near as the country and reach of their capacities in politic affairs will give them leave to do.

The state and form of their government is plain tyrannical, as applying all to the behoof of the prince, and that after a most open and barbarous manner as may appear by the sophismata or secrets of their government afterwards set down, as well for the keeping of the nobility and commons in an under proportion and far uneven balance in their several degrees, as also in their impositions and exactions wherein they exceed all just measure without any regard of nobility or people,

---

grace of God, great lord, emperor, and great duke of all Russia, . . ." See, for example, *Sobranie gosudarstvennykh gramot i dogovorov*, II, 88.

6. Probably Andrei Shchelkalov. See p. 146 below, n. 2.

farther than it giveth the nobility a kind of injust and unmeasured liberty to command and exact upon the commons and baser sort of people in all parts of the realm wheresoever they come, specially in the place where their lands lie or where they are appointed by the emperor to govern under him. Also to the commons some small contentment in that they pass over their lands by descent of inheritance to whither son they will, which commonly they do after our gavelkind[1] and dispose of their goods by gift or testament without any controlment. Wherein, notwithstanding, both nobility and commons are but storers for the prince, all running in the end into the emperor's coffers, as may appear by the practice of enriching his treasury and the manner of exactions set down in the title of his customs and revenues.

Concerning the principal points and matters of state wherein the sovereignty consisteth, as the making and annuling of public laws, the making of magistrates, power to make war or league with any foreign state, to execute or to pardon life, with the right of appeal in all matters both civil and criminal, they do so wholly and absolutely pertain to the emperor, and his council under him, as that he may be said to be both the sovereign commander and the executioner of all these. For as touching any law or public order of the realm, it is ever determined of before any public assembly or parliament be summoned. Where, besides his council, he hath none other to consult with him of such matters as are concluded before hand but only a few bishops, abbots, and friars,[2] to no other end than to make advantage of the people's supersti-

---

1. The custom of dividing a deceased man's property equally among his sons.
2. Fletcher does not take cognizance of the zemskii sobor or estates which met on unusual occasions to consult with or give support to the tsar and duma.

The historians who have made special studies of the zemskii sobor in the period prior to Fletcher's visit have reached widely divergent conclusions on the number of times it met. There is general agreement that the sobor met in 1550, 1566, and 1584 (V. N. Latkin, *Zemskie sobory drevnei Rusi* [St. Petersburg, 1885], pp. 64–89). Recently V. I. Koretskii and M. N. Tikhomirov have suggested that sobors also met in 1575 and 1580 respectively (V. I. Koretskii, "Zemskii sobor 1575 g. i postavlenie Simeona Bekbulatovicha 'velikim kniazem vseia Rusi'," *Istoricheskii arkhiv*, 1959, No. 2, pp. 148–56; M. N. Tikhomirov, "Soslovno-predstavitel'nye uchrezhdeniia (zemskie sobory) v Rossii v XVI v.," *Voprosy istorii*, 1958, No. 5, pp. 3–23, esp. pp. 15–17).

The sobor of 1566 which supported the government's decision to reject Polish offers of a truce and to continue the war was distinguished by the unusual diversity of its delegates. Besides the members of the boiar duma and the sacred council, the delegates included 204 members of the service nobility and 75 representatives of the merchant class (Zimin, *Oprichnina*, p. 167).

tions, even against themselves, which think all to be holy and just that passeth with consent of their bishops and clergymen, whatsoever it be. For which purpose the emperors are content to make much of the corrupt state of the church as now it is among them, and to nourish the same by extraordinary favors and immunities to the bishop's sees, abbeys, and friaries, as knowing superstition and false religion best to agree with a tyrannical state and to be a special means to uphold and maintain the same.

Secondly, as touching the public offices and magistracies of the realm, there is none hereditary, neither any so great nor so little in that country, but the bestowing of it is done immediately by the emperor himself.[3] Insomuch that the very d'iaki or clerks in every head town are for the most part assigned by himself. Notwithstanding, the emperor that now is (the better to intend his devotions) referreth all such matters pertaining to the state wholly to the ordering of his wife's brother, the Lord Boris Fedorovich Godunov.[4]

Thirdly, the like is to be said of the jurisdiction concerning matters judicial, specially such as concern life and death. Wherein there is none that hath any authority or public jurisdiction that goeth by descent or is held by charter, but all at the appointment and pleasure of the emperor, and the same practiced by the judges with such awe and restraint as that they dare not determine upon any special matter, but must refer the same wholly up to the Moscow to the emperor's council. To show his sovereignty over the lives of his subjects, the late emperor Ivan Vasil'evich in his walks or progresses, if he had misliked the face or person of any man whom he met by the way, or that looked upon

3. Fletcher's remark is correct. It should be noted, however, that the tsar usually appointed members of the great noble families to the highest positions at court and in the army.

4. Boris Godunov entered the service ranks in the oprichnina in 1567 or, at the latest, 1570–71 (Kobrin, p. 34). His career was assisted by two fortunate marriages—his own to Mariia, daughter of the tsar's favorite, Maliuta Skuratov-Bel'skii, and that of his sister Irina to Fedor, Ivan's second son and eventual successor. He was raised to the office of *kravchii* (taster) by 1578/79, became a boiar in 1580, and was honored with the post of *koniushii* (master of the horse) at the accession of Fedor in 1584 (*RK*, p. 292; Zimin, "Sostav boiarskoi dumy," p. 78; *DRV*, XX, 60). Within a matter of months, he had made himself the effective ruler of Russia. When Fedor died without an heir in 1598, Boris was elected tsar by a zemskii sobor and reigned until 1605. The classic biography of Godunov is the work of S. F. Platonov, *Boris Godunov* (Petrograd, 1921; French translation, Paris, 1929).

him, would command his head to be struck off, which was presently done, and the head cast before him.

Fourthly, for the sovereign appeal and giving of pardons in criminal matters to such as are convicted, it is wholly at the pleasure and grace of the emperor. Wherein also the empress that now is, being a woman of great clemency and withal delighting to deal in public affairs of the realm (the rather to supply the defect of her husband), doth behave herself after an absolute manner, giving out pardon (specially on her birthday and other solemn times) in her own name by open proclamation, without any mention at all of the emperor.[5] Some there have been of late of the ancient nobility that have held divers provinces by right of inheritance, with an absolute authority and jurisdiction over them to order and determine all matters within their own precinct without all appeal or controlment of the emperor. But this was all annulled and wrung clean from them by Ivan Vasil'evich, father to this emperor.

Chapter 8. The manner of holding their parliaments

Their highest court of public consultation for matter of state is called the sobor, that is, the public assembly. The states and degrees of persons that are present at their parliaments are these in order: (1) the emperor himself; (2) some of his nobility about the number of twenty, being all of his council; (3) certain of the clergymen, etc., about the same number. As for burghers or other to represent the communality, they have no place there, the people being of no better account with them than as servants or bondslaves that are to obey, not to make laws nor to know anything of public matters before they are concluded.[1]

5. It is extremely doubtful that Irina issued pardons on her own authority. In a number of cases, however, documents were issued in her name as well as that of her husband. See, for example, *Dopolneniia k Aktam istoricheskim* (St. Petersburg, 1846–72), I, No. 142.

1. Although he uses the term *sobor*, Fletcher apparently describes not a full meeting of the zemskii sobor but rather a dumnyi sobor or combined session of the boiar duma and the sacred council. The reference to the "burghers" is one reason to doubt that Fletcher is describing a full zemskii sobor, for the merchant class was sometimes represented, as, for example, in 1566.

The court of parliament, called sobor, is held in this manner. The emperor causeth to be summoned such of his nobility as himself thinketh meet, being (as was said) all of his council, together with the patriarch, who calleth his clergy, to wit, the two metropolitans, the two archbishops,[2] with such bishops, abbots, and friars as are of best account and reputation among them. When they are all assembled at the emperor's court, the day is intimated when the session shall begin, which commonly is upon some Friday for the religion of that day.

When the day is come, the clergymen assemble before at the time and place appointed, which is called the *stollie*.[3] And when the emperor cometh attended by his nobility, they arise all and meet him in an out room, following their patriarch, who blesseth the emperor with his two forefingers, laying them on his forehead and the sides of his face, and then kisseth him on the right side of his breast. So they pass on into their parliament house where they sit in this order. The emperor is enthronized on the one side of the chamber. In the next place not far from him at a small square table (that giveth room to twelve persons or thereabouts) sitteth the patriarch with the metropolitans and bishops and certain of the principal nobility of the emperor's council, together with two d'iaki or secretaries (called dumnye d'iaki)[4] that enact that which passeth. The rest place themselves on benches round about the room, every man in his rank after his degree. Then is there propounded by one of the secretaries, who representeth the speaker, the cause of their assembly and the principal matters that they are to consider of; for to propound bills what every man thinketh good for the public benefit, as the manner is in England, the Russe parliament alloweth no such custom nor liberty to subjects.

The points being opened, the patriarch with his clergymen have the prerogative to be first asked their vote or opinion what they think of the points propounded by the secretary. Whereto they answer in order

2. After the creation of the Moscow patriarchate in 1589, the Russian hierarchy included four metropolitans (of Novgorod, Kazan', Rostov, and Krutitsa) and six archbishops (of Vologda, Suzdal', Nizhnii-Novgorod, Smolensk, Riazan' and Tver') (Metr. Makarii, *Istoriia russkoi tserkvi* [St. Petersburg, 1866–83], X, 40).

3. Presumably Stolovaia palata, a reception room in the Kremlin palaces in which the tsar sometimes received the members of the duma, representatives of the clergy, and foreign emissaries of relatively low rank (Kliuchevskii, *Boiarskaia duma*, p. 408).

4. State secretaries who were members of the boiar duma, usually the directors of the most important administrative departments (prikazy).

1

Ivan the Terrible.
A sixteenth-century portrait on wood, now in
the National Museum at Copenhagen.

2

Ivan's farewell audience
with Chancellor; Chancellor's death by shipwreck;
reception of the Russian ambassador by
Philip and Mary. Miniature from the Synodal copy
of the Nikon Chronicle.

3

Providing the Polish-Lithuanian ambassadors
with supplies. Miniature from the Synodal copy
of the Nikon Chronicle.

4

Samoyed sled with reindeer

5

Sleighs

6

Cavalryman shooting

7

Three noble cavalrymen

8

Boris Godunov

9

Tsar Fedor.
Son and successor
of Ivan the Terrible.

10

Prince Dmitrii.
Son of Ivan the Terrible
by his seventh wife,
Mariia Nagaia.

according to their degrees, but all in one form without any discourse, as having learned their lesson before that serveth their turns at all parliaments alike whatsoever is propounded. Commonly it is to this effect: "That the emperor and his council are of great wisdom and experience touching the policies and public affairs of the realm, and far better able to judge what is profitable for the commonwealth than they are which attend upon the service of God only and matters of religion. And therefore it may please them to proceed. That instead of their advice they will aid them with their prayers as their duties and vocations do require," etc. To this or like effect having made their answers every man in his course, up standeth some abbot or friar more bold than the rest (yet appointed beforehand as a matter of form) and desireth the emperor it would please his majesty to command to be delivered unto them what his majesty's own judgment and determinate pleasure is as touching those matters propounded by his d'iak.

Whereto is replied by the said secretary in the emperor's name: "That his highness with those of his noble council upon good and sound advice have found the matters proposed to be very good and necessary for the commonwealth of his realm. Notwithstanding, forasmuch as they are religious men and know what is right, his majesty requireth their godly opinions, yea, and their censures, too, for the approving or correcting of the said propositions and therefore desireth them again to speak their minds freely. And if they shall like to give their consents, that then the matters may pass to a full conclusion."

Hereunto when the clergymen have given their consents (which they use to do without any great pausing), they take their leaves with blessing of the emperor, who bringeth the patriarch on his way so far as the next room and so returneth to his seat till all be made ready for his return homeward.[5] The acts that thus are passed by the sobor or parliament, the d'iaki or secretaries draw into a form of proclamation which they send abroad into every province and head town of the realm to be published there by the dukes and d'iaki, or secretaries, of

5. Fletcher underestimates the freedom of the church leaders to speak out on important issues. Although they did use the formal statement of reverence for the tsar's authority as Fletcher gives it, they sometimes expressed themselves frankly on questions of special importance to the church. In 1580, for example, they initially rejected the tsar's request for a special contribution to the treasury to meet the war emergency and on several occasions they demanded that the government give up plans to recruit or to use western European officers and technicians (Seredonin, pp. 235–37; Kliuchevskii, *Boiarskaia duma,* pp. 522–23).

those places. The session of parliament being fully ended, the emperor inviteth the clergymen to a solemn dinner. And so they depart every man to his home.

Chapter 9. Of the nobility, and by what means it is kept in an under proportion agreeable to that state

The degrees of persons or estates of Russia, besides the sovereign state or emperor himself, are these in their order. First, the nobility, which is of four sorts, whereof the chief for birth, authority, and revenue are called the *udel'nye kniaz'ia*, that is, the exempt or privileged dukes. These held sometime a several jurisdiction and absolute authority within their precincts, much like unto the states or nobles of Germany, but afterwards, reserving their rights upon composition, they yielded themselves to this house of Bela when it began to wax mighty and to enlarge itself by overmatching their neighbors. Only they were bound to serve the emperor in his wars with a certain number of horse. But the late emperor Ivan Vasil'evich, father to this prince, being a man of high spirit and subtle in his kind, meaning to reduce his government into a more strict form, began by degrees to clip off their greatness and to bring it down to a lesser proportion till in the end he made them not only his vassals but his kholopy, that is, his very villeins or bondslaves, for so they term and write themselves in any public instrument or private petition which they make to the emperor. So that now they hold their authorities, lands, lives, and all at the emperor's pleasure, as the rest do.[1]

1. By the death of Ivan III in 1505, most of the independent principalities of north-central Russia had been incorporated into the Muscovite state. When Ivan IV came to the throne, there were only three appanage principalities, two of which had been created by Ivan III and Vasilii III for the support of their younger sons. The only one of these that could claim even a small measure of autonomy was the principality of Staritsa which was broken up in 1566. Its former ruler, Prince Vladimir Andreevich, was executed in 1569. At the time of Fletcher's visit there were probably only two principalities that were a faint reflection of the old appanages—the Uglich domains of Dmitrii, the youngest son of Ivan IV, and the lands of the Nogai princes in the Romanov district (S. B. Veselovskii, "Poslednie udely v severo-vostochnoi Rusi," *Istoricheskie zapiski*, XXII [1947], 101–31).

The means and practice whereby he wrought this to effect against those and other of the nobility (so well as I could note out of the report of his doings) were these and such like. First, he cast private emulations among them about prerogative of their titles and dignities, wherein he used to set on the inferiors to prefer or equal themselves to those that were accounted to be of the nobler houses, where he made his advantage of their malice and contentions the one against the other by receiving devised matter and accusations of secret practice and conspiracies to be intended against his person and state. And so having singled out the greatest of them and cut them off with the good liking of the rest, he fell at last to open practice by forcing of the other to yield their rights unto him.

Second, he divided his subjects into two parts or factions by a general schism. The one part he called the *oprichniki* or selectmen.[2] These were such of the nobility and gentry as he took to his own part to protect and maintain them as his faithful subjects. The other he called *zemskie* or the commons.[3] The zemskie contained the base and vulgar sort with such noblemen and gentlemen as he meant to cut off, as suspected to mislike his government and to have a meaning to practice against him. Wherein he provided that the oprichniki for number and quality of valor, money, armor, etc., far exceeded the other of the zemskii side whom he put (as it were) from under his protection, so that if any of them were spoiled or killed by those of the oprichniki (which he accounted of his own part), there was no amends to be sought for by way of public justice or by complaint to the emperor.

The whole number of both parts was orderly registered and kept in a book, so that every man knew who was a zemskii man and who of the oprichniki. And this liberty of the one part to spoil and kill the other without any help of magistrate or law (that continued seven years)[4] enriched that side and the emperor's treasury and wrought that withal which he intended by this practice, viz., to take out of the way such of the nobility as himself misliked, whereof were slain within one week to the number of three hundred within the city of Moscow. This tyrannical practice of making a general schism and public division among the subjects of his whole realm proceeded (as should seem)

2. Members of the oprichnina, the part of the country under Ivan's direct control after he divided his domains in 1565.
3. Members of the *zemshchina,* the part of the country that remained outside the oprichnina.
4. 1565–72.

from an extreme doubt and desperate fear which he had conceived of most of his nobility and gentlemen of his realm in his wars with the Pole and Krym Tatar, what time he grew into a vehement suspicion (conceived of the ill success of his affairs) that they practiced treason with the Pole and Krym. Whereupon he executed some and devised this way to be rid of the rest.

And this wicked policy and tyrannous practice (though now it be ceased) hath so troubled that country and filled it so full of grudge and mortal hatred ever since, that it will not be quenched (as it seemeth now) till it burn again into a civil flame.

Third, having thus pulled them and seized all their inheritance, lands, privileges, etc., save some very small part which he left to their name, he gave them other lands of tenure of pomest'e (as they call it) that are held at the emperor's pleasure, lying far off in another country,[5] and so removed them into other of his provinces where they might have neither favor nor authority, not being native nor well known there, so that now these of the chief nobility (called udel'nye kniaz'ia) are equaled with the rest, save that in the opinion and favor of the people they are of more account and keep still the prerogative of their place in all their public meetings.[6]

Their practice to keep down these houses from rising again and recovering their dignities are these and such like. First, many of their heirs are kept unmarried perforce that the stock may die with them. Some are sent into Siberia, Kazan', and Astrakhan' under pretense of service and there either made away or else fast clapped up. Some are put into abbeys and shire[7] themselves friars by pretense of a vow to be made voluntary and of their own accord, but indeed forced unto it by fear upon some pretensed crime objected against them, where they are so guarded by some of special trust and the convent itself (upon whose head it standeth that they make no escape), as that they have no hope but to end their lives there. Of this kind there are many of very great

5. In general, Fletcher was correct in stating that the holders of hereditary lands (votchina) who were dispossessed by the oprichnina were given conditional (pomest'e) holdings in exchange. There were, however, cases in which they were given new hereditary estates (P. A. Sadikov, *Ocherki po istorii oprichniny* [Moscow-Leningrad, 1950], pp. 122–23).

6. Platonov used this passage to support his highly controversial view that the oprichnina was designed to destroy the remaining power of the former appanage princes (S. F. Platonov, *Ocherki po istorii smuty v moskovskom gosudarstve XVI–XVII vv.* [St. Petersburg, 1910], pp. 136–37).

7. Declare.

nobility. These and such like ways begun by the Emperor Ivan Vasil'evich are still practiced by the Godunovs, who, being advanced by
the marriage of the empress their kinswoman, rule both the emperor
and his realm (specially Boris Fedorovich Godunov, brother to the empress) and endeavor by all means to cut off or keep down all of the
best and ancientest nobility. Whereof divers already they have taken
away whom they thought likeliest to make head against them and to
hinder their purpose, as Kniaz' Andrei Kurakin-Bulgakov, a man of
great birth and authority in the country.[8] The like they have done with
Petr Golovin (whom they put into a dungeon where he ended his life),
with Kniaz' Vasilii Iur'evich Golitsyn, with Andrei Ivanovich Shuiskii,
accounted among them for a man of a great wisdom.[9] So this last year
was killed in a monastery (whither they had thrust him) one Kniaz' Ivan
Petrovich Shuiskii, a man of great valor and service in that country, who
about five or six years since bare out the siege of the city Pskov, made
by Stephen Bathory, king of Poland, with a 100,000 men, and repulsed
him very valiantly with great honor to himself and his country and disgrace to the Pole.[10] Also Nikita Romanovich, uncle to the emperor by

8. Andrei Petrovich Kurakin-Bulgakov became a boiar in 1584 (*DRV*, XX, 61).
During the Time of Troubles he was a prominent figure, serving as military
governor of Novgorod in 1609 (Platonov, *Ocherki,* p. 366). He died in 1615.
There is little evidence to support Fletcher's claim that Boris persecuted the
Kurakins as a family (Seredonin, p. 103).
9. Petr Ivanovich Golovin was court treasurer from 1576/77 to 1584 (*RK*,
p. 276; *DRV*, XX, 59). In 1582/83 he was raised to the boiar duma with the
rank of okol'nichii (Zimin, "Sostav boiarskoi dumy," p. 78). He fell into disgrace
and died in 1584/85 (*DRV*, XX, 61).
V. Iu. Golitsyn became a boiar in 1573 (Zimin, "Sostav boiarskoi dumy," p.
77). He died while serving as a military commander in Smolensk in 1584/85.
The fact that two of his sons became boiars soon after his death would indicate
that Godunov did not conduct a campaign against the Golitsyns as a family
(Seredonin, p. 103).
In 1581/82 Andrei Ivanovich Shuiskii commanded an expedition against the
Swedes and raised the siege of Oreshek. At the time of Fedor's coronation in
1584 he became a boiar and subsequently commanded forces on the southern
and Swedish frontiers. He was a victim of Godunov's struggle for power with the
Shuiskii family; he was arrested in 1587 and exiled to Kargopol' where he died
(*RBS*).
10. Ivan Petrovich Shuiskii had a long and distinguished military career beginning with the Polotsk campaign of 1563. Ivan IV raised him to the rank of
boiar in 1571 (Zimin, "Sostav boiarskoi dumy," p. 76). In 1573 he took part in the
capture of Weissenstein. He became a national hero when he commanded the
Russian troops that successfully held Pskov against the Polish attack of 1581.
As a reward for his exploits he was granted all of the revenues of the Pskov
district beginning in 1585. His triumph was short-lived. In 1586 one of his

the mother's side, was supposed to have died of poison or some like practice.[11]

The names of these families of greatest nobility are these in their order. The first is of Kniaz' [of] Vladimir, which resteth at this time in one daughter, a widow and without children (mentioned before), sometime wife to Herzog Magnus, brother to the king of Denmark, now closed within a nunnery. The second, Kniaz' Mstislavskii, thrust into a friary and his only son kept from marriage to decay the house.[12] The third, Glinskii, but one left of his house and he without children save one daughter.[13] The fourth, Shuiskii, whereof there are four brethren, young men and unmarried all.[14] The fifth, Trubetskoi, of this house are four living.[15] The sixth, Bulgakov now called Golitsyn house,

servitors denounced him for treason, and Boris Godunov had him exiled to Beloozero where he was murdered in the following year (RBS).

11. Brother-in-law of Ivan IV. He was raised to the rank of okol'nichii in 1559 and was made a boiar in 1565 (Zimin, "Sostav boiarskoi dumy," p. 69). In 1566 he was appointed to the position of dvoretskii, the highest court office, in the court of the zemshchina. In the 1570's he held commands in several campaigns against the Poles and the Swedes. He was still a very prominent figure at court in the last years of the reign of Ivan IV, taking part in the reception of Possevino in 1582 and Bowes in 1583. Illness forced his retirement from public life in 1584 and a year later he died (DRV, XX, 61). In all probability, he died of natural causes since the Russian sources of the period which blame Godunov for a wide variety of outrages do not implicate him in Nikita Romanovich's death (RBS; Seredonin, p. 103).

12. Ivan Fedorovich died in a monastery in 1586. His son, Fedor, married twice but left no descendents at his death in 1622 (A. B. Lobanov-Rostovskii [ed.], Russkaia rodoslovnaia kniga [St. Petersburg, 1895], I, 402).

13. The line of Ivan Mikhailovich Glinskii died out with the death of his daughter. A younger branch of the family, however, was still flourishing in the nineteenth century (ibid., I, 139–41).

14. Ivan Andreevich Shuiskii (d. 1573) had four sons, Vasilii, Dmitrii, Aleksandr, and Ivan. Vasilii became a boiar in 1584 and died in 1612 (DRV, XX, 60). Dmitrii held the office of kravchii (taster) before 1585/86 when he was dismissed from the post; he was made boiar in 1590/91 and died in 1612 (DRV, XX, 59, 62, 64; RBS). Aleksandr was a boiar from 1595/96 and died in 1601 (DRV, XX, 66, 71). Ivan became a boiar in 1595/96 (DRV, XX, 66). None of them left heirs and with the death of Ivan Ivanovich in 1638, the Russian branch of the family died out (P. Dolgorukii [ed.], Rossiiskaia rodoslovnaia kniga [St. Petersburg, 1854], I, 234–36).

15. At the time of Fletcher's visit there were at least five men in the family— Nikita Romanovich (boiar, 1584; died, 1606/07), Timofei Romanovich (boiar, 1584/85; died, 1602/03), Fedor Mikhailovich (boiar, 1568; died, 1600/01), Andrei Vasil'evich (boiar, 1598), and Iurii Nikitich (Zimin, "Sostav boiarskoi dumy," p. 74; DRV, XX, 60–61, 70–72, 81; RK, p. 522).

whereof are five living, but youths all.[16] The seventh, Vorotynskii, two left of that stock.[17] The eighth, Odoevskii, two.[18] The ninth, Teliatevskii, one.[19] The tenth, Tatev, three.[20] These are the names of the chief families called udel'nye kniaz'ia that in effect have lost all now save the very name itself and favor of the people, which is like one day to restore them again if any be left.

The second degree of nobility is of the boiars. These are such as the emperor honoreth, besides their nobility, with the title of counselors. The revenue of these two sorts of their nobles, that riseth out of their lands assigned them by the emperor and held at his pleasure (for of their own inheritance there is little left them as was said before),[21] is about a thousand marks a year, besides pension which they receive of the emperor for their service in his wars to the sum of 700 rubles a year, and none above that sum.[22]

16. Fletcher probably had in mind Ivan Ivanovich (boiar, 1588; died, 1607), Andrei Ivanovich (boiar, 1598; died, 1602/03), Vasilii Vasil'evich (boiar, 1601/02; died, 1619), Ivan Vasil'evich (boiar, 1605; died, 1627), and Andrei Vasil'evich (boiar, 1605/06; died 1611); (DRV, XX, 68, 72, 76–77, 81, 91, 94; Sinbirskii sbornik, I [Moscow, 1844], p. 100; Dolgorukii [ed.], Rossiiskaia rodoslovnaia kniga, I, 285).

17. The senior member of the family in Fletcher's time was Ivan Mikhailovich (boiar, 1591/92; died, 1628). He left one son, Aleksei. The line died out in 1679 (DRV, XX, 64; Lobanov-Rostovskii [ed.], Russkaia rodoslovnaia kniga, I, 118–19).

18. Fletcher probably refers to Ivan "Bol'shoi" Nikitich (boiar, 1605/06; died, 1616), and Ivan "Men'shoi" Nikitich (boiar, 1613/14; died, 1629). There was a third member of the family, Mikhail Nikitich, who died about the time of Fletcher's visit (DRV, XX, 77, 89, 90, 94; RK, p. 360). The family produced many distinguished figures before it died out late in the nineteenth century.

19. In all likelihood, Fletcher refers to Andrei Andreevich (boiar, 1599/1600; died, 1612). His son, Fedor Andreevich, the last of the line, died in 1645 (DRV, XX, 70, 86; Lobanov-Rostovskii [ed.], Russkaia rodoslovnaia kniga, II, 294).

20. In Fletcher's time the most prominent member of the family was Boris Petrovich (boiar, 1605; died 1607). There were besides three brothers, Fedor, Semen, and Ivan Andreevich (DRV, XX, 76, 81; RK, pp. 364, 471, 523). All branches died out by the late seventeenth century (Lobanov-Rostovskii [ed.], Russkaia rodoslovnaia kniga, II, 283–85).

21. Fletcher overemphasizes the extent to which the pomest'e system of conditional landholding had spread. As far as can be determined, the old votchina system under which the nobles held their estates in absolute ownership remained the dominant form of landholding throughout the 16th century in all areas of the Muscovite state except the Novgorod district and the eastern frontier regions (A. A. Zimin, "O politicheskikh predposylkakh voznikoveniia russkogo absoliutizma," in Absoliutizm v Rossii [Moscow, 1964], pp. 22–23).

22. Seredonin (p. 190) thinks 1,000 rubles is too high for the annual income of a boiar and that the average boiar's salary was closer to 400 than 700 rubles a

But in this number the Lord Boris Fedorovich Godunov is not to be reckoned, that is like a "transcendent" and in no such predicament with the rest, being the emperor's brother-in-law, his protector for direction, for command and authority emperor of Russia. His yearly revenue in land and pension amounteth to the sum of 93,700 rubles and more as appeareth by the particulars.[23] He hath of inheritance, which himself hath augmented in Viaz'ma, Dorogobuzh, six thousand rubles a year. For his office of konnik [koniushii] or master of the horse, 1200 rubles or marks raised out of the *koniushennye slobody*[24] or the liberties pertaining to that office, which are certain lands and towns near about the Moscow, besides all the meadow and pasture ground on both sides the bank of the river Moskva, thirty verst up the stream and forty verst downwards. For his pension of the emperor, besides the other for his office, 15,000 rubles. Out of the province or shire of Vaga there is given him for are peculiar, exempted out of the *Posol'skaia chetvert'*[25] 32,000 rubles, besides a rent of furs; out of Riazan' and Seversk (another peculiar), 30,000 rubles; out of Tver' and Torzhok, another exempt place, 8,000 rubles; for rent of bathstoves and bathing houses without the walls of Moscow, 1,500 rubles; besides his pomest'e, or lands which he holdeth at the emperor's pleasure, which far exceedeth the proportion of land allotted to the rest of the nobility.

One other there is of the house of Glinskii that dispendeth in land and pension about 40,000 rubles yearly, which he is suffered to enjoy because he hath married Boris his wife's sister, being himself very simple and almost a natural.[26] The ordering of him and his lands are committed to Boris.

---

year. Fletcher's estimate of 700 rubles falls, however, well within the range of boiar salaries suggested by A. V. Chernov (*Vooruzhennye sily russkogo gosudarstva v XV–XVII vv.* [Moscow, 1954], p. 79).

23. Seredonin (pp. 190–91) suggests that Fletcher's estimate of Godunov's annual revenue is too high. Boris did not have lands in the district of Tver' and Torzhok and probably did not receive revenue from Riazan' and Novgorod-Severskii.

24. Also known as *koniushennye sela*: villages assigned to the master of the horse to provide provisions for the tsar's stables and revenue for the master himself.

25. *Chetfird* of *Posolskoy* in the original text. Also known as *Posol'skii prikaz*: office of foreign affairs.

26. Ivan Mikhailovich Glinskii (d. 1602) was made boiar late in 1585 (*RK*, p. 364). He served in the army against the Crimean Tatars in 1587 and 1591. He was married to Anna Skuratova-Bel'skaia whose younger sister, Mariia, was the wife of Boris Godunov (*RBS*).

In the third rank are the *voevody* or such nobles as are or have been generals in the emperor's wars, which deliver the honor of their title to their posterities also, who take their place above the other dukes and nobles that are not of the two former sorts, viz., of the udel'nye kniaz'ia nor of the boiars.[27]

These three degrees of their nobility, to wit, the udel'nye kniaz'ia, the boiars, and the voevody, have the addition of "vich" put unto their surname, as Boris Fedorovich, etc., which is a note of honor that the rest may not usurp.[28] And in case it be not added in the naming of them, they may sue the *beschest'e* or penalty of dishonor upon them that otherwise shall term them.

The fourth and lowest degree of nobility with them is of such as bear the name of kniaz'ia or dukes but come of the younger brothers of those chief houses through many descents and have no inheritance of their own, save the bare name or title of duke only. For their order is to deliver their names and titles of their dignities over to all their children alike, whatsoever else they leave them, so that the sons of a voevoda or general in the field are called voevody though they never saw the field, and the sons of a kniaz' or duke are called kniaz'ia though they have not one groat of inheritance or livelihood to maintain themselves withal. Of this sort there are so many that the plenty maketh them cheap, so that you shall see dukes glad to serve a mean man for five or six rubles or marks a year, and yet they will stand highly upon their beschest'e or reputation of their honors. And these are their several degrees of nobility.

The second degree of persons is of their syny [deti] boiarskie or the sons of gentlemen, which all are preferred and hold that name by their service in the emperor's wars, being soldiers by their very stock and birth. To which order are referred their d'iaki or secretaries that serve the emperor in every head town, being joined in commission with the dukes of that place.

27. The voevody did not constitute a separate rank of the nobility but were simply military commanders appointed for a particular campaign or provincial governors. The office was not hereditary although, through the workings of mestnichestvo, members of the same families might be appointed to high military commands from generation to generation.

28. According to Staden, the patronymic was used by princes and other nobles ("ist fürstlich und adelich") (Heinrich von Staden, *Aufzeichnungen über den Moskauer Staat,* ed. F. T. Epstein [Hamburg, 1964], p. 195). There is considerable variation in the use of the patronymic in the documents of the late sixteenth and early seventeenth centuries.

The last are their commons whom they call muzhiki, in which number they reckon their merchants and their common artificers. The very lowest and basest sort of this kind (which are held in no degree) are their country people whom they call *krest'iane*. Of the syny [deti] boiarskie (which are all soldiers) we are to see in the description of their forces and military provisions; concerning their muzhiki, what their condition and behavior is, in the title or chapter "Of the common people."

Chapter 10. Of the government of their provinces and shires

The whole country of Russia (as was said before) is divided into four parts which they call chetverti or tetrarchies.[1] Every chetvert' containeth diverse shires and is annexed to a several office whereof it takes the name. The first chetvert' or tetrarchy beareth the name of Posol'skaia chetvert' or the jurisdiction of the office of ambassages, and at this time is under the chief secretary and officer of the ambassages called Andrei Shchelkalov.[2] The standing fee or stipend that he

1. The word chetvert' means "a fourth" but it would nevertheless appear that at the time of Fletcher's visit there were only three such financial offices in existence (Sadikov, *Ocherki*, p. 403).

Fletcher visited Muscovy at a time when the administrative system was in a state of flux. His account, then, falls into the understandable error of oversimplifying the situation. At the end of the sixteenth century, there were, besides the prikazy or government offices that handled one particular type of state business such as foreign affairs or administered special areas like Kazan', offices known as chetverti which collected the revenues from the local authorities of particular areas of the country. These chetverti or *cheti* were often known by the name of the officials who directed them. One, for example, was called the *chet'* of Andrei Shchelkalov. What especially confused Fletcher was the fact that the same bureaucrat might simultaneously be in charge of one or more of the prikazy and one of the cheti. Thus Andrei Shchelkalov was the director of the Posol'skii prikaz and the chet' of Andrei Shchelkalov—two distinct institutions.

2. Shchelkalov was the most powerful bureaucrat of his time. He was one of a thousand service nobles granted estates in the Moscow area in 1550. At the height of his career he was primarily a specialist in foreign affairs. In 1571 he became director of the Posol'skii prikaz and held the post until 1594. Because of his administrative gifts, he was also given a number of other responsibilities, including charge of the Razriadnyi prikaz in 1570 and 1576 (N. P. Likhachev,

receiveth yearly of the emperor for this service is an hundred rubles or marks.

The second is called the *Razriadnaia chetvert'* because it is proper to the *razriad* or high constable.[3] At this time it pertaineth by virtue of office to Vasilii Shchelkalov, brother to the chancellor, but it is executed by one Sapun Abramov.[4] His pension is an hundred rubles yearly.

The third is the *Pomestnaia chetvert'*, as pertaining to that office.[5] This keepeth a register of all lands given by the emperor for service to his noblemen, gentlemen, and others, giveth out and taketh in all assurances for them. The officer at this time is called Eleazar Vyluzgin.[6] His stipend is five hundred rubles a year.

Razriadnye d'iaki XVI veka [St. Petersburg, 1888], pp. 193, 554). He was a member of the duma by 1572 (Zimin, "Sostav boiarskoi dumy," p. 80). As adviser on foreign policy, he was an outspoken opponent of concessions to the English merchants and advocated cooperation with the Hapsburgs. He was deprived of his offices in 1594, probably because he pressed too hard for an alliance with the Empire. After his fall he entered a monastery where he died in about 1597 (*RBS*).

3. Also known as the *Razriadnyi prikaz:* the government department that kept records of the servitors of the state and their duties and directed the organization and supply of the army. In calling the constable "razriad" Fletcher applies the name of the office to its director.

4. Vasilii Shchelkalov, like his brother, gained great influence as a member of the burgeoning Moscow bureaucracy. From the mid-1560's until the first decade of the seventeenth century he occupied a series of important administrative posts. Between 1577 and 1594 he was head of the Razriadnyi prikaz (Likhachev, *Razriadnye d'iaki*, pp. 554–56). He also played an important part in the conduct of foreign affairs. From 1571 on he took part in the reception of virtually every foreign ambassador who visited Moscow. In 1587 he conducted negotiations in Warsaw with members of the Polish Sejm about the conditions under which Fedor might be elected king of Poland. When his brother was disgraced, Vasilii succeeded him as head of the Posol'skii prikaz in 1594 and held the post until 1601 when he, in turn, fell from favor. He was a member of the duma by 1572 (Zimin, "Sostav boiarskoi dumy," p. 80). It was only in 1605 that the False Dmitrii raised him to the rank of okol'nichii. He died in 1610/11 (*RBS*).

Sapun Abramov, also known as Vasilii Tikhonovich Avramov, served in the Razriadnyi prikaz from 1583/84 and in 1594 took charge of it when Vasilii Shchelkalov replaced his brother, Andrei, as head of the Posol'skii prikaz; he directed it until 1605. He was a member of the duma by 1594, and ended his career as a military commander in Karelia (Likhachev, *Razriadnye d'iaki*, pp. 495–97, 555–56).

5. *Chetfird of Pomestnoy* in the original text. Also *Pomestnyi prikaz:* office responsible for the distribution of lands held on service tenure (pomest'e).

6. It is clear from the surviving evidence that Andrei Shchelkalov, Vasilii Shchelkalov, and Druzhina Petelin were in charge of chetverti. Seredonin is convinced that there is enough evidence to show that Vyluzgin administered a fourth chetvert' (pp. 257–58). Sadikov, however, disagrees and argues that there

The fourth is called *Kazanskii dvorets,* as being appropriate to the office that hath the jurisdiction of the kingdoms of Kazan' and Astrakhan' with the other towns lying upon the Volga, now ordered by one Druzhina Petelin, a man of very special account among them for his wisdom and promptness in matters of policy.[7] His pension is one hundred and fifty rubles a year.

From these chetverti or tetrarchies is exempted the emperor's inheritance or votchina (as they call it) for that it pertained from ancient time to the house of Bela, which is the surname of the imperial blood. This standeth of thirty-six towns with their bounds or territories, besides divers peculiar jurisdictions which are likewise deducted out of those chetverti, as the shire of Vaga (belonging to the Lord Boris Fedorovich Godunov) and such like.

These are the chief governors or officers of the provinces, not resident at their charge abroad, but attending the emperor whithersoever he goeth and carrying their offices about with them, which for the most part they hold at Moscow as the emperor's chief seat.

The parts and practice of these four offices is to receive all complaints and actions whatsoever that are brought out of their several chetverti and quarters and to inform them to the emperor's council, likewise to send direction again to those that are under them in their said provinces for all matters given in charge by the emperor and his council to be done or put in execution within their precincts.

For the ordering of every particular province of these four chetverti there is appointed one of these dukes, which were reckoned before in the lowest degree of their nobility, which are resident in the head towns of the said provinces. Whereof every one hath joined with him

---

were only three chetverti in Fletcher's time. He suggests that Vyluzgin, primarily an official of the Pomestnyi prikaz, temporarily took charge of Petelin's chetvert' when the latter was occupied with other matters (Sadikov, *Ocherki,* pp. 403–4). Vyluzgin was the son of a clerk and is first mentioned in an administrative post in 1578. In addition to directing the Pomestnyi prikaz from 1587 to 1601, he took part in the reception of many foreign ambassadors. He was one of the members of the commission sent to investigate the death of Prince Dmitrii in 1591. Despite his humble origins, he married his daughter, Mariia, to Ivan Petrovich Sheremetev, a member of a prominent boiar family (Likhachev, *Razriadnye d'iaki,* pp. 183–84).

7. Also given as Penteleev. Petelin held a wide variety of posts, serving in the *Prikaz bol'shogo prikhoda* (treasury) from 1584–87 and heading the Kazanskii dvorets from 1587 until the late 1590's. His career included a series of diplomatic missions. On three occasions in the 1580's he was sent to Poland on diplomatic errands and he negotiated with the Swedes in 1583 and 1590. He was one of the officials who met Bowes in 1583 (Likhachev, *Razriadnye d'iaki,* pp. 492–94).

in commission a d'iak or secretary to assist him, or rather to direct him, for in the executing of their commission the d'iak doth all.

The parts of their commission are these in effect. First to hear and determine in all civil matters within their precinct, to which purpose they have under them certain officers as *gubnoi starets* [*starosta*][8] or coroners, who, besides the trial of self murders, are to attach felons, and the *sud'ia* or under justices, who themselves also may hear and determine in all matters of the same nature among the country people of their own wards or bailiwicks. But so that in case either party dissent, they may appeal and go farther to the duke and d'iak that reside within the head town, from whom also they may remove the matter to the higher court at Moscow, of the emperor's council, where lie all appeals.[9] They have under them also *sotskii starets* [*starosta*], that is, aldermen or bailiffs of the hundreds.[10]

Secondly, in all criminal matters as theft, murder, treason, etc., they have authority to apprehend, to examine, and to imprison the malefactor; and so, having received perfect evidence and information of the cause, they are to send it ready drawn and orderly digested up to the Moscow to the officer of the chetvert' whereunto that province is annexed, by whom it is referred and propounded to the emperor's council. But to determine in any matter criminal or to do execution upon the party offending is more than their commission will allow them to do.[11]

Thirdly, if there be any public service to be done within that province, as the publishing of any law or common order by way of procla-

---

8. District elder, elected by the local population. The elders were not subordinate to the provincial governors but were instead under the direct supervision of the *Razboinyi prikaz,* the central government office responsible for stamping out brigandage. They did not in fact have jurisdiction over suicide cases (B. N. Chicherin, *Oblastnyia uchrezhdeniia Rossii v XVII veke* [Moscow, 1856], p. 152).

9. The system of appeals in sixteenth-century Russia was very complex. In many cases, appeal against the judgment of a provincial governor could be made to the appropriate prikaz, then, in second instance, to the tsar and the duma. In other situations, cases might be sent directly from the local officials to the prikaz without passing through the governor's hands at all (Seredonin, pp. 277–78).

10. Elected local official, one rank below the gubnoi starosta.

11. Muscovite legislation of the sixteenth century gives contradictory definitions of the governors' judicial prerogatives. Article 71 of the Code of 1550 defines the governors' powers exactly as Fletcher describes. Article 60 of the same code, however, empowers the governors as well as the elected district officials to sentence and execute habitual offenders convicted of robbery or murder without consulting Moscow at all (*PRP*, IV, 247–48, 252).

mation, collecting of taxes and impositions for the emperor, mustering of soldiers and sending them forth at the day and to the place assigned by the emperor or his council, all these and such like pertain to their charge.

These dukes and d'iaki are appointed to their place by the emperor himself and are changed ordinarily at every year's end, except upon some special liking or suit the time be prorogued for a year or two more. They are men of themselves of no credit nor favor with the people where they govern, being neither born nor brought up among them nor yet having inheritance of their own, there or elsewhere. Only of the emperor they have for that service an hundred marks a year he that hath most, some fifty, some but thirty. Which maketh them more suspected and odious to the people because, being so bare and coming fresh and hungry upon them lightly every year, they rack and spoil them without all regard of justice or conscience, which is easily tolerated by the chief officers of the chetverti to the end they may rob them again and have a better booty when they call them to account, which commonly they do at the end of their service, making an advantage of their injustice and oppression over the poor people. There are few of them but they come to the *pytka*[12] or whip when their time is ended, which themselves for the most part do make account of, and therefore they furnish themselves with all the spoil they can for the time of their government that they may have for both turns, as well for the emperor and lord of the chetvert', as to reserve some good part for themselves.

They that are appointed to govern abroad are men of this quality, save that in the four border towns that are of greatest importance are set men of more special valor and trust, two in every town, whereof one is ever of the emperor's privy council. These four border towns are Smolensk, Pskov, Novgorod, and Kazan', whereof three lie towards the Pole and Swede, one bordereth far off upon the Krym Tatar. These have larger commission than the other dukes of the provinces that I spake of before and may do execution in criminal matters, which is thought behooveful for the commonwealth for incident occasions that may happen upon the borders that are far off, and may not stay for direction about every occurrent and particular matter from the emperor and his council. They are changed every year (except as before)

12. Foreign travelers to Muscovy frequently used the term to refer to the *dyba,* a form of torture in which the victim is hung by his hands, which are tied together behind him, and whipped with the *knut.*

and have for their stipend seven hundred rubles a year he that hath most; some have but four hundred. Many of these places that are of greatest importance, and almost the whole country, is managed at this time by the Godunovs and their clients.

The city of Moscow, that is the emperor's seat, is governed altogether by the emperor's council. All matters there, both civil and criminal, are heard and determined in the several courts held by some of the said council that reside there all the year long.

Only for their ordinary matters (as buildings, reparations, keeping of their streets decent and clean, collections, levying of taxes, impositions, and such like) are appointed two gentlemen and two d'iaki or secretaries who hold a court together for the ordering of such matters. This is called the zemskii house.[13] If any townsman suspect his servant of theft or like matter, hither he may bring him to have him examined upon the pytka or other torture. Besides these two gentlemen and secretaries that order the whole city, there are starosty or aldermen for every several company. The alderman hath his sotskii or constable; and the constable hath certain *desiatskie* or decurions under him which have the oversight of ten households apiece, whereby every disorder is sooner spied and the common service hath the quicker dispatch. The whole number of citizens, poor and rich, are reduced into companies. The chief officers (as the d'iaki and gentlemen) are appointed by the emperor himself, the starosta by the gentlemen and d'iaki, the sotskii by the starosta or alderman, and the desiatskie by the constables.[14]

This manner of government of their provinces and towns, if it were as well set for the giving of justice indifferently to all sorts as it is to prevent innovations by keeping of the nobility within order and the commons in subjection, it might seem in that kind to be no bad nor unpolitic way for the containing of so large a commonwealth of that breadth and length as is the kingdom of Russia. But the oppression and slavery is so open and so great that a man would marvel how the nobility and people should suffer themselves to be brought under it while

---

13. *Zemskii dvor.* By the early seventeenth century the zemskii dvor (or prikaz) functioned as the judicial court and the administration of the city of Moscow. Its responsibilities ranged from judging criminals to tracking down runaway peasants and managing the fire brigade. See the Book of Decrees of the Zemskii prikaz in *PRP*, V, 329–92.

14. The starosty, sotskii, and desiatskie were elected by the local communes (Seredonin, pp. 269–70).

they had any means to avoid and repulse it, or being so strengthened as it is at this present, how the emperors themselves can be content to practice the same with so open injustice and oppression of their subjects, being themselves of a Christian profession.

By this it appeareth how hard a matter it were to alter the state of the Russe government as now it standeth. First, because they have none of the nobility able to make head. As for the lords of the four chetverti or tetrarchies, they are men of no nobility but d'iaki advanced by the emperor, depending on his favor and attending only about his own person. And for the dukes that are appointed to govern under them, they are but men of a titular dignity (as was said before), of no power, authority, nor credit save that which they have out of the office for the time they enjoy it, which doth purchase them no favor but rather hatred of the people, for as much as they see that they are set over them not so much for any care to do them right and justice as to keep them under in a miserable subjection and to take the fleece from them, not once in the year (as the owner from his sheep) but to pull and clip them all the year long. Besides, the authority and rule which they bear is rent and divided into many small pieces, being divers of them in every great shire, limited besides with a very short time which giveth them no scope to make any strength nor to contrive such an enterprise if happily they intended any matter of innovation. As for the common people (as may better appear in the description of their state and quality afterwards set down), besides their want of armor and practice of war (which they are kept from of purpose), they are robbed continually both of their hearts and money (besides other means), sometimes by pretense of some service to be done for the common defense, sometimes without any show at all of any necessity of commonwealth or prince, so that there is no means either for nobility or people to attempt any innovation so long as the military forces of the emperor (which are the number of 80,000 at the least in continual pay) hold themselves fast and sure unto him and to the present state. Which needs they must do, being of the quality of soldiers and enjoying withal that free liberty of wronging and spoiling of the commons at their pleasure, which is permitted them of purpose to make them have a liking of the present state. As for the agreement of the soldiers and commons, it is a thing not to be feared, being of so opposite and contrary practice much one to the other. This desperate state of things at home maketh the people for the most part to wish for some foreign invasion, which they suppose to be the only means to rid them of the heavy yoke of this tyrannous government.

Chapter 11. Of the emperor's council

The emperors of Russia give the name of counselor to divers of their chief nobility rather for honors' sake than for any use they make of them about their matters of state. These are called boiars without any addition and may be called counselors at large, for they are seldom or never called to any public consultation.[1] They which are of his special and privy council indeed (whom he useth daily and ordinarily for all public matters pertaining to the state) have the addition of *dumnyi* and are named *dumnyi boiarin* [*dumnye boiare*] or lords of the council, their office or sitting *boarstva* [*boiarskaia duma*].[2]

Their names at this present are these in their order: 1. Kniaz' Fedor Ivanovich Mstislavskii;[3] 2. Kniaz' Ivan Mikhailovich Glinskii;[4] 3. Kniaz' Vasilii Ivanovich Shuiskii-Skopin.[5] (These three are accounted to be of

1. When he writes of boiars who were not members of the duma, Fletcher probably has in mind members of the lower ranks of court servitors. These, however, were not officially called boiars at all (Kliuchevskii, *Boiarskaia duma*, p. 323).

2. Dumnye boiare is, strictly speaking, a redundancy since a boiar was, by definition, a member of the duma. Fletcher's use of the term "boiarskaia duma" is significant because it is not found in any Russian source before the seventeenth century (*ibid.*, p. 323).

3. Fedor Ivanovich Mstislavskii was named to the court post of kravchii in 1575 and in the following year was raised to the rank of boiar (Zimin, "Sostav boiarskoi dumy," p. 77). He served as a commander in campaigns against the Poles in 1581, the Swedes in 1589 and 1592, and the Crimean Tatars in 1591. Boris Godunov appointed him commander-in-chief of the forces sent to oppose the False Dmitrii. Mstislavskii remained loyal to Godunov until his death but then swore allegiance to the pretender. He was one of the leaders in the *coup d'état* against the False Dmitrii in 1606 and was a possible candidate to succeed to the throne but refused to be considered for the honor. After the fall of Vasilii Shuiskii in 1610, he was the leading member of the council of seven boiars that offered the crown to Prince Wladyslaw of Poland.

4. See above, p. 142. Made a boiar in 1585/86 (*DRV*, XX, 62).

5. Probably Vasilii Fedorovich Shuiskii-Skopin (d. 1595) who was a commander in Pskov, along with I. P. Shuiskii, between 1579 and 1582. He held major command posts on the northwestern frontier, particularly in the Novgorod region, in

greater birth than wisdom, taken in, as may seem, for that end rather to furnish the place with their honors and presence than with their advice or counsel.) 4. Kniaz' Vasilii Ivanovich Shuiskii, thought to be more wise than the other of his name;[6] 5. Kniaz' Fedor Mikhailovich; 6. Kniaz' Nikita Romanovich Trubetskoi; 7. Kniaz' Timofei Romanovich Trubetskoi;[7] S. Kniaz' Andrei Grigor'evich Kurakin;[8] 9. Kniaz' Dmitrii Ivanovich Khvorostinin; 10. Kniaz' Fedor Ivanovich Khvorostinin;[9]

the mid-1580's and again during the main operations against the Swedes in the early 1590's (RBS; RK, pp. 346, 364, 414, 453, 459). His appointment to the duma took place in 1577 (Zimin, "Sostav boiarskoi dumy," pp. 77–78).

6. The future tsar was named boiar in 1584.

7. Fedor Mikhailovich Trubetskoi was first mentioned in the sources as a military commander in 1564. During the 1570's he held high command positions in most of the operations on the Livonian front. His membership in the duma dates from 1568 (Zimin, "Sostav boiarskoi dumy," p. 74). Under Fedor and Boris, he continued to play a leading role in military and diplomatic affairs. He died in 1602 (E. E. Trubetskaia, Skazaniia o rode kniazei Trubetskikh [Moscow, 1891], pp. 67–72).

Nikita Romanovich Trubetskoi became a boiar in 1584 (DRV, XX, 60). At the beginning of the Time of Troubles, he was one of Boris Godunov's most loyal supporters and led in the successful defense of Novgorod-Severskii against the attack of the False Dmitrii's forces in 1604. When the rebellion was successful, he swore allegiance to the pretender but emerged in 1606 as a strong supporter of Vasilii Shuiskii. He died in 1608 (Platonov, Ocherki, pp. 247–48, 287–88). Timofei Romanovich Trubetskoi was first mentioned in the military service lists for the year 1572. Thereafter he held many military posts, frequently as a commander in the tsar's regiment. He served in the Livonian campaigns of the late 1570's, the war against the Swedes in 1590–91, and, on many occasions, in the defense forces on the southern frontier. He was made a boiar in 1585 and died in 1602/03 (RK, pp. 244, 261, 277, 293, 341, 392, 419, 439, 441, 455, 471, 497; DRV, XX, 61, 72).

8. Most likely Grigorii Andreevich Kurakin, who became boiar in 1584 (DRV, XX, 60–61).

9. Dmitrii Ivanovich Khvorostinin was one of the greatest Muscovite generals of his time. He is first recorded as serving on the southern frontier in 1559 and from that time he held a position of command in almost every campaign until 1590. Khvorostinin took part in the capture of Polotsk in 1563. In 1569 he was made a member of the duma with the rank of okol'nichii and raised to the rank of boiar in 1584 (DRV, XX, 50, 60). He distinguished himself in battle against the Crimean Tatars in 1570, 1573, and 1577 and against the Swedes in 1572, 1583, and 1590. In 1578 he was one of the commanders who took Oberpalen in Livonia but failed in the attack on Wenden (RBS).

Fedor Ivanovich Khvorostinin served in the Polotsk campaign of 1563. In 1577 he was named to the court office of dvoretskii (lord steward), entered the duma with the rank of okol'nichii in 1584, and became a boiar in 1588/89. In the later years of his career he carried out a number of diplomatic missions, negotiating with Swedish representatives on the Pliussa River in 1589, in 1591 at Ivangorod, and in 1599 with Prince Gustav, the would-be bridegroom of Kseniia Godunova. He met the ambassadors of the Crimea in 1590 and 1593, Lithuania in 1587, Persia in 1594, and the Empire in 1597 (RBS).

11. Bogdan Ivanovich Saburov;[10] 12. Kniaz' Ivan Vasil'evich Sitskii;[11] 13. Kniaz' Fedor Dmitrievich Shestunov;[12] 14. Kniaz' Fedor Mikhailovich Troekurov;[13] 15. Ivan Buturlin;[14] 16. Dmitrii Ivanovich Godunov; 17. Boris Fedorovich Godunov, brother to the empress; 18. Stepan Vasil'evich Godunov; 19. Grigorii Vasil'evich Godunov; 20. Ivan Vasil'evich Godunov;[15] 21. Fedor Sheremetev;[16] 22. Andrei Petrovich

10. Probably Bogdan Iur'evich (d. 1598). Saburov served in the army in Livonia during the early years of the war. He was made a boiar in 1573 (Zimin, "Sostav boiarskoi dumy," p. 77). He served in many military posts, in Kazan' in 1582/83 and 1583/84, Smolensk in 1586–87, through the Swedish war in the early 1590's, and took part in the mobilization at Serpukhov in 1598 (RK, pp. 340, 348, 377, 388, 407, 417, 459, 542).

11. First mentioned in the court rank of stol'nik in 1577. Sitskii was one of the ambassadors who negotiated with Stephen Bathory in 1580–81, first in Velikie Luki and subsequently in Warsaw, in a futile attempt to end the Livonian War. He served in military commands on the southern frontier in 1582 and Novgorod in 1582/83. He became a boiar in 1584/85. In 1601 he fell into disgrace because of his connections with the Romanovs. Boris Godunov stripped him of his rank and exiled him to a remote monastery where he died in 1608 (RBS).

12. Raised to the rank of boiar in 1584. In 1585 he conducted negotiations with the Swedes and in 1586–87 was a member of the delegation that discussed with the Polish representatives the conditions under which Tsar Fedor might ascend the vacant throne of Poland-Lithuania. He died in 1598 (RBS).

13. In 1581 he became a member of the duma with the rank of okol'nichii (Zimin, "Sostav boiarskoi dumy," p. 78). He took part in the reception of Possevino in 1583 and in the following year was sent to the court of the Empire as a member of the Novosil'tsov mission (PDS, I, 917). In 1585/86 he was raised to the rank of boiar (DRV, XX, 62). He was voevoda (military governor) of Astrakhan' from 1588 to 1594 (RK, p. 399, 436, 486).

14. Ivan Mikhailovich (d. 1605) entered the duma in 1585 with the rank of okol'nichii but was never made a boiar. He was killed in Dagestan while leading the expedition of 1604–5 against the Shamkhal of Tarki (RBS).

15. Dmitrii Ivanovich entered the duma in 1575 with the rank of okol'nichii and was raised to the rank of boiar in 1578 (Zimin, "Sostav boiarskoi dumy," p. 78). He died in 1605. Boris was raised to the rank of boiar in 1580 (ibid., p. 78). Stepan Vasil'evich entered the duma with the rank of okol'nichii in 1577 (ibid., p. 78). He became a boiar in 1584 (DRV, XX, 60). In 1586–87 he was one of the representatives who went to Poland to arrange for Tsar Fedor's election to the Polish throne. He was appointed to the office of dvoretskii in 1598 (ibid., XX, 69). When the False Dmitrii seized power in 1605, S. V. Godunov was sent to be a voevoda in Siberia.

G. V. Godunov was in 1584 made a boiar and appointed to the court office of dvoretskii (DRV, XX, 60). He died in 1598. Ivan Vasil'evich became a boiar in 1584 (ibid., XX, 60). In 1589 he took part in the reception of the Imperial ambassador, Warkotsch (PDS, I, 1181–82), and of the Crimean prince, Murat Girey (Sinbirskii sbornik, p. 104). He died in 1601/02 (DRV, XX, 72).

16. F. V. Sheremetev was one of the nobles who in 1550 was granted lands near Moscow on service tenure. He participated in almost every major expedition between 1556 and 1588 but his military career was marked by very few successes

Kleshnin;[17] 23. Ignatii Petrovich Tatishchev;[18] 24. Roman Mikhailovich Pivov;[19] 25. Dementii Ivanovich Cheremisinov;[20] 26. Roman Vasil'evich Alfer'ev;[21] 27. Andrei Shchelkalov; 28. Vasilii Shchelkalov; 29. Eleazar Vyluzgin; 30. Druzhina Petelin; 31. Sapun Abramov.[22]

and several disasters. In 1572 he was sent to defend the southern frontier but fled in the face of the Tatar attack. Later he was one of the commanders whose quarrels impeded the Muscovite attack on Wenden in 1578. Long delays allowed a Polish relief force to attack the besiegers and put them to flight. In the following year, Sheremetev was captured by the Polish forces in the Polotsk area and remained their prisoner until 1583. Despite his lackluster showing in the field, he achieved membership in the duma with the rank of okol'nichii in 1576 and was made a boiar in 1584 (Zimin, "Sostav boiarskoi dumy," p. 78; *DRV*, XX, 60). On two occasions Sheremetev was implicated in intrigues against Boris Godunov. In the first instance, he was sent to a military command in Novgorod in 1584/85 (*RK*, pp. 350, 356). The second time he was forced to enter the Nikolaevskii-Antoniev Monastery in 1590 (*RBS*).

17. In 1584/85 he was named a gentleman of the duma (*dumnyi dvorianin*) and became an okol'nichii in 1586/87 (*DRV*, XX, 61–62). He was a member of the commission sent to investigate the death of Prince Dmitrii in 1591. He died in 1599 (*RBS*).

18. I. P. Tatishchev held a succession of military posts in the late 1570's and early 1580's. In 1583 he was given the rank of dumnyi dvorianin. Along with S. I. Lobanov-Rostovskii and Druzhina Petelin he conducted negotiations with the Swedes at the Pliussa River in 1583. On a later occasion he was one of the officials who met Bowes. In 1589/90 he served in the war against Sweden and then was sent to Poland as ambassador in 1591. Boris Godunov appointed him to the post of court treasurer (kaznachei) in 1600. He died in 1604 (*RBS*).

19. R. M. Pivov was made a gentleman of the duma in 1578 (Zimin, "Sostav boiarskoi dumy," p. 80). In 1586 he was commissioned to accompany the Crimean Tatar prince Murat Girey to Astrakhan' (*Sinbirskii sbornik*, p. 91). He died in 1591/92 (*DRV*, XX, 64).

20. As a member of the oprichnina, Cheremisinov was sent to Novgorod in 1571 to collect money from the ruined city. While on campaign in Livonia, he was captured by the Poles in 1580 and ransomed in 1583. Among his diplomatic activities were negotiations with Bowes in 1583 and with Swedish representatives in 1594 (*RBS*). He became a dumnyi dvorianin in 1577 (Zimin, "Sostav boiarskoi dumy," p. 80). In the service lists, he is designated as kaznachei intermittently from 1584 until the early 1590's. In some instances his name is given alongside that of I. V. Trakhaniotov who is usually regarded as the chief occupant of the position at that time. From 1594 until at least 1597 he served in Astrakhan' under I. M. Buturlin (*RK*, pp. 364, 379, 413, 493, 504, 513).

21. R. V. Alfer'ev (d. 1590), who was *pechatnik* (keeper of the privy seal) in the oprichnina court, was made a gentleman of the duma in 1571 (Zimin, "Sostav boiarskoi dumy," p. 80).

22. For the Shchelkalovs, Vyluzgin, Petelin, and Abramov, see pp. 146–48. Fletcher's list of duma members does not include fourteen names that are given in the so-called Sheremetev list: Andrei Petrovich Kurakin, Fedor Nikitich Iur'ev, Ivan Vasil'evich Gagin, Ivan "Bol'shoi" Petrovich Golovin, Ivan "Kriuk" Fedorovich Kolychov, Petr Semenovich Lobanov-Rostovskii, Nikita Ivanovich Ochin-Pleshcheev,

The four last of these are called dumnye d'iaki or lord secretaries. They are all of the emperor's privy council, though but few of them are called to any consultation for that all matters are advised and determined upon by Boris Fedorovich Godunov, brother to the empress, with some five or six more whom it pleaseth him to call.[23] If they come, they are rather to hear than to give counsel and do so demean themselves. The matters occurrent which are of state done within the realm are informed them at their sittings by the lords of the four chetverti or tetrarchies, whereof mention is made in the chapter concerning the "Government of their Provinces," who bring in all such letters as they receive from the dukes, d'iaki, captains, and other officers of the cities and castles pertaining to their several quarter or chetvert', with other advertisements, and inform the council of them.

The like is done by the chief officer of every several office of record, who may come into the council chamber and inform them as occasion incident to his office doth require. Besides matters of state they consider of many private causes, informed by way of supplication in very great numbers. Whereof some they entertain and determine as the cause or means can procure favor. Some they send to the offices whereto they pertain by common course of law. Their ordinary days for their sitting are Mondays, Wednesdays, and Fridays.[24] Their time of meeting is commonly seven a clock in the morning. If there be any extraordinary occasion that requireth consultation on some other day, they have warning by the clerk of the council, called Dorofei Bushev, who receiveth order from the razriad or high constable of the realm to call them together at the time appointed.

Ivan Ivanovich Saburov, Boris Petrovich Zasekin, Ivan Vasil'evich Trakhaniotov, Aleksandr Nikitich Iur'ev, Baim Vasil'evich Voeikov, Fedor Andreevich Pisemskii, and Bogdan Iakovlevich Bel'skii. Of the men named in Fletcher's list, at least two, Petelin and Abramov, were probably not members of the duma (DRV, XX, 56–63; Seredonin, pp. 218–19).

23. Fletcher's remarks about the importance of the inner council of "some five or six" probably conveys an accurate picture of the workings of the Muscovite government at the time of his visit. The inner duma emerged during the course of the sixteenth century and played an especially important role in the seventeenth when the boiar duma was so enlarged as to become unwieldy. The inner duma handled questions demanding secrecy and issues relating to the imperial household, and prepared important questions for submission to the whole boiar duma (Kliuchevskii, Boiarskaia duma, pp. 322–31; Seredonin, pp. 219–23).

24. Fletcher's statements are the only available evidence from the sixteenth century on the time at which the duma met. It would appear, however, that by the early seventeenth century, the boiars met both in the morning and the evening at least five days a week (Kliuchevskii, Boiarskaia duma, pp. 406–9).

Chapter 12. Of the emperor's customs and other revenues

For the receiving of customs and other rents belonging to the crown there are appointed divers under officers which deliver over the same into the head treasury. The first is the office of *dvortsovyi* or steward of the household. The second is the office of the chetverti, which I comprehend under one though it be divided into four several parts, as was said before. The third is called *bol'shoi prikhod* or the great income.

As touching the first, which is the office of the steward, it receiveth all the rents of the emperor's inheritance or crownland, which they call votchina. The votchina or crownland containeth in it thirty-six towns with the territories or hundreds belonging unto them. Whereof the chief that yield the greatest rents are these: Aleksandrovskaia [Sloboda], Corelska, Tver', Slobodey, Danielska, Mosal'sk, Chara, Sametska, Staraia Russa, Bransove, etc.[1] The inhabitants or tenants of these and the other towns pay, some rent money, some other rent duties (called *obroki*) as certain chetverti or measures of grain, wheat, rye, barley, oats, etc., or of other victual as oxen, sheep, swans, geese, hares, hens, wild fowl, fish, hay, wood, honey, etc. Some are bound to sow for the emperor's provision certain acres of ground and to make the corn ready for his use, having for it an allowance of certain acres of ground for their own proper use.

This provision for the household, specially of grain served in by the tenants, is a great deal more than is spent in his house or in other allowance served out in livery or for the emperor's honor, called *zhalovan'e*, for which use there is bestowed very much both in grain and other victual. This surplus of provision is sold by the steward to the best hand and runneth into the emperor's treasury.

In the time of Ivan Vasil'evich, father to this emperor (who kept a more princely and bountiful house than the emperor now doth), this

---

1. Tver' and Staraia Russa were not part of the tsar's votchina (Seredonin, p. 318). Corelska, Slobodey, Danielska, Chara, Sametska, and Bransove could not positively be identified.

overplus of grain and other incomes into the steward's office yielded to his treasury not past sixty thousand rubles yearly, but riseth now by good husbanding of the steward Grigorii Vasil'evich Godunov to 230,000 rubles a year, and this by the means of the empress and her kindred, specially Boris Fedorovich Godunov, that account it all their own that runneth into the emperor's treasury.[2] Much of this surplusage that riseth out of the rent provision is employed to the payment of the wages of his household officers, which are very many attending at home and purveying abroad.

The second office of receipt, called the chetverti (being divided into four several parts, as before was said), hath four head officers which, besides the ordering and government of the shires contained within their several chetverti, have this also as a part of their office, to receive the *tiaglo*[3] and *podat'*,[4] belonging to the emperor, that riseth out of the four chetverti or quarters. The tiaglo is a yearly rent or imposition raised upon every *vyt'*[5] or measure of grain that groweth within the land, gathered by sworn men and brought into the office. The vyt' containeth sixty chetverti. Every chetvert' is three bushels English or little

2. G. V. Godunov was appointed dvoretskii in 1584 (*DRV*, XX, 60). Fletcher's estimate of court revenue is probably much too high. In the first place, it is hard to believe that the court raised 230,000 rubles a year from the sale of surplus grain and other produce. In addition, fragmentary data from the late sixteenth century indicate that the dues paid to the court probably came to far less than that figure. Moreover, figures from 1613–14 show that, in those years, the annual expenditure of the court was only 9,762 rubles and, even so, court revenues were not sufficient to meet these expenses. Admittedly, Muscovy was in chaos at the end of the Time of Troubles. Nevertheless, the enormous gap between these figures and Fletcher's would suggest that his estimate of revenue is exaggerated even for normal times (Seredonin, pp. 325–39).

3. A general word meaning the sum total of fiscal obligations and labor and service duties imposed by the government on taxpaying citizens.

4. A general term for direct taxes. In the sixteenth century, the word referred primarily to the tax on land usually assessed by the *sokha*, the basic tax assessment unit of land in Muscovite Russia. The sokha varied in size from one locality to another but most commonly, in the late sixteenth century, was equal to 800 chetverti of good land in one field of a property organized on the three-field system, 1,000 chetverti of land of medium quality or 1,200 chetverti of poor land. When used in measuring monastery lands, the sokha was usually equal to 600 chetverti of good land and for the "black lands," 500 chetverti of good land.

5. A tax unit of land used in some areas of Russia. The vyt' was equal to 12 chetverti of good land in one field of a property organized on the three-field system, 14 chetverti of middling land, or 16 to 20 chetverti of poor land. The vyt' was therefore equal to between 65 and 81 acres.

less. The podat' is an ordinary rent of money imposed upon every soke[6] or hundred within the whole realm.

This tiaglo and podat' bring in yearly to the offices of the chetverti a great sum of money as may appear by the particulars here set down. The town and province of Pskov pay yearly for tiaglo and podat' about 18,000 rubles; Novgorod, 35,000 rubles; Torzhok and Tver', 8,000 rubles; Riazan', 30,000 rubles; Murom, 12,000 rubles; Kholmogory and Dvina, 8,000 rubles; Vologda, 12,000 rubles; Kazan', 18,000 rubles; Ustiug, 30,000 rubles; Rostov, 50,000; the city of Moscow, 40,000 rubles; Siberia, 20,000 rubles; Kostroma, 12,000 rubles. The total amounteth to 400,000 rubles or marks a year which is brought in yearly the first day of September, that is reckoned by them the first day of the year.[7]

The third (that is called the bol'shoi prikhod or great income) receiveth all the customs that are gathered out of all the principal towns and cities within the whole realm, besides the fees and other duties which rise out of divers smaller offices which are all brought into this office of bol'shoi prikhod.[8] The towns of most trade that do yield greatest custom are these here set down: Moscow, Smolensk, Pskov, Novgorod Velikii, Staraia Russa, Torzhok, Tver', Iaroslavl', Kostroma,

6. Fletcher appears to have confused the English "soke," a political unit, with the Russian "sokha" described in n. 4 above.

7. Fletcher's information on the income of the chetverti raises questions at several points. First of all, it is difficult to decide whether Fletcher refers to cities and their immediate districts or to entire provinces. Seredonin suggests that, of the places mentioned by Fletcher, only Novgorod and Pskov could be considered as provinces and the rest of the figures must be read as referring to cities and their immediate districts (p. 330). The figures themselves are open to question on several grounds. In the first place, they are out of proportion since, for example, Rostov is listed as providing more revenue than Moscow. Moreover, Siberia is included in the list although the area was not yet under effective Muscovite control. In addition, the individual figures seem much too large. On the basis of contemporary or seventeenth-century data, Seredonin argues that the figures for Novgorod, Pskov, Ustiug, and Kazan' are, in all likelihood, greatly exaggerated (pp. 331–32). Finally, these revenues from direct taxes are much higher than the figures for customs revenue in the next passage. It is generally accepted, however, that in the sixteenth century the Muscovite administration relied predominantly on indirect taxes for its revenue.

8. Fletcher's account of revenues of the bol'shoi prikhod raises doubts on several counts. He indicates that this central financial office received revenue from three sources. The first two of these—the customs duties collected from the towns and the various fees gathered by the smaller prikazy and passed on the bol'shoi prikhod—he considers together. According to his calculations, the customs revenue from the twelve most important cities and towns of Muscovy amounted to 80,500

Nizhnii-Novgorod, Kazan', Vologda. This custom out of the great towns is therefore more certain and easy to be reckoned because it is set and rated precisely what they shall pay for the custom of the year, which needs must be paid into the said office though they receive not so much. If it fall out to be more, it runneth all into the emperor's advantage.

The custom at Moscow for every year is 12,000 rubles; the custom of Smolensk, 8,000 rubles; Pskov, 12,000 rubles; Novgorod Velikii, 6,000 rubles; Staraia Rusa, by salt and other commodities, 18,000 rubles; Torzhok, 800 rubles; Tver', 700 rubles; Iaroslavl', 1,200 rubles; Kostroma, 1,800 rubles; Nizhnii-Novgorod, 7,000 rubles; Kazan', 11,000 rubles; Vologda, 2,000 rubles. The custom of the rest that are towns of trade is sometimes more, sometimes less, as their traffic and dealings with commodities to and fro falleth out for the year.

This may be said for certain, that the three tables of receipts belonging to this office of bol'shoi prikhod when they receive least account for thus much, viz., the first table, 160,000 rubles; the second table, 90,000 rubles; the third, 70,000 rubles, so that there cometh into the office of bol'shoi prikhod at the least reckoning (as appeareth by their books of customs) out of these and other towns and maketh the sum of 340,000 rubles a year. Besides this custom out of the towns of trade, there is received by this office of bol'shoi prikhod the yearly rent of the common bathstoves and *kabaki* or drinking houses which pertain to the emperor, which, though it be uncertain for the just sum, yet because it is certain and an ordinary matter that the Russe will bathe himself as well within as without, yieldeth a large rent to the emperor's treasury.

There is besides a certain mulct or penalty that groweth to the emperor out of every judgment or sentence that passeth in any of his courts of record in all civil matters. This penalty or mulct is twenty

---

rubles a year. Elsewhere he states that the total of such revenues and the miscellaneous dues collected by the smaller prikazy came to 340,000 rubles. This would mean by implication, that customs revenues from the smaller towns and the various dues collected by the smaller prikazy accounted for 259,500 rubles annually—an unreasonably high figure. The third source of the revenue of the bol'shoi prikhod was, according to Fletcher, the surplus left in the prikazy that managed the armed forces after they had met their annual expenses. This surplus he combined, in his calculations, with the income from court fees and the taxes on bathhouses and taverns. The revenue from these combined sources, he states, raised the total income of the bol'shoi prikhod to 800,000 rubles. It is highly unlikely, however that this third combined source of income could have provided 460,000 rubles annually (see Seredonin, pp. 332–35).

den'gi, or pence upon every ruble or mark, and so ten in the hundred, which is paid by the party that is convict by law.[9] He hath besides for every name contained in the writs that pass out of these courts five altyny. An altyn is five pence sterling or thereabouts. This is made good out of the office whence the writ is taken forth. Thence it goeth to the office that keepeth the lesser seal, where it payeth as much more to the emperor's use. This riseth commonly to 3,000 rubles a year or thereabouts. Farther also out of the office of razboinyi [prikaz], where all felonies are tried, is received for the emperor the half part of felons' goods; the other half goeth the one part to the informer, the other to the officers.[10]

All this is brought into the office of bol'shoi prikhod or great income, besides the overplus or remainder that is saved out of the land rents allotted to divers other offices, as namely to the office called razriad, which hath lands and rents assigned unto it to pay the yearly salaries of the soldiers or horsemen that are kept still in pay, which in time of peace when they rest at home not employed in any service is commonly cut off and paid them by halves, sometimes not the half, so that the remainder out of the razriad office that is laid into the emperor's treasury cometh for the most part every year to 250,000 rubles.

In like sort (though not so much) is brought in the surplus out of the *streletskii* offices[11] which hath proper lands for the payment of the *strel'tsy* men or gunners, as well those at Moscow that are of the emperor's guard (12,000 in ordinary pay),[12] as on the borders and other garrison towns and castles. Likewise out of the office of *prechase, shisivoy nemshoy*[13] which hath set allowance of lands to maintain the foreign mercenary soldiers as Poles, Swedes, Dutch, Scots, etc., so out of the office of *pushkarskii*[14] (which hath lands and rents allowed for the

9. 200 den'gi = 1 ruble.

10. The property of a convicted robber was usually divided so that the plaintiff received full compensation for his losses and the remainder was confiscated by the tsar's treasury (*PRP*, V, 198).

11. *Streletskii prikaz.*

12. This figure is reasonable if it is taken to include not only the nobles in the tsar's guard but also the men in their retinues (Seredonin, *Izvestiia inostrantsev o vooruzhennykh silakh moskovskago gosudarstva v kontse XVI v.* [St. Petersburg, 1891], p. 9).

13. Presumably *Inozemnyi* (or *inozemskii*) *prikaz*: the chancellery that registered and paid the salaries of the foreign soldiers in Muscovite service.

14. *Pushkarskii prikaz*: the chancellery responsible for the manufacture and upkeep of cannons and ammunition.

provision of munition, great ordnance, powder, shot, saltpeter, brimstone, lead, and such like) there is left somewhat at the year's end that
runneth into the treasury. All these bring into the office of bol'shoi prikhod that which remaineth in their hand at the year's end, whence it is
delivered into the emperor's treasury, so that the whole sum that groweth to this office of bol'shoi prikhod or the great income (as appeareth
by the books of the said office) amounteth to 800,000 rubles a year or
thereabouts.

All these offices, to wit, the office of the steward, the four chetverti,
and the bol'shoi prikhod deliver in their receipts to the head treasury
that lieth within the emperor's house or castle at the Moscow, where
lie all his monies, jewels, crowns, scepters, plate, and such like, the
chests, hutches, and bags being signed by the emperors themselves
with their own seal, though at this time the Lord Boris Fedorovich Godunov his seal and oversight supplieth for the emperor as in all other
things. The under officer at this time is one Stepan Vasil'evich Godunov, cousin-german to the said Boris, who hath two clerks allowed to
serve under him in the office.[15]

The sum that grow-eth to the emperor's treasury in money only, for every year.	1 Out of the steward's office above the expense of his house, 230,000 rubles. 2 Out of the four chetverti for soke and head money, 400,000 rubles. 3 Out of the bol'shoi prikhod office or great income for custom and other rents, 800,000 rubles.	Sum 1,430,000 rubles clear, besides all charges for his house and ordinary salaries of his soldiers otherwise discharged.[16]

15. At the time of Fletcher's visit, the chief treasurer was Ivan Vasil'evich
Trakhaniotov. It is possible, however, that Stepan Godunov had a special commission to oversee the collection and disposition of state revenues (Seredonin, p.
317).

16. Seredonin argues that the total revenue of the state could not possibly have
been as high as 1,430,000 rubles. At the end of the seventeenth century the income
of the Russian state was only two million rubles despite greatly increased spending and the steady depreciation of the value of the ruble in the intervening century. Moreover, even in the 1630's, military expenditures—the chief expense of the
government—were no greater than 275,000 rubles (Seredonin, p. 323). Seredonin

But besides this revenue that is paid all in money into the emperor's treasury, he receiveth yearly in furs and other duties to a great value out of Siberia, Pechora, Perm', and other places, which are sold or bartered away for other foreign commodities to the Turkish, Persian, Armenian, Georgian, and Bulgarian merchants that trade within his countries, besides others of Christendom. What it maketh in the whole (though the value cannot be set down precisely, as being a thing casual as the commodity may be got), it may be guessed by that which was gathered the last year out of Siberia for the emperor's custom, viz., 466 timber of sables, five timber of martens, 180 black foxes, besides other commodities.[17]

To these may be added their seizures and confiscations upon such as are in displeasure, which riseth to a great sum, besides other their extraordinary impositions and exactions done upon their officers, monasteries, etc., not for any apparent necessity or use of the prince or commonwealth, but of will and custom, yet with some pretense of a Scythian, that is, gross and barbarous policy, as may appear by these few sophismata or counterfeit policies put in practice by the emperors of Russia all tending to this end, to rob their people and to enrich their treasury. To this purpose this byword was used by the late Emperor Ivan Vasil'evich: "that his people were like to his beard; the oftener shaven the thicker it would grow; or like sheep that must needs be shorn once a year at the least to keep them from being overladen with their wool."

Means used to draw the wealth of the land into the emperor's treasury

1. To prevent no extortions, exactions, or briberies whatsoever done upon the commons by their dukes, d'iaki, or other officers in their provinces, but to suffer them to go on till their time be expired and to suck themselves full, then to call them to the pravezh (or whip) for their behavior and to beat out of them all, or the most part, of the booty (as

suggests that Fletcher unintentionally inflates his estimate of state revenue by including the same income under several different categories. Seredonin, himself, estimates that the state revenue in Fletcher's time was about 400,000 rubles in all (pp. 334–35).

17. Fisher, in *The Russian Fur Trade*, pp. 108–9, questions whether the furs were really "customs." He suggests that the furs were actually "tribute" which the emperor regularly exacted from the conquered territories.

the honey from the bee) which they have wrung from the commons and to turn it into the emperor's treasury, but never anything back again to the right owners, how great or evident soever the injury be. To this end the needy dukes and d'iaki that are sent into their provinces serve the turn very well, being changed so often, to wit, once a year, where in respect of their own and the quality of the people (as before was said) they might be continued for some longer time without all fear of innovation. For coming still fresh upon the commons, they suck more eagerly, like Tiberius the emperor's flies that came new still upon an old sore, to whom he was wont to compare his praetors and other provincial officers.

2. To make of these officers that have robbed their people sometimes a public example if any be more notorious than the rest, that the emperor may seem to mislike the oppressions done to his people and transfer the fault to his ill officers.

As among divers other was done by the late Emperor Ivan Vasil'evich to a d'iak[18] in one of his provinces, that, besides many other extortions and briberies, had taken a goose ready dressed full of money. The man was brought to the market place in Moscow. The emperor himself present made an oration: "These good people are they that would eat you up like bread," etc. Then asked he his *palachi* or executioners who could cut up a goose and commanded one of them first to cut off his legs about the middle of the shin, then his arms above his elbows (asking him still if goose flesh were good meat), in the end to chop off his head that he might have the right fashion of a goose ready dressed. This might seem to have been a tolerable piece of justice (as justice goeth in Russia) except his subtle end to cover his own oppressions.

3. To make an open show of want when any great tax or imposition is towards, as was done by this Emperor Fedor Ivanovich by the advice of some about him at the beginning of his reign; when being left very rich (as was thought) by his father, he sold most of his plate and stamped some into coin that he might seem to want money. Whereupon presently out came a taxation.

4. To suffer their subjects to give freely to the monasteries (which for their superstition very many do, specially in their last wills) and to lay up their money and substance in them to keep it more safe, which

18. One manuscript variant identifies the official as I. M. Viskovatyi (Berry, p. 498). On Viskovatyi, see above, p. 24, n. 22.

all is permitted them without any restraint or proviso, as was and is in some countries of Christendom. Whereby their monasteries grow to exceeding great wealth. This they do to have the money of the realm better stored together and more ready for their hand when they list to take it, which many times is done without any noise, the friars being content rather to part from somewhat, as the increase groweth, than to lose all at once, which they were made to doubt of in the other emperor's days.

To this end Ivan Vasil'evich, late emperor, used a very strange practice that few princes would have done in their greatest extremities. He resigned his kingdom to one *Velikii Kniaz'* Simeon, the emperor's son of Kazan', as though he meant to draw himself from all public doings to a quiet private life.[19] Towards the end of the year he caused this new king to call in all charters granted to bishoprics and monasteries, which they had enjoyed many hundred years before, which were all canceled. This done (as in dislike of the fact and of the misgovernment of the new king), he resumed his scepter and so was content (as in favor to the church and religious men) that they should renew their charters and take them of himself, reserving and annexing to the crown so much of their lands as himself thought good.

By this practice he wrung from the bishoprics and monasteries (besides the lands which he annexed to the crown) an huge mass of money, from some forty, from some fifty, from some an hundred thousand rubles.[20] And this as well for the increase of his treasury as to

19. Ivan IV abruptly abdicated in late September or October 1575 and raised Simeon Bekbulatovich, the former khan of Kasimov, to the throne. The change was probably motivated by Ivan's fears of a plot against his life. For several months the new tsar was given full honors as ruler, and Ivan played the role of prince of Moscow. Then in September 1576 Ivan reestablished himself on the throne and granted Simeon lands and the title of great prince of Tver' (*Materialy*, II, 81–82; Tolstoy, pp. 179–88; M. V. Lileev, *Simeon Bekbulatovich, khan kasimovskii, velikii kniaz' vseia Rusi, vposledstvii velikii kniaz' tverskoi. 1567–1616* [Tver', 1891], pp. 18–56. See also Jack M. Culpepper, "The Kremlin Executions of 1575 and the Enthronement of Simeon Bekbulatovich," *Slavic Review*, XXIV [1965], 503–6).

20. Fletcher and Horsey viewed the "reign" of Simeon as a measure directed against church property. The surviving documents of the period, however, present no evidence to support their contention that Ivan IV cancelled the charters of the monasteries in 1575–76, and there are no surviving charters renewing the monasteries' privileges in the years following. As a consequence, many historians have rejected their accounts. In a minority opinion, A. Pavlov, author of the classic study of the monastery land question, defends their position even though he can support their view only by pointing to a possible parallel situation—the cancellation of the monasteries' charters of privilege at the accession of Fedor in 1584

abate the ill opinion of his hard government by a show of worse in another man. Wherein his strange spirit is to be noted, that being hated of his subjects (as himself knew well enough), yet would venture such a practice to set another in his saddle that might have ridden away with his horse while himself walked by on foot.

5. To send their messengers into the provinces or shires where the special commodities of their country grow, as furs, wax, honey, etc. There to forestall and engross sometime one whole commodity, sometime two or more, taking them at small prices what themselves list and selling them again at an excessive rate to their own merchants and to merchants strangers. If they refuse to buy them, then to force them unto it.

The like is done when any commodity, either native or foreign (as cloth of gold, broadcloth, etc.), thus engrossed by the emperor and received into his treasury happeneth to decay or mar by long lying or some other casualty, which is forced upon the merchants to be bought by them at the emperor's price whether they will or no. This last year of 1589 was engrossed all the wax of the country, so that none might deal with that commodity but the emperor only.[21]

6. To take up and engross in like sort sometime foreign commodities (as silks, cloth, lead, pearl, etc.) brought into his realm by Turkish merchants, Armenians, Bulgarians, Poles, English, and other, and then to force his merchants to buy them of his officers at his own price.

7. To make a monopoly for the time of such commodities as are paid him for rent or custom and to enhance the price of them, as furs, corn, wood, etc., what time none must sell of the same kind of commodity till the emperor's be all sold. By this means he maketh of his rent corn, and other provision of victual (as before was said) about 200,000 rubles, or marks a year. Of his rent wood, hay, etc., 30,000 rubles or thereabouts.

8. In every great town of his realm he hath a kabak or drinking

(A. Pavlov, *Istoricheskii ocherk sekuliarizatsii tserkovnykh zemel' v Rossii*, Part I [Odessa, 1871], p. 156).

21. In this passage, Fletcher reflects the complaints of the English merchants in Russia. They were dissatisfied with the Russian government's orders that they could obtain wax only by bartering saltpeter, sulphur, and lead. Besides the limitation this placed on their activities, the order placed them in a poor bargaining position and led to complaints that, for purposes of barter, the government set the price of wax at an absurdly high level and underrated the value of their goods (*Sbornik IRIO*, XXXVIII, 203; Tolstoy, p. 309; Bond, p. cvi).

house where is sold *aqua-vitae* (which they call Russe wine), mead, beer, etc. Out of these he receiveth rent that amounteth to a great sum of money. Some yield 800, some 900, some 1,000, some 2,000 or 3,000 rubles a year. Wherein, besides the base and dishonorable means to increase his treasury, many foul faults are committed. The poor laboring man and artificer many times spendeth all from his wife and children. Some use to lay in twenty, thirty, forty rubles or more into the kabak and vow themselves to the pot till all that be spent, and this (as he will say) for the honor of *gospodar'* or the emperor. You shall have many there that have drunk all away to the very skin and so walk naked, whom they call *nagoi*. While they are in the kabak none may call them forth, whatsoever cause there be, because he hindereth the emperor's revenue.

9. To cause some of his boiars or nobles of his court (whom he useth upon trust) that have houses in the Moscow to feign themselves robbed, then to send for the zemskii men, or aldermen of the city, and to command them to find out the robbery. In default of not finding it, to prave or assess the city for their misgovernment in 8,000, 9,000, or 10,000 rubles at a time. This is many times practiced.

10. In these exactions, to show their sovereignty, sometime they use very plain and yet strange cavilations, as was that of Ivan Vasil'evich, father to this emperor, after this sort. He sent into Perm' for certain loads of cedarwood, whereof he knew that none grew in that country. The inhabitants returned answer they could find none there. Whereupon he assessed their country in 12,000 rubles, as if they concealed the commodity of purpose. Again he sent to the city of Moscow to provide for him a kolpak or measure full of live fleas for a medicine. They returned answer that the thing was impossible, and if they could get them, yet they could not measure them for leaping out. Whereupon he praved or beat out of their shins 7,000 rubles for a mulct.

By like cavilation he extorted from his nobility 30,000 rubles because he missed of his game when he went a-hunting for the hare, as if their hunting and murdering of hares had been the cause of it, which the nobility (as the manner is) praved presently again upon the muzhiki or common people of the country. This may seem a strange kind of extortion by such pleasant cavils to fleece his poor subjects in good sadness, but that it agreeth with the quality of those emperors and the miserable subjection of that poor country. These and such like means are practiced by the emperors of Russia to increase their treasury.

Chapter 13. Of the state
of the commonalty, or vulgar sort of people
in the country of Russia

The condition of the commons and vulgar sort of people may partly be understood by that which already hath been said concerning the manner of their government and the state of the nobility with the ordering of their provinces and chief towns of the land. And first touching their liberty how it standeth with them, it may appear by this, that they are reckoned in no degree at all nor have any suffrage nor place in their sobor or high court of parliament where their laws and public orders are concluded upon, which commonly tend to the oppression of the commons. For the other two degrees, viz., of the nobility and clergy, which have a vote in the parliaments (though far from that liberty that ought to be in common consultations for the public benefit according to the measure and proportion of their degrees), are well contented that the whole burden shall light upon the commons, so they may ease their own shoulders by laying all upon them. Again into what servile condition their liberty is brought, not only to the prince but to the nobles and gentlemen of the country (who themselves also are but servile, specially of late years), it may farther appear by their own acknowledgments in their supplications and other writings to any of the nobles or chief officers of the emperors, wherein they name and subscribe themselves kholopy, that is, their villeins or bondslaves, as they of the nobility do unto the emperor. This may truly be said of them, that there is no servant nor bondslave more awed by his master nor kept down in a more servile subjection than the poor people are, and that universally, not only by the emperor but by his nobility, chief officers, and soldiers, so that when a poor muzhik meeteth with any of them upon the highway he must turn himself about, as not daring to look him on the face, and fall down with knocking of his head to the very ground as he doth unto his idol.

Secondly, concerning the lands, goods, and other possessions of the commons, they answer the name and lie common indeed without any fence against the rapine and spoil not only of the highest but of his nobility, officers, and soldiers. Besides the taxes, customs, seizures, and other public exactions done upon them by the emperor, they are so racked and pulled by the nobles, officers, and messengers sent abroad by the emperor in his public affairs, specially in the iamy (as they call them) and through fair towns, that you shall have many villages and towns of half a mile and a mile long stand all uninhabited, the people being fled all into other places by reason of the extreme usage and exactions done upon them. So that in the way towards Moscow, betwixt Vologda and Iaroslavl' (which is two nineties after their reckoning, little more than an hundred miles English), there are in sight fifty *derevni* or villages at the least, some half a mile, some a mile long, that stand vacant and desolate without any inhabitant. The like is in all other places of the realm, as is said by those that have better traveled the country than myself had time or occasion to do.

The great oppression over the poor commons maketh them to have no courage in following their trades, for that the more they have, the more danger they are in, not only of their goods but of their lives also. And if they have anything, they conceal it all they can, sometimes conveying it into monasteries, sometimes hiding it under the ground and in woods, as men are wont to do where they are in fear of foreign invasion. Insomuch that many times you shall see them afraid to be known to any boiar or gentleman of such commodities as they have to sell. I have seen them sometimes when they have laid open their commodities for a liking (as their principal furs and such like) to look still behind them and towards every door, as men in some fear that looked to be set upon and surprised by some enemy. Whereof asking the cause I found it to be this, that they have doubted lest some nobleman or *syn boiarskii* of the emperor had been in the company and so laid a train for them to prey upon their commodities perforce.

This maketh the people (though otherwise hardened to bear any toil) to give themselves much to idleness and drinking, as passing for no more than from hand to mouth. And hereof it cometh that the commodities of Russia (as was said before), as wax, tallow, hides, flax, hemp, etc., grow and go abroad in far less plenty than they were wont to do, because the people, being oppressed and spoiled of their gettings, are discouraged from their labors. Yet this one thing is much to be noted, that in all this oppression there were three brethren merchants of late that traded together with one stock in common that were found to be worth 300,000 rubles in money, besides lands, cattles, and other commodities, which may partly be imputed to their dwellings far off from the eye of the court, viz., in Vychegda, a thousand miles from Moscow and more.[1] The same are said by those that knew them to have set on work all the year long ten thousand men in making of salt, carriages by cart and boat, hewing of wood, and such like, besides 5,000 bondslaves at the least, to inhabit and till their land.[2]

They had also their physicians, surgeons, apothecaries, and all manner of artificers of Dutch and others belonging unto them. They are said to have paid to the emperor for custom to the sum of 23,000 rubles a year (for which cause they were suffered to enjoy their trade), besides the maintaining of certain garrisons on the borders of Siberia which were near unto them. Wherein the emperor was content to use their purse till such time as they had got ground in Siberia and made it habitable by burning and cutting down woods from Vychegda to Perm', above a thousand verst, and then took it all away from them perforce.

But this in the end being envied and disdained as a matter not standing with their policy to have any so great, specially a muzhik, the emperor began first to pull from them by pieces, sometimes 20,000 rubles at a time, sometime more, till in the end their sons that now are, are well eased of their stock and have but small part of their father's substance, the rest being drawn all into the emperor's treasury. Their names were Iakov, Grigorii, and Semen, the sons of Anika.[3]

For the quality of their people otherwise, though there seemeth to be in them some aptness to receive any art (as appeareth by the natural wits in the men and very children), yet they excel in no kind of

1. In this and the following passages, Fletcher refers to the Stroganov family. His information is inaccurate on several counts. First of all, tax records of the late sixteenth century indicate that the Stroganovs paid taxes of approximately 230 rubles a year, not 23,000 as Fletcher claims. Moreover, although the Stroganovs contributed 423,706 rubles in money and goods to the state treasury as part of national reconstruction at the beginning of the seventeenth century, their enterprises continued to grow and thrive after that time (Seredonin, pp. 208–9).

2. Fletcher exaggerates the number of servants and employees of the Stroganovs. The total number of full-time and seasonal workers in the Stroganov enterprises in the late sixteenth century was about 6,000 (Vvedenskii, *Dom Stroganovykh*, p. 39).

3. Anika's sons inherited his enterprises when he died in 1570. None long survived him: Iakov died in 1577, Grigorii in 1578, and Semen was murdered during a revolt of the family's servitors in 1581 (Vvedenskii, *Dom Stroganovykh*, pp. 44–46, 51).

common art, much less in any learning or literal kind of knowledge, which they are kept from of purpose as they are also from all military practice, that they may be fitter for the servile condition wherein now they are and have neither reason nor valor to attempt innovation. For this purpose also they are kept from traveling that they may learn nothing nor see the fashions of other countries abroad. You shall seldom see a Russe a traveler except he be with some ambassador or that he make an escape out of his country, which hardly he can do by reason of the borders that are watched so narrowly and the punishment for any such attempt, which is death if he be taken and all his goods confiscate. Only they learn to write and to read, and that very few of them. Neither do they suffer any stranger willingly to come into their realm out of any civil country for the same cause, farther than necessity of uttering their commodities and taking in of foreign doth enforce them to do.

And therefore this year 1589 they consulted about the removing of all merchants strangers to the border towns to abide and have their residency there and to be more wary in admitting other strangers hereafter into the inland parts of the realm for fear of infection with better manners and qualities than they have of their own.[4] For the same purpose also they are kept within the bounds of their degree by the laws of their country, so that the son of a muzhik, artificer, or husbandman is ever a muzhik, artificer, etc., and hath no means to aspire any higher, except having learned to write and read he attain to the preferment of a priest or d'iak. Their language is all one with the Slavonian, which is thought to have been derived from the Russe tongue rather than the Russe from the Slavonian. For the people called Slav are known to have had their beginning out of Sarmatia and to have termed themselves of their conquest *slava*, that is, famous or glorious, of the word "slava," which in the Russe and Slavonian tongue signifieth as much as glory or fame. Though afterwards, being subdued and trod upon by divers nations, the Italians their neighbors have turned the word to a contrary signification and term every servant or peasant by the name of

4. In a letter to Queen Elizabeth, Fletcher speaks of the tsar's desire to remove the English trade to the coast: "To this purpose the emperor's council consulted at my being there, and conferred with me about the removing of our merchants' trade from Moscow to Archangel, that lieth 30 miles from the port of Saint Nicholas upon the river Dvina, to feel how it would be taken if it were forced by the emperor" (Berry, pp. 379–80).

slavus, as did the Romans by the Geats and Syrians for the same reason.[5] The Russe character or letter is no other than the Greek somewhat distorted.

Concerning their trades, diet, apparel, and such like, it is to be noted in a several[6] chapter of their private behavior. This order that bindeth every man to keep his rank and several degree wherein his forefathers lived before him is more meet to keep the subjects in a servile subjection and so apt for this and like commonwealths than to advance any virtue or to breed any rare or excellent quality in nobility or commons, as having no farther reward nor preferment whereunto they may bend their endeavors and employ themselves to advance their estate, but rather procuring more danger to themselves the more they excel in any noble or principal quality.

Chapter 14. Of their public justice and manner of proceeding in civil and criminal matters

Their courts of civil justice for matters of contract and other of like sort are of three kinds, the one being subject unto the other by way of appeal. The lowest court that seemeth to be appointed for some ease to the subjects is the office of the gubnoi starosta, that signifieth an alderman, and of the sotskii starosta or bailiff of the soke or hundred, whereof I spake before in the ordering of the provinces. These may end matters among their neighbors within their soke or several hundred where they are appointed under the dukes and d'iaki of the provinces, to whom the parties may remove their matter if they cannot be agreed by the said gubnoi or sotskii starosta.

The second is kept in the head towns of every province or shire by the said dukes and d'iaki that are deputies to the four lords of the chetverti, as before was said. From these courts they may appeal and remove their suits to the chief court that is kept at the Moscow, where

5. Fletcher takes this etymology from Cromer, *De origine et rebus gestis Polonorum,* p. 13: "Slauorum autem etymologiam, uel a Slouo, quod uerbum et sermonem: uel a Slaua, quod famam siue gloriam genti significat, omnes deriuant."
6. Separate.

are resident the officers of the four chetverti. These are the chief justices or judges, every one of them, in all civil matters that grow within their several chetvert' or quarter and may be either commenced originally before them or prosecuted out of the inferior courts of the shires by way of appeal.

Their commencing and proceeding in civil actions is on this manner. First, the plaintiff putteth up his supplication wherein he declareth the effect of his cause or wrong done unto him. Whereupon is granted unto him a *vypis'* or warrant which he delivereth to the pristav or sergeant to do the arrest upon the party whom he meaneth to implead, who upon the arrest is to put in sureties to answer the day appointed or else standeth at the sergeant's devotion to be kept safe by such means as he thinketh good.

The sergeants are many and excel for their hard and cruel dealing towards their prisoners. Commonly, they clap irons upon them, as many as they can bear, to wring out of them some larger fees. Though it be but for sixpence, you shall see them go with chains on their legs, arms, and neck. When they come before the judge, the plaintiff beginneth to declare his matter after the content of his supplication. As for attorneys, counselors, procurators, and advocates to plead their cause for them, they have no such order, but every man is to tell his own tale and plead for himself so well as he can.

If they have any witness or other evidence, they produce it before the judge. If they have none or if the truth of the cause cannot so well be discerned by the plea or evidence on both parts, then the judge asketh either party which he thinketh good, plaintiff or defendant, whether he will kiss the cross upon that which he avoucheth or denieth. He that taketh the cross, being so offered by the judge, is accounted clear and carrieth away the matter. This ceremony is not done within the court or office, but the party is carried to the church by an officer and there the ceremony is done, the money in the meanwhile hanging upon a nail or else lying at the idol's feet, ready to be delivered to the party as soon as he hath kissed the cross before the said idol.

This kissing of the cross, called *krestnoe tselovanie,* is as their corporal oath and accounted with them a very holy thing which no man will dare to violate or profane with a false allegation. If both parties offer to kiss the cross in a contradictory matter, then they draw lots. The better lot is supposed to have the right and beareth away the matter, so the party convicted is adjudged to pay the debt or penalty whatsoever and withal to pay the emperor's fees, which is twenty pence upon every mark as before hath been noted.

When the matter is thus ended, the party convicted is delivered to the sergeant, who hath a writ for his warrant out of the office to carry him to the pravezh or righter of justice if presently he pay not the money or content not the party. This pravezh or righter is a place near to the office where such as have sentence passed against them and refuse to pay that which is adjudged are beaten with great cudgels on the shins and calves of their legs. Every forenoon from eight to eleven they are set on the pravezh and beaten in this sort till the money be paid. The afternoon and nighttime they are kept in chains by the sergeant, except they put in sufficient sureties for their appearance at the pravezh at the hour appointed. You shall see forty or fifty stand together on the pravezh all on a row and their shins thus becudgeled and bebasted every morning with a piteous cry. If after a year's standing on the pravezh the party will not or lack wherewithal to satisfy his creditor,[1] it is lawful for him to sell his wife and children, either outright or for a certain term of years. And if the price of them do not amount to the full payment, the creditor may take them to be his bondslaves for years or forever, according as the value of the debt requireth.[2]

Such kind of suits as lack direct evidence or stand upon conjectures and circumstances to be weighed by the judge draw of great length and yield great advantage to the judge and officers. If the suit be upon a bond or bill they have for the most part good and speedy justice. Their bonds or bills are drawn in a very plain sort after this tenor. "I, Ivan Vasil'evich, have borrowed of Afanasii Dementio[3] the sum of one hundred rubles of going money of Moscow, from the *kreshchenie* (or hallowing of the water) until the *Sbornoe Voskresen'e* (or Counsel

1. Legislation of the period usually stipulated one month as the longest period for which the debtor could be subjected to pravezh (*PRP*, IV, 360).

2. Fletcher's remark is not quite accurate. The law stipulated that a debtor who could not meet his obligations was to be given to his creditor to serve as a bondsman until the debt was paid. By the law of 1560, however, a debtor could not be forced to become a permanent bondsman (*polnyi kholop*) (A. Iakovlev, *Kholopstvo i kholopy v moskovskom gosudarstve XVII v.* [Moscow-Leningrad, 1943], I, 49). Kliuchevskii suggests, however, that creditors may have resorted to selling the debtor's wife and children into full bondage in order to get around this law prohibiting the enslaving of the debtor himself ("Proiskhozhdenie krepostnogo prava v Rossii," *Sochineniia*, VII [Moscow, 1959], 259).

3. Perhaps Afanasii Dem'ianov.

Sunday),[4] without interest. And if this money rest unpaid after that day, then he shall give interest upon the said money after the common rate as it goeth among the people, viz., for every five, the sixth ruble. Upon this there are witnesses, Nikita Sidorov, etc. Subscribed: This bill have I written, Gavriil Iakovlev syn, in the year 7096."[5] The witnesses and debtor (if he can write) endorse their names on the back side of the bill. Other signing or sealing have they none.

When any is taken for a matter of crime (as treason, murder, theft, and such like) he is first brought to the duke and d'iak, that are for the province where the party is attached, by whom he is examined. The manner of examination in such cases is all by torture, as scourging with whips made of sinews or white leather (called the pytka) as big as a man's finger, which giveth a sore lash and entereth into the flesh, or by tying to a spit and roasting at the fire, sometimes by breaking and wresting one of their ribs with a pair of hot tongs, or cutting their flesh under the nails, and such like.

The examination thus taken with all the proofs and evidences that can be alleged against the party, it is sent up to the Moscow to the lord of the chetvert', or fourthpart under whom the province is, and by him is presented to the council table to be read and sentenced there, where only judgment is given in matter of life and death and that by evidence upon information, though they never saw nor heard the party, who is kept still in prison where the fact was committed and never sent up to the place where he is tried. If they find the party guilty, they give sentence of death according to the quality of the fact, which is sent down by the lord of the chetvert' to the duke and d'iak to be put in execution.[6] The prisoner is carried to the place of execution with his hands bound and a wax candle burning held betwixt his fingers.

Their capital punishments are hanging, heading, knocking on the head, drowning, putting under the ice, setting on a stake, and such like. But for the most part the prisoners that are condemned in summer are kept for the winter to be knocked in the head and put under the ice. This is to be understood of common persons. For theft and murder,

---

4. The first Sunday in Lent.
5. I.e., 1587/88.
6. The laws against brigandage empowered the local authorities, in some cases the governors and in other cases the elected officials, to pass and execute death sentences without consulting the central administration in advance.

if they be committed upon a poor muzhik by one of nobility, are not lightly punished nor yet is he called to any account for it. Their reason is because they are accounted their kholopy or bondslaves. If by some syn boiarskii or gentleman soldier a murder or theft be committed, peradventure he shall be imprisoned at the emperor's pleasure. If the manner of the fact be very notorious he is whipped perchance, and this is commonly all the punishment that is inflicted upon them.

If a man kill his own servant, little or nothing is said unto him for the same reason, because he is accounted to be his kholop or bondslave and so to have right over his very head. The most is some small mulct to the emperor if the party be rich, and so the quarrel is made rather against the purse than against the injustice. They have no written law, save only a small book that containeth the time and manner of their sitting, order in proceeding, and such other judicial forms and circumstances, but nothing to direct them to give sentence upon right or wrong.[7] Their only law is their *speaking law*, that is, the pleasure of the prince and of his magistrates and officers, which showeth the miserable condition of this poor people, that are forced to have them for their law and direction of justice, against whose injustice and extreme oppression they had need to be armed with many good and strong laws.

Chapter 15. Their forces for the wars, with the chief officers and their salaries

The soldiers of Russia are called syny [deti] boiarskie or the sons of gentlemen, because they are all of that degree by virtue of their military profession. For every soldier in Russia is a gentleman, and none are gentlemen but only the soldiers that take it by descent from their ancestors, so that the son of a gentleman (which is born a soldier) is ever a gentleman and a soldier withal and professeth nothing else but military matters. When they are of years able to bear arms,

7. The Code of 1550 was the basis of Muscovite legal practice at the time of Fletcher's visit. Although its creators concentrated on legal procedure, they also dealt with crimes and their punishment.

they come to the office of razriad or great constable and there present
themselves, who entereth their names and allotteth them certain lands
to maintain their charges, for the most part the same that their fathers
enjoyed.[1] For the lands assigned to maintain the army are ever certain,
annexed to this office without improving or detracting one foot. But
that if the emperor have sufficient in wages, the rooms being full so far
as the land doth extend already, they are many times deferred and
have nothing allowed them except some one portion of the land be divided into two, which is a cause of great disorder within that country
when a soldier that hath many children shall have sometimes but one
entertained in the emperor's pay, so that the rest, having nothing, are
forced to live by unjust and wicked shifts that tend to the hurt and
oppression of the muzhik or common sort of people.[2] This inconvenience groweth by maintaining his forces in a continual succession. The
whole number of his soldiers in continual pay is this. First, he hath of
his *dvoriane,* that is, pensioners or guard of his person, to the number
of 15,000 horsemen with their captains and other officers that are always in a readiness.[3]

Of these 15,000 horsemen there are three sorts or degrees, which differ as well in estimation as in wages one degree from another. The first
sort of them is called *dvoriane bol'shie* or the company of head pensioners that have some an hundred, some fourscore rubles a year, and
none under seventy. The second sort are called *srednie dvoriane* or the
middle rank of pensioners. These have sixty or fifty rubles by the year,
none under forty. The third and lowest sort are the deti boiarskie, that is, the low pensioners. Their salary is thirty rubles a year for

1. Usually officials from Moscow went out to register newcomers to the service
ranks in their own district. The records of the registration were then sent to the
Razriadnyi prikaz (Chernov, *Vooruzhennye sily,* pp. 74–76).

2. Fletcher is essentially correct in his analysis of the pomest'e system in the late
sixteenth century. The land fund available to the government for distribution was
not fixed. The shortage arose from the fact that, although there was plenty of available land in the country as a whole, there was little populated and cultivated land
left to give out in the areas where it was advantageous to settle the members of the
gentry army. Consequently, younger sons of the gentry sometimes received very
small holdings or none at all. (S. V. Rozhdestvenskii, *Sluzhiloe zemlevladenie v
moskovskom gosudarstve XVI veka* [St. Petersburg, 1897], p. 271).

3. Surviving data suggest that there were never 15,000 nobles and deti boiarskie
in the tsar's guard. The figure may be accurate if it includes both the nobles who
served in the tsar's corps (*tsarskii polk*) and their retinues (Seredonin, p. 344). On
the size of the Muscovite army as a whole, see above, p. 27.

him that hath most; some have but five and twenty, some twenty, none under twelve, whereof the half part is paid them at the Moscow, the other half in the field by the general when they have any wars and are employed in service. When they receive their whole pay it amounteth to 55,000 rubles by the year.[4]

And this is their wages, besides lands allotted to every one of them, both to the greater and the less according to their degrees, whereof he that hath least hath to yield him twenty rubles or marks by the year. Besides these 15,000 horsemen that are of better choice (as being the emperor's own guard when himself goeth to the wars, not unlike the Roman soldiers called *Praetoriani*) are a hundred and ten men of special account for their nobility and trust, which are chosen by the emperor and have their names registered, that find among them for the emperor's wars to the number of 65,000 horsemen with all necessaries meet for the wars after the Russe manner.[5]

To this end they have yearly allowance made by the emperor for themselves and their companies to the sum of 40,000 rubles. And these 65,000 are to repair to the field every year on the borders towards the Krym Tatar, except they be appointed for some other service, whether there be wars with the Tatars or not.[6] This might seem peradventure somewhat dangerous for some state to have so great forces under the command of noblemen to assemble every year to one certain place, but the matter is so used as that no danger can grow to the emperor or his state by this means: 1. Because these noblemen are many, to wit, an hundred and ten in all and changed by the emperor so oft as he thinketh good. 2. Because they have their livings of the emperor, being otherwise but of very small revenue, and receive this yearly pay of 40,000

4. Fletcher's figures are not consistent. He states that there were 15,000 nobles and deti boiarskie in the tsar's guard. If the minimum salary of these soldiers were twelve rubles, the total of their salaries would be at least 180,000 rubles, not 55,000 as Fletcher concludes. Moreover, Fletcher's estimate of the salary of the average serving man in the ranks seems too high. Chernov suggests that the ordinary gentleman in service was paid between 4 and 14 rubles a year (*Vooruzhennye sily*, pp. 78–79).

5. Seredonin (p. 345) suggests that Fletcher refers here to the officials who were in charge of overseeing the gentry soldiers of the various regions and paying them their salaries.

6. Fletcher's figure is probably too high to describe the normal distribution of troops. In the early seventeenth century, for example, about 10,000 men were usually stationed on the southern frontier (P. N. Miliukov, *Gosudarstvennoe khoziaistvo Rossii v pervoi chetverti XVIII stoletiia i reforma Petra Velikago* [St. Petersburg, 1905], pp. 33–34).

rubles when it is presently to be paid forth again to the soldiers that are under them. 3. Because for the most part they are about the emperor's person, being of his council either special or at large. 4. They are rather as paymasters than captains to their companies, themselves not going forth ordinarily to the wars, save when some of them are appointed by special order from the emperor himself. So the whole number of horsemen that are ever in a readiness and in continual pay are 80,000, a few more or less.

If he have need of a greater number (which seldom falleth out), then he entertaineth of those syny [deti] boiarskie that are out of pay so many as he needeth; and if yet he want of his number, he giveth charge to his noblemen that hold lands of him to bring into the field every man a proportionable number of his servants (called kholopy, such as till his lands) with their furniture, according to the just number that he intendeth to make, which, the service being done, presently lay in their weapons and return to their servile occupations again.[7]

Of footmen that are in continual pay he hath to the number of 12,000, all gunners called strel'tsy, whereof 5,000 are to attend about the city of Moscow or any other place where the emperor shall abide, and 2,000 (which are called *stremiannye strel'tsy* or gunners at the stirrup) about his own person at the very court or house where himself lodgeth. The rest are placed in his garrison towns till there be occasion to have them in the field and receive for their salary or stipend every man seven rubles a year, besides twelve measures apiece of rye and oats. Of mercenary soldiers that are strangers (whom they call *nemtsy*) they have at this time 4,300 of Poles; of Circassian that are under the Poles about 4,000 whereof 3,500 are abroad in his garrisons;[8] of Dutch and Scots about 150; of Greeks, Turks, Danes, and Swedes, all in one band, an 100 or thereabouts. But these they use only upon the Tatar side and against the Siberians, as they do the Tatar soldiers (whom they hire sometimes but only for the present) on the other side against the Pole and Swede,[9] thinking it best policy so to use their service upon the contrary border.

7. The decree of 1556 obligated all noble landowners to provide one cavalryman for every 100 chetverti of good land he held (*PSRL*, XIII, i, 268–69). Some members of the lower classes also served in the armed forces. The special forces, strel'tsy, and Cossacks were non-noble in origin and the peasantry sometimes had to provide levies of auxiliary troops (Chernov, *Vooruzhennye sily*, pp. 93–94).

8. Presumably Cossacks from the Ukraine.

9. The Muscovite government also made use of Tatar units as guards along the southern frontier.

The chief captains or leaders of these forces, according to their names and degrees, are these which follow. First, the *bol'shoi voevoda*,[10] that is, the great captain or lieutenant general under the emperor. This commonly is one of the four houses of the chief nobility of the land, but so chosen otherwise as that he is of small valor or practice in martial matters, being thought to serve that turn so much the better if he bring no other parts with him save the countenance of his nobility, to be liked of by the soldiers for that and nothing else. For in this point they are very wary, that these two, to wit, nobility and power, meet not both in one, specially if they see wisdom withal or aptness for policy.

Their great voevoda or general at this present in their wars is commonly one of these four: Kniaz' Fedor Ivanovich Mstislavskii, Kniaz' Ivan Mikhailovich Glinskii, Cherkasskii, and Trubetskoi, all of great nobility but of very simple quality otherwise, though in Glinskii (as they say) there is somewhat more than in the rest. To make up this defect in the voevoda or general there is some other joined with him as lieutenant general, of far less nobility but of more valor and experience in the wars than he, who ordereth all things that the other countenanceth. At this time their principal man and most used in their wars is one Kniaz' Dmitrii Ivanovich Khvorostinin, an ancient and expert captain and one that hath done great service (as they say) against the Tatar and Pole.[11] Next under the voevoda and his lieutenant general are four other that have the marshaling of the whole army divided among them and may be called the marshals of the field.

Every man hath his quarter or fourth part under him, whereof the first is called the *pravyi polk* or right wing; the second is the *levyi polk* or left wing; the third is *rusnoy polskoy* or the broken band, because out of this there are chosen to send abroad upon any sudden exploit, or

10. Commander of the great or central corps and commander-in-chief of the whole army.

11. In 1588 and 1589 Mstislavskii commanded the detachments at Serpukhov and the southern army as a whole. Trubetskoi and Cherkasskii, in 1589, were chief commanders in Tula and Novgorod respectively. When the army mustered in 1589/90 for the war with Sweden, Mstislavskii commanded the whole army, Cherkasskii, the tsar's guard, and Trubetskoi, the right wing of the main force. Glinskii held no command positions in these years but had been chief commander on the southern frontier in 1587 (*Sinbirskii sbornik*, p. 93). As Fletcher indicates, Khvorostinin held very important subordinate posts. He was second-in-command at Tula in 1587/88 and again in 1588/89 under Trubetskoi. Later in 1589 he was second-in-command to Cherkasskii in Novgorod; and in the orders for the muster against Sweden in 1589/90, he was designated second-in-command of the forward corps (*RK*, pp. 391, 394, 400–7, 415–17).

to make a rescue, or supply, as occasion doth require; the fourth, *storozhevoi polk* or the warding band.[12] Every one of these four marshals have two other under them (eight in all) that twice every week at the least must muster and train their several wings or bands and hold and give justice for all faults and disorders committed in the camp.

And these eight are commonly chosen out of the one hundred and ten (which I spake of before) that receive and deliver the pay to the soldiers. Under these eight are divers other captains, as the *golovy*, captains of thousands, five hundreds, and hundreds; the *piatidesiatskie*[13] or captains of fifties; and the desiatskie or captains of tens.[14]

Besides the voevoda or general of the army (spoken of before), they have two other that bear the name of voevoda,[15] whereof one is the master of the great ordnance (called *nariadnyi voevoda*), who hath divers under officers necessary for that service; the other is called the *voevoda gulavoy* or the walking captain, that hath allowed him 1,000 good horsemen or principal choice to range and spy abroad and hath the charge of the running castle which we are to speak of in the chapter following. All these captains and men of charge must once every day resort to the bol'shoi voevoda or general of the army to know his pleasure and to inform him if there be any requisite matter pertaining to their office.

12. In the normal alignment of the Muscovite forces, there were five corps in each army. Fletcher omits the *bol'shoi polk* from his list and refers to the advance regiment (*peredovoi polk*) as the *rusnoy polskoy*. The latter term was not used in the documents of the period.

13. Or perhaps *piatidesiatniki* (*Petyde Setskoy* in the original text).

14. Fletcher's list of subordinate officers applies with some accuracy to the units of strel'tsy but not to the rest of the army. The musketeers were divided into units of 100, 50, and 10 under the command of *sotniki, piatidesiatniki,* and *desiatniki* respectively (Seredonin, p. 362). The smallest unit of the gentry cavalry was the *sotnia* or hundred.

15. Actually, each of the five corps of the army was under the command of a voevoda. Usually another voevoda served with each section as well (Seredonin, p. 362).

Chapter 16. Of their mustering and levying of forces, manner of armor, and provision of victual for the wars

When wars are towards, which they fail not of lightly every year with the Tatar and many times with the Pole and Swede, the four lords of the chetverti send forth their summons in the emperor's name to all the dukes and d'iaki of the provinces to be proclaimed in the head towns of every shire that all the syny [deti] boiarskie or sons of gentlemen make their repair to such a border where the service is to be done, at such a place and by such a day, and there present themselves to such and such captains. When they come to the place assigned them in the summons or proclamation, their names are taken by certain officers that have commission for that purpose from the razriad or high constable as clerks of the bands.

If any make default and fail at the day, he is mulcted and punished very severely. As for the general and other chief captains, they are sent thither from the emperor's own hand with such commission and charge as he thinketh behooveful for the present service. When the soldiers are assembled they are reduced into their bands and companies under their several captains of tens, fifties, hundreds, thousands, etc., and these bands into four polki or legions (but of far greater numbers than the Roman legions were) under their four great leaders, which also have the authority of marshals of the field, as was said before.

Concerning their armor, they are but slightly appointed. The common horseman hath nothing else but his bow in his case under his right arm and his quiver and sword hanging on the left side, except some few that bear a case of dags or a javelin or short staff along their horse side. The under captains will have commonly some piece of armor besides, as a shirt of mail or such like. The general with the other chief captains and men of nobility will have their horse very richly furnished, their saddles of cloth of gold, their bridles fair bossed and tasseled with gold and silk fringe, bestudded with pearl and precious stones, themselves in very fair armor, which they call *bulatnyi*, made of fair shining steel, yet covered commonly with cloth of gold and edged round with ermine fur, his steel helmet on his head of a very great price, his sword, bow, and arrows at his side, his spear in his hand, with another fair helmet and his *shestoper* or horseman's scepter carried before him. Their swords, bows, and arrows are of the Turkish fashion. They practice like the Tatar to shoot forwards and backwards as they fly and retire.

The strel'tsy [strelets] or footman hath nothing but his piece in his hand, his striking hatchet at his back, and his sword by his side. The stock of his piece is not made cleaver-wise, but with a plain and straight stock, somewhat like a fowling piece; the barrel is rudely and unartifically made, very heavy, yet shooteth but a very small bullet. As for their provision of victual, the emperor alloweth none either for captain or soldier, neither provideth any for them except peradventure some corn for their money. Every man is to bring sufficient for himself to serve his turn for four months, and, if need require, to give order for more to be brought unto him to the camp from his tenant that tilleth his land or some other place. One great help they have, that for lodging and diet every Russe is prepared to be a soldier beforehand, though the chief captains and other of account carry tents with them after the fashion of ours with some better provision of victual than the rest. They bring with them commonly into the camp for victual a kind of dried bread (which they call *sukhar'*) with some store of meal, which they temper with water and so make it into a ball or small lump of dough called *tolokno*. And this they eat raw instead of bread. Their meat is bacon or some other flesh or fish dried after the Dutch manner. If the Russe soldier were as hardy to execute an enterprise as he is hard to bear out toil and travail, or were otherwise as apt and well trained for the wars as he is indifferent for his lodging and diet, he would far excel the soldiers of our parts. Whereas now he is far meaner of courage and execution in any warlike service, which cometh partly of his servile condition that will not suffer any great courage or valor to grow in him, partly for lack of due honor and reward which he hath no great hope of whatsoever service or execution he do.

Chapter 17. Of their
marching, charging, and other martial discipline

The Russe trusteth rather to his number than to the valor of his soldiers or good ordering of his forces. Their marching or leading is without all order, save that the four polki or legions (whereinto their army is divided) keep themselves several under their ensigns and so thrust all on together in a hurry as they are directed by their general. Their ensign is the image of Saint George. The bol'shie dvoriane or chief horsemen have every man a small drum of brass at his saddle bow, which he striketh when he giveth the charge or onset.

They have drums besides of a huge bigness, which they carry with them upon a board laid on four horses that are sparred together with chains,[1] every drum having eight strikers or drummers, besides trumpets and shawms[2] which they sound after a wild manner much different from ours. When they give any charge or make any invasion, they make a great halloo or shout altogether as loud as they can, which, with the sound of their trumpets, shawms, and drums, maketh a confused and horrible noise. So they set on first discharging their arrows, then dealing with their swords, which they use in a bravery to shake and brandish over their heads before they come to strokes.

Their footmen (because otherwise they want order in leading) are commonly placed in some ambush or place of advantage where they may most annoy the enemy with least hurt to themselves. If it be a set battle or if any great invasion be made upon the Russe borders by the Tatar, they are set within the running or moving castle (called *beza*[3] or *guliai-gorod*) which is carried about with them by the voevoda gulavoy (or the walking general) whom I spake of before. This walking or moving castle is so framed that it may be set up in length (as occasion doth require) the space of one, two, three, four, five, six, or seven miles, for so long it will reach. It is nothing else but a double wall of wood to defend them on both sides behind and before, with a space of

1. Fasten or secure.
2. A wind instrument of the oboe class.
3. There is no such word in modern Russian. Perhaps Fletcher intended *oboz*, which in archaic Russian usage can mean the device he describes.

three yards or thereabouts betwixt the two sides, so that they may
stand within it and have room enough to charge and discharge their
pieces and to use their other weapons. It is closed at both ends and
made with loopholes on either side to lay out the nose of their piece or
to push forth any other weapon. It is carried with the army wheresoever it goeth, being taken into pieces and so laid on carts sparred
together and drawn by horse that are not seen by reason that they are
covered with their carriage as with a shelf or penthouse. When it is
brought to the place where it is to be used (which is devised and chosen out before by the walking voevoda), it is planted so much as the
present use requireth, sometimes a mile long, sometimes two, sometimes three or more, which is soon done without the help of any car-
penter or instrument because the timber is so framed to clasp together
one piece within another, as is easily understood by those that know
the manner of the Russe building.

In this castle standeth their shot, well fenced for advantage, specially against the Tatar that bringeth no ordnance nor other weapon
into the field with him save his sword and bow and arrows. They have
also within it divers field pieces which they use as occasion doth require. Of pieces for the field they carry no great store when they war
against the Tatar; but when they deal with the Pole (of whose forces
they make more account) they go better furnished with all kind of munition and other necessary provisions. It is thought that no prince of
Christendom hath better store of munition than the Russe emperor.
And it may partly appear by the artillery house at Moscow where are
of all sorts of great ordnance, all brass pieces, very fair, to an exceeding great number.

The Russe soldier is thought to be better at his defense within some
castle or town than he is abroad at a set pitched field, which is ever
noted in the practice of his wars, and namely at the siege of Pskov
about eight years since, where he repulsed the Polish king Stephen
Bathory with his whole army of 100,000 men and forced him in the end
to give over his siege with the loss of many of his best captains and
soldiers. But in a set field the Russe is noted to have ever the worse of
the Poles and Swedes.

If any behave himself more valiantly than the rest or do any special
piece of service, the emperor sendeth him a piece of gold stamped
with the image of Saint George on horseback, which they hang on their
sleeves and set in their caps. And this is accounted the greatest honor
they can receive for any service they do.

Chapter 18. Of their colonies
and maintaining of their conquests or purchases
by force

The Russe emperors of late years have very much enlarged their dominions and territories. Their first conquest after the dukedom of Moscow (for before that time they were but dukes of Vladimir, as before was said) was the city and dukedom of Novgorod on the west and northwest side, which was no small enlargement of their dominion and strengthening to them for the winning of the rest. This was done by Ivan, great-grandfather to Fedor now emperor, about the year 1480. The same began likewise to encroach upon the countries of Lithuania[1] and Livonia, but the conquest, only intended and attempted by him upon some part of those countries, was pursued and performed by his son Vasilii, who first won the city and dukedom of Pskov, afterwards the city and dukedom of Smolensk and many other fair towns with a large territory belonging unto them, about the year 1514.[2] These victories against the Letts or Lithuanians in the time of Alexander their duke he achieved rather by advantage of civil dissensions and treasons among themselves than by any great policy or force of his own.[3] But all this was lost again by his son Ivan Vasil'evich, about eight or nine years past, upon composition with the Polish king Stephen Bathory, whereunto he was forced by the advantages which the Pole had then of him by reason of the foil he had given him before and the disquiet-

---

1. In 1478 Ivan III annexed Novgorod, in 1485, Tver'.
2. Pskov was annexed in 1510, Smolensk captured in 1514.
3. Fletcher is here referring to the conquests of Ivan III, not his son Vasilii III. Soon after Alexander (1492–1505) was elected grand duke of Lithuania, Ivan annexed parts of Lithuania along the Ugra and Oka rivers near Dorogobuzh and Mtsensk. To forestall further aggrandizement, Alexander concluded a treaty with Ivan in 1494, by which the areas already gained by Ivan were ceded to him; and in return Ivan agreed to maintain a perpetual peace with Lithuania and to give his daughter, Elena, in marriage to Alexander, provided she would remain free to practice her Orthodox religion. In 1499 the Tatars attacked the southern borders of Lithuania; and Ivan invaded Lithuania, alleging that Alexander had endeavored to regulate Elena's spiritual life and had persecuted members of the Orthodox church. In 1503 a treaty was signed, by which Alexander ceded Novgorod-Severskii, Chernigov, Starodub, Briansk, Dorogobuzh, and several other towns to Ivan.

ness of his own state at home.[4] Only the Russe emperor at this time
hath left him on that side his country the cities of Smolensk, Vitebsk,
Chernigov, and Belgorod in Lithuania, in Livonia, not a town nor one
foot of ground.

When Vasilii first conquered those countries he suffered the natives
to keep their possessions and to inhabit all their towns, only paying
him a tribute under the government of his Russe captains. But by their
conspiracies and attempts not long after he was taught to deal more
surely with them. And so coming upon them the second time, he killed
and carried away with him three parts of four, which he gave or sold
to the Tatars that served him in those wars, and instead of them placed
there his Russes, so many as might overmatch the rest, with certain
garrisons of strength besides. Wherein notwithstanding this oversight
was committed, for that taking away with him the upland or country
people that should have tilled the ground and might easily have been
kept in order without any danger by other good policies, he was driven
afterwards many years together to victual the country (specially the
great towns) out of his own country of Russia, the soil lying there in
the meanwhile waste and untilled.[5]

The like fell out at the port of Narva in Livonia,[6] where his son Ivan
Vasil'evich devised to build a town and a castle on the other side the
river (called Ivangorod) to keep the town and country in subjection.[7]
The castle he caused to be so built and fortified that it was thought to
be invincible. And when it was finished, for reward to the architect
(that was a Pole) he put out both his eyes to make him unable to
build the like again. But having left the natives all within their own
country without abating their number or strength, the town and castle
not long after was betrayed and surrendered again to the king of Sweden.

On the southeast side they have got the kingdoms of Kazan' and As-

4. The war with Poland-Lithuania ended in 1582. Along the Lithuanian frontier,
defeat in the Livonian war cost Ivan his own previous gains but not those of his
father.
5. Perhaps a reference to the policy of Ivan III and Vasilii III of deporting the
leading citizens of the principalities which they annexed and resettling them in the
center of Muscovite territory. Settlers from these central regions were sent to replace
them.
6. Liefland throughout the original text.
7. Ivan III began the construction of Ivangorod in 1492. The fortress was ceded to
Sweden in 1583.

trakhan'. These were won from the Tatar by the late Emperor Ivan Vasil'evich, father to the emperor that now is, the one about thirty-five, the other about thirty-three years ago. Northward out of the country of Siberia he hath laid unto his realm a great breadth and length of ground from Vychegda to the river of Ob, about a thousand miles space, so that he is bold to write himself now "The great commander of Siberia."

The countries likewise of Perm' and Pechora are a divers people and language from the Russe, overcome not long since, and that rather by threatening and shaking of the sword than by any actual force, as being a weak and naked people without means to resist.[8]

That which the Russe hath in his present possession he keepeth on this sort. In his four chief border towns of Pskov, Smolensk, Astrakhan', and Kazan', he hath certain of his council, not of greatest nobility but of greatest trust, which have more authority within their precincts for the countenancing and strengthening of their government there than the other dukes that are set to govern in other places, as was noted before in the manner of ordering their provinces. These he changeth sometime every year, sometime every second or third year, but exceedeth not that time except upon very special trust and good liking of the party and his service, lest by enlarging of their time they might grow into some familiarity with the enemy (as some have done), being so far out of sight.

The towns besides are very strongly fenced with trenches, castles, and store of munition, and have garrisons within them to the number of two or three thousand apiece. They are stored with victual, if any siege should come upon them, for the space of two or three years beforehand. The four castles of Smolensk, Pskov, Kazan', and Astrakhan' he hath made very strong to bear out any siege, so that it is thought that those towns are impregnable.

As for the countries of Pechora and Perm' and that part of Siberia which he hath now under him, they are kept by as easy means as they were first got, viz., rather by showing than by using of arms. First, he hath stored the country with as many Russes as there are natives and hath there some few soldiers in garrison, enough to keep them under. Secondly, his officers and magistrates there are of his own Russe peo-

8. When Ivan III annexed Novgorod, he took over these northern areas that were part of the city's traditional domains. The original inhabitants of Perm' and Pechora were mainly Komi, who speak an Ugro-Finnic language.

ple, and he changeth them very often, viz., every year twice or thrice, notwithstanding there be no great fear of any innovation. Thirdly, he divideth them into many small governments, like a staff broke in many small pieces, so that they have no strength being severed, which was but little neither when they were all in one. Fourthly, he provideth that the people of the country have neither armor nor money, being taxed and pilled so often as he thinketh good, without any means to shake off that yoke or to relieve themselves.

In Siberia (where he goeth on in pursuing his conquest) he hath divers castles and garrisons to the number of six thousand soldiers of Russes and Poles and sendeth many new supplies thither to plant and to inhabit as he winneth ground.[9] At this time besides he hath gotten the king's brother of Siberia, allured by certain of his captains, to leave his own country by offers of great entertainment and pleasanter life with the Russe emperor than he had in Siberia. He was brought in this last year and is now with the emperor at Moscow well entertained.[10]

This may be said of the Russe practice wheresoever he ruleth, either by right of inheritance or by conquest. First, he bereaveth the country of armor and other means of defense, which he permitteth to none but to his boiars only. Secondly, he robbeth them continually of their money and commodities and leaveth them bare with nothing but their bodies and lives, within certain years' compass. Thirdly, he renteth and divideth his territories into many small pieces by several governments, so that none hath much under him to make any strength though he had other opportunities. Fourthly, he governeth his countries by men of small reputation and no power of themselves and strangers in those places where their government lieth. Fifthly, he changeth his governors once a year ordinarily, that there grow no great liking nor entireness betwixt the people and them, nor acquaintance with the enemy if they lie towards the borders. Sixthly, he appointeth in one and the same place adversary governors, the one to be as controller of the other, as the dukes and d'iaki where, by means of their envies and emulations, there is less hurt to be feared by their agreement and himself is better informed what is done amiss. Seventhly, he

9. In the 1580's and 1590's the Muscovite government extended its authority into western Siberia by building a network of military outposts on the main rivers of the region. Tiumen' was founded on the Tura River in 1585 and Tobol'sk in 1587 on the Irtysh River near its junction with the Tobol.

10. Muhammad Kul, nephew of Kuchum, khan of the Tatar principality of Sibir', was captured during Ermak's raid into Siberia in 1582. See Horsey, below, p. 33.

sendeth many times into every province secret messengers of special trust about him, as intelligences to pry and harken out what is doing and what is amiss there. And this is ordinary, though it be sudden and unknown what time they will come.

Chapter 19. Of the Tatars and other borderers to the country of Russia, with whom they have most to do in war and peace

T heir neighbors with whom they have greatest dealings and intercourse, both in peace and war, are first the Tatar; secondly, the Poles whom the Russe calleth *Liakhi,* noting the first author or founder of the nation, who was called Laches or Leches, whereunto is added *po,* which signifieth people, and so is made *Polaches,* that is, the people or posterity of Laches, which the Latins after their manner of writing call *Polanos;*[1] the third are the Swedes. The Poles and Swedes are better known to these parts of Europe than are the Tatars that are farther off from us (as being of Asia) and divided into many tribes, different both in name and government one from another. The greatest and mightiest of them is the Krym Tatar, whom some call the great khan, that lieth south and southeastward from Russia and doth most annoy the country by often invasions, commonly once every year, sometimes entering very far within the inland parts. In the year 1571 he came as far as the city of Moscow with an army of 200,000 men[2] without any battle or resistance at all, for that the Russe emperor (then Ivan Vasil'evich), leading forth his army to encounter with him, marched a wrong way, but as it was thought of very purpose, as not daring to ad-

1. Fletcher follows Cromer's etymology of the word "Polanos" in *De origine et rebus gestis Polonorum,* p. 20: "Duplex autem nominis huius ratio assignatur: uel enim a Pole, quod et planiciem, et uenationem Slauis significat, Polanos et Polacos appellari uolunt, propterea quod et planam fere apertamque regionem ij tenent, et apprime tenentur uenandi studio: uel a conditore ac primo duce gentis Lecho siue Lacho, Polacos, quasi Polachos, hoc est, posteritatem Lachi, dici autumant."
2. This figure is probably much too high. The most reasonable contemporary estimate of the size of the Tatar force is 40,000 ("Poslanie Ioganna Taube i Elerta Kruze" [hereafter Taube & Kruze], *Russkii istoricheskii zhurnal,* Book 8 [1922], 52).

venture the field by reason that he doubted his nobility and chief captains of a meaning to betray him to the Tatar.

The city he took not but fired the suburbs, which by reason of the building (which is all of wood without any stone, brick, or lime, save certain out rooms) kindled so quickly and went on with such rage as that it consumed the greatest part of the city, almost within the space of four hours, being of thirty miles or more of compass. Then might you have seen a lamentable spectacle besides, the huge and mighty flame of the city all on light fire, the people burning in their houses and streets, but most of all of such as labored to pass out of the gates farthest from the enemy, where meeting together in a mighty throng and so pressing every man to prevent another, wedged themselves so fast within the gate and streets near unto it as that three ranks walked one upon the other's head, the uppermost treading down those that were lower, so that there perished at that time (as was said) by the fire and the press the number of 800,000 people or more.[3]

The Krym, thus having fired the city and fed his eyes with the sight of it all on a light flame, returned with his army and sent to the Russe emperor a knife (as was said) to stick himself withal, upbraiding this loss and his desperate case as not daring either to meet his enemy in the field nor to trust his friends or subjects at home.[4] The principal cause of this continual quarrel betwixt the Russe and the Krym is for the right of certain border parts claimed by the Tatar but possessed by the Russe. The Tatar allegeth that besides Astrakhan' and Kazan' (that are the ancient possession of the East Tatar), the whole country from his bounds north and westward so far as the city of Moscow, and Moscow itself, pertaineth to his right, which seemeth to have been true by the report of the Russes themselves that tell of a certain homage that was done by the Russe emperor every year to the great Krym or khan, the Russe emperor standing on foot and feeding the Krym's horse, himself sitting on his back, with oats out of his own cap instead of a bowl or manger, and that within the castle of Moscow. And this homage (they say) was done till the time of Vasilii, grandfather to this man, who, surprising the Krym emperor by a stratagem, done by one of his

3. An absurdly high estimate since the total population of the city was probably a little over 100,000. More reasonable contemporary estimates range from 20,000 to 60,000 (Zimin, *Oprichnina*, p. 457).

4. Fletcher may well have heard this story from Horsey who gives a more melodramatic version in his memoirs. See below, p. 27.

nobility called Ivan Dmitrievich Bel'skii, was content with this ransom, viz., with the changing of this homage into a tribute of furs, which afterwards also was denied to be paid by this emperor's father.[5]

Hereupon they continue the quarrel, the Russe defending his country and that which he hath won, the Krym Tatar invading him once or twice every year, sometime about Whitsuntide but oftener in harvest. What time if the great khan or Krym come in his own person, he bringeth with him a great army of 100,000 or 200,000 men. Otherwise they make short and sudden roads into the country with lesser numbers, running about the list of the border as wild geese fly, invading and retiring where they see advantage.

Their common practice (being very populous) is to make divers armies and, so drawing the Russe to one or two places of the frontiers, to invade at some other place that is left without defense. Their manner of fight or ordering of their forces is much after the Russe manner (spoken of before), save that they are all horsemen and carry nothing else but a bow, a sheaf of arrows, and a falcon sword after the Turkish fashion. They are very expert horsemen and use to shoot as readily backward as forward. Some will have a horseman's staff like to a boar spear besides their other weapons. The common soldier hath no other armor than his ordinary apparel, viz., a black sheepskin with the wool side outward in the day time and inward in the night time, with a cap of the same. But their *mirza*[6] or noblemen imitate the Turk both in apparel and armor. When they are to pass over a river with their army they tie three or four horses together and, taking long poles or pieces of wood, bind them fast to the tails of their horse; so sitting on the poles they drive their horse over. At handy strokes (when they come to join battle) they are accounted far better men than the Russe people, fierce by nature, but more hardy and bloody, by continual practice of war, as men knowing no arts of peace nor any civil practice.

Yet their subtlety is more than may seem to agree with their barbarous condition. By reason they are practiced to invade continually and

5. According to Herberstein, the Tatar invaders received from Vasilii a promise to pay regular tribute. Later when the Crimean forces laid siege to Riazan', the governor of the town tricked the Tatars into giving him the document, then drove them away before they could recover it (Herberstein, II, 64–65). Dmitrii Fedorovich Bel'skii (d. 1551) commanded the Muscovite troops that resisted the Crimean invasion of 1521. He became a boiar in 1522 and thereafter fought many important campaigns including those against Kazan' in 1549 and 1550 (*RBS*).

6. Originally, son of a prince; in common usage, a noble.

to rob their neighbors that border about them, they are very pregnant and ready-witted to devise stratagems upon the sudden for their better advantage, as in their war against Bela, the fourth king of Hungary, whom they invaded with 500,000 men and obtained against him a great victory. Where, among other having slain his chancellor called Nicholas Schinick, they found about him the king's privy seal. Whereupon they devised presently to counterfeit letters in the king's name to the cities and towns next about the place where the field was fought, with charge that in no case they should convey themselves and their goods out of their dwellings, where they might abide safely without all fear of danger, and not leave the country desolate to the possession of so vile and barbarous an enemy as was the Tatar nation, terming themselves in all reproachful manner. For notwithstanding he had lost his carriages with some few stragglers that had marched disorderly, yet he doubted not but to recover that loss with the access of a notable victory if the savage Tatar durst abide him in the field. To this purpose having written their letters in the Polish character, by certain young men whom they took in the field, and signed them with the king's seal, they dispatched them forth to all the quarters of Hungary that lay near about the place. Whereupon the Hungarians that were now flying away with their goods, wives, and children upon the rumor of the king's overthrow, taking comfort of these counterfeit letters, stayed at home, and so were made a prey, being surprised on the sudden by this huge number of these Tatars, that had compassed them about before they were aware.[7]

When they besiege a town or fort they offer much parley and send many flattering messages to persuade a surrender, promising all things that the inhabitants will require; but being once possessed of the place, they use all manner of hostility and cruelty. This they do upon a rule they have, viz., that justice is to be practiced but towards their own. They encounter not lightly but they have some ambush, whereunto, having once showed themselves and made some short conflict, they retire as repulsed for fear and so draw the enemy into it if they can. But the Russe being well acquainted with their practice is more wary of them. When they come a-roving with some small number they set on horseback counterfeit shapes of men that their number may seem greater.

7. The source for this interesting story is Bonfinius, *Rerum Ungaricarum decades quatuor cum dimidia,* p. 296. The invasion took place in 1241.

When they make any onset their manner is to make a great shout, crying all out together "Allah billah, Allah billah"—"God help us, God help us." They condemn death so much as that they choose rather to die than to yield to their enemy and are seen, when they are slain, to bite the very weapon when they are past striking or helping of themselves, wherein appeareth how different the Tatar is in his desperate courage from the Russe and Turk. For the Russe soldier, if he begin once to retire, putteth all his safety in his speedy flight. And if once he be taken by his enemy, he neither defendeth himself nor entreateth for his life, as reckoning straight to die. The Turk commonly when he is past hope of escaping falleth to entreaty and casteth away his weapon, offereth both his hands and holdeth them up, as it were to be tied, hoping to save his life by offering himself bondslave.

The chief booty the Tatars seek for in all their wars is to get store of captives, specially young boys, and girls, whom they sell to the Turks or other their neighbors. To this purpose they take with them great baskets made like bakers' panniers to carry them tenderly; and if any of them happen to tire or to be sick on the way, they dash him against the ground or some tree and so leave him dead. The soldiers are not troubled with keeping the captives and the other booty, for hindering the execution of their wars, but they have certain bands that intend nothing else, appointed of purpose to receive and keep the captives and the other prey.

The Russe borders (being used to their invasions lightly every year in the summer) keep few other cattle on the border parts save swine only, which the Tatar will not touch nor drive away with him, for that he is of the Turkish religion and will eat no swine's flesh. Of Christ our Savior they confess as much as doth the Turk in his *Alcoran*, viz., that he came of the angel Gabriel, and the Virgin Mary, that he was a great prophet and shall be the judge of the world at the last day. In other matters likewise they are much ordered after the manner and direction of the Turk, having felt the Turkish forces when he won from them Azov and Kaffa, with some other towns about the Euxine, or Black Sea, that were before tributaries to the Krym Tatar.[8] So that now the emperor of the Kryms for the most part is chosen some one of the nobility whom the Turk doth commend, whereby it is brought now to that pass that the Krym Tatar giveth to the Turk the tenth part of the spoil which he getteth in his wars against the Christians.

8. The Turks captured Azov in 1471 and Kaffa in 1475.

Herein they differ from the Turkish religion, for that they have certain idol puppets made of silk or like stuff of the fashion of a man which they fasten to the door of their walking houses to be as Januses or keepers of their house. And these idols are made not by all, but by certain religious women which they have among them for that and like uses.[9] They have besides the image of their king or great khan, of an huge bigness, which they erect at every stage when the army marcheth, and this every one must bend and bow unto as he passeth by it, be he Tatar or stranger. They are much given to witchcraft and ominous conjectures upon every accident which they hear or see.

In making of marriages they have no regard of alliance or consanguinity. Only with his mother, sister, and daughter a man may not marry; and though he take the woman into his house and accompany with her, yet he accounteth her not for his wife till he have a child by her. Then he beginneth to take a dowry of her friends of horse, sheep, kine, etc. If she be barren after a certain time, he turneth her home again.

Under the emperor they have certain dukes whom they call mirza or *divei-mirza* that rule over a certain number of 10,000, 20,000, or 40,000 apiece, which they call hordes. When the emperor hath any use of them to serve in his wars, they are bound to come and to bring with them their soldiers to a certain number, every man with his two horses at the least, the one to ride on, the other to kill when it cometh to his turn to have his horse eaten. For their chief victual is horseflesh, which they eat without bread or any other thing with it. So that if a Tatar be taken by a Russe he shall be sure lightly to find a horse leg or some other part of him at his saddle bow.[10]

This last year when I was at the Moscow came in one *Kiriach-mirza*, nephew to the emperor of the Kryms that now is (whose father was emperor before), accompanied with three hundred Tatars and his two wives, whereof one was his brother's widow.[11] Where being enter-

9. John Smith gives a similar description of felt dolls which were objects of veneration. He also states that the Tatars did reverence to fire, air, water, and the dead (*The true travels, adventures and observations of Captain John Smith in Europe, Asia, Africa and America from Anno Domini 1593 to 1629* [London, 1630], pp. 26–27).

10. According to Biezdfedea, Tatar warriors lived on dried millet, mares' milk, cheese, and dried mares' meat while on campaign (Samuel Purchas, *Purchas, His Pilgrimes,* III [London, 1625], 640). *Divei-mirza* is actually a proper name.

11. Perhaps the Crimean prince known to the Russians as "Murza Kirei" who was received by Tsar Fedor on June 21, 1586 (*Sinbirskii sbornik*, p. 91).

tained in very good sort after the Russe manner, he had sent unto his lodging for his welcome, to be made ready for his supper and his companies, two very large and fat horses, ready flayed in a sled. They prefer it before other flesh because the meat is stronger (as they say) than beef, mutton, and such like. And yet (which is marvel), though they serve all as horsemen in the wars and eat all of horseflesh, there are brought yearly to the Moscow to be exchanged for other commodities thirty or forty thousand Tatar horse which they call *koni*. They keep also great herds of kine and stocks of black sheep, rather for the skins and milk (which they carry with them in great bottles) than for the use of the flesh, though sometimes they eat of it. Some use they have of rice, figs, and other fruits. They drink milk or warm blood and for the most part card them both together. They use sometimes as they travel by the way to let their horse blood in a vein and to drink it warm as it cometh from his body.

Towns they plant none nor other standing buildings but have walking houses, which the Latins call *veii*, built upon wheels like a shepherd's cottage. These they draw with them whithersoever they go, driving their cattle with them. And when they come to their stage or standing place, they plant their cart houses very orderly in a rank and so make the form of streets and of a large town.[12] And this is the manner of the emperor himself, who hath no other seat of his empire but an *agora*, or town of wood, that moveth with him whithersoever he goeth. As for the fixed and standing building used in other countries, they say they are unwholesome and unpleasant.

They begin to move their houses and cattle in the springtime from the south part of their country towards the north parts. And so driving on till they have grazed all up to the farthest part northward, they return back again towards their south country (where they continue all the winter) by ten or twelve miles a stage, in the meanwhile the grass being sprung up again to serve for their cattle as they return. From the border of the Shalcan[13] towards the Caspian Sea to the Russe frontiers, they have a goodly country, specially on the south and southeast parts, but lost for lack of tillage.

12. Biezdfedea gives a very similar description of Tatar houses (Purchas III, 633).
13. Probably the principality of Tarki on the coast of the Caspian Sea south of the mouth of the Terek River. The ruler of Tarki was known by the title of *shamkhal*. Russian as well as foreign sources frequently confused the title of the prince with the name of his domain.

Of money they have no use at all and therefore prefer brass and steel before other metals, specially *bulat*,[14] which they use for swords, knives, and other necessaries. As for gold and silver they neglect it of very purpose (as they do all tillage of their ground), to be more free for their wandering kind of life and to keep their country less subject to invasions, which giveth them great advantage against all their neighbors, ever invading and never being invaded.[15] Such as have taken upon them to invade their country (as of old time Cyrus and Darius Hystaspis on the east and southeast side) have done it with very ill success, as we find in the stories written of those times.[16] For their manner is, when any will invade them, to allure and draw them on by flying and recoiling (as if they were afraid) till they have drawn them some good way within their country. Then when they begin to want victual and other necessaries (as needs they must where nothing is to be had) to stop up the passages and enclose them with multitudes. By which stratagem (as we read in Laonicus Chalcocondyles in his Turkish story) they had well nigh surprised the great and huge army of Tamerlane but that he retired with all speed he could towards the river Tanaïs or Don, not without great loss of his men and carriages.[17]

In the story of Pachymeres the Greek (which he wrote of the emperors of Constantinople from the beginning of the reign of Michael Palaeologus to the time of Andronicus the elder) I remember he telleth to the same purpose of one Nogas, a Tatarian captain under Kazan', the emperor of the East Tatars (of whom the city and kingdom of Kazan' may seem to have taken the denomination) who refused a present of pearl and other jewels sent unto him from Michael Palaeologus, asking withal for what use they served and whether they were good to keep away sickness, death, or other misfortunes of this life or no.[18] So that it seemeth they have ever, or long time, been of that mind to value things no further than by the use and necessity for which they serve.

14. Damascus steel.

15. Biezdfedea states that only copper coins were minted in the Crimea. The use of foreign coins of gold and silver was prohibited by law (Purchas III, 640).

16. Herodotus, IV.120–42. It was only because Histaeus of Miletus advised the Ionians not to tear down the bridge across the Ister that Darius escaped from the Scythians.

17. Laonicus Chalcocondyles, *Atheniensis historiarum. Interprete Conrado Clausero* (Paris, 1650), Book III, p. 73. *Tamerlane:* Timur (1336–1405).

18. Georgius Pachymeres, *Michael Palaeologus* (Rome, 1666), p. 237. Michael Palaeologus was emperor of Byzantium, 1261–82. Andronicus II ruled 1282–1328.

For person and complexion they have broad and flat visages of a
tanned color into yellow and black, fierce and cruel looks, thin-haired
upon the upper lip and pit of the chin, light and nimble-bodied with
short legs, as if they were made naturally for horsemen, whereto they
practice themselves from their childhood, seldom going afoot about
any business. Their speech is very sudden and loud, speaking as it
were out of a deep hollow throat. When they sing you would think a
cow lowed or some great bandog howled. Their greatest exercise is
shooting, wherein they train up their children from their very infancy,
not suffering them to eat till they have shot near the mark within a certain scantling. They are the very same that sometimes were called *Scy-
thae nomades,* or the Scythian shepherds, by the Greeks and Latins.[19]
Some think that the Turks took their beginning from the nation of the
Krym Tatars, of which opinion is Laonicus Chalcocondyles, the Greek
historiographer, in his first book of his Turkish story, wherein he followeth divers very probable conjectures, the first taken from the very
name itself, for that the word Turk signifieth a shepherd or one that
followeth a vagrant and wild kind of life.[20] By which name these Scythian Tatars have ever been noted, being called by the Greeks σχύθαι
νόμαδες or the Scythian shepherds. His second reason, because the
Turks (in his time) that dwelt in Asia the less, to wit, in Lydia, Caria,
Phrygia, and Cappadocia, spake the very same language that these Tatars did that dwelt betwixt the river Tanaïs or Don and the country of
Sarmatia, which (as is well known) are these Tatars called Kryms. At
this time also the whole nation of the Turks differ not much in their
common speech from the Tatar language. Thirdly, because the Turk
and the Krym Tatar agree so well together, as well in religion as in
matter of traffic, never invading or injuring one another, save that the
Turk (since Laonicus his time) hath encroached upon some towns
upon the Euxine Sea that before pertained to the Krym Tatar.
Fourthly, because Ortogules,[21] son to Oguzalpes and father to
Othman[22] the first of name of the Turkish nation, made his first roads
out of those parts of Asia upon the next borderers till he came towards

19. Cf. the following passage with Fletcher's *The Tartars or Ten Tribes,* ll. 228–
29 (Berry, p. 326).
20. Chalcocondyles, *Atheniensis historiarum,* Book I, pp. 4–5. Fletcher follows
Chalcocondyles' account very closely. Cf. *The Tartars or Ten Tribes,* ll. 253–76
(Berry, pp. 326–27).
21. Ertogrul, a semi-legendary Turkish leader.
22. Osman I (1288–1326), founder of the Ottoman dynasty.

the countries about the hill Taurus, where he overcame the Greeks that inhabited there and so enlarged the name and territory of the Turkish nation, till he came to Euboea and Attica and other parts of Greece. This is the opinion of Laonicus, who lived among the Turks in the time of Amurat,[23] the sixth Turkish emperor, about the year 1400, when the memory of their original was more fresh and therefore the likelier he was to hit the truth.

There are divers other Tatars that border upon Russia, as the Nogais, the Cheremiss, the Mordvinians, the Circassians, and the Shalcans,[24] which all differ in name more than in regimen or other condition from the Krym Tatar, except the Circassians[25] that border southwest towards Lithuania and are far more civil than the rest of the Tatars, of a comely person and of a stately behavior, as applying themselves to the fashion of the Poles. Some of them have subjected themselves to the kings of Poland and profess Christianity. The Nogais lieth eastward and is reckoned for the best man of war among all the Tatars, but very savage and cruel above all the rest. The Cheremiss Tatar, that lieth betwixt the Russe and the Nogais are of two sorts, the *Lugovoi,* that is, of the valley, and the *Nagornyi,* or of the hilly country.[26] These have much troubled the emperors of Russia. And therefore they are content now to buy peace of them under pretense of giving a yearly pension of Russe commodities to their mirza or divei-mirza that are chief of their tribes. For which also they are bound to serve them in their wars under certain conditions. They are said to be just and true in their dealings, and for that cause they hate the Russe people, whom they account to be double and false in all their dealing. And therefore the common sort are very unwilling to keep agreement with them, but that they are kept in order by their mirza or dukes for their pensions' sake.

The most rude and barbarous is counted the Mordvinian Tatar, that hath many self-fashions and strange kinds of behavior differing from the rest. For his religion, though he acknowledge one god, yet his man-

23. Murad II (1421–51).
24. Presumably the inhabitants of the domains of the Shamkhal of Tarki.
25. Cossacks.
26. On the division of the Cheremiss into two groups, see also Staden, *Aufzeichnungen über den Moskauer Staat,* pp. 13–14. The Lugovoi Cheremiss lived on the lower, that is, the left bank of the middle Volga; the Nagornyi inhabited the right bank.

ner is to worship for god that living thing that he first meeteth in the morning and to swear by it all that whole day, whether it be horse, dog, cat, or whatsoever else it be. When his friend dieth he killeth his best horse; and having flayed off the skin, he carrieth it on high upon a long pole before the corpse to the place of burial. This he doeth (as the Russe sayeth) that his friend may have a good horse to carry him to heaven, but it is likelier to declare his love towards his dead friend in that he will have to die with him the best thing that he hath.

Next to the kingdom of Astrakhan', that is the farthest part south-eastward of the Russe dominion, lieth the Shalcan and the country of Media, whither the Russe merchants trade for raw silks, sindon,[27] saffian, skins, and other commodities. The chief towns of Media where the Russe tradeth are Derbent (built by Alexander the Great as the inhabitants say) and Shemakha, where the staple is kept for raw silks. Their manner is in the springtime to revive the silkworms (that lie dead all the winter) by laying them in the warm sun, and, to hasten their quickening that they may sooner go to work, to put them into bags and so to hang them under their children's arms. As for the worm called *chrivisin* (as we call it crimson) that maketh colored silk, it is bred not in Media but in Assyria. This trade to Derbent and Shemakha for raw silks and other commodities of that country, as also into Persia and Bulgaria down the river Volga and through the Caspian Sea, is permitted as well to the English as to the Russe merchants by the emperor's last grant at my being there, which he accounteth for a very special favor, and might prove indeed very beneficial to our English merchants if the trade were well and orderly used.[28]

The whole nation of the Tatars are utterly void of all learning and without written law.[29] Yet certain rules they have which they hold by tradition, common to all the hordes for the practice of their life, which are of this sort. 1. To obey their emperor and other magistrates whatsoever they command about the public service. 2. Except for the public behoof, every man to be free and out of controlment. 3. No private man to possess any lands but the whole country to be as a common. 4. To neglect all daintiness and variety of meats and to content them-

27. A fine linen fabric.
28. See Tolstoy, p. 347.
29. Biezdfedea, who spent nine months in the Crimea, was impressed by the effectiveness and fairness with which the khans dispensed justice under Islamic law (Purchas III, 638–39).

selves with that which cometh next to hand for more hardness and readiness in the executing of their affairs. 5. To wear any base attire and to patch their clothes, whether there be any need or not, that when there is need it be no shame to wear a patched coat. 6. To take or steal from any stranger whatsoever they can get, as being enemies to all men, save to such as will subject themselves to them. 7. Towards their own horde and nation to be true in word and deed. 8. To suffer no stranger to come within the realm. If any do, the same to be bond-slave to him that first taketh him, except such merchants and other as have the Tatar bull or passport about them.

Chapter 20. Of the Permians, Samoyeds, and Lapps

The Permians and Samoyeds that lie from Russia north and north-east are thought likewise to have taken their beginning from the Tatar kind.[1] And it may partly be guessed by the fashion of their countenance, as having all broad and flat faces as the Tatars have, except the Circassians. The Permians are accounted for a very ancient people. They are now subject to the Russe. They live by hunting and trading with their furs, as doth also the Samoyed that dwelleth more towards the North Sea. The Samoyed hath his name (as the Russe saith) of eating himself, as if in times past they lived as the cannibals, eating one another, which they make more probable because at this time they eat all kind of raw flesh whatsoever it be, even the very carrion that lieth in the ditch. But as the Samoyeds themselves will say, they were called Samoie, that is, of themselves, as though they were *indigenae* or people bred upon that very soil that never changed their seat from one place to another as most nations have done. They are subject at this time to the emperor of Russia.

I talked with certain of them and find that they acknowledge one god but represent him by such things as they have most use and good by, and therefore they worship the sun, the olen', the los', and such like. As for the story of Zlata Baba or the Golden Hag (which I have read

1. The Permians or Komi are a people of the Ugro-Finnic language group and the Samoyeds are several related groups that speak Uralic languages.

in some maps[2] and descriptions of these countries to be an idol after the form of an old woman) that, being demanded by the priest, giveth them certain oracles concerning the success and event of things, I found it to be but a very fable. Only in the province of Obdoria upon the seaside near to the mouth of the great river Ob there is a rock which naturally (being somewhat helped by imagination) may seem to bear the shape of a ragged woman with a child in her arms (as the rock by the North Cape the shape of a friar), where the Obdorian Samoyeds use much to resort by reason of the commodity of the place for fishing, and there sometime (as their manner is) conceive and practice their sorceries and ominous conjecturings about the good or bad speed of their journeys, fishings, huntings, and such like.

They are clad in sealskins, with the hairy side outwards, down as low as the knees, with their breeches and netherstocks of the same, both men and women. They are all black-haired, naturally beardless. And therefore the men are hardly discerned from the women by their looks, save that the women wear a lock of hair down along both their ears. They live in a manner a wild and a savage life, roving still from one place of the country to another without any property of house or land more to one than to another. Their leader or director in every company is their *pop* or priest.

On the north side of Russia next to Karelia lieth the country of Lappia, which reacheth in length from the farthest point northward (towards the North Cape) to the farthest part southeast (which the Russe calleth Sviatoi Nos or Holy Nose, the Englishmen, Cape Grace) about 345 verst or miles. From Sviatoi Nos to Kandalaksha by the way of Varzuga (which measureth the breadth of that country) is ninety miles or thereabouts.[3] The whole country in a manner is either lakes or mountains, which towards the seaside are called Tundra[4] because they are all of hard and craggy rock, but the inland parts are well furnished with woods that grow on the hills' sides, the lakes lying between. Their

2. Herberstein in his map of 1549 only shows the figure of Zlata Baba, but Anton Wied's map of 1555 and Jenkinson's map of 1562 have descriptions below the figure.

3. The length of the coast of the Kola Peninsula from Sviatoi Nos to Kandalaksha is about 640 versts or about 415 miles (Serbina [ed.], *Kniga Bol'shomu Chertezhu,* pp. 149–50). The distance overland from Sviatoi Nos to Varzuga and thence to Kandalaksha is considerably shorter but still a good deal more than Fletcher suggests.

4. Fletcher uses the generic Russian term for the Arctic plain as the proper name of the coastal mountains.

diet is very bare and simple. Bread they have none but feed only upon fish and fowl. They are subject to the emperor of Russia and the two kings of Sweden and Denmark, which all exact tribute and custom of them (as was said before), but the emperor of Russia beareth the greatest hand over them and exact of them far more than the rest. The opinion is that they were first termed Lapps of their brief and short speech. The Russe divideth the whole nation of the Lapps into two sorts. The one they call *Novremanskoy* [*Norvezhskie*] *Lopari,* that is, the Norwegian Lapps, because they be of the Danish religion.[5] For the Danes and Norwegians they account for one people. The other that have no religion at all, but live as brute and heathenish people without God in the world, they call *dikie Lopari* or the wild Lapps.

The whole nation is utterly unlearned, having not so much as the use of any alphabet or letter among them. For practice of witchcraft and sorcery they pass all nations in the world, though for the enchanting of ships that sail along their coast (as I have heard it reported) and their giving of winds good to their friends and contrary to other whom they mean to hurt by tying of certain knots upon a rope (somewhat like to the tale of Aeolus his windbag) is a very fable, devised (as may seem) by themselves to terrify sailors for coming near their coast. Their weapons are the longbow and handgun, wherein they excel, as well for quickness to charge and discharge as for nearness at the mark, by reason of their continual practice (whereto they are forced) of shooting at wild fowl. Their manner is in summertime to come down in great companies to the seaside, to Vardo, Kola, Kegor, and the bay of Vaida Guba,[6] and there to fish for cod, salmon, and buttfish, which they sell to the Russes, Danes, and Norwegians, and now of late to the Englishmen that trade thither with cloth, which they

5. The Norwegians first attempted to Christianize the Lapps in the thirteenth century (Bjorn Collinder, *The Lapps* [Princeton, N.J., 1949], p. 19). The most celebrated early Russian missionaries to the Lapps were the sixteenth-century monks, Theodorit and Trifon. Theodorit, a monk of the Solovetskii Monastery, carried on his mission from a hermitage on the Kola River for roughly two decades after 1527 and is reputed to have won over two thousand converts. From about 1520 until his death in 1583, Trifon worked from a settlement on the Pechenga River that grew into the Pechenga Monastery (P. Shestakov, "Prosvetiteli loparei archimandrit Feodorit i sv. Trifon pechengskii," *Zhurnal Ministerstva narodnago prosveshcheniia,* CXXXIX [1868], 242–96).

6. A small inlet on the northwest corner of the Rybachii Peninsula and the settlement on its shore.

exchange with the Lapps and Karelians for their fish, oil, and furs, whereof also they have some store. They hold their mart at Kola on Saint Peter's Day, what time the Captain of Vardo (that is resident there for the king of Denmark) must be present, or at least send his deputy, to set prices upon their stockfish, train oil, furs, and other commodities, as also the Russe emperor's customer or tribute-taker to receive his custom, which is ever paid before anything can be bought or sold. When their fishing is done, their manner is to draw their carbasses[7] or boats on shore, and there to leave them with the keel turned upwards till the next springtide. Their travel to and fro is upon sleds drawn by the olen' deer, which they use to turn a-grazing all the summertime in an island called Kil'din (of a very good soil compared with other parts of that country), and towards the wintertime when the snow beginneth to fall they fetch them home again for the use of their sled.

Chapter 21. Of their ecclesiastical state, with their church offices

Concerning the government of their church, it is framed altogether after the manner of the Greek, as being a part of that church and never acknowledging the jurisdiction of the Latin church usurped by the Pope. That I may keep a better measure in describing their ceremonies than they in the using them (wherein they are infinite), I will note briefly: first, what ecclesiastical degrees or offices they have with the jurisdiction and practice of them; secondly, what doctrine they hold in matter of religion; thirdly, what liturgy or form of service they use in their churches with the manner of their administering the sacraments; fourthly, what other strange ceremonies and superstitious devotions are used among them.

Their offices or degrees of churchmen are as many in number and the same in a manner both in name and degree that were in the western churches. First they have their patriarch, then their metropolitans,

7. From the archaic Russian word *karbas*, a large rowboat with sails, used to transport goods on the White Sea and the northern rivers.

their archbishops, their *vladyki* or bishops, their *protopopy* or archpriests, their *popy* or priests, their deacons, friars, monks, nuns, and eremites.

Their patriarch or chief director in matter of religion until this last
year was of the city of Constantinople, whom they called the patriarch
of Scio because, being driven by the Turk out of Constantinople (the
seat of his empire), he removed to the isle Scio, sometimes called
Chios, and there placed his patriarchal see, so that the emperors and
clergy of Russia were wont yearly to send gifts thither and to acknowledge a spiritual kind of homage and subjection due to him and to that
church.[1] Which custom they have held (as it seemeth) ever since they
professed the Christian religion. Which how long it hath been I could
not well learn, for that they have no story or monument of antiquity
(that I could hear of) to show what hath been done in times past
within their country concerning either church or commonwealth
matters.[2] Only I hear a report among them that about three hundred
years since there was a marriage betwixt the emperor of Constantinople and the king's daughter of that country, who at the first denied to
join his daughter in marriage with the Greek emperor because he was
of the Christian religion. Which agreeth well with that I find in the
story of Laonicus Chalcocondyles concerning Turkish affairs in his
fourth book, where he speaketh of such a marriage betwixt John, the
Greek emperor, and the king's daughter of Sarmatia.[3] And this argueth
out of their own report that at that time they had not received the
Christian religion, as also that they were converted to the faith and withal perverted at the very same time, receiving the doctrine of the gospel corrupted with superstitions even at the first when they took it from
the Greek church, which itself then was degenerate and corrupted with
many superstitions and foul errors both in doctrine and discipline, as
may appear by the story of Nicephorus Gregoras in his eighth and

1. The patriarchal see was located in Constantinople. Fletcher may have been
misled by an incident in the career of Jeremiah II. Before his journey to Russia,
Jeremiah was deposed twice, in 1579–80 and 1584–86. On the second occasion, he
was exiled to Rhodes. In 1586 he was restored to the patriarchal throne.

2. The conventional date for the conversion of Russia is 988. Fletcher was ap-
parently unaware of the extensive chronicle account of the conversion of Vladimir.
His ignorance of the existence of Russian chronicles is difficult to explain since
Horsey knew of them and claimed to have read them.

3. Chalcocondyles, *Atheniensis historiarum,* Book IV, p. 92. A reference to the
marriage of Emperor John VIII (1425–48) and Anna, daughter of Vasilii I of
Moscow.

ninth books.[4] But as touching the time of their conversion to the Christian faith, I suppose rather that it is mistaken by the Russe for that which I find in the Polish story, the second book, the third chapter, where is said that about the year 990 Vladimir, duke of Russia, married one Anne, sister to Basil and Constantinus, brothers and emperors of Constantinople.[5] Whereupon the Russe received the faith and profession of Christ, which though it be somewhat more ancient than the time noted before out of the Russe report,[6] yet it falleth out all to one reckoning touching this point, viz., in what truth and sincerity of doctrine the Russe received the first stamp of religion, for as much as the Greek church at that time also was many ways infected with error and superstition.

At my being there, the year 1588, came unto the Moscow the patriarch of Constantinople or Scio called Jeremiah, being banished (as some said) by the Turk, as some other reported, by the Greek clergy deprived. The emperor, being given altogether to superstitious devotions, gave him great entertainment. Before his coming to Moscow he had been in Italy with the Pope as was reported there by some of his company.[7] His errand was to consult with the emperor concerning these points. First, about a league to pass betwixt him and the king of Spain, as the meetest prince to join with him in opposition against the Turk. To which purpose also ambassages had passed betwixt the Russe and the Persian.[8] Likewise from the Georgians to the emperor of Russia to join league together for the invading of the Turk on all sides of his dominions, taking the advantage of the simple quality of the Turk that now is.[9] This treaty was helped forward by the emperor's ambas-

4. Nicephori Gregorae, *Romanae hoc est Byzantinae historiae libri XI* (Basel, 1562), Books VIII–IX, pp. 127–210.

5. Cromer, *De origine et rebus gestis Polonorum*, pp. 49–50. The rulers referred to are Vladimir I (978–1015), Basil II Bulgaroctonus (976–1025), and Constantine VIII (976–1028).

6. The Russian Primary Chronicle tells the same story but assigns it to the year 988 (Likhachev [ed.], *Povest' vremennykh let*, I, 76–77).

7. When he visited Moscow, Jeremiah was patriarch. There is no evidence that he had previously been in Italy. His appearance in Moscow apparently had no connection with the attempts of the Hapsburgs to draw Russia into an anti-Turkish alliance.

8. Between 1587 and 1590 the Muscovite government negotiated with Persia for the formation of an anti-Turkish alliance. The alliance was, however, never formally concluded.

9. The Muscovite government made an alliance with the Caucasian principality of Kakhetia in 1587.

sador of Almaine, sent at the same time to solicit an invasion upon the
parts of Poland that lie towards Russia and to borrow money of the
Russe emperor to pursue the war for his brother Maximilian against
the Sweden's son, now king of Poland.[10] But this consultation concerning a league betwixt the Russe and the Spaniard (which was in some
forwardness at my coming to Moscow and already one appointed for
ambassage into Spain)[11] was marred by means of the overthrow
given to the Spanish king by her majesty the queen of England this
last year,[12] which made the Russe emperor and his council to give a
sadder countenance to the English ambassador at that time, for that
they were disappointed of so good a policy as was this conjunction supposed to be betwixt them and the Spanish.

His second purpose (whereto the first served as an introduction)
was, in revenge of the Turk and the Greek clergy that had thrust him
from his seat, to treat with them about the reducing of the Russe
church under the Pope of Rome. Wherein it may seem that coming
lately from Rome he was set on by the Pope, who hath attempted the
same many times before, though all in vain, and namely in the time of
the late Emperor Ivan Vasil'evich by one Anthony[13] his legate, but
thought this belike a far better means to obtain his purpose by treaty
and mediation of their own patriarch. But this not succeeding, the patriarch fell to a third point of treaty concerning the resignation of his
patriarchship and translation of the see from Constantinople or Scio to
the city of Moscow, which was so well liked and entertained by the
emperor (as a matter of high religion and policy) that no other treaty
(specially of foreign ambassages) could be heard or regarded till that
matter was concluded.[14]

10. A reference to Warkotsch's visit to Moscow in 1589. Maximilian was younger
brother of Emperor Rudolf II (1576–1612), and a contender for the Polish throne
in the interregnum following the death of Stephen Bathory in 1586. One Polish
faction proclaimed him king but the nobles who supported Sigismund Vasa rallied
and won the decisive battle with Maximilian's supporters in 1588. The Hapsburg
prince was imprisoned and went free in 1589 only at the cost of renouncing his
claims to the throne. Sigismund III Vasa reigned until 1632.

11. Petr Ragon, the tsar's interpreter.

12. The defeat of the Spanish Armada in 1588.

13. Antonio Possevino, who in 1582 mediated the truce between Muscovy and
Poland-Lithuania.

14. The issue was not the resignation of the existing patriarch of Constantinople
but rather the creation of an entirely new office, patriarch of Moscow. N. F. Kapterev
suggests that Fletcher may have confused the desire of the Russian government

The reasons wherewith the patriarch persuaded the translating of his see to the city of Moscow were these in effect. First, for that the see of the patriarch was under the Turk that is enemy to the faith and therefore to be removed into some other country of Christian profession. Secondly, because the Russe church was the only natural daughter of the Greek at this time and holdeth the same doctrine and ceremonies with it, the rest being all subject to the Turk and fallen away from the right profession. Wherein the subtle Greek to make the better market of his broken ware advanced the honor that would grow to the emperor and his country to have the patriarch's seat translated into the chief city and seat of his empire. As for the right of translating the see and appointing his successor he made no doubt of it but that it pertained wholly to himself.

So the emperor and his council with the principal of his clergy being assembled at the Moscow, it was determined that the metropolitan of Moscow should become patriarch of the whole Greek church and have the same full authority and jurisdiction that pertained before to the patriarch of Constantinople or Scio.[15] And that it might be done with more order and solemnity, the 25 of January 1588,[16] the Greek patriarch, accompanied with the Russe clergy, went to the great church of Precheste, or Our Lady, within the emperor's castle (having first wandered through the whole city in manner of a procession and blessing the people with his two fingers), where he made an oration and delivered his resignation in an instrument of writing and so laid down his patriarchal staff, which was presently received by the metropolitan of Moscow and divers other ceremonies used about the inauguration of this new patriarch.

The day was held very solemn by the people of the city, who were commanded to forebear their works and to attend this solemnity. The Greek patriarch that day was honored with rich presents sent him from the emperor and empress, of plate, cloth of gold, furs, etc., carried with great pomp through the streets of Moscow, and at his departing received many gifts more both from the emperor, nobility, and clergy.

and hierarchy to bring the premier patriarchate to Moscow with what actually happened (*Kharakter otnoshenii Rossii k pravoslavnomu vostoku v XVI i XVII stoletiiakh* [Sergiev Posad, 1914], p. 53).

15. The new patriarch of Moscow was one of five patriarchs of the Orthodox church. The patriarch of Constantinople continued to be recognized as the first among them.

16. Actually January 26, 1589 (Makarii, *Istoriia russkoi tserkvi*, X, 26).

Thus the patriarchship of Constantinople or Scio (which hath continued since the Council of Nicaea)[17] is now translated to Moscow, or
they made believe that they have a patriarch with the same right and
authority that the other had, wherein the subtle Greek hath made good
advantage of their superstition and is now gone away with a rich booty
into Poland, whether their patriarchship be current or not.

The matter is not unlike to make some schism betwixt the Greek and
Russe church if the Russe hold this patriarchship that he hath so well
paid for and the Greeks elect another withal as likely they will,
whether this man were banished by the Turk or deprived by order of
his own clergy,[18] which might happen to give advantage to the Pope
and to bring over the Russe church to the see of Rome (to which end
peradventure he devised this stratagem and cast in this matter of
schism among them) but that the emperors of Russia know well
enough by the example of other Christian princes what inconvenience
would grow to their state and country by subjecting themselves to the
Romish see. To which end the late Emperor Ivan Vasil'evich was very
inquisitive of the Pope's authority over the princes of Christendom and
sent one of very purpose to Rome to behold the order and behavior of
his court.[19]

With this patriarch Jeremiah was driven out at the same time by the
great Turk, one Demetrio, archbishop of Larissa, who is now in England and pretendeth the same cause of their banishment by the Turk,
to wit, their not admitting of the Pope's new calendar[20] for the alteration of the year, which how unlikely it is may appear by these circumstances. First, because there is no such affection nor friendly respect
betwixt the Pope and the Turk as that he should banish a subject for

17. At the Council of Nicaea (325) and at the Council of Constantinople (381),
the patriarch of Constantinople was granted the place of honor next to the bishop
of Rome.

18. After the creation of the patriarchate of Moscow, the main point of dispute
between Moscow and Constantinople was the question of the proper place of the
Moscow patriarchate in the hierarchy of patriarchal sees.

19. Perhaps a reference to the diplomatic mission of Istoma Shevrigin to Rome
in 1581. The envoy was instructed to remind the Pope of the previous relations
between Moscow and the Holy See and to elicit his support for the tsar's attempts
to end the Livonian War which had taken a disastrous turn. In particular, the
Muscovite government requested the Pope to use his influence with the king of
Poland to persuade him to end the war with Muscovy (PDS, X, 1–38).

20. Jeremiah, in a circular letter, prohibited the introduction of the Gregorian
calendar (A. N. Mouravieff, A History of the Church of Russia [trans. R. W. Black-
more; Oxford, 1842], p. 136).

not obeying the Pope's ordinance, specially in a matter of some sequel for the alteration of times within his own countries. Secondly, for that he maketh no such scruple in deducting of times and keeping of a just and precise account from the incarnation of Christ, whom he doth not acknowledge otherwise than I noted before. Thirdly, for that the said patriarch is now at Naples in Italy, where it may be guessed he would not have gone within the Pope's reach and so near to his nose if he had been banished for opposing himself against the Pope's decree.[21]

This office of patriarchship now translated to Moscow beareth a superior authority over all the churches not only of Russia and other the emperor's dominions but throughout all the churches of Christendom that were before under the patriarch of Constantinople or Scio, or at least the Russe patriarch imagineth himself to have the same authority. He hath under him as his proper diocese the province of Moscow, besides other peculiars. His court or office is kept at the Moscow.

Before the creation of this new patriarch they had but one metropolitan that was called the metropolitan of Moscow. Now for more state to their church and new patriarch they have two metropolitans, the one of Novgorod Velikii, the other of Rostov.[22] Their office is to receive of the patriarch such ecclesiastical orders as he thinketh good and to deliver the charge of them over to the archbishops, besides the ordering of their own diocese.

Their archbishops are four: of Smolensk, Kazan', Pskov, and Vologda. The parts of their office is all one with the metropolitans, save that they have an under-jurisdiction as suffragans to the metropolitans and superiors to the bishops. The next are the vladyki or bishops that are but six in all: of Krutitskii [diocese], of Riazan', of Tver' and Torzhok, of Kolomenskii [diocese], of Vladimir, of Suzdal'.[23] These have every one a very large diocese, as dividing the rest of the whole country among them.

The matters pertaining to the ecclesiastical jurisdiction of the metropolitans, archbishops, and bishops are the same in a manner that are

21. Patriarch Jeremiah returned to Constantinople and was still there when Fletcher's book was published.

22. In 1589 the archbishops of Novgorod, Rostov, Kazan', and Krutitsa were raised to the dignity of metropolitan.

23. After the church council of 1589, there were six archbishops (of Nizhnii-Novgorod, Riazan', Tver', Smolensk, Suzdal', and Vologda), and eight bishops (of Kolomna, Pskov, Rzhev, Ustiug Velikii, Beloozero, Briansk, Dmitrov, and an unnamed see [Chernigov]) (Sobranie gosudarstvennykh gramot i dogorov, II, 98–99).

used by the clergy in other parts of Christendom. For besides their authority over the clergy and ordering such matters as are mere ecclesiastical, their jurisdiction extendeth to all testamentary causes, matters of marriage and divorcements, some pleas of injuries, etc. To which purpose also they have their officials or commissaries (which they call *boiarin* [*boiare*] *vladychnye*) that are laymen of the degree of dukes or gentlemen that keep their courts and execute their jurisdiction, which, besides their other oppressions over the common people, reign over the priests as the dukes and d'iaki do over the poor people within their precincts. As for the archbishop or bishop himself, he beareth no sway in deciding those causes that are brought into his court. But if he would moderate any matter he must do it by entreaty with his gentleman official. The reason is because these boiars or gentlemen officials are not appointed by the bishops but by the emperor himself or his council and are to give account of their doings to none but to them. If the bishop can entreat at his admission to have the choice of his own official it is accounted for a special great favor.[24] But to speak it as it is, the clergy of Russia, as well concerning their lands and revenues as their authority and jurisdiction, are altogether ordered and overruled by the emperor and his council, and have so much and no more of both as their pleasure doth permit them. They have also their assistants or several councils (as they call them) of certain priests that are of their diocese, residing within their cathedral cities, to the number of four and twenty apiece.[25] These advise with them about the special and necessary matters belonging to their charge.

Concerning their rents and revenues to maintain their dignities, it is somewhat large. The patriarch's yearly rents out of his lands (besides other fees) is about 3,000 rubles or marks, the metropolitans' and archbishops' about 2,500, the bishops', some a 1,000, some 800, some 500, etc. They have had some of them (as I have heard say) ten or twelve thousand rubles a year, as had the metropolitan of Novgorod.

Their habit or apparel (when they show themselves in their pontificalibus after their solemnest manner) is a miter on their heads after the popish fashion, set with pearl and precious stone, a cope on their

24. Fletcher somewhat exaggerates the powers of the lay officials of the church. They performed their functions under the supervision of the bishops and were, for example, not empowered to judge cases of a purely religious nature.

25. The number of members of a bishop's council was variable. In 1594, for example, the council in Moscow had 52 members of various ranks (Seredonin, p. 296).

backs, commonly of cloth of gold embroidered with pearl, and a cro-
sier's staff in their hands, laid overall with plate of silver double gilded,
with a cross or shepherd's crook at the upper end of it. Their ordinary
habit otherwise when they ride or go abroad is a hood on their heads
of black color that hangeth down their backs and standeth out like a
bongrace[26] before. Their upper garment (which they call *riasa*) is a
gown or mantle of black damask with many lists or guards of white
satin laid upon it, every guard about two fingers broad, and their cro-
sier's staff carried before them. Themselves follow after, blessing the
people with their two forefingers with a marvelous grace.

The election and appointing of the bishops and the rest pertaineth
wholly to the emperor himself. They are chosen ever out of the monasteries, so that there is no bishop, archbishop, nor metropolitan but hath
been a monk or friar before. And by that reason they are and must all
be unmarried men, for their vow of chastity when they were first shorn.
When the emperor hath appointed whom he thinketh good, he is invested in the cathedral church of his diocese with many ceremonies,
much after the manner of the popish inauguration. They have also
their deans and their archdeacons.

As for preaching the word of God or any teaching or exhorting such
as are under them, they neither use it nor have any skill of it, the
whole clergy being utterly unlearned both for other knowledge and in
the word of God. Only their manner is twice every year, viz., the first
of September (which is the first day of their year) and on Saint John
Baptist's Day, to make an ordinary speech to the people, every metropolitan, archbishop, and bishop in his cathedral church, to this or like
effect: "That if any be in malice towards his neighbor, he shall leave
off his malice; if any have thought of treason or rebellion against his
prince, he beware of such practice; if he have not kept his fasts and
vows nor done his other duties to the Holy Church, he shall amend
that fault," etc. And this is a matter of form with them, uttered in as
many words and no more in a manner than I have here set down. Yet
the matter is done with that grace and solemnity in a pulpit of purpose
set up for this one act as if he were to discourse at large of the whole
substance of divinity. At the Moscow the emperor himself is ever present at this solemn exhortation.

26. A shade or curtain worn on the front of women's bonnets to protect the complexion from the sun.

As themselves are void of all manner of learning, so are they wary
to keep out all means that might bring any in, as fearing to have their
ignorance and ungodliness discovered. To that purpose they have persuaded the emperors that it would breed innovation and so danger to
their state to have any novelty of learning come within the realm.
Wherein they say but truth, for that a man of spirit and understanding,
helped by learning and liberal education, can hardly endure a tyrannical government. Some years past in the other emperor's time there
came a press and letters out of Poland to the city of Moscow, where a
printing house was set up with great liking and allowance of the emperor himself. But not long after the house was set on fire in the nighttime, and the press and letters quite burnt up, as was thought by the
procurement of the clergymen.[27]

Their priests (whom they call popy) are made by the bishops without any great trial for worthiness of gifts before they admit them or
ceremonies in their admission, save that their heads are shorn (not
shaven for that they like not) about an hand breadth or more in the
crown and that place anointed with oil by the bishop, who in his admission putteth upon the priest first his surplice, and then setteth a
white cross on his breast of silk or some other matter, which he is to
wear eight days and no more, and so giveth him authority to say and
sing in the church and to administer the sacraments.[28]

They are men utterly unlearned, which is no marvel forasmuch as
their makers, the bishops themselves (as before was said), are clear of
that quality and make no farther use at all of any kind of learning, no,
not of the scriptures themselves, save to read and to sing them. Their
ordinary charge and function is to say the liturgy, to administer the sacraments after their manner, to keep and deck their idols, and to do
the other ceremonies usual in their churches. Their number is great because their towns are parted into many small parishes without any discretion for dividing them into competent numbers of households and
people for a just congregation, as the manner in all places where the
means is neglected for increasing of knowledge and instruction towards

27. The first printing press in Moscow was established by Ivan Fedorov in 1553.
Ivan IV encouraged his efforts which led to the founding of an official printing
office in 1563. The first printers abruptly moved their operations to Lithuania in
1565, quite possibly because of incidents such as Fletcher describes. Printing was
resumed in Moscow three years later and thereafter continued without interruption
(Tikhomirov, p. 97).

28. In the Orthodox service, the candidate for priestly orders is neither tonsured
nor anointed with oil.

God, which cannot well be had where, by means of an unequal partition of the people and parishes, there followeth a want and unequality of stipend for a sufficient ministry.

For their priests it is lawful to marry for the first time. But if the first wife die a second he cannot take but he must lose his priesthood and his living withal.[29] The reason they make out of that place of Saint Paul to Timothy (I. 3:2), not well understood, thinking that to be spoken of divers wives successively that the apostle speaketh of at one and the same time.[30] If he will needs marry again after his first wife is dead, he is no longer called pop but *raspop* or priest quondam. This maketh the priests to make much of their wives, who are accounted as the matrons and of best reputation among the women of the parish.

For the stipend of the priest their manner is not to pay him any tenths of corn or ought else, but he must stand at the devotion of the people of his parish and make up the incomes towards his maintenance so well as he can by offerings, shrifts, marriages, burials, dirges, and prayers for the dead and the living, which they call *molitva*. For, besides their public service within their churches, their manner is for every private man to have a prayer said for him by the priest upon any occasion of business whatsoever, whether he ride, go, sail, plow, or whatsoever else he doeth, which is not framed according to the occasion of his business but at random, being some of their ordinary and usual church prayers. And this is thought to be more holy and effectual if it be repeated by the priest's mouth rather than by his own. They have a custom besides to solemnize the saint's day that is patron to their church once every year. What time all their neighbors of their country and parishes about come in to have prayers said to that saint for themselves and their friends and so make an offering to the priest for his pains. This offering may yield them some ten pounds a year, more or less as the patron or saint of that church is of credit and estimation among them. The manner is on this day (which they keep anniversary) for the priest to hire divers of his neighbor priests to help him, as having more dishes to dress for the saint than he can well turn his hand unto. They use besides to visit their parishioners' houses, with holy water and perfume, commonly once a quarter; and so, having sprinkled and becensed the good man and his wife with the rest of their household and household stuff, they receive some devotion, more

29. A parish priest whose wife died was normally expected to become a monk.
30. "A bishop then must be blameless, the husband of one wife, vigilant, sober, of good behavior, given to hospitality, apt to teach."

or less as the man is of ability. This and the rest laid altogether may make up for the priest towards his maintenance about thirty or forty rubles a year, whereof he payeth the tenth part to the bishop of the diocese.

The pop or priest is known by his long tufts of hair hanging down by his ears, his gown with a broad cape, and a walking staff in his hand. For the rest of his habit he is appareled like the common sort. When he saith the liturgy or service within the church he hath on him his surplice, and sometimes his cope if the day be more solemn. They have, besides their popy or priests, their *chernye popy* (as they call them), that is, black priests, that may keep their benefices though they be admitted friars withal within some monastery. They seem to be the very same that were called regular priests in the Popish church. Under the priest is a deacon in every church that doeth nothing but the office of a parish clerk. As for their protopopy or archpriests and their archdeacons (that are next in election to be their protopopy) they serve only in the cathedral churches.

Of friars they have an infinite rabble far greater than in any other country where popery is professed. Every city and good part of the country swarmeth full of them. For they have wrought, as the popish friars did by their superstition and hypocrisy, that if any part of the realm be better and sweeter than other there standeth a friary or a monastery dedicated to some saint.

The number of them is so much the greater not only for that it is augmented by the superstition of the country but because the friar's life is the safest from the oppressions and exactions that fall upon the commons, which causeth many to put on the friar's weed as the best armor to bear off such blows. Besides such as are voluntary, there are divers that are forced to shire themselves friars upon some displeasure. These are for the most part of the chief nobility. Divers take the monasteries as a place of sanctuary, and there become friars to avoid some punishment that they had deserved by the laws of the realm. For if he get a monastery over his head, and there put on a cowl before he be attached, it is a protection to him forever against any law for what crime soever, except it be for treason.[31] But this proviso goeth withal

31. Monks were under the legal jurisdiction of the church authorities for all but the most serious crimes: robbery, brigandage, and murder. For less important criminal matters and for civil suits, they were as liable as ordinary laymen, but the trial procedures and punishments were in their cases handled by church courts.

that no man cometh there (except such as are commanded by the emperor to be received) but he giveth them lands or bringeth his stock with him and putteth it into the common treasury. Some bring a thousand rubles and some more. None is admitted under three or four hundred.[32]

The manner of their admission is after this sort. First, the abbot strippeth him of all his secular or ordinary apparel. Then he putteth upon him next to his skin a white flannel shirt with a long garment over it down to the ground girded unto him with a broad leather belt. His uppermost garment is a weed of *garus* or say,[33] for color and fashion much like to the upper weed of a chimney sweeper. Then is his crown shorn a hand breadth or more close to the very skin, and these or like words pronounced by the abbot whiles he clippeth his hair: "As these hairs are clipped off and taken from thy head, so now we take thee and separate thee clean from the world and worldly things," etc. This done, he anointeth his crown with oil and putteth on his cowl and so taketh him in among the fraternity. They vow perpetual chastity and abstinence from flesh.[34]

Besides their lands, that are very great, they are the greatest merchants in the whole country and deal for all manner of commodities. Some of their monasteries dispend in lands one thousand or two thousand rubles a year. There is one abbey called Troitsa that hath in lands and fees the sum of 100,000 rubles or marks a year.[35] It is built in manner of a castle, walled round about with great ordnance planted on the wall, and containeth within it a large breadth of ground and great variety of building. There are of friars within it (besides their officers and other servants) about seven hundred. The empress that now is hath many vows to Saint Sergius, that is patron there, to entreat him to make her fruitful, as having no children by the emperor her husband. Lightly every year she goeth on pilgrimage to him from the Moscow on foot, about eighty English miles,[36] with five or six thousand women

32. Fletcher's figures are far too high. According to the records of the Solovetskii Monastery, the fee for being tonsured varied between 2 and 16 rubles, depending on the wealth of the candidate (A. A. Savich, *Solovetskaia votchina XV-XVI v.* [Perm', 1927], p. 213).

33. A fine textile of mixed silk and wool or entirely of wool.

34. A postulant who is consecrated a monk is tonsured but not anointed.

35. The Holy Trinity Monastery of St. Sergius was founded about 1340.

36. Sixty versts or about 41 miles. (Petrov, "Geograficheskie spravochniki," p. 103).

attending upon her, all in blue liveries, and four thousand soldiers for her guard. But Saint Sergius hath not yet heard her prayers, though (they say) he hath a special gift and faculty that way.

What learning there is among their friars may be known by their bishops that are the choice men out of all their monasteries. I talked with one of them at the city of Vologda, where to try his skill I offered him a Russe Testament and turned him to the first chapter of Saint Matthew's gospel, where he began to read in very good order. I asked him first what part of scripture it was that he had read. He answered that he could not well tell. How many evangelists there were in the New Testament? He said he knew not. How many apostles there were? He thought there were twelve. How he should be saved? Whereunto he answered me with a piece of Russe doctrine, that he knew not whether he should be saved or no, but if God would *pozhalovat'* him or gratify him so much as to save him, so it was; he would be glad of it; if not, what remedy? I asked him why he shore himself a friar. He answered, because he would eat his bread with peace. This is the learning of the friars of Russia, which though it be not to be measured by one, yet partly it may be guessed by the ignorance of this man what is in the rest.

They have also many nunneries, whereof some may admit none but noblemen's widows and daughters when the emperor meaneth to keep them, unmarried, from continuing the blood or stock which he would have extinguished. To speak of the life of their friars and nuns, it needs not to those that know the hypocrisy and uncleanness of that cloister brood. The Russe himself (though otherwise addicted to all superstition) speaketh so foully of it that it must needs gain silence of any modest man.

Besides these, they have certain eremites (whom they call holy men) that are like to those gymnosophists for their life and behavior, though far unlike for their knowledge and learning.[37] They use to go stark naked save a clout about their middle, with their hair hanging long and wildly about their shoulders, and many of them with an iron collar or chain about their necks or middle, even in the very extremity of winter. These they take as prophets and men of great holiness, giv-

37. What follows is an unflattering description of the *iurodivyi* or holy fool. "Gymnosophists" was the name given by the Greeks to certain ancient Hindu philosophers who pursued asceticism to the point of regarding food and clothing as detrimental to purity of thought.

ing them a liberty to speak what they list without any controlment, though it be of the very highest himself. So that if he reprove any openly in what sort soever, they answer nothing but that it is *po grek-ham*, that is, for their sins. And if any of them take some piece of sale ware from any man's shop as he passeth by to give where he list, he thinketh himself much beloved of God and much beholding to the holy man for taking it in that sort.

Of this kind there are not many because it is a very hard and cold profession to go naked in Russia, specially in winter. Among other at this time they have one at Moscow that walketh naked about the streets and inveigheth commonly against the state and government, especially against the Godunovs that are thought at this time to be great oppressors of that commonwealth. Another there was that died not many years ago, whom they called Vasilii, that would take upon him to reprove the old emperor for all his cruelty and oppressions done towards his people.[38] His body they have translated of late into a sumptuous church near the emperor's house in Moscow and have canonized him for a saint. Many miracles he doth there (for so the friars make the people to believe), and many offerings are made unto him not only by the people but by the chief nobility and the emperor and empress themselves, which visit that church with great devotion. But this last year, at my being at Moscow, this saint had ill luck in working his miracles. For a lame man that had his limbs restored (as it was pretended by him) was charged by a woman that was familiar with him (being then fallen out) that he halted but in the daytime and could leap merrily when he came home at night, and that he had intended this matter six years before. Now he is put into a monastery, and there raileth upon the friars that hired him to have this counterfeit miracle practiced upon him. Besides this disgrace, a little before my coming from thence there were eight slain within his church by fire in a thunder, which caused his bells (that were tingling before all day and night long as in triumph of the miracles wrought by Vasilii their saint) to ring somewhat softlier and hath wrought no little discredit to this miracle worker. There was another of great account at Pskov, called Nikola of Pskov, that did much good when this emperor's father came to sack the town upon suspicion of their revolting and rebellion against

---

38. Vasilii the Blessed (1469–1552) was a holy fool who achieved great renown during his lifetime. It is from him that the great church that Ivan IV built on the edge of Red Square has received its popular name. His feast day is August 2.

him. The emperor, after he had saluted the eremite at his lodging, sent him a reward. And the holy man to requite the emperor sent him a piece of raw flesh, being then their Lent time, which the emperor seeing, bid one to tell him that he marveled that the holy man would offer him flesh to eat in the Lent when it was forbidden by order of Holy Church. "And doth Ivashka (which is as much to say, as Jack) think," quoth Nikola, "that it is unlawful to eat a piece of beast's flesh in Lent and not to eat up so much man's flesh as he hath done already?" So threatening the emperor with a prophecy of some hard adventure to come upon him except he left murdering of his people and departed the town, he saved a great many men's lives at that time.[39]

This maketh the people to like very well of them, because they are as pasquils to note their great men's faults that no man else dare speak of. Yet it falleth out sometime that for this rude liberty which they take upon them after a counterfeit manner by imitation of prophets, they are made away in secret, as was one or two of them in the last emperor's time for being over bold in speaking against his government.

Chapter 22. Of their liturgy, or form of church service, and their manner of administering the sacraments

Their morning service they call *zautrenia*, that is, matins. It is done in this order. The priest entereth into the church with his deacon following him. And when he is come to the middle of the church, he beginneth to say with a loud voice, "*Blagoslovi, Vladyka*," that is, "bless us, Heavenly Pastor," meaning of Christ. Then he addeth, "in the name of the Father, and of the Son, and of the Holy Ghost, one very God in Trinity," and "*Gospodi pomilui*," or "Lord have mercy upon us, Lord have mercy upon us, Lord have mercy upon us," repeated three times. This done, he marcheth on towards the chancel, or Sanctum Sanctorum as they use to call it, and so entereth into the *tsarskiia dveri* or the heavenly door, which no man may enter into but the priest only. Where standing at the altar or table (set near to the

39. See Horsey's account of the same incident, p. 268 below.

upper wall of the chancel) he sayeth the Lord's prayer and then again "*Gospodi pomilui*" or "Lord have mercy upon us, Lord have mercy upon us," etc., pronounced twelve times, then, "praised be the Trinity, the Father, the Son, and Holy Ghost forever and ever." Whereto the deacons and people say "Amen." Next after, the priest addeth the psalms for that day and beginneth with "O come let us worship and fall down before the Lord," etc., and therewithal himself with the deacons and people all turn themselves towards their idols or images that hang on the wall and crossing themselves bow down three times, knocking their heads to the very ground. After this he readeth the ten commandments and Athanasius' Creed out of the service book.

This being done, the deacon that standeth without the heavenly door or chancel readeth a piece of a legend out of a written book (for they have it not in print) of some saint's life, miracles, etc. This is divided into many parts for every day in the year and is read by them with a plain singing note not unlike to the popish tune when they sung their Gospels. After all this (which reacheth to an hour and an half or two hours of length) he addeth certain set collects or prayers upon that which he hath read out of the legend before and so endeth his service. All this while stand burning before their idols a great many of wax candles (whereof some are of the bigness of a man's waist) vowed or enjoined by penance upon the people of the parish.[1]

About nine of the clock in the morning, they have another service called *obednia* or compline, much after the order of the popish service that bare that name. If it be some high or festival day they furnish their service beside with "Blessed be the Lord God of Israel," etc., and "We praise Thee, O God," etc., sung with a more solemn and curious note.

Their evening service is called *vechernia*, where the priest beginneth with "Blagoslovi, Vladyka," as he did in the morning, and with the psalms appointed for the vechernia. Which being read, he singeth "My

---

1. J. G. King, *The Rites and Ceremonies of the Greek Church in Russia* (London, 1772), pp. 97–121, gives the complete order of service. Fletcher's description of the services of the Orthodox church may well be based on hearsay rather than on observation. Many foreigners who visited Muscovy remarked that they were unable to attend church functions either because they were forbidden by their hosts or because they were afraid that the worshippers would react to their presence in a hostile manner. It is distinctly possible that Fletcher never attended a celebration of the liturgy; the order of service that he gives is quite different from the usual practice of the Russian church.

soul doth magnify the Lord," etc. And then the priest, deacons, and people all with one voice sing "Gospodi pomilui" or "Lord have mercy upon us" thirty times together. Whereunto the boys that are in the church answer all with one voice, rolling it up so fast as their lips can go, "*verii, verii, verii, verii*" or "praise, praise, praise," etc., thirty times together with a very strange noise. Then is read by the priest and upon the holidays sung, the first psalm, "Blessed is the man," etc. And in the end of it is added "Alleluia" repeated ten times. The next in order is some part of the Gospel read by the priest, which he endeth with "Alleluia" repeated three times. And so, having said a collect in remembrance of the saint of that day, he endeth his evening service.[2] All this while the priest standeth above at the altar or high table within the chancel or Sanctum Sanctorum whence he never moveth all the service time. The deacon or deacons (which are many in their cathedral churches) stand without the chancel by the tsarskiia dveri or heavenly door, for within they may not be seen all the service time, though otherwise their office is to sweep and keep it and to set up the wax candles before their idols. The people stand together the whole service time in the body of the church and some in the church porch, for pew or seat they have none within their churches.

The sacrament of baptism they administer after this manner.[3] The child is brought unto the church, and this is done within eight days after it is born; if it be the child of some nobleman it is brought with great pomp in a rich sled or wagon with chairs and cushions of cloth of gold and such like sumptuous show of their best furniture. When they are come to the church the priest standeth ready to receive the child within the church porch with his tub of water by him and then beginneth to declare unto them that they have brought a little infidel to be made a Christian, etc. This ended, he teacheth the witnesses, that are two or three, in a certain set form out of his book what their duty is in bringing up the child after he is baptised, viz., that he must be taught to know God and Christ the Savior, and because God is of great majesty and we must not presume to come unto him without mediators (as the manner is when we make any suit to an emperor or great prince), therefore they must teach him what saints are the best and chief mediators, etc. This done, he commandeth the devil in the name of God after a conjuring manner to come out of the water, and so after certain

2. For order of service see *ibid.*, pp. 59–76.
3. For order of service see *ibid.*, pp. 208–20.

prayers he plungeth the child thrice over head and ears. For this they hold to be a point necessary, that no part of the child be undipped in the water.

The words that bear with them the form of baptism uttered by the priest when he dippeth in the child are the very same that are prescribed in the Gospel and used by us, viz., "In the name of the Father and of the Son, and of the Ghost." For that they should alter the form of the words and say "by the Holy Ghost," as I have heard that they did following certain heretics of the Greek church, I found to be untrue as well by report of them that have been often at their baptisms as by their book of liturgy itself wherein the order of baptism is precisely set down.

When the child is baptized, the priest layeth oil and salt tempered together upon the forehead and both sides of his face and then upon his mouth, drawing it along with his finger over the child's lips (as did the popish priests), saying withal certain prayers to this effect, "that God will make him a good Christian," etc. All this is done in the church porch. Then is the child (as being now made a Christian and meet to be received within the church door) carried into the church, the priest going before, and there he is presented to the chief idol of the church, being laid on a cushion before the feet of the image, by it (as by the mediator) to be commended unto God. If the child be sick or weak (specially in the winter) they use to make the water lukewarm. After baptism the manner is to cut off the hair from the child's head and having wrapped it within a piece of wax, to lay it up as a relic or monument in a secret place of the church.

This is the manner of their baptism, which they account to be the best and perfectest form, as they do all other parts of their religion, received (as they say) by tradition from the best church, meaning the Greek. And therefore they will take great pains to make a proselyte or convert either of an infidel or of a foreign Christian by rebaptizing him after the Russe manner. When they take any Tatar prisoner, commonly they will offer him life with condition to be baptized. And yet they persuade very few of them to redeem their life so because of the natural hatred the Tatar beareth to the Russe and the opinion he hath of his falsehood and injustice. The year after Moscow was fired by the Krym Tatar, there was taken a divei-mirza, one of the chief in that exploit, with three hundred Tatars more, who had all their lives offered them if they would be baptized after the Russe manner, which they refused all to do with many reproaches against those that persuaded them. And so being carried to the river Moskva (that runneth through the city) they were all baptized after a violent manner, being thrust down with a knock on the head into the water through an hole made in the ice for that purpose. Of Livonians that are captives there are many that take on them this second Russe baptism to get more liberty, and somewhat besides towards their living, which the emperor ordinarily useth to give them.

Of Englishmen since they frequented the country there was never any found that so much forgot God, his faith, and country, as that he would be content to be baptized Russe for any respect of fear, preferment, or other means whatsoever, save only Richard Relph that, following before an ungodly trade by keeping a kabak (against the order of the country) and being put off from that trade and spoiled by the emperor's officers of that which he had, entered himself this last year into the Russe profession and so was rebaptized, living now as much an idolater as before he was a rioter and unthrifty person.[4]

Such as thus receive the Russe baptism are first carried into some monastery to be instructed there in the doctrine and ceremonies of the church where they use these ceremonies. First they put him into a new and fresh suit of apparel made after the Russe fashion and set a coronet or, in summer, a garland upon his head. Then they anoint his head with oil and put a wax candlelight into his hand and so pray over him four times a day the space of seven days. All this while he is to abstain from flesh and white meats. The seven days being ended he is purified and washed in a bathstove, and so the eighth day he is brought into the church where he is taught by the friars how to behave himself in presence of their idols by ducking down, knocking of the head, crossing himself, and such like gestures which are the greatest part of the Russe religion.

The sacrament of the Lord's supper they receive but once a year, in their great Lent time a little before Easter.[5] Three at the most are admitted at one time and never above. The manner of their communicating is thus. First, they confess themselves of all their sins to the priest, whom they call their ghostly father. Then they come to the church and

4. Relph was a servant of the Russia Company who had used his position to engage in private trade in defiance of the company's monopoly. He returned to England in the mid-1580's but soon went back to Russia where he settled down in the situation that Fletcher describes (Willan, *Early History*, pp. 190–96).

5. Every member of the Russian church is expected to communicate at least once a year. The obligation is frequently satisfied during Lent.

are called up to the communion table that standeth like an altar, a little removed from the upper end of the church, after the Dutch manner. Here first they are asked of the priest whether they be clean or no,
that is, whether they have never a sin behind that they left uncon-
fessed. If they answer "no," they are taken to the table where the priest
beginneth with certain usual prayers, the communicants standing in
the meanwhile with their arms folded one within another like peniten-
tiaries or mourners. When these prayers are ended, the priest taketh a
spoon and filleth it full of claret wine. Then he putteth into it a small
piece of bread and tempereth them both together and so delivereth
them in the spoon to the communicants that stand in order, speaking
the usual words of the sacrament, "Eat this," etc.; "Drink this," etc.,
both at one time without any pause.

After that, he delivereth them again bread by itself and then wine
carded together with a little warm water, to represent blood more
rightly (as they think) and the water withal that flowed out of the side
of Christ. Whiles this is in doing the communicants unfold their arms
and then, folding them again, follow the priest thrice round about the
communion table and so return to their places again. Where, having
said certain other prayers, he dismisseth the communicants with charge
to be merry and to cheer up themselves for the seven days next following. Which being ended, he enjoineth them to fast for it as long time
after, which they use to observe with very great devotion, eating
nothing else but bread and salt, except a little cabbage and some other
herb or root, with water or *kvas* (mead) for their drink.

This is their manner of administering the sacraments, wherein what
they differ from the institution of Christ and what ceremonies they
have added of their own, or rather borrowed of the Greeks, may easily
be noted.

Chapter 23. Of the doctrine of the Russe church, and what errors it holdeth

Their chiefest errors in matter of faith I find to be these. First,
concerning the word of God itself they will not read publicly
certain books of the canonical Scripture, as the books of Moses, spe-

cially the four last, Exodus, Leviticus, Numbers, and Deuteronomy, which they say are all made disauthentic and put out of use by the coming of Christ, as not able to discern the difference betwixt the moral and the ceremonial law. The books of the prophets they allow of but read them not publicly in their churches for the same reason, because they were but directors unto Christ and proper (as they say) to the nation of the Jews. Only the book of Psalms they have in great estimation and sing and say them daily in their churches. Of the New Testament they allow and read all except the Revelation, which therefore they read not (though they allow it) because they understand it not, neither have the like occasion to know the fulfilling of the prophecies contained within it concerning especially the apostasy of the anti-Christian church as have the western churches. Notwithstanding they have had their antichrists of the Greek church; any may find their own falling off and the punishments for it by the Turkish invasion in the prophecies of that book.

Secondly (which is the fountain of the rest of all their corruptions, both in doctrine and ceremonies), they hold with the papists that their church traditions are of equal authority with the written word of God. Wherein they prefer themselves before other churches, affirming that they have the true and right traditions delivered by the apostles to the Greek church and so unto them.

3. That the church (meaning the Greek and specially the patriarch and his synod as the head of the rest) have a sovereign authority to interpret the Scriptures and that all are bound to hold that interpretation as sound and authentic.

4. Concerning the divine nature and the three persons in the one substance of God, that the Holy Ghost proceedeth from the Father only and not from the Son.

5. About the office of Christ they hold many foul errors and the same almost as doth the popish church, namely, that he is the sole mediator of redemption but not of intercession. Their chief reason (if they be talked withal) for defense of this error is that unapt and foolish comparison betwixt God and a monarch or prince of this world that must be sued unto by mediators about him, wherein they give special preferment to some above others, as to the blessed Virgin, whom they call *Prechistaia* or undefiled, and Saint Nicholas, whom they call *skoryi pomoshchnik* or the speedy helper and say that he hath three hundred angels of the chiefest appointed by God to attend upon him. This hath

brought them to an horrible excess of idolatry after the grossest and profanest manner, giving unto their images all religious worship of prayer, thanksgiving, offerings, and adoration with prostrating and knocking their heads to the ground before them as to God himself. Which because they do to the picture, not to the portraiture of the saint, they say they worship not an idol but the saint in his image and so offend not God, forgetting the commandment of God that forbiddeth to make the image or likeness of anything for any religious worship or use whatsoever. Their church walls are very full of them, richly hanged and set forth with pearl and stone upon the smooth table, though some also they have embossed that stick from the board almost an inch outwards. They call them *chudotvortsy* or their miracle workers, and when they provide them to set up in their churches, in no case they may say that they have bought the image but exchanged money for it.

6. For the means of justification they agree with the papists that it is not by faith only apprehending Christ but by their works also, and that *opus operatum* or the work for the work sake must needs please God. And therefore they are all in their numbers of prayers, fasts, vows, and offerings to saints, alms, deeds, crossings, and such like and carry their numbering beads about with them continually, as well the emperor and his nobility as the common people, not only in the church but in all other public places, specially at any set or solemn meeting, as in their fasts, law courts, common consultations, entertainment of ambassadors, and such like.

7. They say with the papists that no man can be assured of his salvation till the last sentence be passed at the day of judgment.

8. They use auricular confession and think that they are purged by the very action from so many sins as they confess by name and in particular to the priest.

9. They hold three sacraments, of baptism, the Lord's Supper, and the last anointing or unction. Yet concerning their sacrament of extreme unction, they hold it not so necessary to salvation as they do baptism, but think it a great curse and punishment of God if any die without it.

10. They think there is a necessity of baptism and that all are condemned that die without it.

11. They rebaptize as many Christians (not being of the Greek church) as they convert to their Russe profession, because they are di-

vided from the true church, which is the Greek, as they say.

12. They make a difference of meats and drinks, accounting the use of one to be more holy than of another. And therefore in their set fasts they forbear to eat flesh and white meats (as we call them) after the manner of the popish superstition, which they observe so strictly and with such blind devotion as that they will rather die than eat one bit of flesh, eggs, or such like, for the health of their bodies in their extreme sickness.

13. They hold marriage to be unlawful for all the clergymen except the priests only, and for them also after the first wife as was said before. Neither do they well allow of it in laymen after the second marriage, which is a pretense now used against the emperor's only brother, a child of six years old, who therefore is not prayed for in their churches (as their manner is otherwise for the prince's blood) because he was born of the sixth marriage and so not legitimate.[1] This charge was given to the priests by the emperor himself by procurement of the Godunovs, who make him believe that it is a good policy to turn away the liking of the people from the next successor.

Many other false opinions they have in matter of religion. But these are the chief, which they hold partly by means of their traditions (which they have received from the Greek church) but specially by ignorance of the Holy Scriptures. Which, notwithstanding, they have in the Polish tongue (that is all one with theirs, some few words excepted), yet few of them read them with that godly care which they ought to do; neither have they (if they would) books sufficient of the Old and New Testament for the common people but of their liturgy only or book of common service, whereof there are great numbers.

All this mischief cometh from the clergy, who, being ignorant and godless themselves, are very wary to keep the people likewise in their ignorance and blindness, for their living and bellies' sake, partly also from the manner of government settled among them, which the emperors (whom it specially behooveth) list not to have changed by any innovation but to retain that religion that best agreeth with it. Which, notwithstanding, it is not to be doubted but that having the word of God in some sort (though without the ordinary means to attain to a true sense and understanding of it), God hath also his number

---

1. A layman could normally marry 3 times. The "emperor's only brother" was Prince Dmitrii, the child of Ivan's seventh (not sixth) marriage.

among them, as may partly appear by that which a Russe at Moscow said in secret to one of my servants, speaking against their images and other superstitions, "that God had given unto England light today and might give it tomorrow, if he pleased, to them."

As for any inquisition or proceeding against men for matter of religion, I could hear of none save a few years since against one man and his wife who were kept in a close prison the space of twenty-eight years till they were overgrown into a deformed fashion for their hair, nails, color of countenance, and such like, and in the end were burned at Moscow in a small house set on fire. The cause was kept secret, but like it was for some part of truth in matter of religion, though the people were made to believe by the priests and friars that they held some great and damnable heresy.

Chapter 24. Of the manner of solemnizing their marriages

The manner of making and solemnizing their marriages is different from the manner of other countries. The man, though he never saw the woman before, is not permitted to have any sight of her all the time of his wooing, which he doth not by himself but by his mother or some other ancient woman of his kin or acquaintance. When the liking is taken (as well by the parents as by the parties themselves, for without the knowledge and consent of the parents the contract is not lawful) the fathers on both sides, or such as are to them instead of fathers, with their other chief friends have a meeting and conference about the dowry, which is commonly very large after the ability of the parents, so that you shall have a market man (as they call them) give a thousand rubles or more with his daughter.

As for the man, it is never required of him nor standeth with their custom to make any jointer in recompense of the dowry. But in case he have a child by his wife she enjoyeth a third deal after his decease. If he have two children by her or more, she is to have a courtesy more at the discretion of the husband. If the husband depart without issue by his wife, she is returned home to her friends without anything at all save only her dowry if the husband leave so much behind him in

goods. When the agreement is made concerning the dowry, they sign
bonds one to the other, as well for the payment of the dowry as the
performing of the marriage by a certain day. If the woman were never
married before, her father and friends are bound besides to assure her
a maiden, which breedeth many brabbles and quarrels at law if the
man take any conceit concerning the behavior and honesty of his wife.

Thus, the contract being made, the parties begin to send tokens the
one to the other, the woman first, then afterwards the man, but yet see
not one another till the marriage be solemnized. On the eve before the
marriage day the bride is carried in a *kolymaga* or coach or in a sled
(if it be winter) to the bridegroom's house with her marriage apparel
and bedstead with her which they are to lie in. For this is ever provided by the bride and is commonly very fair with much cost bestowed
upon it. Here she is accompanied all that night by her mother and
other women, but not welcomed nor once seen by the bridegroom
himself.[1]

When the time is come to have the marriage solemnized, the bride
hath put upon her a kind of hood made of fine knitwork or lawn that
covereth her head and all her body down to the middle. And so accompanied with her friends, and the bridegroom with his, they go to
church all on horseback, though the church be near hand and themselves but of very mean degree. The words of contract and other ceremonies in solemnizing the marriage are much after the order and with
the same words that are used with us, with a ring also given to the
bride. Which being put on and the words of contract pronounced, the
bride's hand is delivered into the hand of the bridegroom, which standeth all this while on the one side of the altar or table and the bride on
the other. So the marriage knot being knit by the priest, the bride cometh to the bridegroom (standing at the end of the altar or table) and
falleth down at his feet, knocking her head upon his shoe in token of
her subjection and obedience. And the bridegroom again casteth the
lap of his gown or upper garment over the bride in token of his duty to
protect and cherish her.

Then, the bridegroom and bride standing both together at the table's
end, cometh first the father and the other friends of the bride and bow
themselves down low to the bridegroom, and so likewise his friends

1. Traditionally the bride did not go to the groom's house on the eve of the
wedding. Fletcher may have mistaken the dispatch of part of the dowry to the
bridegroom's house for the arrival of the bride (Seredonin, p. 155).

bow themselves to the bride in token of affinity and love ever after betwixt the two kindreds. And withal the father of the bridegroom offereth to the priest a loaf of bread, who delivereth it straight again to the father and other friends of the bride with attestation before God and their idols that he deliver the dowry wholly and truly at the day appointed and hold love ever after one kindred with another. Whereupon they break the loaf into pieces and eat of it to testify their true and sincere meanings for performing of that charge and thenceforth to become as grains of one loaf or men of one table.

These ceremonies being ended the bridegroom taketh the bride by the hand, and so they go on together with their friends after them towards the church porch, where meet them certain with pots and cups in their hands with mead and Russe wine. Whereof the bridegroom taketh first a *charka* or little cupful in his hand and drinketh to the bride, who, opening her hood or veil below and putting the cup to her mouth underneath it (for being seen of the bridegroom), pledgeth him again. Thus returning altogether from the church, the bridegroom goeth not home to his own but to his father's house, and she likewise to hers, where either entertain their friends apart. At the entering into the house they use to fling corn out of the windows upon the bridegroom and bride in token of plenty and fruitfulness to be with them ever after.

When the evening is come the bride is brought to the bridegroom's father's house and there lodgeth that night with her veil or cover still over her head. All that night she may not speak one word (for that charge she receiveth by tradition from her mother and other matrons her friends) that the bridegroom must neither hear nor see her till the day after the marriage. Neither three days after may she be heard to speak save certain few words at the table in a set form with great manners and reverence to the bridegroom. If she behave herself otherwise it is a great prejudice to her credit and life ever after and will highly be disliked of the bridegroom himself.

After the third day they depart to their own and make a feast to both their friends together. The marriage day and the whole time of their festival the bridegroom hath the honor to be called *molodoi kniaz'* or young duke and the bride *molodaia kniaginia* or young duchess.

In living with their wives they show themselves to be but of a barbarous condition, using them as servants rather than wives, except the noblewomen which are or seem to be of more estimation with their husbands than the rest of meaner sort. They have this foul abuse contrary to good order and the word of God itself, that upon dislike of his wife or other cause whatsoever the man may go into a monastery and shire himself a friar by pretense of devotion and so leave his wife to shift for herself so well as she can.

Chapter 25. Of the other ceremonies of the Russe church

The other ceremonies of their church are many in number, especially the abuse about the sign of the cross, which they set up in their highways, in the tops of their churches, and in every door of their houses, signing themselves continually with it on their foreheads and breasts with great devotion as they will seem by their outward gesture, which were less offense if they gave not withal that religious reverence and worship unto it which is due to God only and used the dumb show and signing of it instead of thanksgiving and of all other duties which they owe unto God. When they rise in the morning they go commonly in the sight of some steeple that hath a cross on the top and, so bowing themselves towards the cross, sign themselves withal on their foreheads and breasts. And this is their thanksgiving to God for their night's rest, without any word speaking except peradventure they say "Gospodi pomilui" or "Lord have mercy upon us." When they sit down to meat and rise again from it the thanksgiving to God is the crossing of their foreheads and breasts, except it be some few that add peradventure a word or two of some ordinary prayer impertinent to that purpose. When they are to give an oath for the deciding of any controversy at law they do it by swearing by the cross and kissing the feet of it, making it as God whose name only is to be used in such trial of justice. When they enter into any house (wherever there is an idol hanging on the wall) they sign themselves with the cross and bow themselves to it. When they begin any work, be it little or much, they arm themselves first with the sign of the cross. And this commonly is all their prayer to God for good speed of their business. And thus they serve God with crosses after a cross and vain manner, not understanding what the cross of Christ is nor the power of it. And yet they think all strangers Christians to be no better than Turks in comparison of themselves (and so they will say) because they bow not themselves when they meet with the cross nor sign themselves with it as the Russe manner is.

They have holy water in like use and estimation as the popish church hath. But herein they exceed them in that they do not only hallow their holy water stocks and tubs full of water but all the rivers of the country once every year. At Moscow it is done with great pomp and solemnity, the emperor himself being present at it, with all his nobility, marching through the streets towards the river of Moskva in manner of procession in this order as followeth. First go two deacons with banners in their hands, the one of Precheste (or Our Lady), the other of Saint Michael fighting with his dragon. Then follow after the rest of the deacons and the priests of Moscow, two and two in a rank, with copes on their backs and their idols at their breasts carried with girdles or slings made fast about their necks. Next the priests come their bishops in their pontificalibus, then the friars, monks, and abbots, and after, the patriarch in very rich attire with a ball or sphere on the top of his miter to signify his universality over that church. Last cometh the emperor with all his nobility. The whole train is of a mile long or more. When they are come to the river a great hole is made in the ice, where the market is kept, of a rod and a half broad with a stage round about it to keep off the press. Then beginneth the patriarch to say certain prayers and conjureth the devil to come out of the water, and so casting in salt and censing it with frankincense maketh the whole river to become holy water. The morning before all the people of Moscow use to make crosses of chalk over every door and window of their houses lest the devil being conjured out of the water should fly into their houses.

When the ceremonies are ended you shall see the black guard of the emperor's house and then the rest of the town with their pails and buckets to take off the hallowed water for drink and other uses. You shall also see the women dip in their children over head and ears, and many men and women leap into it, some naked, some with their clothes on, when some man would think his finger would freeze off if he should but dip it into the water. When the men have done they bring their horse to the river to drink of the sanctified water, and so make them as holy as a horse. Their set day for this solemn action of hallowing their rivers is that we call Twelfthday.[1] The like is done by other bishops in all parts of the realm.

Their manner is also to give it to their sick in their greatest extremity, thinking it will either recover them or sanctify them to God. Whereby they kill many through their unreasonable superstition, as did the Lord Boris his only son at my being at the Moscow, whom he killed (as was said by the physicians) by pouring into him cold holy water and presenting him naked into the church to their Saint Vasilii in the cold of the winter in an extremity of sickness.

They have an image of Christ which they call *nerukotvornyi*, which signifieth as much as "made without hands," for so their priests and superstition withal persuadeth them it was. This in their processions they carry about with them on high upon a pole enclosed within a pyx made like a lantern and do reverence to it as to a great mystery.

At every brewing their manner is likewise to bring a dish of their wort[2] to the priest within the church, which being hallowed by him is poured into the brewing and so giveth it such a virtue as when they drink of it they are seldom sober. The like they do with the first fruits of the corn in harvest.

They have another ceremony on Palm Sunday of ancient tradition, what time the patriarch rideth through the Moscow, the emperor himself holding his horse bridle and the people crying "Hosanna" and spreading their upper garments under his horse feet. The emperor hath of the patriarch for his good service of that day two hundred rubles of standing pension. Another pageant they have much like to this the week before the nativity of Christ, when every bishop in his cathedral church setteth forth a show of the three children in the oven, where the angel is made to come flying from the roof of the church with great admiration of the lookers-on, and many terrible flashes of fire are made with rosin and gunpowder by the Chaldeans (as they call them) that run about the town all the twelve days disguised in their players' coats and make much good sport for the honor of the bishop's pageant. At the Moscow the emperor himself and the empress never fail to be at it, though it be but the same matter played every year without any new invention at all.

1. The blessing of the waters on the Feast of the Epiphany (King, *Rites and Ceremonies*, pp. 387–93).
2. The infusion of malt or other grain that after fermentation becomes beer.

Besides their fasts on Wednesdays and Fridays throughout the whole year (the one because they say Christ was sold on the Wednesday, the other because he suffered on the Friday), they have four great fasts or lents every year. The first, which they call their great lent, is at the same time with ours; the second about midsummer; the third in harvest time; the fourth about Hallowtide, which they keep not of policy but of mere superstition. In their great lent for the first week they eat nothing but bread and salt and drink nothing but water, neither meddle with any matter of their vocation, but intend their shriving and fasting only. They have also three vigils or wakes in their great lent which they call *stoianiia*,[3] and the last Friday their great vigil as they call it. What time the whole parish must be present in the church and watch from nine a clock in the evening till six in the morning, all the while standing save when they fall down and knock their heads to their idols, which must be an hundred and seventy times just through the whole night.

About their burials also they have many superstitious and profane ceremonies, as putting within the finger of the corpse a letter to Saint Nicholas,[4] whom they make their chief mediator and, as it were, the porter of heaven gates, as the papists do their Peter.

In wintertime when all is covered with snow and the ground so hard frozen as that no spade or pickax can enter, their manner is not to bury their dead but to keep the bodies (so many as die all the wintertime) in an house in the suburbs or outparts of the town which they call *bozhii dom*, that is, God's house, where the dead bodies are piled up together like billets on a woodstack, as hard with the frost as a very stone, till the springtide come and resolveth the frost, what time every man taketh his dead friend and committeth him to the ground.

They have besides their years and month's minds for their friends departed. What time they have prayers said over the grave by the priest, who hath a penny ordinary for his pains. When any dieth they have ordinary women mourners that come to lament for the dead party and stand howling over the body after a profane and heathenish manner, sometimes in the house, sometimes bringing the body into the backside, asking him what he wanted and what he meant to die. They

3. Probably the *Andreevo stoianie,* the service on the Thursday before Palm Sunday at which the Great Canon of Andrew of Crete is read in its entirety.

4. See Chancellor's account, p. 38 above.

bury their dead as the party used to go, with coat, hose, boots, hat, and
the rest of his apparel.

Many other vain and superstitious ceremonies they have which were
long and tedious to report. By these it may appear how far they are
fallen from the true knowledge and practice of Christian religion, having exchanged the word of God for their vain traditions and brought
all to external and ridiculous ceremonies without any regard of spirit
and truth which God requireth in his true worship.

Chapter 26. Of the emperor's domestic or private behavior

The emperor's private behavior, so much as may be or is meet to
be known, is after this manner. He riseth commonly about four a
clock in the morning. After his appareling and washing in cometh his
ghostly father or priest of his chamber, which is named in their tongue
otets dukhovnyi, with his cross in his hand wherewith he blesseth
him, laying it first on his forehead, then upon his cheeks or sides of his
face, and then offereth him the end of it to kiss. This done the clerk of
the cross (called *krestnyi d'iak* Porfirii) bringeth into his chamber a
painted image representing the saint for that day. For every day with
them hath his several saint, as it were the patron for that day. This he
placeth among the rest of his image gods wherewithal his chamber is
decked as thick almost as the wall can bear, with lamps and wax candles burning before them. They are very costly and gorgeously decked
with pearl and precious stone. This image being placed before him, the
emperor beginneth to cross himself after the Russe manner, first on the
forehead, then on both sides of his breast with "*Gospodi pomilui, pomilui menia Gospodi, sokhrani menia greshnogo ot zlogo deistviia,*" which
is as much to say as "Help me, O Lord my God, Lord comfort me, defend and keep me a sinner from doing evil," etc. This he directeth
towards the image or saint for that day, whom he nameth in his
prayer together with Our Lady (whom they call Prechistaia), Saint
Nicholas, or some other to whom he beareth most devotion, bowing
himself prostrate unto them with knocking his head to the very ground.
Thus he continueth the space of a quarter of an hour or thereabouts.

Then cometh again the ghostly father or chamber priest with a silver bowl full of holy water, which they call in Russe *sviataia voda*, and a sprinkle of basil (as they call it) in his hand, and so all to besprinkleth first the image gods and then the emperor. This holy water is brought fresh every day from the monasteries far and near, sent to the emperor from the abbot or prior in the name of the saint that is patron of that monastery as a special token of good will from him.

These devotions being ended he sendeth in to the empress to ask whether she hath rested in health, etc., and after a little pause goeth himself to salute her in a middle room betwixt both their chambers. The empress lieth apart from him and keepeth not one chamber nor table with the emperor ordinarily save upon the eve of their lents or common fasts, what time she is his ordinary guest at bed and board. After their meeting in the morning they go together to their private church or chapel where is said or sung a morning service (called zautrenia) of an hour long or thereabouts. From the church he returneth home and sitteth him down in a great chamber to be seen and saluted by his nobility, such as are in favor about the court. If he have to say to any of them or they to him, then is the time. And this is ordinary except his health or some other occasion alter the custom.

About nine in the morning he goeth to another church within his castle where is sung by priests and choristers the high service (called obednia or compline) which commonly lasteth two hours, the emperor in the meantime talking commonly with some of his council, nobility, or captains which have to say to him or he to them. And the council likewise confer together among themselves as if they were in their council house. This ended, he returneth home and recreateth himself until it be dinnertime.

He is served at his table on this manner. First, every dish (as it is delivered at the dresser) is tasted by the cook in the presence of the high steward or his deputy and so is received by the gentlemen waiters (called zhil'tsy[1]) and by them carried up to the emperor's table, the high steward or his deputy going before. There it is received by the sewer (called *erastnoy*),[2] who giveth a taste of every dish to the taster,

1. Members of the lowest rank of Moscow service personnel.
2. Probably kravchii. The tasters were usually young members of high noble families, many of whom later in their careers were elevated to membership in the boiar duma (M. A. D'iakonov, *Ocherki obshchestvennago i gosudarstvennago stroia drevnei Rusi* [St. Petersburg, 1912], pp. 272–73).

and so placeth it before the emperor. The number of his dishes for his ordinary service is about seventy, dressed somewhat grossly with much garlic and salt much after the Dutch manner. When he exceedeth upon some occasion of the day or entertainment of some ambassador he hath many more dishes. The service is sent up by two dishes at a time, or three at the most, that he may eat it warm, first the baked, then the roast meats, and last the broths. In his dining chamber is another table where sit the chief of his nobility that are about his court and his ghostly father or chaplain. On the one side of the chamber standeth a cupboard or table of plate very fair and rich, with a great cistern of copper by it full of ice and snow wherein stand the pots that serve for that meal. The taster holdeth the cup that he drinketh in all dinnertime and delivereth it unto him with a say when he calleth for it. The manner is to make many dishes out of the service after it is set on the table and to send them to such noblemen and officers as the emperor liketh best. And this is counted a great favor and honor.

After dinner he layeth him down to rest where commonly he taketh three hours sleep except he employ one of the hours to bathing or boxing. And this custom for sleeping after dinner is an ordinary matter with him as with all the Russes. After his sleep he goeth to evensong (called vechernia) and, thence returning, for the most part recreateth himself with the empress till suppertime with jesters and dwarfs, men and women that tumble before him and sing many songs after the Russe manner. This is his common recreation betwixt meals, that he most delights in. One other special recreation is the fight with wild bears, which are caught in pits or nets and are kept in barred cages for that purpose against the emperor be disposed to see the pastime. The fight with the bear is on this sort. The man is turned into a circle walled round about where he is to quit himself so well as he can, for there is no way to fly out. When the bear is turned loose he cometh upon him with open mouth. If at the first push he miss his aim, so that the bear come within him, he is in great danger. But the wild bear being very fierce hath this quality that giveth advantage to the hunter. His manner is when he assaileth a man to rise upright on his two hinder legs and so to come roaring with open mouth upon him. And if the hunter then can push right into the very breast of him betwixt his forelegs (as commonly he will not miss), resting the other end of their boar spear at the side of his foot and so keeping the pike still towards the face of the bear, he speedeth him commonly at one blow. But many times these hunters come short and are either slain or miserably torn with the teeth and talons of the fierce beast. If the party quit himself well in this fight with the bear he is carried to drink at the emperor's cellar door, where he drinketh himself drunk for the honor of Gospodar'. And this is his reward for adventuring his life for the emperor's pleasure. To maintain this pastime the emperor hath certain huntsmen that are appointed for that purpose to take the wild bear. This is his recreation commonly on the holy days. Sometimes he spendeth his time in looking upon his goldsmiths and jewelers, tailors, embroiderers, painters, and such like, and so goeth to his supper. When it draweth towards bedtime his priest sayeth certain prayers, and then the emperor blesseth and crosseth himself, as in the morning, for a quarter of an hour or thereabouts, and so goeth to his bed.

The emperor that now is (called Fedor Ivanovich) is for his person of a mean stature, somewhat low and gross, of a sallow complexion, and inclining to the dropsy, hawk-nosed, unsteady in his pace by reason of some weakness of his limbs, heavy and inactive, yet commonly smiling almost to a laughter. For quality otherwise simple and slow witted but very gentle and of an easy nature, quiet, merciful, of no martial disposition nor greatly apt for matter of policy, very superstitious and infinite that way. Besides his private devotions at home he goeth every week commonly on pilgrimage to some monastery or other that is nearest hand. He is of thirty-four years old or thereabouts and hath reigned almost the space of six years.[3]

Chapter 27. Of the emperor's private or household officers

The chief officers of the emperor's household are these which follow. The first is the office of the boiarin koniushii or master of the horse, which containeth no more than is expressed by the name, that is, to be overseer of the horse and not *magister equitum* or master of the horsemen. For he appointeth other for that service as occasion

3. Fedor was born in 1557; he became tsar in 1584, and died in 1598.

doth require as before was said. He that beareth that office at this time is Boris Fedorovich Godunov, brother to the empress. Of horse for service in his wars (besides other for his ordinary uses) he hath to the number of ten thousand, which are kept about Moscow.

The next is the lord steward of his household, at this time one Grigorii Vasil'evich Godunov.[1] The third is his treasurer that keepeth all his monies, jewels, plate, etc., now called Stepan Vasil'evich Godunov.[2] The fourth, his controller, now Andrei Petrovich Kleshnin.[3] The fifth, his chamberlain. He that attendeth that office at this time is called Istoma Bezobrazov, *postel'nichii*.[4] The sixth, his tasters, now Fedor Aleksandrovich and Ivan Vasil'evich Godunov.[5] The seventh, his harbingers, which are three noblemen and divers other gentlemen that do the office under them. These are his ordinary officers and offices of the chiefest account.

Of gentlemen beside that wait about his chamber and person (called *zhil'tsy-striapchie*)[6] there are two hundred, all noblemen's sons. His ordinary guard is two thousand harquebusiers ready with their pieces charged and their match lighted, with other necessary furniture, continually day and night, which come not within the house but wait without in the court or yard where the emperor is abiding. In the nighttime there lodgeth next to his bedchamber the chief chamberlain with one or two more of best trust about him. A second chamber off there lodge six other of like account for their trust and faithfulness. In the third chamber lie certain young gentlemen, of these two hundred, called zhil'tsy-striapchie, that take their turns by forties every night.

1. G. V. Godunov was appointed to the post of dvoretskii in 1584 (*DRV*, XX, 60).

2. According to the Sheremetev list of Muscovite courtiers and their ranks, Ivan Vasil'evich Trakhaniotov was appointed treasurer (kaznachei) in 1586/87. S. V. Godunov was promoted to the rank of boiar in 1584 and is not mentioned again in the lists until 1598 when he appears as dvoretskii (*DRV*, XX, 60, 69).

3. In 1586/87 A. P. Kleshnin was named to the rank of okol'nichii, the second rank in the boiar duma (*DRV*, XX, 62). See above, pp. 155–56.

4. Istoma Osipovich Bezobrazov was appointed postel'nichii (chamberlain) in 1582 and retained the post through the reign of Fedor (*DRV*, XX, 60).

5. The taster at the time of Fletcher's visit was Aleksandr Nikitich Romanov-Iur'ev (*DRV*, XX, 63). His appointment to the post took place in 1586. He was raised to the rank of boiar in 1599. In the following year his household treasurer denounced him to the government as a traitor. Boris Godunov consequently exiled him to a settlement on the coast of the White Sea where he died in 1602 (*RBS*).

6. The words are usually applied to two different ranks of court servitors.

There are grooms besides that watch in their course and lie at every gate and door of the court, called *istopnik*.[7]

The harquebusiers or gunners, whereof there are two thousand, as was said before, watch about the emperor's lodging or bedchamber by course two hundred and fifty every night, and two hundred and fifty more in the courtyard and about the treasure house. His court or house at the Moscow is made castle-wise, walled about with great store of fair ordnance planted upon the wall, and containeth a great breadth of ground within it with many dwelling houses which are appointed for such as are known to be sure and trusty to the emperor.

Chapter 28. Of the private behavior or quality of the Russe people

The private behavior and quality of the Russe people may partly be understood by that which hath been said concerning the public state and usage of the country. As touching the natural habit of their bodies they are for the most part of a large size and of very fleshly bodies, accounting it a grace to be somewhat gross and burly, and therefore they nourish and spread their beards to have them long and broad. But for the most part they are very unwieldy and inactive withal, which may be thought to come partly of the climate and the numbness which they get by the cold in winter and partly of their diet, that standeth most of roots, onions, garlic, cabbage, and such like things that breed gross humors, which they use to eat alone and with their other meats.

Their diet is rather much than curious. At their meals they begin commonly with a charka or small cup of *aqua vitae* (which they call Russe wine) and then drink not till towards the end of their meals, taking it in largely and altogether with kissing one another at every pledge. And therefore after dinner there is no talking with them, but every man goeth to his bench to take his afternoon's sleep, which is as ordinary with them as their night's rest. When they exceed and have variety of dishes the first are their baked meats (for roast meats they

7. Stoker, servant responsible for tending the heating stoves of the palace.

use little) and then their broths or pottage. To drink drunk is an ordinary matter with them every day in the week. Their common drink is mead; the poorer sort use water and a thin drink called *kvas,* which is nothing else (as we say) but water turned out of his wits with a little bran mashed with it.

This diet would breed in them many diseases but that they use bathstoves or hot houses instead of all physic commonly twice or thrice every week. All the wintertime and almost the whole summer they heat their *pechi,* which are made like the German bathstoves, and their potlads, like ovens, that so warm the house that a stranger at the first shall hardly like of it. These two extremities, specially in the winter of heat within their houses and of extreme cold without, together with their diet, maketh them of a dark and sallow complexion, their skins being tanned and parched both with cold and with heat, specially the women that for the greater part are of far worse complexions than the men. Whereof the cause I take to be their keeping within the hot houses and busying themselves about the heating and using of their bathstoves and pechi.

The Russe because that he is used to both these extremities of heat and of cold can bear them both a great deal more patiently than strangers can do. You shall see them sometimes (to season their bodies) come out of their bathstoves all on a froth and fuming as hot almost as a pig at a spit, and presently to leap into the river stark naked or to pour cold water all over their bodies, and that in the coldest of all the wintertime. The women to mend the bad hue of their skins use to paint their faces with white and red colors so visibly that every man may perceive it. Which is made no matter because it is common and liked well by their husbands, who make their wives and daughters an ordinary allowance to buy them colors to paint their faces withal and delight themselves much to see them of foul women to become such fair images. This parcheth the skin and helpeth to deform them when their painting is off.

They apparel themselves after the Greek manner. The nobleman's attire is on this fashion. First, a *taf'ia* or little night cap on his head that covereth little more than his crown, commonly very rich wrought of silk and gold thread and set with pearl and precious stone. His head he keepeth shaven close to the very skin except he be in some displeasure with the emperor. Then he suffereth his hair to grow and hang down upon his shoulders, covering his face as ugly and deformedly as he can. Over the taf'ia he weareth a wide cap of black fox (which they account for the best fur) with a tiara or long bonnet put within it standing up like a Persian or Babylonian hat. About his neck (which is seen all bare) is a collar set with pearl and precious stone about three or four fingers broad. Next over his shirt (which is curiously wrought because he strippeth himself unto it in the summertime while he is within the house) is a *zipun* or light garment of silk made down to the knees, buttoned before, and then a *kaftan* or a close coat buttoned and girt to him with a Persian girdle whereat he hangs his knives and spoon. This commonly is of cloth of gold and hangeth down as low as his ankles. Over that he weareth a loose garment of some rich silk, furred and faced about with some gold lace, called a *feriaz'*. Another over that of camlet[1] or like stuff called an *okhaben'*, sleeved and hanging low and the cape commonly brooched and set all with pearl. When he goeth abroad he casteth over all these (which are but slight though they seem to be many) another garment called an odnoriadka, like to the okhaben' save that it is made without a collar for the neck. And this is commonly of fine cloth or camel's hair. His buskins (which he weareth instead of hose with linen folds under them instead of boot hose) are made of a Persian leather called saffian embroidered with pearl. His upper stocks commonly are of cloth of gold. When he goeth abroad he mounteth on horseback though it be but to the next door, which is the manner also of the boiars or gentlemen.

The boiarskii or gentleman's attire is of the same fashion but differeth in stuff, and yet he will have his kaftan or undercoat sometimes of cloth of gold, the rest of cloth or silk.

The noblewoman (called *zhena boiarskaia*) weareth on her head first a cowl of some soft silk (which is commonly red) and over it a frontlet called *ubrus* of white color, over that her cap (made after the coif fashion of cloth of gold) called *shapka zemskaia*,[2] edged with some rich fur and set with pearl and stone, though they have of late begun to disdain embroidering with pearl about their caps because the d'iaki and some merchants' wives have taken up the fashion. In their ears they wear earrings (which they call *ser'gi*) of two inches or more compass, the matter of gold set with rubies or sapphires or some like precious stone. In summer they go often with kerchiefs of fine white

---

1. A fine fabric, commonly of Angora.
2. The adjective probably should be *zhenskaia*: woman's.

lawn or cambric fastened under the chin with two long tassels pendant, the kerchief spotted and set thick with rich pearl. When they ride or go abroad in rainy weather they wear white hats with colored bands called *shliapa zemskaia*. About their necks they wear collars of three or four fingers broad set with rich pearl and precious stone. Their upper garment is a loose gown called *opashen'*, commonly of scarlet, with wide loose sleeves, hanging down to the ground, buttoned before with great gold buttons, or at least silver and gilt nigh as big as a walnut, which hath hanging over it fastened under the cap a large broad cape of some rich fur that hangeth down almost to the middle of their backs. Next under the opashen' or upper garment they wear another called a *letnik* that is made close before with great wide sleeves, the cuff or half sleeve up to the elbows, commonly of cloth of gold, and under that a feriaz' zemskaia which hangeth loose buttoned throughout to the very foot. On the hand wrists they wear very fair bracelets about two fingers broad of pearl and precious stone. They go all in buskins of white, yellow, blue, or some other colored leather embroidered with pearl. This is the attire of the noblewoman of Russia when she maketh the best show of herself. The gentlewoman's apparel may differ in the stuff but is all one for the making or fashion.

As for the poor muzhik and his wife they go poorly clad. The man with his odnoriadka or loose gown to the small of the leg tied together with a lace before, of coarse white or blue cloth, with some shuba or long waistcoat of fur or of sheepskin under it, and his furred cap and buskins. The poorer sort of them have their odnoriadka or upper garment made of cow's hair. This is their winter habit. In the summertime commonly they wear nothing but their shirts on their backs and buskins on their legs. The woman goeth in a red or blue gown when she maketh the best show and with some warm shuba of fur under it in the wintertime, but in the summer nothing but her two shirts (for so they call them), one over the other whether they be within doors or without. On their heads they wear caps of some colored stuff, many of velvet or of cloth of gold, but for the most part kerchiefs. Without earrings of silver or some other metal and her cross about her neck you shall see no Russe woman be she wife or maid.

As touching their behavior and quality otherwise they are of reasonable capacities if they had those means that some other nations have to train up their wits in good nurture and learning, which they might borrow of the Poles and other their neighbors but that they refuse it of a very self pride as accounting their own fashions to be far the best, partly also (as I said before) for that their manner of bringing up (void of all good learning and civil behavior) is thought by their governors most agreeable to that state and their manner of government, which the people would hardly bear if they were once civilized and brought to more understanding of God and good policy. This causeth the emperors to keep out all means of making it better and to be very wary for excluding of all peregrinaty that might alter their fashions, which were less to be disliked if it set not a print into the very minds of his people. For as themselves are very hardly and cruelly dealt withal by their chief magistrates and other superiors, so are they as cruel one against another, specially over their inferiors and such as are under them. So that the basest and wretchedest krest'ianin (as they call him) that stoopeth and croucheth like a dog to the gentleman and licketh up the dust that lieth at his feet is an intolerable tyrant where he hath the advantage. By this means the whole country is filled with rapine and murder. They make no account of the life of a man. You shall have a man robbed sometime in the very streets of their towns if he go late in the evening, and yet no man to come forth out of his doors to rescue him though he hear him cry out. I will not speak of the strangeness of the murders and other cruelties committed among them that would scarcely be believed to be done among men, specially such as profess themselves Christians.

The number of their vagrant and begging poor is almost infinite, that are so pinched with famine and extreme need as that they beg after a violent and desperate manner with "give me and cut me, give me and kill me" and such like phrases. Whereby it may be guessed what they are towards strangers that are so unnatural and cruel towards their own. And yet it may be doubted whether is the greater, the cruelty or intemperancy that is used in that country. I will not speak of it because it is so foul and not to be named. The whole country overfloweth with all sin of that kind, and no marvel, as having no law to restrain whoredoms, adulteries, and like uncleanness of life.

As for the truth of his word the Russe for the most part maketh small regard of it so he may gain by a lie and breach of his promise. And it may be said truly (as they know best that have traded most with them) that from the great to the small (except some few that will scarcely be found) the Russe neither believeth anything that another man speaketh nor speaketh anything himself worthy to be believed.

These qualities make them very odious to all their neighbors, specially to the Tatars that account themselves to be honest and just in comparison of the Russe. It is supposed by some that do well consider of the state of both countries that the offense they take at the Russe government and their manner of behavior hath been a great cause to keep the Tatar still heathenish and to mislike (as he doth) of the Christian profession.

The Travels
of Sir Jerome Horsey

Sir Jerome Horsey

Introduction

Sir Jerome Horsey's longest work, his *Travels,* is a puzzle.[1] If any Englishman could claim to have inside information about sixteenth-century Muscovy, it was this one. Not only did Horsey work for years as a successful, although unscrupulous, commercial agent; he also ingratiated himself with Ivan IV and Boris Godunov and found satisfaction in running their diplomatic errands. In the course of his many-sided career he undoubtedly built up a store of facts and anecdotes that a modern historian would give a great deal to possess. When he wrote down his recollections, however, something must have been lost. From so well-informed a memoirist, the *Travels* is a grave disappointment: the work is diffuse and often misleading, if we may judge by the testimony of the other sources of the period.

Both the ambiguous quality of Horsey's career and the circumstances in which he wrote the *Travels* may help to explain this disap-

1. Horsey's other writings include his description of the coronation of Tsar Fedor and his subsequent mission to London in 1585–86 as Fedor's ambassador (Bond, pp. 269–80), an account of his second and third missions to Russia (Bond, pp. 288–311), and a number of letters.

pointing discrepancy. Although we know very little of Horsey before his first Russian journey, in 1573, his activities thereafter are, to say the least, amply documented. Horsey went to Russia as an employee of the Russia Company and lived there almost continuously until his final expulsion in 1591. Nothing is known of the first seven years of his stay, yet the time was not wasted. By 1580, it seems, he had learned to speak Russian fluently (writing was never his forte, even in English) and had attracted the attention of Ivan IV. In that year the tsar sent him secretly to England for a supply of "powder, saltpeter, lead, and brimstone."

The mission of 1580 set the pattern for Horsey's complex operations in the following years. Apart from his personal qualities—apparently a delicate blend of ruthlessness and charm—he proved, as an Englishman who knew Russia well, to be an ideal link between the two countries. On occasion each sovereign employed him as his emissary to the other: in 1585 the Muscovite government chose him to convey to Queen Elizabeth the news of Fedor's accession to the throne, and the queen selected him as her messenger to Muscovy in 1586 and again in 1590.

Sometimes his patrons entrusted him with tasks that lay well outside the bounds of normal diplomatic activity. Boris Godunov once sent him to Livonia to establish contact with Mariia Vladimirovna, the widow of Prince Magnus and a member of the imperial family of Moscow, and to convince her to leave Polish protection and return to Russia. Horsey carried out his instructions to perfection and the lady was soon safely confined in a Muscovite convent. On the English side, Sir Francis Walsingham seems to have employed him to manage his private trading ventures in Russia.[2]

It was never easy to juggle so many commissions and loyalties. For most of his career in diplomacy, Horsey had to fight hard to retain the confidence of the patrons upon whom depended his position of prestige and influence. The first storm broke in 1585. While he was in England as Tsar Fedor's ambassador, an employee of the Russia Company named John Finch caused him acute embarrassment by charging that, while both were in Russia, Horsey had falsely denounced him to the Muscovite authorities who thereupon arrested and tortured him.[3] When the Privy Council looked into the matter, however, Finch confessed that his accusations were false.

---

2. Willan, *Early History*, pp. 201–4.
3. Finch's petition to the Lords of the Council in 1585. *Calendar of State Papers, Foreign* (May 1585–May 1586), p. 268.

The setback did not deter Horsey's critics and, in the years following, their accusations piled up ominously. The first witnesses were representatives of the Russia Company whose testimony boiled down to
the charge that Horsey had undermined the Company's operations in
Russia in order to fill his own purse. In the first place, they alleged, he
made use of his long experience and extensive contacts in Russia to set
up a private trading enterprise which competed with his own employ-
ers and, on occasion, went so far as to defraud fellow employees
whose ignorance of Russian made them vulnerable. Moreover, if any-
one threatened to expose his shady dealings, he would go to great
lengths to cover his tracks. When other members of the Company tried
to look into his affairs, the allegations continued, he saw to it that the
Muscovite government seized their property and, in several cases, even
arranged for their arrest and torture by suggesting that they were
agents of a hostile power. As John Horneby claimed on a later occasion:

I myself endured (through Horsey's procuring) both imprisonment
and extreme torture by whipping, racking, and roasting, in such cruel
sort as I cannot endure to make particular relation of it and if the
now emperor (being then the chiefest of the nobility) had not showed
me his gracious favor I had been tortured to death, being innocent
and guiltless of any such matter as I was charged withal.[4]

As if to clinch the case, the Company's spokesmen charged that Horsey was a menace to England's national interest. As the directors of the
Company were well aware, Elizabeth and her ministers cultivated
good relations with Muscovy primarily so that English merchants could
provide the crown with Russian naval stores. The Company's indict-
ment struck at a very sensitive spot when it suggested that if the Muscovite government uncovered Horsey's flamboyant transactions, which
were often floated with money borrowed from Russians, the tsar might
retaliate by curtailing all of the Company's operations in his territories.
At first, these charges, although embarrassing, were not a serious
threat to Horsey's status: as long as he retained the trust of his patrons
in both England and Muscovy, he could still perform his diplomatic
shuttle service between the two courts. His position, nevertheless, was

---

4. Bond, pp. 315–27, 330–34; the quotation is given in Charles Sisson, "Englishmen in Shakespeare's Muscovy or the Victims of Jerome Horsey," *Mélanges en
l'honneur de Jules Legras* (Paris, 1939), p. 242. Testimony before the Court of
Chancery in 1597.

hardly enviable. By 1587 the outcry against him had reached such an intensity that the Privy Council began a formal investigation of the Company's allegations. Horsey, who was once again in England, abruptly disappeared and, for several months, the queen's ministers were not sure of his whereabouts.[5]

When he came to the surface in Moscow in 1588 he had suffered a fatal loss of credit. His chief protector, Boris Godunov, had lost faith in him and had joined the ranks of his accusers. After that the tsar's government attacked him with a persistence and savagery that rivalled the onslaughts of the Russia Company. Its formal accusations concentrated on two issues. In financing his trading ventures, Horsey apparently fell deeply in debt not only to private citizens but to the tsar's treasury as well. By ill-advised talk, moreover, he managed to give the impression that he was planning to protect the English stranglehold on Russia's overseas trade in the north by conducting pirate raids against any ships of another nationality that should approach Russian waters.[6] One recent incident must have caused Horsey embarrassment even though it was of too delicate a nature to mention in formal denunciations of his conduct. In 1586 he fulfilled what he thought to be the wishes of Godunov and brought an English midwife to attend the Empress Irina, Godunov's sister. What the lady needed, however, was rather some remedy to help her conceive.[7]

As a final sign of their displeasure, the Muscovite authorities arrested Horsey in 1589 and sent him back to England in the custody of Giles Fletcher. With that, his usefulness as a diplomatic agent came to an end.

At first he would not recognize that the game was over. By appealing to the queen and her advisers for one more chance to put right his affairs in Russia, he won appointment as ambassador to Muscovy in 1590 in spite of the bitter protests of the Russia Company. The mission was a total fiasco. When Horsey appeared at the court, Andrei Shchelkalov expressed doubts about the authenticity of Elizabeth's letters to Tsar Fedor and soon he was sent to rusticate in Iaroslavl' while the tsar received a Polish embassy. As he waited in vain for a summons to return to Moscow, he realized at last that his old patrons would never again take him into their confidence. In 1591 he left Russia for the last

5. Bond, p. 313; *Calendar of State Papers, Foreign* (Jan.–June 1588), pp. 94–95.
6. Tolstoy, pp. 396–97; Bond, p. cxii.
7. Bond, p. 321.

time with ambivalent feelings of disappointment at his failure and relief that he had escaped a worse fate.[8]

Even in retirement he could not hide from the old accusations. When he sued a Dutchman, Jan van de Valle, in 1592 to recover debts incurred when both were living in Russia, the defense called as character witnesses many of his enemies from the Russia Company. Before the trial ended, their testimony wove the long-standing charges against Horsey into a lurid pattern of mendacity, cruelty, and greed.[9]

During each wave of denunciations, Horsey defended himself coolly and tenaciously. At first sight, his tactics seem strange, for he rarely attempted to disprove the statements of his accusers. He came to grips only with the charges of the Muscovite government—from his point of view, the most serious of all—and explained that they were the result of misunderstanding of his words and of the unprovoked illwill of Shchelkalov.[10] On the whole he chose instead to draw attention away from the accusations against him by pointing to his accomplishments in the service of his sovereign. This was his theme, for example, in his report on his last mission to Muscovy. "Hereby it may seen, my good lord, that I have discharged my duty to my uttermost ability . . . ."[11]

In the midst of these controversies, Horsey began to write his *Travels*, a detailed account of his diplomatic career and of the main events in the recent history of Muscovy. He apparently worked on the treatise intermittently over a period of more than thirty years. The only clues to the date of composition of the work are found in the text itself. The dedication to Walsingham (p. 262) who died in 1590, suggests that he began to write in the interval between his return to England with Fletcher in 1589 and his departure on his final mission in 1590. It may well be that he began to write in the hope that a description of his past services would add weight to his pleas to be sent back to Moscow. Whatever his motives for beginning his work, many years passed before he finished it: he must have written the final pages of the manuscript in 1621 or later since he noted that "Since changing another course, I have lived for above thirty years' space in that fruitful region

8. Horsey's disappointment and frustration at the failure of his mission, and his fears for his own safety, are clearly evident in a letter he wrote to Lord Burghley from Iaroslavl', in April, 1591 (Bond, pp. 360–64).

9. Sisson's summary of the trial is found in *Mélanges en l'honneur de Jules Legras*, pp. 231–47.

10. Bond, pp. 307–8, 337–41.

11. Bond, p. 372.

of Buckinghamshire . . ." (p. 369).[12] Apart from the dedication, there is no indication of the readers for whom he wrote. When finished, the work was quickly forgotten.

Horsey probably wrote the *Travels* as a final answer to his accusers. Even though he made no unequivocal statement of his purpose in recounting the main events of his career, the tone and theme of the *Travels* link it to the letters which he wrote in his own defense at the height of the campaign against him. In each case, the dominant motif is his resolute service to his country. At the end of the *Travels,* he captured his conviction in the felicitous turn of phrase with which he described his retirement: "In the mean I must be contented, as an old ship that hath done good service, to be laid up in the dock unrigged . . . (p. 369)."

Horsey's diplomatic memoirs, the largest part of the *Travels,* is a set of variations on this central theme. In describing each of the most important events of his career, he portrayed his activities in simple and consistent terms: he undertook every mission with diligence and resourcefulness and completed it with conspicuous success. One might reasonably assume that, in order to give substance to such a flattering appraisal of its hero and author, Horsey's memoir would present a full account of his triumphs and either explain away his defeats or ignore them entirely.

A comparison of the *Travels* with the other sources of information on Anglo-Russian relations indicates that Horsey did precisely this. On the whole, his treatment of the period of unqualified success, the years between 1580 and 1585, seems to be a reasonable appraisal of his achievements. His account of his secret mission to England in 1580, an episode mentioned in no other source, is quite consistent with what we know of the desperate military situation facing Ivan IV and of his previous attempts to elicit Queen Elizabeth's support.

A note of personal animosity dominates his description of Sir Jerome Bowes' embassy to Moscow in 1583–84. Yet, in outline, Horsey's account is in harmony with Bowes' own reports on the mission. The special element in Horsey's presentation is his insistence that the difficul-

12. On his return to England in 1591 Horsey retired to an estate in Buckinghamshire. Between 1592 and 1620 he was a member of parliament for various boroughs. In 1603 he was knighted, and in 1604 was made one of the receivers of the king's lands for life. He was high sheriff of Buckinghamshire in 1610 (*DNB* and Bond, pp. cxxviii–cxxxiv).

ties which Bowes encountered during the negotiations were entirely
the result of his own tactlessness. In fairness to Bowes, it would seem
that, in spite of his notorious irascibility, he was badly received in Moscow primarily because Elizabeth had sent him to reject Ivan's offer of
an alliance and the tsar took no pains to hide his displeasure at the re-
buff. In the end, after weeks of wrangling, Ivan IV suddenly changed
his tactics and granted Bowes new commercial privileges which Fedor
confirmed after his accession to the throne. According to Horsey's account of the episode, Fedor's advisers were furious with the ambassador
and allowed him to leave for England only because Horsey convinced
Boris Godunov that it was to the advantage of the Muscovite government to overlook Bowes' unseemly conduct and to maintain good relations with England. As is so often the case, we cannot check the accuracy of Horsey's claims. There is no question that he had attached himself to Godunov and was most likely in a position to intervene privately
on Bowes' behalf. At the same time, he wrote as an embattled man
and may well have given in to the temptation to exaggerate the extent
of his assistance to a fellow Englishman in distress.

When he described the stormy last years of his diplomatic activity, he
yielded completely to his desire to vindicate himself. His account of
the period between 1585 and 1591 exaggerates his triumphs and mentions only a few of the many trials he faced. With relish he told the
story of his successful defense against Finch's accusations. When describing the concessions which he won for the Russia Company in
1587, however, he gave himself credit for several privileges which
Fedor granted not in 1587 but in 1589 to Fletcher.[13] It is perhaps
equally significant that he did not mention that by 1589 the Muscovite
government was insisting it had granted no privileges at all in 1587.[14]

Horsey's diplomatic memoir comes to a grand climax in the story of
his journey to Russia in 1590–91. This picaresque tale begins with a
brilliant send-off from Elizabeth's court and encompasses elaborate negotiations with the Danish government, an incognito interview with
the dowager queen of Poland, and narrow escapes from Jesuit assassins
and a decaying crocodile. Through these vicissitudes Horsey advanced

13. The 1587 privileges are published in Hakluyt III, 348–53, and in Bond,
pp. 281–87; the 1589 grant is summarized in Tsar Fedor's letter to Elizabeth,
printed by Tolstoy, pp. 347–53, and in Fletcher's report on his mission, in Bond,
pp. 348–49, and Berry, pp. 373–75.
14. Bond, p. 333.

triumphantly until he reached Muscovy. There he was barred from the
court through the intrigues of Andrei Shchelkalov and, after several
months of threats and insults, considered himself fortunate to be allowed to leave Russia without suffering further indignities. How much
of the story is true is impossible to determine. It is important to note,
first, that Horsey made no mention at all of his secret departure from
England at the end of 1587 or the beginning of 1588 nor of the fact
that he was expelled from Muscovy in 1589. In relating his futile attempts to deal with the Muscovite government he once again omitted
details more important than most of those which he included. Other
evidence, for example, supports his claim that Shchelkalov vigorously
opposed close ties with England but also indicates that Horsey's arro-
gance and financial chicanery had made him an easy target. Moreover,
although the story shows that Horsey knew a great deal about the
courts of northern Europe and their diplomacy, it includes a number of
incidents that could not possibly have happened as he described them;
for example, Horsey could not have met Frederick II of Denmark in
1590 because the king had died two years earlier. Errors and distor-
tions of this magnitude, and the boastful gusto with which Horsey described his last journey, all indicate that the concluding sections of his
memoirs are to be read with great caution.

On the whole, therefore, it would be very dangerous to place too
much faith in Horsey's account of the relations between England and
Muscovy. The *Travels* adds interesting details on a number of episodes
but its contribution can be appraised only when compared with the
official correspondence between the two courts and the private letters
of the statesmen who protected him and the tradesmen who brought
accusations against him.

Horsey's work is considerably more reliable in the passages in which
his honor and credibility are not at stake. His description of Muscovite
politics and court life shows few signs of prejudice and offers an eyewitness view of many episodes of the 1570's and 1580's, probably the
most poorly documented decades in the history of the Muscovite state.
When Horsey allows partisanship to intrude, his feelings are clearly
stated and easy to understand: he hated Andrei Shchelkalov and was
partial to Boris Godunov, his chief protector until he fell from grace.

Unfortunately objectivity is not the only desirable quality in a historical narrative. Stylistic flaws, in Horsey's case, wreaked even more
havoc than partisanship. Horsey, who was, by his own admission, no

scholar, often muddled the sequence of events, in some cases juxtaposing episodes that occurred more than a decade apart. The errors in chronology admittedly occur chiefly in the opening section of the work which describes the course of recent Russian history up to the time of his arrival in Muscovy. The extent of Horsey's confusion, however, suggests that, even in the core of the *Travels*, we cannot be sure that events followed one another in the order in which Horsey treats them. His lack of precision extended to his choice of words as well. What troubles a modern reader is not his excessive use of sensational and hackneyed detail, which can easily be overlooked, but rather his annoying vagueness at important points in his narrative.

To take literally the details of Horsey's work can easily lead to misconceptions. A recent article provides a good illustration of the allure and danger of the *Travels* as a historical source. In reassessing the traditional interpretation of the rise of the zemskii sobor (estates-general), S. O. Shmidt argued that the sobor probably met much more frequently than historians have hitherto believed. To support his case, he examined a number of sources, including Horsey's work, in which he found passages that seemed to him to prove that meetings of the sobor took place in 1571 and 1576. The case for a 1571 sobor rests on part of Horsey's description of Ivan's flight from Moscow during the Crimean invasion:

> The Russe emperor fled still farther off with his two sons and treasure to a great town called Vologda, where he thought himself more secure, five hundred miles off. Much amazed and perplexed for this great disaster befallen him, he, accompanied with his metropolitans, bishops, and clergymen, his chief princes and ancient nobility now called for and summoned to a council royal, and the enemy gone, dissolved his army that fought not a stroke for him (pp. 272–73).

From this passage it is not at all clear what kind of council Ivan called. It could as easily have been a dumnyi sobor, a combined meeting of the boiar council and the leaders of the church, as a full zemskii sobor.

In another case, Shmidt argues that a sobor met in 1576 to urge Ivan to resume the crown that he had given up in favor of Simeon Bekbulatovich a few months earlier. Once again, the argument rests on a fragment from the *Travels*. After his description of the enthronement of Simeon, Horsey continued, "His clergy, nobility, and commons must now petition Ivan Vasil'evich that he would be pleased to take the crown and government upon him again, upon many conditions and authentical instruments confirmed by act of parliament in very solemn new inauguration" (p. 275). Later in the same passage, Horsey stated that Ivan thereupon began to rule as tsar and restored the privileges and charters of each estate of the realm. On this point as well, Horsey's vagueness destroys the significance of his observations. Did a meeting of the petitioners actually occur? He does not say and the reference to an "act of parliament" does not clarify his explanation. Therefore, while there is nothing intrinsically unreasonable about Shmidt's thesis, his case fails on these two points because Horsey's work, the only direct support for his suppositions, is too imprecise to prove his point.[15]

Horsey's work is not always so misleading. In many cases, his report of events coincides with the testimony of other sources and supplements them. A particularly good case is his handling of the church council which Ivan IV called in 1580 to force the great monasteries to agree not to accept any further bequests of land. Although his description of the council is exceptionally verbose, even by his own demanding standards, and is interrupted by a grotesque tale of the martyrdom of several prominent monks in a bear pit, the core of the story is consistent with the few other records of the council: Horsey's paraphrase of the tsar's speech opening the council and his description of the response of the leaders of the church are very close in content and in tone to the Russian original.

Where Horsey excels is in recording the mood of Muscovite society during the recurrent crises of the 1570's and 1580's. The description of the Crimean raid on Moscow in 1571 captures the confusion and terror inspired by a disaster in which large parts of the city were destroyed and many thousands perished. Although not a witness of the tragedy, he may well have set down the impressions of English or Russian acquaintances who survived it.

Court politics held a special interest for him and inspired some of his most perceptive observations. He apparently shared Fletcher's feeling that Muscovite society was living in fear of an explosion. In his

15. S. O. Shmidt, "K istorii soborov XVI v.," *Istoricheskie zapiski*, LXXVI (1965), 144–45. V. I. Koretskii has taken even greater liberties with Horsey's imprecise terminology in his article, "Zemskii sobor 1575 g. i postavlenie Simeona Bekbulatovicha 'Velikim kniazem vsei Rusi'," *Istoricheskii arkhiv*, 1959, No. 2, 148–56. Both Shmidt and Koretskii suffered from their reliance on N. A. Belozerskaia's century-old Russian translation of the *Travels*. Miss Belozerskaia cleaned up Horsey's rough prose by tidying up his disorderly syntax and sharpening his imprecise vocabulary and, in the process, she altered the meaning of many passages.

view, however, the danger lay in a breakdown in the orderly succession to the throne and a destructive clash between rival factions of courtiers. In his most evocative passage, he described the aftermath of the death of Ivan the Terrible—the sense of relief mixed with a terrible fear that unknown forces would intervene and cause the downfall of the ruling elite and perhaps of the tsardom itself. The fears of the court proved to be unjustified and Fedor was duly installed as tsar. It was only after the coronation that the struggle for power among Ivan's favorites broke out in full fury. Horsey recorded Boris Godunov's victorious struggle with his court adversaries and his emergence as the real ruler of Russia. In describing Godunov's path to power, he included statements that were probably based on rumors prevalent in Russia at the time. He claimed, for example, that Godunov at one time planned to flee to England and that conspirators had tried to murder Prince Dmitrii, the youngest son of Ivan IV, even before his mysterious death in 1591. Whether or not such plans were actually entertained, the currency of the rumors is a symptom of the ferocity of the struggles at the court and the ominous expectations of society concerning their outcome. All of the rising tension was concentrated in the reaction to Dmitrii's death in 1591. Horsey shared the conviction of most of his contemporaries that the deed was the work of agents of Godunov, a view that contributed to the collapse of Muscovite government and society after Godunov assumed the throne at the end of the century.

In Horsey's *Travels*, the leading figures of Muscovy are lively and complex people. His assessment of Ivan the Terrible is particularly significant since it differs from the view prevalent in the writings of the period. It is a portrait that might have appealed to Ivan himself. The tsar was monstrously cruel and vindictive—and Horsey gives his readers more than their share of torture, rape, and plunder. Yet he was also a man of wit and lively intelligence, a statesman whose ambition added large territories to his domains and whose humanity brought enlightened reforms to the mass of his subjects. His cruelty, although perhaps intensified by a sadistic element in his character, was essential to his success as a ruler. For to the lord of an enormous realm and the master of rebellious nobles, gentleness would have been fatal. To be great, Ivan had to be terrible.

Boris Godunov is also a figure fraught with contradictions. When Horsey pictured him during the early years of Fedor's reign, he was charming and magnanimous. In the first years of power, Boris also displayed ruthlessness toward his enemies, partly as a result of his position as chief adviser to a "silly prince" under whose rule the state might be fatally weakened if some strong hand did not take control of the government. At the same time, Horsey displayed considerable sympathy for Godunov's defeated rivals and in the later passages describing the coming of the Time of Troubles, Boris, now branded as the murderer of Prince Dmitrii, was a sinister figure, dominated by ambition and greed. This picture of Godunov as a humane man corrupted by ambition had wide currency and received its classic statement in Pushkin's play and Mussorgsky's opera, *Boris Godunov*. Only since Platonov's studies at the turn of the century has Boris emerged as a more consistently sympathetic figure, overwhelmed by forces beyond his control.

Horsey's *Travels* is a puzzling patchwork of sharp insights and glaring errors. Its contradictory qualities reflect the extraordinary character of its author and hero. From an inauspicious beginning, Horsey rose to prominence in an age in which the practice of international diplomacy was changing rapidly. England and Muscovy had not yet exchanged resident ambassadors, but needed more regular and flexible contact than occasional ambassadorial visits could provide. One solution was the employment of a skilled courier whose commission, open or secret, could be adjusted to meet the demands of the moment. Horsey was just the man for so demanding a role: his knowledge of both countries offered him the opportunity to serve two masters—the queen and the tsar. His audacity prompted him to take up the game and his shrewdness permitted him to play it successfully for a decade. We cannot be sure how much he learned about the countries he visited and the statesmen he knew, for his *Travels* gives us only hints of what he might have recorded. When he wrote, it seems, he was still playing out the old game and, if not winning as before, then at least keeping the world at bay. His work is an embattled *apologia pro vita sua*, probably composed in haste and, in large part, long after the events. The modern reader may regret that the *Travels* is not more systematic and less partisan. If it were, however, it would not be the work of Jerome Horsey.

Horsey's *Travels* exists in a single manuscript in the British Museum, Harleian MS 1813. The work has been edited only once, by Edward A. Bond, *Russia at the Close of the Sixteenth Century* (London, 1856), pp. 153–266. The *Travels* has been translated into Russian:

N. A. Belozerskaia (trans.) and N. I. Kostomarov (ed.), "Zapiski o Moskovii XVI veka," *Biblioteka dlia chteniia*, 1865, Nos. 4–6 (text incomplete). Iu. Tolstoi (trans.), "Razskaz ili povestvovanie o puteshestviiakh, dolzhnostiakh, sluzhbakh i peregovorakh sera Eremeia Gorseia, v kotorykh on provel pochti tselykh vosemnadtsat' let," *Chteniia v Imperatorskom obshchestve istorii i drevnostei rossiiskikh pri Moskovskom universitete*, 1877, Book I, part iv, 1–30; 1907, Book II, part iii, pp. i–iv, 31–110. The complete Belozerskaia-Kostomarov version appeared as *Rossiia v kontse shestnadtsatago stoletiia. Zapiski o Moskovii XVI veka sera Dzheroma Gorseia* (St. Petersburg, 1909).

Sir Jerome Horsey

Travels

I
To the right honorable
Sir Francis Walsingham, knight,
principal secretary of estate
unto her majesty

Having found and felt your love and favor so great[1] towards the furthering of my well doing and preferment since the happy time my most worthy friend and kinsman, Sir Edward Horsey,[2] first brought my acquaintance unto your honor; and knowing your noble disposition and desire to understand the estate and foreign occurrences, and according to your advice and instructions (heretofore given me), I hold it no less a duty of thankfulness in me to render an account of such things as most properly are due unto your place, of all others to be advertised of; and for the encouragement of others that may reap some benefit by the knowing and doing the like, I have thought good, by way of discourse or treatise, first unto your honor, and next to you, my right worthy good friends, that are desirous to know my observations in my travels, employments, and negotiations of the most rare and remarkable things of the known countries and king-

1. Walsingham (1530?–90) was Secretary of State from 1573–90. See Conyers Read, *Mr. Secretary Walsingham* (Oxford, 1925).
2. Horsey (d. 1583) was a naval and military commander, a confidant of the earl of Leicester, ambassador in the Netherlands, and a member of the privy council (*DNB*).

doms in the north and northwestern parts of Europe, Asia, and Scythia, as Russia, Muscovy, Tatary, with all those continent territories and kingdoms adjacent, Poland, Transylvania, Lithuania, and Livonia, Sweden, Denmark, situated between the Northern Ocean and the Baltic Sea; the empire and imperial spacious principalities of high Germany; of the five upper and nether united cantons, Cleve, Westphalia, Friesland; the low countries of Bass Germany, commonly called Flanders, Brabant, Zeeland, and Holland, consisting of the seventeen United Provinces; their chief cities and towns of traffic and commerce, both inland and maritime, their commodities, their universities and ancient monuments, their climates and situations, laws, languages, religion, discipline of church and commonwealth, and natural disposition of the people. All which I mind to contract in four several and distinct treatises, as compendious and methodical as my observation and seventeen years' experience will give me leave.

II

The first, after I had been and seen some part of France and the Low Countries in their flourishing but most troublesome time of war, I arrived in Muscovy, commonly called Russia. Though but a plain grammarian, and having some smack in the Greek, I attained by the affinity thereof in short time to the ready and familiar knowledge of their vulgar speech, the Slavonian tongue, the most copious and elegant language in the world. With some small abbreviation and pronunciation it comes near the Polish, Latvian, Transylvanian, and all those adjacent countries;[1] and it will serve in Turkey, Persia, even to the known Indies, etc. I read in their chronicles, written and kept in secret by a great prime prince of that country named Kniaz' Ivan Fedorovich Mstislavskii, who, out of his love and favor, imparted unto me many secrets observed in the memory and process of his time, which was fourscore years, of the state, nature, and government of that commonwealth;[2] of which I made good use when discourse among

1. Of the languages Horsey mentions, only Polish is related to Russian.
2. It is very unlikely that Horsey made significant use of the Russian chronicles. Had he really studied the chronicles, the historical passages in his work would

them served, committing matters done in former ages (in the latter end of Vasilii Andreevich his reign,[3] styled then but great duke of Vladimir, Russia, Muscovy, etc., the catalogue whereof I refer to a more fitter place), that he had enlarged his countries and dominions very much in his time, both upon the Pole, Swede, and especially upon the Tatars, the great Scythian Krym or khan,[4] left his countries and people in great peace and tranquility, strong and rich, and his princes in charge of government to defend his countries and kingdoms, divided into four parts, and his two sons, the eldest of five years age,[5] called Velikii Kniaz' Ivan Vasil'evich, to reign and govern after him, the other, of two years of age, duke of a territory called Vaga.[6] This great duke of all Russia, Ivan Vasil'evich, grew up comely in person, indued with great wit, excellent gifts, and graces fit for government of so great a monarchy, married at twelve years Anastasiia Romanova, daughter to a gentleman of good rank; Nikita Romanovich, her brother, highly advanced.[7] This empress became wise and of such holiness, virtue, and government, as she was honored, beloved, and feared of all her subjects. He being young and riotous, she ruled him with admirable affability and wisdom, that, with the prowess and courage of his princes, bishops, and council, he cast off the yoke of homage his predecessors always did unto the great Scythian emperor of the Kryms,[8] conquered

surely be more accurate. Mstislavskii, one of the last appanage princes, was made boiar in 1549 (Zimin, "Sostav boiarskoi dumy," p. 61). In the Kazan' campaign and the invasion of Livonia, he was one of the chief commanders of the Russian forces. During the oprichnina, he and I. D. Bel'skii were the leaders of the boiar council that ruled the zemshchina. After the Tatar invasion of 1571, he was accused of treason but escaped with a light penalty (Zimin, *Oprichnina*, pp. 463–64). He remained a boiar until the end of Ivan's reign and was one of the inner circle that arranged the orderly succession of Fedor. He soon fell out with Boris Godunov and was exiled to a monastery where he died in 1586 (*DRV*, XX, 62).

3. Presumably this refers to Vasilii III Ivanovich.

4. Vasilii III absorbed into his domains Pskov and the principality of Riazan'. In 1514 his armies captured Smolensk. On the east, he fought a series of indecisive wars with the Khanate of Kazan'. He made no conquests at the expense of the Crimean Tatars; on the contrary, Khan Muhammad Girey inflicted on Vasilii his worst defeat—a disastrous raid deep into Russian territory in 1521.

5. In 1533 when his father died, Ivan IV was three years old.

6. The principality of Prince Iurii Vasil'evich consisted of Uglich, Bezhetskii Verkh, Kaluga, Malyi Iaroslavets, Kremensk, Medyn', and Mezetsk (S. B. Veselovskii, "Poslednie udely v Severo-Vostochnoi Rusi," *Istoricheskie zapiski*, XXII [1947], 101).

7. Ivan married in February, 1547, at the age of sixteen.

8. Perhaps a reference to the Muscovite tradition that Ivan III repudiated the suzerainty of the Golden Horde in 1480.

the empire and emperors of Kazan' and Astrakhan', 2,700 miles from
his city of Moscow down the great river Volga, near the Mare Caspian
Sea,[9] conquered, in a short space after, all the princes and their countries of Tatary of divers sorts and brought a great people under his
subjection, the dissolution [devastation][10] whereof to this day is most
mournfully sung and spoken of among those nations. Through which
conquest he gathered great strength and got great fame, and thereby
assumed to himself two several crowns and empiredoms, and by a general council of all his princes, nobles, prelates, and people was crowned
and styled the emperor, great monarch, and great duke of Kazan', Astrakhan', Moscow, Vladimir, Novgorod, Russia, and a great rabblement
more of the names of his provinces, which he would have all kings' ambassadors recite and acknowledge with whom he had any correspondence. But yet he had continual wars with the Krym Tatar, who did
sore annoy him and his subjects with their yearly incursions. As he
grew in years and greatness, so did his conquests increase and augment; he got from the king of Poland the famous cities of Polotsk,
Smolensk, Dorogobuzh, Viaz'ma, and many other towns,[11] with much
riches and infinite numbers of people captives, seven hundred miles
within their confines; Belorussia and Lithuania, goodly towns of traffic,
and countries yielding great commodities, wax, flax, and hemp, tallow,
hides, corn, and cattle abundance; many nobles and of the gentry and
merchants bought and sold and put to great ransoms; so that he grew
very puissant, proud, mighty, cruel, and bloody in his conquests. And
when his good queen died, Empress Anastasiia, who was canonized a
saint and so worshiped in their churches to this day, having by her two
sons, Ivan and Fedor, then he married one of the Circassian princesses,
by whom he had no issue that he would be known of.[12] The manner
and solemnity of this marriage was so strange and heathenly as credit
will hardly be given to the truth thereof. Therefore I will forbear to
repeat the narration out of their own histories and come nearer the
times of my own knowledge.

9. Ivan's armies conquered Kazan' in 1552, Astrakhan' in 1556.
10. Alternate readings in the ms. will be contained in square brackets in the text.
11. Ivan III annexed Viaz'ma in 1494 and Dorogobuzh in 1503. Smolensk was
captured in 1514 in the reign of Vasilii III. Ivan IV's army took Polotsk in 1563
but lost it again in 1579 to the Poles under Bathory. Except for a short period in
the mid-seventeenth century, Polotsk remained in the Polish-Lithuanian commonwealth until the first partition in 1772.
12. Anastasiia died in 1560, and in 1561 Ivan married Mariia, daughter of
Temriuk, prince of Kabarda.

He having strengthened himself, not only by his conquests of those empiredoms, as their speech terms them, of Kazan' and Astrakhan', bringing captive the chief and most of all their princes and mightiest men of war, but also by this late marriage gotten an invincible power and strength of these Tatars, resolute and better soldiers than themselves; as well to make use of them to suppress and curb such of his princes and nobles as he perceived were in discontentment and in mutiny against him for his most cruel slaughtering, murdering, and incessant massacring, robbing, and putting to death of his nobility; swelling in ambition, boasting beyond all sense [reason] what conquest he intended, sets forward with an army of a hundred thousand horse and fifty thousand foot, cannon and all artillery, munition, victuals, and all other provisions accordingly,[13] towards Livonia and Sweden, the confines of that part of Christendom; kills and murders men, women, and children that crosseth his army between him and Novgorod and Pskov, two greatest mart [maritime or trade] towns for traffic of all the eastern parts, with the Narva, standing triangle-wise in equal distance at the end or gulf of the Baltic eastern sea, heretofore belonging to the freedom of Livonia, governed by a freer or absolute state, where he built a strong castle, I mean at the Narva, called Ivangorod,[14] to command the town; and caused the eyes of the builder to be pulled [bored] out for his so rare architecture. From Pskov[15] he enters the confines of Livonia, sends Kniaz' Mikhail Glinskii with the cannon to besiege the first castle, called Neuhausen, takes it and the soldiers captives and puts in three hundred soldiers for garrison thereof, to whom he gave the spoil and pillage,[16] besieges and takes other small towns and castles in his way to Dorpat, a great and strong town of traffic, batters and besieges it; they yield with a dejective flag of truce; four thousand Tatars carry away eight thousand captives, men, women, and children, the treasure and merchandises taken and sent to Novgorod for the emperor's use.[17]

13. Contemporary sources give widely varying estimates of the size of the Russian army that invaded Livonia. In any case, Horsey's figure is far too large, since the total strength of the Russian army on all fronts was about 150,000 (Zimin, *Reformy*, p. 448).

14. Ivangorod was built in 1492 by Ivan III.

15. Vobsko in the original text.

16. On June 30, 1558, Russian forces under Petr Ivanovich Shuiskii and Andrei Mikhailovich Kurbskii captured Neuhausen (*PSRL*, XIII, ii, 303–4; *PL*, II, 236).

17. In the summer of 1558 a Russian army laid siege to Dorpat (Tartu). When further resistance seemed hopeless, the bishop and the leading citizens of the town

He goes forward, severing his army into four troops, without resistance, and ten thousand to guard and draw his ordnance over rivers and standing ozera frozen hard and all over; takes many castles, towns, and villages, riches, cattle, and people in his way to Pernau, Hapsal, Leal, Wenden, Goldingen, Mitau, and many other strong towns standing near the Eastern Sea, to the number of thirty walled towns within two hundred miles compass.[18] O the lamentable outcries and cruel slaughters, drowning and burning, ravaging of women and maids, stripping them naked without mercy or regard of the frozen weather, tying and binding them by three and by four at their horses' tails, dragging them, some alive, some dead, all bloodying the ways and streets, lying full of carcasses of the aged men and women and infants; some goodly persons clad in velvet, damask, and silks, with jewels, gold, and pearl hid about them; the fairest people in the world, by reason of their generation, country, and climate, cold and dry. There was infinite numbers thus sent and dragged into Russia. The riches, in money and merchandises and other treasure, that was conveyed and carried out of these cities and country and out of six hundred churches robbed and destroyed, was invaluable. Thus the emperor and his cruel and hellish Tatars, having ranged and ransacked this goodly country and miserable people, came at last to the capital and chief city called Reval, by him Steucoll, standing and built very strong upon a high rocky mountain upon the edge of the Baltic Sea over against Stockholm in Sweden; besieges it with twenty thousand men; batters it with twenty cannons; the soldiers, men, and women within the town make up the breaches in the night that were battered in the day, with carrying and casting hot and cold water, which continually froze so thick as the emperor, after six weeks' siege and twenty thousand cannon shot, did little prevail; wherewith, and with the loss of six thou-

made an agreement to surrender on condition that the people be allowed to remain there and live according to their own customs (*PL*, II, 236–37). The tsar agreed to spare the town but ordered that the bishop and some of the most prominent citizens be deported into Russia (*PSRL*, XIII, ii, 304–5). In 1565, however, large numbers of people were taken from Dorpat and resettled in the interior of Russia in the districts of Nizhnii-Novgorod, Vladimir, Kostroma, and Uglich (*PSRL*, XIII, ii, 397; *PL*, II, 248).

18. The Russian army captured Pernau in 1575 and Hapsal and Leal in 1576. In 1578 an army under the command of Ivan Iur'evich Golitsyn unsuccessfully besieged Wenden (now Cesis). The tsar's forces did not capture Goldingen (now Kuldiga) and Mitau (now Jelgava) during the Livonian war.

sand men, he hasted his retreat and left it with shame.[19] The sudden thaw and inundation of the great land waters made him to lose a great deal of his artillery, booty, and baggage, and at least thirty thousand men in his retiring, so that he, being overcome with fury and madness of this repulse and loss of the most and best part of his huge army and ordnance, he hasted to put in execution the most bloody and cruelest massacre that ever was heard of in any age. He comes to the Narva, robs and spoils the town of all their riches, wealth, and merchandises, kills and murders men, women, and children, and gives the spoil to his Tatar army. Thence to Pskov or Vobsko[20] where he intended to do the like because he was incensed, and easily made believe those two towns and Novgorod had conspired his death and practiced with his enemies the overthrow of his army, and by their treacherous means and intelligence he was beaten from the siege of Reval and sustained that loss of men and munition; but that there met him an impostor or magician, which they held to be their oracle, a holy man named Nikola Sviatoi, who, by his bold imprecations and exorcisms, railings, and threats, terming him the emperor bloodsucker, the devourer and eater of Christian flesh, and swore by his angel that he should not escape death of a present thunderbolt if he or any of his army did touch a hair in displeasure of the least child's head in that city, which God, by his good angel, did preserve for better purpose than his rapine; therefore to get him thence before the fiery cloud, God's wrath, were raised, hanging over his head as he might behold, being in a very great and dark storm at that instant. These words made the emperor to tremble, so as he desired prayers for his deliverance and forgiveness of his cruel thoughts.[21] I saw this impostor or magician, a foul creature, went

19. It is not clear whether Horsey refers to the first Russian attacks on Reval (now Tallinn) in 1558 and 1559 or to one of the later attempts to take the city. If this passage describes the initial attacks, Horsey's version bears little resemblance to the sober account of the Livonian Chronicle (*Scriptores rerum Livonicarum* [Riga and Leipzig, 1853, 1848], Vol. II, 56, 62).

20. Horsey confuses the sequence of events. Muscovite forces captured Narva on May 11, 1558 (*PSRL*, XIII, i, 295). The first attack on Reval was made in the same year. The campaign against Pskov was an extension of Ivan's punitive expedition against Novgorod in 1570. Horsey may have been confused by the fact that in 1570 the Muscovite army made another unsuccessful attack on Reval.

21. The Pskov Chronicle gives a somewhat different account of Ivan's visit to Pskov in 1570. According to this story, the iurodivyi Nikola urged the citizens of the city to prepare to welcome the tsar with full hospitality. When Ivan entered the city, he went to receive Nikola's blessing but instead was given a stern warning not to murder the citizens nor to despoil the property of the church. At first the tsar paid no attention but when his favorite horse suddenly died, he became frightened and left the city. He remained in the outskirts for some time and allowed

naked both in winter and summer; he endured both extreme frost and heat, did many strange things through the magical illusions of the devil, much followed, feared, and reverenced, both of prince and people. But the emperor, returning to the great city of Novgorod where all his captives and prisoners remained he being mightily displeased against this city above all others, the inhabitants, for revenge of their treasons and treacheries, as joining with the discontented nobility, he chargeth it with thirty thousand Tatars and ten thousand gunners of his guard, without any respect ravished all the woman and maids, ransacked, robbed, and spoiled all that were within it of their jewels, plate, and treasure, murdered the people young and old, burned all their household stuff, merchandises, and warehouses of wax, flax, tallow, hides, salt, wines, cloth, and silks, set all on fire, with wax and tallow melted down the kennels in the streets, together with the blood of seven hundred thousand men, women, and children, slain and murdered; so that with the blood that ran into the river, and of all other living creatures and cattle, their dead carcasses did stop as it were the stream of the river Volga, being cast therein. No history maketh mention of so horrible a massacre. Which being thus done and destroyed, the city left desolate and waste, he returned with his army and Livonian captives towards his city Moscow. In the way he employs his captains and other officers to drive and take out of the towns and villages within fifty miles' compass all sorts of people, gentlemen, peasants, merchants, and monks, old and young, with their families, goods, and cattles, to go cleanse and inhabit this great and ruinated city of Novgorod, exposing them to a new slaughter; for many of them died with pestilence of the infected new and noisome air and place they came unto, which could not be replenished with people to any purpose, though many sent out of divers ages, remote towns, and places to inhabit there.[22]

his men to loot all but church property. Church treasure he placed under his own control (*PL*, I, 115–16).

22. Horsey's account of Ivan's expedition against Novgorod clashes with other contemporary records on a number of counts. He greatly exaggerates the number of troops involved; Schlichting's figure of 1,000 is much more likely (*Novoe izvestie o Rossii vremeni Ivana Groznogo. "Skazanie" Al'berta Shliktinga* [hereafter Schlichting] [Leningrad, 1934], p. 28). Moreover, Novgorod is situated on the Volkhov River. The most interesting feature of the passage is the description of the repopulation of the city with settlers from other regions and the difficulties these new inhabitants faced. The estimate of the number of victims is absurdly high: modern scholars' estimates range up to 40,000. (See, for example Zimin, *Oprichnina*, pp. 300–2).

III

This cruelty bred such a general hatred, distress, fear, and discontentment through his kingdom that there were many practices and devices how to destroy this tyrant, but he still did discover their plots and treasons by ennobling and countenancing all the rascalest and desperate soldiers he could pick out to affront the chief nobility.[1] He employed most of his time and these soldiers, after he had divided his spoils and settled his treasure and house in the city of Moscow and in the strongest, greatest, and trustiest monasteries, to ransack and spoil and massacre the chief nobility and richest officers and other the best sort of his merchants and subjects; his hands and heart, now so hardened and imbrued, did put many of them to most horrible and shameful deaths and tortures—a base and servile people without courage. And now distrusting the fidelity of his late conquered Tatars, did place them in garrisons in and upon the confines of his last conquered towns and castles in Livonia and Sweden. Suspecting some insurrection at home, and especially the approaching power of his ancient enemy the Scythian khan, emperor of the Kryms, incited and stirred up, as he found out, by his own nobility and subjects, he levies out of all his provinces most remote a huge army consisting of Poles, Swedes, and his own one hundred thousand horse and fifty thousand foot (as well for his own safety and strength, whereof he much upon just cause feared) to encounter and defend his enemy the Krym, that was a-preparing to invade his countries.[2] In the meantime he discards his Circassian wife, shires her a nun, and puts her in a monastery, and chooseth out of many a subject of his own, Nataliia, daughter to Kniaz' Fedor Bulgakov, a chief lieutenant or voevoda of great trust and experience

---

1. Presumably this passage refers to the special forces of the oprichnina. Horsey is wrong in stating that the oprichniki were mainly of low social origin. Some historians, like V. B. Kobrin, suggest that there was a slightly higher proportion of men of minor noble origin in the oprichnina than in the zemshchina. Zimin, however, argues that the proportion of boiars and service nobles was about the same in both halves of the government and administration (Zimin, *Oprichnina*, pp. 358–59).

2. Horsey's estimate of the size of the Russian forces is much too high.

in his wars.[3] But he soon after lost his head, and his daughter within a year shorn a nun also. The time approacheth; news come his enemy the Krym was onward the field—though fearful to him, yet pleasing news to the most of his princes and people that lived in this thrall and misery. It was God that suffereth this wicked people, who live, flow, and wallow in the very height of their lust and wickedness of the crying sodomitical sins, to be thus justly punished and plagued with the tyranny of so bloody a king; God, I say, hath now appointed a time and prepared out of his great justice a fearful revenge and spectacle to all generations, both for prince and people.[4] The Scythian emperor takes the opportunity, enters the confines of Russia, stands with an army of two hundred thousand soldiers,[5] all horsemen, within fifty miles compass upon the river's side, Oka, facing the Emperor Ivan Vasil'evich his army of one hundred thousand gallant generals and soldiers, who keep the fords and passages very strong with great artillery, munition, supply of men and arms, victuals, and all other provision plentiful. Upon hope and secret intelligence they are encouraged and venture to swim and pass the partition river without repulse. The emperor's army dare not (it is death to exceed their commission) stirs not beyond their bounds of twenty-five miles compass to defend the enemy's approach upon what advantage soever. The enemy being come at this side the river have no let, but speed towards Moscow, but ninety miles off, where the emperor thinks himself secure. But the enemy approaching the great city Moscow, the Russe emperor flies, with his two sons, treasure, household, servants, and personal guard of twenty thousand

3. No other source supports Horsey's statement that Mariia Temriukovna was sent to a convent. Apparently she was still Ivan's wife when she died on September 1, 1569. The rest of Horsey's information is also completely wrong. He evidently refers to Ivan's third wife, Marfa Vasil'evna Sobakina, who was chosen from among a group of girls assembled for the tsar's inspection. She was married on October 28, 1571, and died on November 13 of the same year. Veselovskii suggests that she was poisoned despite the elaborate security measures which the tsar had taken to protect the Aleksandrovskaia Sloboda. Before the wedding, several of her relatives, Tver' gentry, were raised to high rank. After her death, they soon fell from grace. In 1575 six of her kinsmen were executed and her father, Vasilii "Bol'shoi" Stepanovich Sobakin, was forced to enter a monastery (Veselovskii, *Issledovaniia*, p. 300).

4. Horsey's account is essentially similar to the other accounts of the sack of Moscow in 1571. The disaster showed the incompetence of the oprichnina forces to defend their country and was one of the factors that led Ivan to abandon his experiment in government.

5. See Fletcher, above, pp. 191–92.

gunners, towards a strong monastery, Troitsa, sixty miles off, upon Ascension Day.[6] The enemy fires St. John's Church high steeple, at which instant happened a wonderful stormy wind, through which all the churches, houses, and palaces within the city and suburbs thirty miles compass, built most of fir and oak timber, was set on fire and burned within six hours' space, with infinite thousands men, women, and children burned and smothered to death by the fiery air, and likewise in the stone churches, monasteries, vaults, and cellars, very few escaping both without and within the three walled castles. The river and ditches about Moscow stopped and filled with the multitudes of people, loaded with gold, silver, jewels, chains, earrings, bracelets, and treasure, that went for succor even to save their heads above water. Notwithstanding, so many thousands were there burned and drowned as the river could not be rid nor cleansed of the dead carcasses with all the means and industry could be used in twelve months after; but those alive, and many from other towns and places, every day were occupied within a great circuit to search, dredge, and fish, as it were, for rings, jewels, plate, bags of gold and silver, by which many were enriched ever after. The streets of the city, churches, cellars, and vaults lay so thick and full of dead and smothered carcasses as no man could pass for the noisome smells and putrefaction of the air long after. The emperor of the Kryms and his army beheld this goodly fire, lodged and solaced himself in a fair monastery by the riverside, four miles of the city, called Simonov monastery, took the wealth and riches they had and of all such as fled from the fire. Though little the better by firing of that within the city, they did the exploit they came for, returned with a number of captives and loaded with that they had gotten, fearing to be set on by the army at Serpukhov.[7] But they escaped over the river again the way they came.

The Russe emperor fled still farther off with his two sons and treasure to a great town called Vologda, where he thought himself more secure, five hundred miles off. Much amazed and perplexed for this great disaster befallen him, he, accompanied with his metropolitans, bishops, and clergymen, his chief princes and ancient nobility now called for

---

6. The sources give contradictory accounts of Ivan's whereabouts during the Tatar raid. Some state that he headed for Iaroslavl' but stopped in Rostov (*PSRL*, XIII, i, 301; Staden, p. 70). Others claim that he actually took refuge in Iaroslavl' ("Poslanie Ioganna Taube i Elerta Kruze" [hereafter Taube & Kruze], *Russkii istoricheskii zhurnal*, Book 8 [1922], 52).

7. Circapur in the original text.

and summoned to a council royal, and the enemy gone, dissolved his army that fought not a stroke for him; examined, racked, and tortured many of the voevody and chief captains; puts some to death; confiscated their goods and lands; destroyed their race and families; set a course for cleansing, repairing, and replenishing of the city of Moscow, which was an infinite labor and work to consult of.[8] In the midst of which, this his great enemy, Devlet Girey, sends him an ambassador attended with many mirza, noblemen after their account, all well horsed, clad but in sheepskins coats girt to them, with black caps of the same, bow and arrows, with curious rich scimitars by their sides. They had a guard to keep them in dark rooms; stinking horse flesh and water was their best food, without bread or beer or bed. The time was come he must have audience; much disgrace and base usage was offered them; they endured, puffed, and scorned it. The emperor, with his three crowns before him in his royal estate, with his princes and nobles about him, commanded his sheepskin coat and cap to be taken off him and a golden robe and rich cap to be put on him. The ambassador well contented, he enters his presence; his followers kept back in a space with grates of iron between the emperor and them, at which the ambassador chafes with a hellish, hollow voice, looking fierce and grimly. Four captains of the guard bring him near the emperor's seat. Himself, a most ugly creature, without reverence thunders out, says his master and lord, Devlet Girey, great emperor of all the kingdoms and khans the sun did spread his beams over, sent to him, Ivan Vasil'evich, his vassal and great duke over all Russia by his permission, to know how he did like the scourge of his displeasure by sword, fire, and famine; had sent him for remedy (pulling out a foul rusty knife) to cut his throat withal. They hasted him forth of the room without answer and would a taken off his golden gown and cap but he and his company strived with them so stoutly that he would not suffer them. Guarded to the place from whence they were brought, the emperor fell into such an agony, sent for his ghostly father, tore his own hair and beard for madness. The chief captain prayed his majesty's leave to cut them all

8. After the catastrophe of 1571 Ivan ordered the execution of a number of prominent figures including Mikhail Cherkasskii, V. I. Temkin-Rostovskii, V. P. Iakovlev, I. P. Iakovlev, S. V. Iakovlev, P. V. Zaitsev, L. A. Saltykov, F. I. Saltykov, I. F. Gvozdev-Rostovskii, G. B. Griaznoi, Andrei Ovtsyn, Bulat Artsybashev, and I. F. Vorontsov (Zimin, *Oprichnina*, pp. 459–62; Heinrich von Staden, *Aufzeichnungen über den Moskauer Staat*, ed. F. T. Epstein [Hamburg, 1964], pp. 49–50; Taube & Kruze, p. 54).

in pieces but had no answer. After he had kept this ambassador some time with some better usage, sent him away with this message: "Tell the miscreant and unbeliever, thy master, it is not he; it is for my sins and the sins of my people against my God and Christ; he it is that hath given him, a limb of Satan, the power and opportunity to be the instrument of my rebuke, by whose pleasure and grace I doubt not of revenge and to make him my vassal or long be." He answered, "He would not do him so much service to do any such message for him."[9] Whereupon the emperor not long after did address a wise, noble gentleman for his ambassador, Afanasii Fedorovich Nagoi, who was kept there and endured much penury [misery] for the space of seven years.[10]

The emperor was loth to come to the city of Moscow, though he sent for the chief merchants, handicrafts, and tradesmen from all other his cities and towns within his kingdom to build and inhabit there and draw traffic thither, took away all impositions, gave them freedom of customs, set seven thousand masons and workmen to build a fair stone wall round about the Moscow, which was finished in four years' space, very strong and beautiful and furnished with very fair and goodly pieces of brass ordnance, settled his offices and officers of justice and governors therein, in manner and form as heretofore it was, as time did permit. Himself kept much at Vologda upon the river Dvina[11] and at Sloboda Aleksandrovskaia, conferred much with Eleazar Bomelius, a doctor of physic,[12] sent for skillful builders, architects, carpenters, joiners, and masons, goldsmiths, physicians, apothecaries, and such like, out of England, having some purpose in his head which will shortly discover itself, builds a treasure house of stone, great barks and barges, to convey and transport upon sudden occasion treasure to Solovetskii monastery, standing upon the North Seas the direct way into England.

9. Taube and Kruze also mention that a Tatar emissary was sent to Ivan after the raid of 1571 and presented him with a knife. In their version, the gift was a sign of respect (Taube & Kruze, p. 54). Devlet Girey (*Chigaley Mursoye* in the original text) was khan of the Crimea, 1551–77.

10. Afanasii Fedorovich Nagoi was ambassador to the Crimean court between 1563 and 1572. Again Horsey has scrambled the order of events.

11. Vologda is actually on the Vologda River, a tributary of the Sukhona.

12. Born in Westphalia, Bomelius studied medicine in England and gained a reputation as an astrologer. His activities led to prison in London, but he was rescued by Sovin, the Russian ambassador, and entered Russian service, where he became a confidant of Ivan IV. He was a member of the oprichnina and was suspected by contemporaries of poisoning some of Ivan's enemies at the tsar's command. In 1579 he fell from favor and was tortured to death (*DNB* and *RBS*).

He had so fleeced his merchants by taking their commodities to exchange with strangers for cloth of gold, dollars, pearl, jewels, etc., which he continually took into his treasury without paying little or nothing, by that means borrowing great sums of cities, towns, and monasteries, exhausting all their wealth by great impositions and customs to augment and increase his own treasure, became so odious and in such a desperate case as he devised how to prevent and alter his estate. To annihilate and frustrate all this he had engaged his crown unto, made a separation and division of his towns, offices, and subjects, called this oprichnina and the other zemshchina, established a new king or emperor, named Tsar Simeon, the emperor's son of Kazan', resigned his style and lent him his crown; transfers all authority thereunto incident; crowns him, but with no solemnity nor consent of peers;[13] causeth his subjects to address themselves and their affairs, petitions, and suits to him; and in his name all privileges, charters, instruments, and writings to be called in and new to be published in his name and under his seal. They plead in all courts of justice in his name; coins money, receives customs and casual fines and certain revenues for the maintenance of his house, officers, and servants; is liable to all debts and matters concerning his office of treasury. He sits[14] in majesty; the old Emperor Ivan comes and prostrates himself. Causeth his metropolitans, bishops, priors, noblemen, and officers to do the like, and all ambassadors to resort before him, which some refused. Was married unto the daughter of Kniaz' Ivan Fedorovich Mstislavskii, prime prince of the blood royal. These things being thus controverted and changed, the old emperor would take no notice of any debts owing in his time—letters patents, privileges to towns and monasteries all void. His clergy, nobility, and commons must now petition Ivan Vasil'evich that he would be pleased to take the crown and government upon him again, upon many conditions and authentical instruments confirmed by act of parliament in a very solemn new inauguration. He was contented, at which infinite gifts and presents were of all men of any worth sought out for to give unto him, amounting and valued to be a great treasure. He was freed of all old debts and former charge whatsoever. Too tedious to recite any more of this tragedy.[15] But that the

13. The oprichnina was established in 1565; Simeon was enthroned in 1575.
14. *sits.* sets in the original text.
15. See Fletcher, above, p. 166.

device of his own head might have set him clear beside the saddle, if it had continued but a little longer, it is happy he is become invested again *in statu quo prius*. Regrants privileges, jurisdictions, charters to towns, monasteries, and noblemen and merchants, upon new composition, for which great sums and fines were obtained; sends an army of Tatars, governed by his own captains, to reconquer, as he terms it, the towns in Livonia, which King Stephen had lately taken from him; propounded a marriage to Duke Magnus with his brother's daughter, Kniaz' Andrei;[16] sends for his said brother out of his province of Vaga; had him in jealousy; himself living so tyrannically and in the hatred of his subjects, the other, Kniaz' Andrei, had gotten their hearty affections, which he well perceived. When he came to his presence, he laid himself prostrate to his foot; he took him up and kissed him. "O cruel brother," with tears, says the story, "this is a Judas kiss; thou hast sent for me to no good end; take thy fill," and so parted for that time. Died the next day; was buried in Micholsea crest in the Moscow solemnly.[17] This marriage must go forward, having some relation to foreign aid. Herzog Magnus was eldest son to Christian, duke of Holstein, born before he was elected king of Denmark; this King Frederick born after, between whom grew such hatred and dissention as he was enforced to exchange with him for the dukedom of Holstein an island called Osel

16. Horsey has further confused the sequence of events. Stephen Bathory's offensive began in 1578 and 1579. Ivan promised Prince Magnus the hand of one of the daughters of Vladimir Andreevich in 1570; Magnus actually married another daughter in 1573, considerably before the events just described. Magnus (1540–83) was the second son of Christian III of Denmark. In 1559 he gave up his inheritance in Schleswig-Holstein in favor of his elder brother Frederick II. In return, Frederick promised to support Magnus' plans to take over the island of Osel (Saaremaa) in the eastern Baltic and use it as a base for carving out a domain in Livonia. Magnus arrived in Osel in 1560 and quickly found himself beleaguered by the other powers competing for possession of the Baltic provinces. In 1569 he began to work for an alliance with Ivan IV against their common enemy, Sweden. In the following year the tsar received him, recognized him as "king of Livonia," and promised him the hand of a princess of the ruling house of Moscow, Evfemiia, daughter of Prince Vladimir Andreevich. The alliance proved a disastrous failure. In 1570 Magnus led a force of Muscovite troops and his own retainers against Reval but failed to capture it even after a long siege. From that point, Magnus' military fortunes steadily declined and in 1578 he swore allegiance to the king of Poland. Before long he was deprived of the remainder of his lands (*Dansk Biografisk Leksikon;* Zimin, *Oprichnina,* p. 433).

17. Vladimir Andreevich, the tsar's cousin, was poisoned on October 9, 1569 (Taube & Kruze, pp. 46–47; *Materialy,* II, 78; Zimin, *Oprichnina,* p. 290). "Micholsea crest" probably indicates the Cathedral of the Archangel Michael in the Moscow Kremlin.

in Livonia, his right in Riga and Reval, King John of Sweden competitor thereof; also many other towns and castles in Livonia, which the emperor of Russia had won and spoiled from them both. He makes up the match and marries his niece, Elena,[18] to Herzog Magnus, gives him in dowry with her all his interest, towns, castles, and possessions in Livonia, doth establish him therein, styles and calls him Corcell[19] Magnus, which is King Magnus, gives him a hundred good horse, well furnished, two hundred thousand rubles, which is 600,000 dollars in money, gold and silver vessel, plate and jewels and rich apparel, gratifies and gives liberal gifts to all followers and servants, conducts and sends, with him many of his nobles and ladies with two thousand horse, the said king and queen, who saw them safely settled and seated in their estates in that his great town of Dorpat in Livonia.

I fear I shall fill my discourse with too much of this narration if I be larger; I will therefore leave the rest for his proper place hereafter and go onward with the story of the emperor's life. Instead of the alliance and amity he aimed at the king of Denmark and king of Sweden, wars follows, both of them putting him to distress and the king of Poland also, who got from him the Narva and besieged Pskov, two of the chiefest towns he had of traffic in those parts.[20] The Dane and Swede encroacheth upon his part, being all three competitors in certain territories upon the northern coasts, Vardo, Kola, Solovetskii, Varzuga, etc. Puts him from his customs and traffic and offers to trouble and deny the English merchants also in their passage for fishing upon those coasts and trading with him at St. Nicholas and Kholmogory.[21]

The emperor Ivan Vasil'evich sends for all his nobles' and gentlemen's fairest daughters, maidens, throughout his kingdoms and chooseth out among them a wife for his eldest son, Tsarevich Ivan. Her

18. Magnus married Mariia, younger daughter of Vladimir Andreevich, in 1573.
19. Presumably *korol.*
20. Narva fell to the Swedes in 1581 and Pskov was besieged in the same year.
21. In about 1580 the Danish government laid claim to certain territories on the Arctic coast on the Russian side of the present Norwegian-Soviet frontier. Queen Elizabeth wrote to Ivan IV in 1582 reporting these claims and asked for an explanation. The tsar answered that the areas had long been part of Muscovy and requested English help in fighting off any Danish attempt to capture them (*Sbornik IRIO*, XXXVIII, 8–10). In the same year the Danish government expressed concern over England's trade with Russia via the northern route and revived the claim that the sea between Norway and Iceland was part of Danish territorial waters (*Calendar of State Papers, Foreign*, 1581–82, p. 647; 1582, p. 534). *Vardo:* Wardhouse in the original text.

name was Nataliia, daughter to Ivan Sheremetev, a voevoda of a good family. Great feastings and trumps was at the solemnizing of this marriage, though worth the relating, yet not so pertinent to the discourse in hand.[22]

IV

This emperor lived in great danger and fear of treasons and his making away, which he daily discovered, and spent much time in the examination, torturing, execution, and putting to death such noble captains and officers that were found practicers against him. Kniaz' Ivan Kurakin being found drunk, as was pretended, in Wenden, a fast town in Livonia, when King Stephen besieged it, being voevoda thereof, was stripped naked, laid in a cart, whipped through the market with six whips of wire, which cut his back, belly, and bowels, so he was whipped with to death.[1] Another, as I remember, called Ivan Obrossimov, a master of his horse, was hanged on a gibbet naked by the heels [hair of his head]; the skin and flesh of his body from top to toe cut off and minced with knives into small gobbets by four palachi; the one, wearied with his long carving, thrust his knife somewhat far into his bowels the sooner to dispatch him, was presently had to another place of execution and that hand cut off, which being not well seared he died the next day.[2] Many other were knocked in the heads, cast into the pools and lakes near Sloboda, their flesh and carcasses fed upon by such huge overgrown pikes, carps, and other fishes, so fat as any other [anything but fat] could hardly be discerned upon them. That was the valley compared to Gehenna or Tophet, where the faithless Egyptians

22. At the same time as he made arrangements to marry Marfa Sobakina, Ivan chose a bride for his son. Tsarevich Ivan married the lady, Evdokiia Saburova, on November 4, 1571 (Taube & Kruze, p. 52; Zimin, *Oprichnina*, p. 466).

1. The story is impossible. Ivan Andreevich Bulgakov-Kurakin was forced to enter a monastery in 1565 and probably died soon after (Veselovskii, *Issledovaniia*, p. 403). Bathory besieged Wenden in 1578.

2. Horsey's memory apparently betrayed him. It is impossible to discover what incident, if any, was the basis of this anecdote. The last regular holder of the office of master of the horse (koniushii) was I. P. Fedorov-Cheliadnin, who was executed in 1568. Boris Godunov used the title after 1584 (A. A. Zimin, "O sostave dvortsovykh uchrezhdenii russkogo gosudarstva kontsa XV i XVI v.," *Istoricheskie zapiski*, LXIII [1958], 199).

did sacrifice their children to the hideous devils. Kniaz' Boris Tulupov, a great favorite of that time, being discovered to be a treason worker [traitor] against the emperor and confederate with the discontented nobility, was drawn upon a long sharp made stake, soaped to enter [so made as that it was thrust into] his fundament through his body, which came out at his neck, upon which he languished in horrible pain for fifteen hours alive and spake unto his mother, the duchess, brought to behold that woeful sight. And she, a goodly matronly woman, upon like displeasure given to one hundred gunners, who defiled her to death one after the other; her body, swollen and lying naked in the place commanded his huntsmen to bring their hungry hounds to eat and devour her flesh and bones, dragged everywhere; the emperor at that sight saying, "Such as I favor I have honored and such as be traitors will I have thus done unto."[3] The friends of the duke's fortunes and servants of his favors lamentably mourning at this disaster and sudden change. I could enumerate many and much more that have felt the like severity and cruelty of this emperor's heavy hand of displeasure, but I forbear to trouble the modest ears and Christian patience of such as shall read it.

This emperor's delight, hands and heart being thus imbrued in blood, making his chief exercise to devise and put in execution new torments, tortures, and deaths upon such as he took displeasure against and had in most jealousy, those especially of his nobility of best credit and most beloved of his subjects, he countenancing the most desperate captains, soldiers, and decayed sort to affront them and breed faction; whereby indeed there grew such factions and jealousy as they durst not trust one another to ruinate and displace him as they were willing to do; all which he perceived and knew that his estate and case for safety grew every day more desperate and in danger than other and, troubled much how to shun and escape the same, was very inquisitive with one Eleazar Bomelius, as you have heard, sometimes a cozening imposter, doctor of physic in England, a rare mathematician, magician, and of others, what years Queen Elizabeth was of, what likely of success there might be if he should be a suitor unto her for himself. And though he was much disheartened, not only for that he had two wives living and that many kings and great princes that had been suitors to

3. Tulupov was a commander in several military operations after 1570. In 1573 he was made a member of the boiar duma with the rank of okol'nichii (Kobrin, p. 79). He was executed in 1575 (Zimin, "Sostav boiarskoi dumy," p. 77).

her majesty and could not prevail, yet he magnified himself, his person, his wisdom, greatness, and riches above all other princes, would give the assay, and presently puts that empress, his last wife, into a nunnery to live there as dead to the world.⁴ And, as you have formerly read, having it in his thoughts long before to make England in case of extremity his safest refuge, built and prepared many goodly barks, large barges or boats, at Vologda, and drawn and brought his most richest treasure thither to be embarked in the same to pass down the river Dvina and so into England by the English ships upon a sudden, leaving his eldest son, Tsarevich Ivan, to govern and pacify his so troubled estate.⁵ For that purpose he did devise to raise a new treasure to leave unto him, the better to establish his strength as he thought after him, would now put in practice that he had often in purpose; called for the principal priors, abbots, archimandrites, and hegumens of the ablest, richest, and chief monasteries and religious houses of his kingdom, which were very many, and told them that which he was to say was best known to themselves;⁶ he had spent the most part of his time,

4. There is no evidence besides Horsey's word to indicate that Ivan wanted to marry Elizabeth herself. He was advised by Dr. Robert Jacob that he might make an English marriage with the queen's cousin, Lady Mary Hastings. During the negotiations he made clear that he was ready to rid himself of Mariia Nagaia, his seventh wife, but was careful not to do so until he was sure of her successor. The plan for an English marriage came to nothing (*Sbornik IRIO*, XXXVIII, 3–6).

5. Horsey is the only source which states that Ivan was building a fleet at Vologda. His account is, however, widely accepted by historians (see A. V. Chernov, *Vooruzhennye sily russkogo gosudarstva XV–XVII vv.* [Moscow, 1954], pp. 67–68).

At certain moments in his reign, Ivan IV seriously considered taking refuge in England. In 1567, for example, he requested Elizabeth to exchange formal guarantees that either one of them could seek asylum in the other's domains if he were driven from his own country.

6. In the account that follows Horsey probably refers to the church council of 1580. Although his version is full of details that seem to be of his own invention, he clearly understood the basic issues. Like Horsey's version of the tsar's speech, the official resolution of the council denounced the monasteries for accepting bequests of land when they could not utilize what they already owned. The resolution likewise referred to the war emergency and accused the monasteries of hindering the nation's struggle by their greed. The council therefore decreed that the monasteries were not to accept any further bequests of land (*Akty, sobrannye v bibliotekakh i arkhivakh Rossiiskoi Imperii Arkheograficheskoiu ekspeditsieiu Imperatorskoi Akademii Nauk*, I [St. Petersburg, 1836], 372–73). Pavlov and Veselovskii accept the essential accuracy of Horsey's account of the council. Pavlov, indeed, goes so far as to suggest that, in his version of the council's proceedings, he may actually have included his own translations of some sections of the decree that were omitted in the surviving Russian text (A. Pavlov, *Istoricheskii ocherk sekuliarizatsii tserkovnykh zemel' v Rossii*, Part I [Odessa, 1871], pp. 145–49). In

wits, vigor, and youth in warfaring for their wealth and safety, preservation, and defense of his kingdoms and people; what dangers and troubles he had passed was not unknown unto them, above many others. They, apart to whom[7] he makes his moan, have only reaped the benefit thereof. By which his treasures have been exhausted and theirs increased; their safeties, peace, and tranquillity preserved, and his lessened and daily endangered by foreign enemies and practices, both at home and abroad, which he[8] was very sensible they were too well acquainted with. How could he or they any longer subsist without their essential assistance? Their willingness must be the touchstone and trial of their fidelity, as well as their contemplations, which proved of no force. Their pretended prayers prevailed not; whether for their iniquities, his sins and people's, or both, he leaves to the divine knowledge. The utility of their holy thoughts and actions must now be the supply out of their infinite abundance; yea, the urgent necessity and miserable estate both of him and people doth now require their devotion; the souls of their own patrons and donors, saints and holy workers of wonders, for redemption of their souls and sins, commands it. Prepare therefore your thoughts with holy resolutions, without sophistical or exorcisms of refusal.

A high and provincial convocation was called in the great consistory of the Holy Ghost; the oath of sovereignty was ministered in the city of Moscow, some fearing he did aim at all; and after long debate the particulars of their allegations and reasons very profoundly set down, as appeareth in the original, and prepared for the king's audience. The emperor had false spies that brought him intelligence of all. He forced delays of excuse; in the mean he thunders out his thrasonical[9] threats to their ears, conveyed by his secret instigators; calls forty of the most capital and pragmatical priors and prelates; tells them in this substance too long to particularize: "We understand of your consultations and resolutions you are the principal of your perverse partisans. The mild re-

---

his treatment of the application of the council's decisions, Veselovskii argues that the government was successful in limiting the acquisition of land by the monasteries. In the years immediately following the council, the monasteries received land only from donors who had secured the tsar's prior consent or in such small quantities that the transaction would not be noticed (Veselovskii, *Feodal'noe zemlevladenie,* pp. 100–3).

7. *whom.* home in the original text.
8. *he.* one in the original text.
9. *thrasonical.* thrononicall in the original text.

lation of the ill estate and misery of my people and ill success of my affairs hath nothing moved nor mollified your compassion. What shall we render for your reward? The nobility and people cry out with their complaints that you have gotten, wherewith you do maintain your hierarchy, all the treasure of the land by trading in all kind of merchandises, chaffering and taking the benefit of all other men's travels, having privileges to pay no customs to our crown nor charge of wars, and, by terrifying of the noblest, ablest, and best sort of our subjects their dying consciences, have gotten the third part, by due computation, of the towns, royalties, and villages of this kingdom into your possessions by your witchery and enchantments and sorcery. You buy and sell the souls of our people. You live a most idle life in all pleasure and delicacy, commit most horrible sins, extortion, bribery, and excess usury. You abound in all the bloody and crying sins, oppression, gluttony, idleness, and sodomy, and worse, if worse, with beasts. Maybe your prayers avail not neither for me nor my people. We have much to answer before God to suffer you to live, and so many more worthy to die for you; God forgive my partakership with you. Did not the Pope of late, by the earnest contemplation of his nuncio,[10] persuade to have the supremacy over you and to dispose of all your places, preeminences, and revenues? Hath not the Greek church oftentimes solicited us for the change of your metropolitan see by the mediation of the patriarch of Alexandria? Yea, and as often have I been moved for your dissolution to the reparation and reestablishing of thousands of my ancient and poorest nobility, from whose ancestors most of your revenues came and to whom it most justly belongs, that have left and spent their honors, lives, and livings for your safeties and enrichments, and my rich people and subjects impoverished through your rapine and devilish illusions, and by which of the contrary a flourishing commonwealth would be established and sustained, a fair example by that valorous King Henry the eighth of England, your revenues being much more beside your standing treasury than your prodigal and luxurious maintenance can expend. By which means my nobility and serviceable subjects are decayed and our treasure so exhausted that we are enforced by the secret inspiration of the souls and holy saints, the holy workers of wonders, whom you profess and hold that infinite treasure, not yours, that lies as a dead talent in your custodies, put to no religious use; in their names and all the souls of the donors and benefactors

10. Apparently a reference to Possevino, whose ultimate goal was the union of the Russian church with Rome.

thereof, I conjure and command that by such a day (lest then you all be, through the plague and just punishment of God, devoured by wild beast of the forest, who attend the execution of your judgment with a more sudden and fearful death than befell the falsehood of Ananias and Sapphira's denial)[11] you bring us a faithful and true inventory what treasure and yearly revenues every of your houses have in their possessions. Necessity will permit no delay nor excuse. By which time we will call a parliament or council royal of all our princes and nobles, metropolitans, bishops, priors, archimandrites, and hegumens, to be not only judges in the truth of their souls what urgent necessity and utility there is at this present for a mass of treasure to be employed for defense of our realm—the king and princes of Poland and Lithuania, the king of Sweden, and the king of Denmark all combining and our rebels confederating with that mighty power prepared by the Krym—but also to be ear and eyewitnesses of the discharge of our duty to God and his angels, to incite you in their name and his poor distressed peoples, for whose necessities, redemption, and preservation of you all, we are thus enforced so earnestly to mediate and implore, as it were, their so miserable estates, which lies in your hands and powers yet in time to remedy and relieve."

I am the larger because the matter is enforced, as you perceive, with such great efficacy as to hear the sequel will countervail your patience in reading. The chief bishops, priors, and abbots assembled and dissembled often times together, much perplexed and divided, seeking and devising with the discontented nobility how to turn head and make a war of resistance, but there wanted such a head or general that had courage sufficient to guide or lead such an army as could encounter his puissant power, they altogether unprovided both of horse and arms. The emperor took opportunity and advantage of this practice and made good use thereof. Proclaims the heads of all those houses to be traitors. To make them more hateful summoned, nay, sent for twenty of the principalest, chargeth them with odious and horrible crimes and treacheries upon such pregnant and apparent proofs as was manifestly known and published to be true, exclaimed upon and condemned of all sorts of people in general. Now come we to the merry tragedy to requite your patience all this while. The emperor commands his great bears, wild, fierce, and hungry, to be brought out of their dark caves and cages, kept of purpose for such his delights and pastimes at Sloboda Velikaia, upon St. Isaiah's Day, in a spacious place

11. Acts V: 1–11.

high walled. About seven of those principal rebellious big fat friars were brought forth, one after another, with his cross and beads in his hands, and, through the emperor's great favor, a boar spear of five foot in length in the other hand for his defense, and a wild bear was let loose, ranging and roaring up against the walls with open mouth, scenting the friar by his fat garments, made more mad with the cry and shouting of the people, runs fiercely at him, catches and crushes his head, body, bowels, legs, and arms as a cat doth a mouse, tears his weeds in pieces till he came to his flesh, blood, and bones, and so devours his first friar for his prey. The bear also shot and killed with pieces by the gunners pell-mell. And so another friar and a fresh bear was singly hand to hand brought forth till they were all seven devoured in manner as the first was, saving one friar, more cunning than the rest, bestirred his boar spear so nimbly, setting the end thereof in the ground, guiding it to the breast of the bear that ran himself through upon it, and yet not escaped devouring after the bear was hurt, both dying in the place. This friar was canonized for a valiant saint by the rest of his living brothers of Troitsa monastery.[12] This pastime was not for the time so pleasing unto the emperor and other beholders thereof as terrible and displeasing to all the rabblement and consistory of friars and monks that were convocated and so combined together as you have heard, whereof seven more were promised to be burned, etc. The metropolitans, bishops, monks, and friars, of all houses that had offices and charge, resorted with petitions and their prostrations to pacify and stay the emperor's further displeasure and fury, were not only contented to suffer and allow his ghostly father to absolve him, but also to acknowledge those detestable friars that had committed and perpetrated such detestable crimes and offenses, as was manifestly proved against them, had condignly suffered for their wicked deserts, hoping it would not only be an example but an amendment to all other that professed such holy orders of worldly sequestration. The said metropolitans, bishops, priors, archimandrites, and hegumens, heads, treasurers, and all other officers of all the chief

12. There is no evidence that prominent members of the clergy were executed as a direct result of the council of 1580–81. Seredonin suggests that Horsey may have based this story on tales he heard about the execution of leading churchmen on other occasions (Seredonin, p. 31). The story about the bears may be a confused version of a legend about the death of Archbishop Leonid of Novgorod in 1575. According to one account, Leonid was dressed in a bearskin and hunted down by dogs (PL, II, 262).

monasteries[13] and nunneries and religious houses did, in the names of
the whole, for themselves and souls of their holy saints, founders, and
workers of holy wonders, of whom they held their lives and being, together with his imperial, most sacred, and most gracious commiseration
and permission (for whom and his good success they all poured out
unto the Holy Trinity their devout vows and daily prayers), they presented unto his imperial majesty and prostrated before his throne of
mercy a true and a perfect inventory of all the treasure, monies, towns
and lands, and other revenues that do particularly belong to every particular holy soul and saint that did endow and commend the same unto
their custody and everlasting keeping successively for the maintenance
of those holy seminaries and sanctuaries, hoping and assuredly believing his sacred soul, in commemoration of all ages, will not suffer perpe-
tration or violation of those things in his age, which must pass away
with the accounts thereof before the Trinity, as those have done; if otherwise minded, that it would please him to give them an authentical
discharge to publish to all posterities to come.

I have with my best skill translated this much *verbatim* out of the
original. Their enchantments prevented dissolution, but not prevailed
against the emperor's resolute demand of three hundred thousand
marks sterling, which he by the means of this conjuration obtained, besides many precincts, towns, villages, lands, and royalties, at least as
much more worth to dispose of, though with great grudge and dislike,
yet to the pacification of many his discontented nobles, raising and
enabling thereby most of his trusties, captains, and servitors the better to
serve his turn in all his designs. This practice and policy of his, though
condemned and much disliked of some, yet reckoned the most commendable tyranny that ever he used of other some and least dangerous.

V

W ell, this turn being served to raise a standing treasure for his
son without diminishing any part of his own, he hath still an eye
and aim to England. His infinite treasure and mind is prepared; but

13. *monasteries.* monsterous in the original text.

neither his ambassador, Andrei Sovin, did discharge the trust reposed in his delivery of his mind, darkly expressed by work of mouth, which he durst not commit to paper, as it seems; neither did Mr. Jenkinson nor Mr. Thomas Randolph in their particular negotiations so thoroughly understand, move, or break the matter as he expected.[1] So that he himself kept it not so secret but that his eldest son, Tsarevich Ivan, and their favorites and nobles took notice of it. Which the emperor perceiving, and to put out all jealousy thereof in their minds, married again the fifth wife, the daughter of Fedor Nagoi, a very beautiful young maiden of a noble house and great family, by whom he had a third son called Dmitrii Ivanovich,[2] spent now his time still in pacifying his discontented nobles and people, kept two armies afoot and yet at but small charge; for his princes and nobles went most upon their own charge, and gentlemen and common syny [deti] boiarskie had certain portions of land, corn, and money allowed them yearly, and this issued out of certain revenues put apart for that purpose, and escheats, robberies, and customs, pensions duly paid them whether they go to war or no, without diminution of any his crown revenues or great standing treasure.[3] The one army consisting most of Tatars,[4] which he employed against the king and princes of Poland and Sweden, by whom he was now environed, for the country of Livonia,[5] which he had so ransacked and showed so much cruelty in conquering it before; the other army consisting commonly of one hundred thousand horse,[6] most of his own

1. Horsey refers to the negotiations which took place between 1567 and 1572 when Ivan withdrew his request for mutual guarantees of asylum. The English envoys disappointed Ivan because they brought no answering request for asylum from Elizabeth but above all because they would not accept his plans for an alliance.

2. Again Horsey confuses the time sequence in his narrative. Ivan married Mariia Nagaia, his seventh wife, in 1581.

3. The land grants of the gentry cavalrymen ranged between 20 and 700 chetverti and the annual salary between 4 and 14 rubles (Chernov, *Vooruzhennye sily*, p. 78).

4. The total number of Tatars in the Russian army was no higher than 10,000. They must, therefore, have been a minority in the army in the major western campaigns (Seredonin, *Izvestiia inostrantsev o vooruzhennykh silakh moskovskago gosudarstva v kontse XVI v.* [St. Petersburg, 1891], p. 13).

5. Lioland in the original text.

6. This figure is much too large, since the total number of troops engaged in major operations on the western front was, at most, between 40,000 and 60,000 (Chernov, *Vooruzhennye sily*, pp. 94–95).

natural subjects, saving some few Poles, Swedes, Dutch, and Scots, employed against his great enemy the Krym Tatar, which commonly doth not last above three months, May, June, and July, every year. He lost most part of all the towns he had conquered in Livonia,[7] regained by that most valorous king Stephen Bathory; but the emperor had fleeced and carried away all the riches and principal people before, whose cruelty and tyranny used there is most lamentably set forth in the Livonian history. The goodliest country, flowing with milk and honey and all other commonwealth commodities, nothing wanting, and the fairest women and best conditioned people to converse with in the world, but much given to pride, luxury, and idleness and pleasure, for which sins God hath so plagued and routed out that nation that infinite numbers are carried captives and sold for slaves into Persia, Tatary, Turkey, and the farthest part of the Indies. It was my fortune, by special favor, to buy and redeem divers, both men, women, and children, of those captived people for small sums of money, some merchants of good quality, and got leave to convey and send them, some into Livonia,[8] some to Hamburg and Lübeck. On the other side, King John of Sweden[9] by his general, Lorent Forusbaeck, and Pontus, a French captain,[10] besieged the Narva both by sea and land and took it and the strong castle also of Ivangorod, his best maritime town of traffic, no

7. Liffland in the original text. Between 1578 and 1581 the armies of Sweden and Poland drove the Russians out of all of Livonia.

8. Liefland in the original text.

9. Johan III reigned from 1568 to 1592.

10. Pontus de la Gardie was born in France in 1520. After a number of adventures, he entered Swedish service and in 1568 served as steward of Duke Johan who soon became king. In the following year he served in the same post in the household of Queen Katarina. Between 1573 and 1576 he was continually in Livonia in various military capacities. He was sent as ambassador to the emperor and the Pope in 1576. In 1581 he was made governor of Swedish-held Livonia and in that capacity led the expedition that swept through Estonia and captured Narva and Ivangorod. He participated in the negotiations that led to a truce with Russia in 1583. In 1585 he died while on service in Livonia (*Svenskt Biografiskt Lexikon*).

By Lorent Forusbaeck, Horsey apparently had in mind Jürgen Farensbach (1552–1602), a Livonian noble, who served in the Muscovite army on the Oka in 1572 (Staden, *Aufzeichnungen über den Moskauer Staat*, 34*, n. 2). Subsequently, as an official of the Danish crown, he was governor of Osel from 1579 or 1580 to 1584 (K. Erselev, *Danmarks len og lensmand i det sextend aarhundrede (1513–1596)* [Copenhagen, 1879], p. 14). In the 1580's he entered Polish service and maintained this allegiance for the rest of his career (*Svenskt Biografiskt Lexikon*).

such cruelty showed by them.[11] The emperor's soldiers and army, far greater in number, ranged far into the Swedes' country and did much spoil and rapine, brought many captives away to remote places in his land, Livonians,[12] French, Scots, Dutchmen, and some English. The emperor settling and seating a great many of them in the city of Moscow to inhabit by themselves without the city, and by my mediation and means, being then conversant and familiar in the court, well known and respected of the best favorites and officers of that time, I procured liberty to build them a church and contributed well thereunto; got unto them a learned preaching minister and divine service and meeting of the congregation every sabbath day, but after their Lutheran profession; grew in short time in favor and familiar, and in good like, of the Russe people, living civilly but in doleful and mourning manner for their evil loss of goods, friends, and country. At which time, among other nations, there were four score and five poor Scots soldiers left of seven hundred sent from Stockholm, and three Englishmen in their company, brought among other captives in most miserable manner piteous to behold. I labored and employed my best endeavors and credit not only to succor them, but with my purse and pains and means got them to be well placed at Bolvanovka near the Moscow; and although the emperor was much inflamed with fury and wrath against them, torturing and putting many of those Swedish soldiers to death,[13] most lamentably to behold, I procured the emperor to be told of the difference between those Scotsmen now his captives and the Swedes, Poles, and Livonians, his enemies. They were a nation strangers, remote, adventurous, and warlike people, ready to serve any Christian prince for maintenance and pay, as they would appear and prove if it pleased his majesty to employ and spare them such maintenance, now out of heart and clothes and arms, as they may show themselves and valor against his mortal enemy the Krym Tatar. It seems some use was made of this advice, for shortly the best soldiers and men-at-arms of these strangers were spared and put apart, and captains of each nation appointed to govern the rest—Jamy Lingett for the Scottish men, a

11. At the climax of a successful offensive on both shores of the Gulf of Finland, a Swedish army under Pontus de la Gardie stormed Narva in the late summer of 1581. The Swedes thus cut off all foreign trade with Russia through the Baltic since Narva had been the only significant port in Russian hands.

12. Liefflanders in the original text.

13. Staden and Schlichting also describe the massacre of foreign prisoners of war. In their accounts, the victims are Poles (Staden, *Aufzeichnungen über den Moskauer Staat*, p. 38; Schlichting, pp. 44–45).

valiant honest man. Money, clothes, and daily allowance for meat and drink was given them, horse, hay, and oats; swords, piece, and pistols were they armed with. Poor snakes afore, look now cheerfully. Twelve hundred of them did better service against the Tatar than twelve thousand Russes with their short bow and arrows. The Krym, not knowing then the use of piece and pistols, struck dead off their horses with shot they saw not, cried, "Away with those new devils that come with their thundering puffs," whereat the emperor made good sport. Then had they pensions and lands allowed them to live upon, married and matched with the Livonian fair women, increased into families and live in favor of the prince and people. O! how glad was I that the emperor took no notice of those few Englishmen taken captive among them! An opportune quarrel to my life, that was so well known and conversant in their court, but especially a fit prey for the emperor to seize upon the English merchants' goods, having then a stock in company for at least one hundred thousand marks sterling in his country. For, but a little before, the king had sold to one Thomas Glover,[14] a chief agent for that company, a wife born of a noble house in Poland, Basmanovey, taken captive at Polotsk, for ten thousand Hungarian ducats in gold; and yet shortly after, falling into some displeasure, robbed him of sixteen thousand pounds more in cloth, silk, wax, furs, and other merchandises, and sent him and his dear wife empty out of his land. But letting many other such acts of his pass, let us return to our more proper discourse.

VI

The emperor expecting some return of his letters out of England and news by Daniel Sylvester,[1] a thing thought upon that God would make an example of. He arrived with the queen's letters at St.

14. Glover was chief agent of the Russia Company in Russia from 1562 to 1567. He remained in Russia as an interloper, because, as he says, the Company is "bent to use rigor and cruelty towards him than by any reward to consider his long and painful travail, which causes him to bethink himself better before he departs from hence" (*Calendar of State Papers, Foreign*, 1566–68, p. 309).

1. Before his mission of 1575–76 Sylvester had been Jenkinson's interpreter during his last mission to Russia and subsequently been sent to Moscow as a courier in 1573 (Willan, *Early History*, pp. 125–26). On the mission of 1575–76 he

Nicholas, passed up to Kholmogory, where, preparing and making clothes fit for his present posting up to the emperor with those letters and message from the queen, the tailor sewing[2] on a new yellow satin jacket or japonne in an upper room of his lodging in the English house, and the tailor gone scarce down the stairs, a thunderbolt came and struck him dead, piercing down the collar of the inside of his new coat out the right side of his body, not outwardly seen. A flash of lightning killed also his boy and dog by him, burnt his desk, letters, house, all at instant. Whereat the emperor was much amazed when he heard of it, saying, "God's will be done!" but raged and was in desperate case; his enemies besetting and besieging three parts of his country, the Pole, Swede, and the Krym; King Stephen Bathory threatening he would visit him at his great city Moscow shortly. He made preparation accordingly, only doubting of some want of powder, saltpeter, lead, and brimstone, and knew not how to be furnished thereof, the Narva shut up, but out of England.[3] The difficulty[4] was how he should convey and send his letters to the queen, his countries environed and passages shut up. Sent for me and told me he had a message of honor, weight, and secrecy to employ me in to the queen's majesty of England, perceiving I had attained to the familiar phrase of his language, the Polish, and Dutch tongues. Questioned with me of divers things; liked my ready answers; asked me if I had seen his great vessels and barks built and prepared at Vologda. I told him I had. "What traitor hath showed them you?" "The fame of them was such, and people flocking to see them upon a festival day, I ventured with thousands more to behold

carried two letters with him from the queen, dated May 9 and May 10, 1575. The letters covered some of the points dealt with in instructions given to Sylvester. They are printed in Tolstoy, pp. 160–65. They also emphasized the secret nature of the impending negotiations. See Baker MSS 32, fols. 63–65, Cambridge University Library, and Willan, *Early History*, p. 127. Sylvester was killed in 1576.

2. saienge in the original text. Bond, in his edition, emends the text to read "essaying"; but the sense of the passage surely calls for "sewing."

3. In the 1580's the Russian government took steps to encourage the English merchants to bring in increased quantities of munitions. For example, in the negotiations with Bowes, Andrei Shchelkalov offered to renew the English trading monopoly on several conditions, one of which was the export to Russia of sufficient quantities of specified war materials (*Sbornik IRIO*, XXXVIII, 89). Finally in 1589, in the privileges granted to Fletcher, the Russian government stipulated that the English could no longer buy wax but could only barter it for saltpeter, powder, or sulphur (Bond, p. 350).

4. *difficulty*. difficult in the original text.

the curious beauty, largeness, and strange fashion of them." "Why, what mean you by those words, strange fashion?" "For that the portraiture of lions, dragons, eagles, elephants, and unicorns were so lively made and so richly set forth with gold, silver, and curious colors of painting, etc." "A crafty youth commends his own countrymen's artifice," said the emperor to his favorite standing by. "It is true; it seems you have taken good view of them; how many of them?" "It please your majesty I saw but twenty." "You shall see forty, ere long be, no worse. I commend you. No doubt you can relate as much in foreign place, but much more to be admired if you knew what inestimable treasure they are inwardly to be beautified with. It is reported your queen, my sister, hath the best navy of ships in the world." "It is true, and please your majesty." "Why have you dissembled with me then?" "For strength and greatness to break and cut through the great ocean, turbulent seas." "How framed so?" "For art, sharp-keeled, not flat-bottomed, so thick and strong-sided that a cannon shot can scarce pierce through." "What else?" "Every ship carries cannon and forty brass pieces of great ordnance, bullets, muskets, powder, chainshot, pikes, and armor of defense, wild fireworks, stanchions for fights, a thousand mariners and men at arms, soldiers, captains, and officers of all sorts to guide and govern; discipline and daily divine prayers, beer, bread, beef, fish, bacon, pease, butter, cheese, vinegar, oatmeal, aqua-vitæ, wood, water, and all other provisions plentiful, fit, and necessary for food and maintenance of men; anchors, cables, tackles, masts, five or six great sails spread, ancients, flags, costly silk banners displayed with the queen's ensigns and arms, whereat all other kings' ships bend and bow; drums, trumpets, tabor, pipe, and other instruments of warlike designs and defiance to the enemy; able to assault and batter the strongest maritime towns and castles that are; most terrible and warlike for the aid, conduction, and defense of her majesty's alliance and friends. Most noble emperor, this is the frame, form, and fashion of one of the triumphant ships of her majesty's navy royal."

I had the grace of spirit and speech in the essential delivery of this, as he often cast his head and eye aside upon the hearers and standers by, not with any applaud to myself nor great admiration. "How many such hath the queen as you describe?" "Forty, and please your majesty." "It is a good navy royal, as you term it. It can transport forty thousand soldiers to a friend." Gave me in charge to prepare myself and be silent and secret, and daily to attend till he were provided and prepared for my dispatch; commanded Eleazar Vyluzgin,[5] his secret secretary, to take from me in writing the description I made of the queen's navy royal, unto whom I presented also a ship, curiously made, set forth and drawn with all his sails spread, banners and ensigns displayed, ordnance gilt, and all things in a warlike fashion, made and given me by Mr. John Chappell of Lübeck and London.[6]

At this time he was very much busied by searching out a notable treason in practice and purpose against him by Eleazar Bomelius, the bishop of Novgorod, and some others, discovered by their servants, tortured upon the pytka or rack, letters written in ciphers, Latin and Greek, sent three manner of ways to the kings of Poland and Sweden. The bishop upon examination confessed all. Bomelius denied all, hoping to fare the better by means of some his confederates, as it was thought favorites near about the king, whom the emperor had appointed to attend his son Tsarevich Ivan to examine the said Bomelius upon the rack; his arms drawn back disjointed, and his legs stretched from his middle loins, his back and body cut with wire whips; confessed much and many things more than was written or willing the emperor should know. The emperor sent word they should roast him. Taken from the pytka and bound to a wooden pole or spit, his bloody cut back and body roasted and scorched till they thought no life in him, cast into a sled brought through the castle, I pressed among many others to see him; cast up his eyes naming Christ; cast into a dungeon and died there. He lived in great favor and pomp, a skillful mathematician, a wicked man, and practicer of much mischief. Most of the nobles were glad of his dispatch, for he knew much by them. He had conveyed great riches and treasure out of the country by way of England

5. See Fletcher, above, p. 147.

6. Chappell described himself as "John Chappell of London, draper." In the late 1560's he traded at Narva as an interloper. He later entered the service of the Russia Company and went to Russia in 1584 as assistant to Robert Peacock. Soon he was sent to Kazan', apparently to look into the private trading operations of employees of the company. As a result of this journey, the Russian authorities arrested him and accused him of writing treasonous letters to the governments of Sweden and Denmark (Willan, *Early History*, pp. 96, 105, 189, 191–92, 195–96; *Sbornik IRIO*, XXXVIII, 181–82). When the English government vigorously protested his arrest, he was released in 1587 (*Sbornik IRIO*, XXXVIII, 190). Subsequently, the directors of the company charged Horsey with responsibility for Chappell's arrest (Bond, p. 319).

to Wesel in Westphalia, where he was born, though brought up in Cambridge. An enemy always to our nation. He had deluded the emperor, making him believe the queen of England was young, and that it was very feasible for him to marry her, whereof he was now out of hope. Yet heard she had a young lady in her court of the blood royal named the Lady Mary Hastings, of which we shall speak more hereafter. The bishop of Novgorod was condemned of his treason and of coining money and sending it and other treasure to the king of Poland and Sweden, of buggery, of keeping witches and boys and beasts, and other horrible crimes. All his goods, horses, money, and treasure was confiscated to the king, which was much; himself to everlasting imprisonment; lived in a cave with irons on his head and legs, made and painted pictures and images, combs and saddles, with bread and water. Eleven of his confederate servants hanged at his palace gate at Moscow and his women witches shamefully dismembered and burned.[7] He was loath to take notice of all those that were confederated in this treason, passed it over with admonitions, and declaring his pleasure and intent to marry his second son, Tsarevich Fedor, his eldest son having no issue, a great work to advise on with his princes and prelates because of his simplicity, yet did what pleased himself. But having them together, his stomach full of their treasonable purposes, must evaporate somewhat for revenge. "O disloyal and most treacherous subjects! this day must now be double celebrated, the day of our Savior's Ascension, fresh in memory of sacrificing so many hundred thousand innocent souls, presented in red letters to the view of the whole world upon the theater of your rebellion. Nay, what coal can sufficiently note to all posterities this mournful and dismal day? What law of forgetfulness can wipe out the remembrance of thy shame, ingratitude, and treachery? What lotion can wash away the spots of thy pollution, filthiness and villainy? What fire shall ever consume the memory of the rebellious tyrannies and seditions of this so fatal and abominable conspiracies," etc. He was three hours enlarging this theme and style, and with

---

7. Horsey lumped together two similar incidents that occurred at different times. The Novgorod bishop may be either Pimen or his successor Leonid. Pimen was accused of conspiring to surrender Novgorod to the Poles and was imprisoned in 1570 during Ivan's sack of the city. He died in the Venevskii Monastery in 1571 (*NL*, 107, 344–45; Zimin, *Oprichnina*, pp. 299–300). Leonid was deposed and executed in 1575. Bomelius was then at the height of his power; he fell under suspicion of treason and was tortured to death in 1579.

great eloquence and bold utterance after their phrase and method and emphacy; darting still at many present of confederates in this last conspiracy; promising and protesting to leave them a naked, a disloyal, and distressed people, and a reproach to all the nations of the world; the enemies at hand to destroy us; God and his prodigious creatures in the heavens fight against us; the scarcities and famine witness it when no judgments, plagues, and punishments from the same God by him did move no remorse nor amendment in them. The original itself says too long to recite. Little was answered, less done, at this assembly, but all prostrating themselves to his sacred and most royal majesty and mercy, desiring God to bless his holy purpose and intention in this marriage of his noble son, prince Tsarevich Fedor. For whom he chose out of a great and famous family, powerful and most trusty to the emperor, a beautiful young lady named Irina, daughter to Fedor Ivanovich Godunov, and after the solemnity and great feasting and triumphs, the emperor dismissed all those nobles and prelates with good words and more favorable countenance, which was held for a mutual reconciliation and forgiveness of all.[8]

VII

N ow the emperor's letters and instructions were ready, himself and Sava Frolov, chief secretary of estate, closing them up in one of the false sides of a wooden bottle filled full with aqua-vitæ, to hang under my horse mane, not worth three pence; appointed me four hundred Hungarian ducats in gold to be sewed in my boots and quilted in some of my worst garments.[1] "I forbear to tell you of some secrets of my pleas-

8. The confusion of historians over the date of Fedor's marriage to Irina Godunova is a good illustration of the scarcity and confusion of the sources on the late sixteenth century. Most historians of previous generations have assumed that Fedor married in 1580. Recently, however, some Soviet writers have stated insistently that the marriage must have taken place as early as 1574/75 since the legend on a piece of embroidery that Irina made in those years indicates that she was already Fedor's wife (Zimin, "Sostav boiarskoi dumy," p. 78; *Materialy*, II, 163, n. 88).

1. Horsey set off in 1580. Sava Frolov was a clerk (*pod'iachii,* assistant to a d'iak or state secretary) who played an important role in the negotiations with Bowes in 1583–84 (*RK*, p. 276).

ure, for fearing thou passing through my enemies countries now in combustion, thou fall into their hands, may be enforced to discover that I
would not have known. What thou shalt say to Queen Elizabeth, my
loving sister, the bottle thou carriest with thee shall declare unto thee
when thou comest in safe place to make it open. In the mean and always be thou trusty and faithful, and thy reward shall be my goodness
and grace from me hereafter." I fell prostrate, laid my head on his foot
with a heavy heart to be thus exposed to so apparent misery and not
avoidable danger. A gentleman of good rank attended me. My sled and
horse and twenty servants posted that night ninety miles to Tver',
where victuals and fresh horse were prepared, and so to Novgorod and
Pskov and to Neuhausen, six hundred miles in three days; where entering into Livonia[2] my gentleman and servants take their leaves, desiring some token of my safe conducting thither. I bid them hie them
away, lest then the enemy round about us might take them and hinder
my service. The sentinel brought me to the stateholder or lieutenant of
the castle; he and his complices strictly examined and searched me;
coming from their enemy's country they could not but suspect me. I
told them I was glad I was come into their hands out of the vale of
misery, the Muscovites' country, not without some ransom. They laid
their heads together, and in the third day they appointed me a guide
and suffered me with more humanity to pass. The guard and waiters
expected some reward, but I prayed them to spare me; my purse was
not answerable to my willingness. I was three days a passing in great
danger by land and frozen meres to Osel in Livonia,[3] an island of the
king of Denmark's, large and spacious; taken by ragamuff soldiers, who
used me very roughly, carried me to Sonneburg and so to Arensburg
the chief town and castle in those parts; brought and delivered me to
the stateholder's lieutenant, sick, aged, and crabbed; attended his pleasure, hardly kept as a spy, the snakes creeping in my lodging upon bed
and board; hens and poultry pecking at them upon the floor and in the
milk pans, a strange sight to me; the soil was such, did no harm; but
the fear what should become of me made me to think the less of that.
The time came I was called before the governors. The chief was a very
grave gentleman in good favor with the king; he ruled all, soldiers
about him with halberds and swords; did examine me; the questions

2. Lieffland in the original text.
3. Liffland in the original text.

were many. I was a subject of the queen of England, who had peace
and amity with all Christian princes, especially and most entirely with
the majesty of Denmark. Yea, but that would not serve. We confederated most with the Muscovite against Christendom. Asked my name
and quality. I framed him an answer. Committed me to the custody
whence I was brought; dismissed his company, which was many; sends
his son, a proper fine gentleman, for me in private; had a letter in his
hand; asked my name again. I told him. "I have received sundry letters
from my friends, and one of late from a beloved daughter I have, captive with the emperor in the Moscow. She writes of much Christian
friendship and favor she hath found at an English gentleman's hands
named after your name, that negotiates in that court from the queen of
England."[4] "Is your daughter called Madelyn van Uxell."[5] "Yea, indeed,
sir," says he. "I am the same she writes of. I know her well, and was in
good health within this ten days." "O! sir, she is my dear and beloved
daughter, whom I cannot have ransomed, though the majesty of Denmark hath written in her behalf." Claps me about the neck, crying, and
his son in like manner. "God's angel hath brought your goodness to me;
however, you appear here no better secured, that I might render you
my thanks and friendship for your benevolence and favor towards me
and mine. This island hath heard of your worthy name and goodness,
and what it can afford you shall command." It seems he was very joyful
and I no less glad of this good hap. Caused me to be brought to a
pleasant lodging; his son next day showed his stables of great horse, his
armor, munition, and library; sent for divers of his friends; feasted me;
made ready his letters and passports with many ceremonial loving en-
tertainments; gave me a fair German clock, and his son and servants to
guide me out of all danger; commended his daughter, with prayer and
tears I would continue my goodness towards her, etc.

I haste on my way. A *domherr*[6] met me, a man of good account in
Livonia. Marveled I was so meanly attended; knew me, and told his
company of my quality, which might have done me hurt, and my

4. Johan Yxkull (d. 1582 or 1583), a Livonian noble, was, when in Danish
service, governor of Osel from 1576 to 1579 or 1580. There is no record that he
had a daughter who was a prisoner in Russia but, given the international situation,
Horsey's story could well be true in essence. See Johannes Lossius, *Drei Bilder aus
dem livländischen Adelsleben*, Vol. II, *Jürgen und Johan Uexküll im Getriebe
der livländischen Hofleute* (Leipzig, 1878).
5. Probably Yxkull (or Üksküll).
6. Canon.

aqua-vitæ bottle, too, girded close under my cassock by day and in the night my best pillow under my head. Past all danger as I thought; came to Pilten, a strong castle upon the Baltic Sea, where King Magnus lay, of whom you have heard before. He used me but roughly, by reason I could not drink excessively with him. He having spent and given most of his towns, castles, jewels, money, horse, and plate he had in dower with the emperor's niece riotously to his followers and adopted daughters, and not long after died miserably,[7] leaving his queen and only daughter in very poor estate. And thenceforward through the duke of Courland's country and duke of Prussia to Königsberg, Elbing,[8] and Danzig in Poland, Pomerania, and Mecklenburg, and so to the imperial town of Lübeck where I was known and exceedingly well and honorably entertained. Now I had gotten some better attendance, four or five servants, Dutch and English, taken up at Elbing[9] and Danzig. Here the burgomaster and lords of the town sent me by their recorder a present of fish and flesh and wines of all sorts, with a long oration of the favors I had done and showed to them and theirs. The next day divers now worthy merchants and their friends came with their thanks and acknowledgment my means of their redemption, being by my only means and purse freed of their captivity from the Muscovite, presented to me a fair bowl of silver gilt with a cover, in it rix-dollars and Hungarian ducats of gold. I poured out the gold and silver, returning that unto them again more prodigal than wise, put up the cup, and gave them my thanks; brought me their town book, prayed me to write therein my name and place of birth and abode, to the end that they and their posterities might honor my name forever.

Coming to Hamburg, but ten miles[10] of Lübeck, the Hamburgers having heard of my entertainment at Lübeck, those that had been in the same predicament and freed also by means of their captivity presented me their thanks and friendly remembrances. The burgomaster and *ratsherren*[11] feasted me; and the others gave me a fair tablecloth of damask work, two dozen of napkins, and a long towel of the same. Thus much more for my own remembrance than proper to the dis-

---

7. Magnus died in 1583.
8. Melvin in the original text.
9. Melvin in the original text.
10. Thirty-three miles.
11. Aldermen.

course I have taken in hand, for which I crave pardon, and yet a digression of some dependency upon the same.

Coming from Hamburg into England, I opened my aqua-vitæ bottle; took out and sweetened the emperor's letters and directions as well as I could, but yet the queen smelled the savor of the aqua-vitæ when I delivered them unto her majesty, declaring the cause for her highness more satisfaction. I had access three or four several times and some discourse by means of the lord treasurer and Sir Francis Walsingham, and some honorable countenance also of my lord of Leicester, most by Sir Edward Horsey his love and countenance, my especial noble good friend and kinsman. The Company trading Muscovy gave me good entertainment and presents; provided, by her majesty's order, all those things which the emperor had given in his directions, but in nowise to acquaint them with any other secret matter, with which and her majesty's dispatch commanded me to be sworn esquire of her body, gave me her picture, and her hand to kiss.

VIII

I departed in company of thirteen tall ships, met with the king of Denmark's near the North Cape, fought with them and put them to the worst.[1] Arrived at St. Nicholas; posted over Vaga and came to Sloboda Aleksandrovskaia, where I delivered the queen's letters to the emperor and her pleasure in secret. Who commended my speed and business done for him, gave me allowance, and promised his great goodness for recompense when he came to the city of Moscow. Took there all those commodities into his treasury, copper, lead, powder, saltpeter, brimstone, and other things, to the value of £9,000, and paid them ready money for all.

His majesty came to the city of Moscow; cast his displeasure upon

---

1. Although some historians have expressed doubt about Horsey's story, it is consistent with the international situation of the time. In the early 1580's the Danish government tried to compensate for its loss of revenues from the Sound tolls by charging duty on all ships sailing around the northern coast of Norway. Danish attempts to enforce their right to tax English shipping led to several skirmishes. The issue was settled by a compromise in 1583.

some noblemen and governors thereof; set a parasite of his and sent with him two hundred gunners to rob Nikita Romanovich our next neighbor, brother to the good empress Anastasiia, his first wife; took from him all his armor, horse, plate, and goods, to the value of forty thousand pounds; seized his lands and left him and his so poor and needy as he sent to the English house the next day for as much coarse cotton as made him a gown to cover himself and children withal, and for some other relief.[2] Sent Semen Nagoi, another of instruments of mischief, to rob and spoil one Andrei Shchelkalov, a great bribing officer, who brought his fair young wife out, repudiated her, cut and gashed her naked back with his scimitar.[3] Killed his trusty servant Ivan Lottish and beat out of his shins the said Andrei Shchelkalov five thousand rubles in money. At which time he did also take displeasure against those Dutch or Livonian people whom he had planted and placed with their wives and children and families without the city of Moscow, which he brought from the Narva and Dorpat, merchants and gentlemen of good account, and gave them liberty of religion and church there. Set a thousand gunners in the night to rob and take the spoil of them, stripped them naked, most barbarously ravished and deflowered both young and old women without respects, carrying divers of the youngest and fairest maids to serve their wicked lusts away with

2. Horsey's story is not consistent with the other evidence on the official functions and ceremonial ranking of Nikita Romanovich in the years between 1581 and 1584. In 1581, for example, he occupied one of the most honored places at the tsar's banquet in honor of Possevino, the Papal emissary. He also conducted some of the negotiations with Possevino in 1581 and 1582 and with Sir Jerome Bowes in the following two years (*PDS*, X, 80, 193–95, 336, 345; *Sbornik IRIO*, XXXVIII, 91–93, 116 ff.).

3. The career of Semen Fedorovich Nagoi was marked by sharp and sudden changes of fortune. In 1570/71 he was governor of Ryl'sk and fought a rearguard action against the invading Crimean Tatars. He was a commander on the Livonian front in 1573. When Ivan IV married Mariia Nagaia in 1581, Nagoi, now brother-in-law of the tsar, assumed a prominent position at court. His glory was of short duration. When Fedor came to the throne in 1584, Mariia and her infant son, Dmitrii, were exiled to Uglich. In the same year, Nagoi was made military commander of Vasil'gorod, a small fortress on the Volga between Nizhnii-Novgorod and Kazan'. He was reappointed to the post annually between 1584 and 1586/87 and again in 1589/90. After the death of his nephew, Dmitrii, in 1591, the government exiled him to one of his estates. The first False Dmitrii allowed him to return to court and made him a boiar. His fate after 1606 is unknown (*RK*, pp. 231, 233, 245, 348–49, 378, 390, 436; *RBS*). For Shchelkalov, see Fletcher, above, p. 146.

them; some escaping came to the English house, where they were covered, clad, and relieved, but in danger of displeasure in so doing. Well!
God would not leave this cruelty and barbarism unpunished. Not long
after he, the emperor, fell out in rage with his eldest son Tsarevich
Ivan for having some commiseration of these distressed poor Christians, and but for commanding an officer to give a gentleman a warrant
for five or six post horses, sent in his affairs without the king's leave,
and some other jealousy of greatness and too good opinion of the people as he thought. Struck him in his fury a box on the ear, and thrust at
him with his piked staff, who took it so tenderly, fell into a burning
fever, and died within three days after. Whereat the emperor tore his
hair and beard like a mad man, lamenting and mourning for the loss of
his son.[4] But the kingdom had the greatest loss, the hope of their comfort, a wise, mild, and most worthy prince of heroical condition, of
comely presence twenty-three years of age,[5] beloved and lamented of
all men; was buried in Michaela Sweat Archangel church,[6] with jewels,
precious stones, and pearl put into his tomb with his corpse, worth fifty
thousand pounds, watched by twelve citizens every night by change,
dedicated unto his Saint John and Michael Archangel to keep both
body and treasure.

IX

N ow was the Emperor more earnest to send into England about
this long conceited match and marriage than ever; addressed
one Fedor Pisemskii, a noble, grave, wise, and trusty gentleman,[1] to

---

4. See Fletcher, above, p. 128.
5. Tsarevich Ivan was killed in November, 1581, at the age of twenty-seven.
6. The Cathedral of the Archangel Michael.
1. Fedor Andreevich Pisemskii was ambassador in the Crimea between 1564
and 1573. Ivan IV made him a member of the oprichnina in 1571 as a reward
for his services. In 1583/84 and 1584/85 Pisemskii was civil governor of Chernigov
and later held military posts in Novgorod and Pskov. He became a member of
the boiar duma in 1589/90. He died in 1591 (Kobrin, p. 57; D. S. Likhachev [ed.],
Puteshestviia russkikh poslov XVI–XVII vv. [Moscow-Leningrad, 1954], pp. 386–
87; RK, pp. 348, 350, 359, 410, 414, 433). Pisemskii's mission to England took
place in 1582–83. He returned to Russia in the spring of 1583. For Pisemskii's
account of his visit to England, see Sbornik IRIO, XXXVIII, 3–70, or Likhachev
(ed.), Puteshestviia russkikh poslov XVI–XVII vv., pp. 100–55.

confer and desire of the queen the Lady Mary Hastings, daughter to that noble Henry, Lord Hastings, earl of Huntington, whom he heard was her kinswoman and of the blood royal, as he termed it; and that it would please her majesty to send some noble ambassador to treat with him about it. His ambassador went forward; took shipping at St. Nicholas; arrived in England magnificently received; had audience of the queen; delivered his letters commendatory. Her majesty caused that lady to be attended on with divers great ladies and maids of honor and young noblemen, the number of each appointed to be seen by the said ambassador in York House garden. She put on a stately countenance accordingly. The ambassador, attended with divers other noblemen and others, was brought before her ladyship; cast down his countenance; fell prostrate to her feet, rose, ran back from her, his face still towards her, she and the rest admiring at his manner. Said by an interpreter it did suffice him to behold the angel he hoped should be his master's spouse; commended her angelical countenance, state, and admirable beauty. She after was called by her familiar friends in court the empress of Muscovy. Sir William Russell, the earl of Bedford's third son, a noble, wise, and comely gentleman, was chosen her majesty's ambassador to the emperor.[2] But he and his honorable friends better considering of it made his unwillingness the means for another. Then the company of merchants entreated for Sir Jerome Bowes, only for presence and person, and repented afterwards.[3] He was well set forth most at their charge.

X

These two ambassadors, the queen's and the emperor's, with leave and letters were dispatched from her majesty, well shipped, arrived at St. Nicholas in Russia. The Russe ambassador posted overland, delivered his letters and account of his ambassage to his master the emperor, which was joyfully received. The other, Sir Jerome Bowes,

2. Russell (1558–1613), son of Francis Russell, second earl of Bedford, was lieutenant-general of cavalry under Leicester in the expedition to the Netherlands in 1585. He was Lord Deputy of Ireland, 1594 to 1597 (*DNB*).

3. Bowes (d. 1616) was ambassador to Russia in 1583. He was a tough, irascible person and his quarrels with the tsar made his embassy almost legendary. See Willan, *Early History*, pp. 163–69.

embarked by the merchants, passed slowly up the river Dvina, a thousand miles to Vologda. The emperor sent one Mikhail Protopopov,[1] a pensioner, well attended, to meet him and to make provision of victual, etc., for his passage, furnished with carts and post-horses for himself, baggage, and company. At Iaroslavl' another equerry of the stable met him with two fair ambling geldings for himself to mount on when pleased him. Was very honorably received at the Moscow by a duke, Kniaz' Ivan Sitskii,[2] attended with three hundred horse well appointed; brought to his lodging. The king's secretary, Sava Frolov, sent from the emperor to congratulate his welcoming, with many dishes of meat for his supper, promising he should be well accommodated. The next day the emperor sent a nobleman, Ignatii Tatishchev,[3] to visit Sir Jerome Bowes, to know how he did and what he did and what he wanted should be supplied, and to tell him he longed to see him, and if he were not overwearied with his journey he should have his presence and audience upon Saturday following two days' respite. He answered that he hoped he should be able to attend his majesty.

Accordingly about nine of the clock upon that day the streets were filled with people, and a thousand gunners, clad in red, yellow, and blue garments, set in ranks by the captains on horseback with bright pieces, harquebuses, in their hands, from the ambassador's door to the emperor's palace. Kniaz' Ivan Sitskii, mounted upon a fair jennet richly clad and decked, having a fair gelding led before him well furnished, sent for the ambassador to mount upon, attended with three hundred gentlemen on horseback richly furnished also. The ambassador, displeased the duke's horse was better than his, mounted on his own footcloth and with his thirty men liveried in stammel cloaks well set forth, each having a piece of his present, being most plate, marched onward to the king's palace; where met him another duke and told him the emperor stayed for him; who answered he came as fast as he could. By the way the people, partly guessing at his message generally disliked, cried *Carluke*[4] in mocking at him, which is "crane's legs." The passages, terraces, and rooms he was conducted through were all beset with merchants and gentlemen with golden coats. His men entering before him with their presents the room the king sat in, they put at one side. The

1. See *Sbornik IRIO*, XXXVIII, 71ff.
2. See Fletcher, above, p. 155.
3. See Fletcher, above, p. 156.
4. It is difficult to guess what Horsey meant by this word.

emperor sits[5] in his majesty, richly clad, with his three crowns before
him; four young noblemen, called *ryndy*, shining in cloth of silver with
four scepters or bright silver hatchets of each side the emperor; the
prince and other his great dukes and noblest of rank setting round
about him. The emperor stood up; the ambassador makes his curtsies
and speech, delivers the queen's letters. The emperor receiving puts off
his imperial cap, asked how his sister Queen Elizabeth did. The ambassador answering, sat down upon a form at one side the emperor, covered with a carpet. After some little time of pause and view of each
other was dismissed in manner as he came, and his dinner of two hundred dishes of meats sent after him by a gentleman of quality, which,
being delivered and rewarded, left Sir Jerome Bowes at his repast.

XI

I f I should be so large in the rest, the matter not being short would
take up too much time; some secret meetings and conferences and
some public there were. The king feasted, great allowance of all provisions daily made him; all things granted him, and yet nothing would
please him, made great displeasure. A reconciliation of accounts between the emperor's officers and the company of merchants was made,
all their *doléances* heard and remedied, their privileges and all things
granted, and the emperor resolved to send a nobleman his ambassador
to the queen. If Sir Jerome Bowes had known the measure and taken
the opportunity of time, the king, so inflamed with the effecting of his
desire, would yield to anything propounded;[1] yea, promise that, if this
marriage did take effect with the queen's kinswoman, her issue should

---

5. sets in the original text.
1. Horsey's version of the negotiations is grossly unfair to his enemy, Bowes.
When Ivan realized that the envoy had instructions to evade his demands, he
accused the English traders of malpractice and subversion and finally raged that
Bowes was no ambassador at all. For a long time, it seemed as though Ivan would
refuse to renew the trade concessions. Only when Bowes came for his farewell
audience did the tsar relent and renew them (*Sbornik IRIO*, XXXVIII, 90–132).
Elizabeth had given Bowes a nearly impossible assignment, to give nothing and to
get everything in return. His rudeness intensified the problems of the negotiations
but did not create them.

inherit the crown.[2] The princes and nobles, especially those of nearest alliance to the prince's wife, the family of the Godunovs, much grieved and offended at this, found by secret practice and plotted a remedy to cross and overthrow all these designs. The king in fury, much distracted and doubting, caused many witches' magicians presently to be sent for out of the north, where there is store between Kholmogory and Lapland. Threescore were brought post to the Moscow, placed and guarded, and daily dieted and daily visited and attended on by the emperor's favorite, Bogdan Bel'skii, who was only trusted by the emperor to receive and bring from them their divinations or oracles upon the subjects that was given them in charge.[3] This favorite was now revolted in faith to the king, wholly seeking now and serving the turns of the sun-rising, wearied and tired with the devilish tyrannical practices, horrible influences, and wicked devices of this Heliogabalus.[4] The soothsayers tell him that the best signs, [constellations], and strongest planets of heaven was against the emperor, which would produce his end by such a day, but he durst not to tell him so; he fell in rage and told them they were very likely to be all burned that day. The emperor began grievously to swell in his cods, with which he had most horribly offended above fifty years together, boasting of thousand virgins he had deflowered and thousands of children of his begetting destroyed.

Carried every day in his chair into his treasury. One day the prince beckoned to me to follow. I stood among the rest venturously and heard him call for some precious stones and jewels. Told the prince and nobles present before and about him the virtue of such and such,

2. This statement is not true. Ivan offered to set up appanage principalities (*udely*) for any sons of the proposed marriage but made it clear that he would not change the order of the succession to the throne (*Sbornik IRIO*, XXXVIII, 7).

3. One of the members of an impoverished boiar family from the Iaroslavl' district, Bel'skii came to prominence in the last two years of the oprichnina. He was one of the oprichniki who remained in Ivan's favor, became a duma member in 1566/67, and in 1578/79 was appointed to the office of *oruzhnichii* (armorer). In 1584 he intrigued against the other leading figures of the court and when riots broke out in Moscow demanding his punishment, he was exiled to Nizhnii-Novgorod. In the reign of Boris Godunov he was given the rank of okol'nichii and subsequently the False Dmitrii made him boiar. Tsar Vasilii Shuiskii removed him from the court by appointing him governor of Kazan'. He was killed there in 1610 (Veselovskii, *Issledovaniia*, pp. 202, 204; *RK*, pp. 276, 295, 349).

4. Heliogabalus ruled from 218–222 A.D., under the name M. Aurelius Antoninus. A prince of incredible folly, superstition, and vice, he was slain by soldiers and succeeded by his cousin Alexander Severus.

which I observed, and do pray I may a little digress to declare for my own memory sake.

"The loadstone you all know hath great and hidden virtue, without which the seas that compass the world are not navigable nor the bounds nor circle of the earth cannot be known. Muhammad, the Persians' prophet, his tomb of steel hangs in their Ropata at Derbent most miraculously."[5] Caused the waiters to bring a chain of needles touched by this loadstone, hanged all one by the other. "This fair coral and this fair turquoise you see; take in your hand; of his nature are orient colors; put them on my hand and arm. I am poisoned with disease; you see they show their virtue by the change of their pure color into pall; declares my death. Reach out my staff royal, an unicorn's horn garnished with very fair diamonds, rubies, sapphires, emeralds, and other precious stones that are rich in value, cost seventy thousand marks sterling of David Gower from the folkers of Augsburg. Seek out for some spiders." Caused his physician, Johan Eilof,[6] to scrape a circle thereof upon the table; put within it one spider and so one other and died, and some other without that ran alive apace from it. "It is too late, it will not preserve me. Behold these precious stones. This diamond is the orient's richest and most precious of all other. I never affected it; it restrains fury and luxury and abstinacy and chastity; the least parcel of it in powder will poison a horse given to drink, much more a man." Points at the ruby. "O! this is most comfortable to the heart, brain, vigor, and memory of man, clarifies congealed and corrupt blood." Then at the emerald. "The nature of the rainbow, this precious stone is an enemy to uncleanness. Try it; though man and wife cohabit in lust together, having this stone about them, it will burst at the spending of nature. The sapphire I greatly delight in; it preserves and increaseth courage, joys the heart, pleasing to all the vital senses, precious and very sovereign for the eyes, clears the sight, takes away bloodshot, and strengthens the muscles and strings thereof." Then takes the onyx in

5. *Ropata:* an archaic Russian word meaning a temple or mosque. Probably a reference to the great mosque in Derbent, which dates from the 8th century.

6. Johan Eilof (or Eylof) was court physician in the last years of Ivan IV. He was a Dutch Anabaptist and attracted the ire of Possevino in 1581 by doing his best to warn Ivan against negotiating with the Papacy. In addition to his services at court, he conducted a trading enterprise with his son (V. A. Kordt, "Ocherk snoshenii moskovskago gosudarstva s respublikoiu Soedinennykh Niderlandov po 1631 g.," *Sbornik IRIO,* CXVI, pp. cclxxxvii–cclxxxviii). *Physician:* physicians in the original text.

hand. "All these are God's wonderful gifts, secrets in nature, and yet reveals them to man's use and contemplation, as friends to grace and virtue and enemies to vice. I faint; carry me away till another a time."

In the afternoon peruseth over his will and yet thinks not to die; he hath been bewitched in that place and often times unwitched again, but now the devil fails. Commands the master of his apothecary and physicians to prepare and attend for his solace and bathing, looks for the goodness of the sign, send his favorite to his witches again to know their calculations. He comes and tells them the emperor will bury or burn them all quick for their false illusions and lies. The day is come; he is as heart whole as ever he was. "Sir, be not so wrathful. You know the day is come and ends with the setting of the sun." He hastes him to the emperor; made great preparation for the bath. About the third hour of the day the emperor went into it, solaced himself and made merry with pleasant songs as he useth to do, came out about the seventh hour well refreshed; brought forth, sets him down upon his bed, calls Rodion Birkin, a gentleman whom he favored, to bring the chess board.[7] He sets his men, his chief favorite and Boris Fedorovich Godunov and others about him. The emperor in his loose gown, shirt, and linen hose faints and falls backward. Great outcry and stir; one sent for aqua-vitæ, another to the apothecary for marigold and rosewater and to call his ghostly father and the physicians. In the mean he was strangled and stark dead.[8] Some show of hope was made for recovery to still the outcry. The said Bogdan Bel'skii and Boris Fedorovich, unto whom the emperor had bequeathed, the first, of four other noblemen and brother to this Emperor Fedor Ivanovich his wife and empress that must now succeed, the government of all, go out upon the terrace, accompanied so suddenly at hand with so many and other multitudes of the nobility, his familiar friends, as it was strange to behold. Cried out to the captains and gunners to keep their guard strong and the gates sure about the palace, with their pieces and matches lighted; the gates of the castle presently shut and well watched. I offered myself, men, powder, and pistols to attend the prince protector; he accepted me among his family and servants, passing by with a cheerful countenance upon me said, "Be faithful and fear not."

7. Birkin was a member of a Riazan' gentry family who assisted in the reception of Possevino in 1582 and was an army commander at Pronsk in 1585. In 1587 he and Petr Pivov were sent to Georgia as ambassadors (*RBS*; *RK*, pp. 350–54; *PDS*, X, 70–71).

8. Ivan died on March 18, 1584.

XII

The metropolitans, bishops, and other of the nobility flocked into the castle, holding it for a day of jubilee for their redemption; it was who could press first to the book and cross to take oath and vow faith to this new emperor, Fedor Ivanovich. It was admirable what dispatch there was in six or seven hours: the treasuries sealed up and new officers added to the old of this family. Twelve thousand gunners, and captains over them, set for a garrison about the walls of the great city of Moscow; a guard given me to keep the English house; and the ambassador, Sir Jerome Bowes, who trembled and expected hourly nothing but death and confiscation, his gates, windows, and servants shut up, made spare of the plenty he had before. Boris Fedorovich, now lord protector; three other chief boiars joined assistance with him for the government, Kniaz' Ivan Mstislavskii, Kniaz' Ivan Vasil'evich Shuiskii,[1] and Nikita Romanovich, by the old emperor's will; began to manage and dispose of all affairs, take inventories of all the treasure everywhere, gold, silver, and jewels, a survey of all the offices and books of revenues; new treasurers, new counselors, new officers in all courts; new lieutenants, captains, and garrisons in all places of charge; and in the castles, towns, and countries of most importance were placed such out of that family as was best to be trusted; and so likewise the attendance about the empress his sister, by which means he became most wonderful safe and strong. Great was his observation magnified, beloved, feared, and honored of all men, and he showed and behaved himself both to the princes and nobility and to all sorts of the people so affable and loving as did procure, draw, and increase the same.

I was sent for and asked what they[2] should do with Sir Jerome Bowes, his business being at an end. I told the lords it stood with the honor of the king and kingdom to dismiss him with all safety and humanity according to the law of nations; otherwise it would be ill taken, and perhaps procure such displeasure as would not be soon pacified; all which I submitted to their wiser and better considerations. They all

1. Presumably F. I. Msistislavskii and V. I. Shuiskii. See pp. 154, n. 6, 263–64, n. 2, and 365, n. 15.
2. *they.* the in the original text.

reviled at him saying he had deserved death, but that the emperor and empress were now of a more merciful disposition; they would have sent a message by me to prepare his dispatch, with some other words of displeasure, which I prayed might be done by some other his majesty's servants.

The lord Boris Fedorovich sent for me at evening, whom I found playing at chess with a prince of the blood, Kniaz' Ivan Glinskii.[3] Took me aside, "Speak little in defense of Bowes, I advise you, the lords take it ill. Go show yourself and pacify such and such. Your answer was well considered of; many persuade revenge of his behavior. I'll do my best to make all well, and tell him so from me." I went to those noblemen accordingly and did endeavor to pacify them. They told me my partaking with Sir Jerome Bowes would do me more hurt than I was aware of, knowing how things stood and so distasteful to all, especially those chief officers that had suffered so much for his arrogancy. They could not but love me for ancient knowledge, and the more because Boris Fedorovich did favor me so well. "Therefore meddle you little with that business." And yet I did not leave to deal effectually underhand for him, for his case was very dangerous. I entreated he might be sent for and dispatched, being cooped up and kept close as a prisoner, all allowances taken from him. In the end he was sent for when other greater affairs of state was passed over; not attended upon, but with a mean messenger had into a withdrawing room where many of the lords were; used him with no respect, charged him with heinous matter practiced against the crown and estate, would suffer nor spend time for his answer, railed upon, especially by the two Shchelkalovs, great officers, and some others who had endured most displeasure and beatings of the emperor for his complaints and unreasonable and needless finding faults, from time to time, so much to disquiet the king and state, as never any ambassador did; and told him it were very requisite, for example of all others that should so much forget themselves and the place employed in, to cut off his legs and cast his withered carcass into the river, pointing out of the window under him; but that God hath given us now a more merciful emperor that wills no revenge, whose eyes he should see for Queen Elizabeth sake, but put off your sword, which he refused; it was against his orders and oath. They would enforce him else, coming into the presence of so sacred and peaceable a

3. See Fletcher, above, pp. 142, 153.

prince, his soul being clad with mourning not fitted for the sight of arms; and so put on patience, being single was brought to the emperor, who by the mouth of his chancellor commended him to Queen Elizabeth. Wherewith Sir Jerome Bowes was conveyed to his lodging, three days given for his departure out of the city of Moscow; perhaps he should have a letter sent after him. Sir Jerome Bowes had now little means, less money, but what was supplied him, glad of so peaceable a dismissment, and wished himself out of their reach. I made means to get him thirty carts for his own stuff and servants and as many posthorses. I asked the lord protector's leave to see and speak with him and to bring him out of the city. A mean syn boiarskii was appointed to guard him and to look narrowly to him, who used him with small humanity and much against the height of his mind and stoutness of his heart to endure. I with my servants and good friends accompanied him, well mounted and appointed, out of the city of Moscow; otherwise both he and others feared some disgrace. I pitched my tent or pavilion ten miles off, and, with the provision I had ready there of all sorts of wines and mead, I took leave of him and his company; prayed me to have an eye and ear to his safety, doubting of some treachery towards him upon the way, and so did I, though I said little. Wonderfully perplexed with fear, he thanked me for that I had done; he would cause the queen and my friends to give me thanks, and himself and his friends should never forget it; his own hand and letter written at Pereiaslavl' upon the way confirms and prays the continuance of my care. God bears me witness I wrought effectually for his safety and good. I procured the prince protector to send his letters after him to the queen, and a timber of sables, a gift from himself. When he came to St. Nicholas and aboard the ship, he used exceeding intemperate, rash, and indiscreet words to the gentleman that conducted him thither, cutting both sables and letters in pieces, and sent many proud and opprobrious words of the emperor and his council.[4] After he was gone for taking his part those great officers of estate, the Shchelkalovs, of friends became my mortal enemies. I am the larger, because you shall perceive hereafter how well Sir Jerome Bowes requited me. The state

4. Russian diplomatic sources confirm Horsey's account of Bowes' stormy departure from Russia (*Sbornik IRIO*, XXXVIII, 145) and the ambassador admitted that he had returned the tsar's gifts (Tolstoy, p. 235). It is hardly surprising that the agents of the Russia Company feared that they might suffer for Bowes' insulting behavior.

and government of this new commonwealth, so much altered as it was termed new, having put on, as it were, a new face so contrary to the old, every man living in peace, enjoying and knowing his own, good officers placed, justice ministered everywhere. Yet God hath a great plague in store for this people; what shall we say? The natural disposition of this nation was so wicked and vile that if the old emperor had not held so hard a hand and severe government over them, he could never have lived so long, for their treacherous and treasonable practices and still discovered. Little would we think now that this so great a treasure so left would be so soon consumed, and this kingdom, emperor, and princes and people so speedily ruinated. Ill gotten, soon lost.

XIII

This emperor, Ivan Vasil'evich, reigned above sixty years.[1] He conquered Polotsk, Smolensk, and many other great towns and castles, seven hundred miles southwest from the city of Moscow into the countries of Lithuania, belonging to the crown of Poland. He conquered also as much and as many towns and castles eastward Livonia and other dominions of the king of Sweden and Poland; he conquered the kingdom of Kazan' and the kingdom of Astrakhan', and all the regions and great people of the Nogai[2] and Circassian Tatars,[3] and many other of that kind inhabiting above two thousand miles of each side that famous river of Volga, southward even to the Mare Caspian Sea. He freed himself from the servile tribute and homage that he and his

1. Actually 51 years (1533–84).
2. In the 1540's the leaders of the Great Horde of the Nogai became allies of Muscovy and remained so during the conquest of Kazan' and Astrakhan'. In spite of interruptions and strains, the alliance continued throughout the following decades: the tsar's government paid subsidies to the Nogai princes; and the Nogais, on occasions, sent detachments to serve with the Muscovite army.
3. In the years between 1552 and 1557, a number of princes of Kabarda in the northern Caucasus swore allegiance to Ivan IV in a bid for Muscovite support. In 1557 Temriuk, one of these princes, appealed for support against a rival Caucasian ruler, the Shamkhal of Tarki. His alliance with Moscow was strengthened by the marriage of Ivan to his daughter Mariia in 1561.

predecessors did yearly pay and perform to the great Scythian emperor, the khan or Krym Tatar, not without some yearly charge for defense of their yearly incursions. He conquered the kingdom of Siberia[4] and all those adjacent countries northwards above 1,500 miles, so that he hath mightily enlarged his country and kingdoms every way, so peopled and inhabited as great trade and traffic is maintained with all nations for the several commodities each country yields, whereby his customs and crown revenues are not only increased, but those towns and provinces richly maintained. So spacious and large is now the dominions of this empire as it can hardly be held within one regiment, but to be divided again into several kingdoms and principalities, and yet under one complete monarchical sovereignty, and then too overmighty for all his neighbor princes. This did he aim at, was in good hope and way to make it feasible. But the boundless ambition and wisdom of man seemed but foolishness to the preventing pleasure and power of the Almighty, as the sequel declareth.[5] This emperor reduced the ambiguities and uncertainties of their laws and pleadings into a most perspicuous and plain form of a written law, for every man universal to understand and plead his own cause without any advocate, and to challenge upon a great mulct to the crown judgment without delay. This emperor established and published one universal confession of faith, doctrine, and discipline of church, consonant to the three symbolic, as they term it, or orthodox creeds most agreeable to the apostolical order used in the primitive church, allowed in the opinion of the best and ancientest fathers, Athanasius and others, in their Nicene, best and most approved councils.[6] He and his ancestors acknowledging their

4. Ermak Timofeev and his band of Cossacks, retainers of the Stroganov family, overran the Tatar khanate of Sibir' in 1582. Effective Russian control of the area was established more slowly. In the 1580's and 1590's, the Muscovite government founded a series of forts at strategic points in western Siberia. Then in 1598 regular Muscovite troops defeated Kuchum, the last khan, who had tried to revive the Tatar state, and from that time, western Siberia was under firm Russian control.

5. Probably a paraphrase of I Corinthians III:19: "For the wisdom of this world is foolishness with God."

6. Horsey uses a Protestant turn of phrase to describe the activities of the church council of 1550–51. Its resolutions were concerned chiefly with regularizing liturgical practice and tightening ecclesiastical discipline. The references are to Athanasius (298–373), Archbishop of Alexandria and a defender of orthodox doctrine against the Arian heresy, and to the first council of Nicaea (325), which promulgated the Nicene creed.

original and fundamental laws of religion of Christian belief to be grounded upon the Greek church, deriving their antiquity from their apostle, St. Andrew, and patron, St. Nicholas, which church since, by reason of their dissenting and dissipation in late ages, have fallen and erred from the essential points both in substance of doctrine and ceremony.

Whereupon this emperor hath acquitted this see of Moscow from that society, and consequently of the oblations and synodals heretofore contributed to the necessity of that church, and by the help of the Trinity hath inspired the hollow heart of the patriarch Ερεμιας to resign over the patriarchship of Constantinople or Scio to the μετραπολεταν see of Moscow to save that charge.[7] The emperor utterly denies and disclaims the doctrine of the Pope, holds it of all Christian churches to be the most erroneous; goes together with his ambition, both grounded upon invention, to maintain an hierarchy never allowed him, marveling that any prince Christian will yield him any supremacy or secular authority. All which, and largely more, did he cause his metropolitans, archbishops and bishops, archimandrites and hegumens, to declare and deliver to his nuncio Pater Antonio Possevino, the great Jesuit, at the church door of Prechista, articulated in the city of Moscow.[8] This emperor hath built in his time above forty fair stone churches, richly bedecked and adorned within, and the turrets all gilt with fine pure gold. He hath built above sixty monasteries and nunneries, endowed them with bells and ornaments and maintenance to pray for his soul.

He built a goodly steeple of hewn stone in the inner castle of Moscow, called *Blaveshina Collicalits*[9] with thirty great sweet-sounding bells in it, which serves to all those cathedral and goodly churches standing round about it, ringing all together every festival day, which

7. Under pressure of the Muscovite government, the patriarch of Constantinople, Jeremiah, consecrated Iov, the metropolitan of Moscow, as patriarch in 1589. Jeremiah did not resign his own see but created an entirely new patriarchate. Ερεμιας: Ερεμ in the original text.

8. Probably a reference to Ivan's debate with Possevino on February 21, 1582. Horsey may have combined this with a reference to an incident of March 4 when the tsar requested Possevino to accompany him to a celebration of the liturgy and the nuncio, after a brief period of confusion, declined the invitation (P. Pierling, *La Russie et le Saint-Siège* [Paris, 1897], II, 166–73, 177–80).

9. Apparently a reference to the Bell Tower of Ivan the Great, the oldest section of which was built between 1532 and 1543.

are many, and very dolesomely at every midnight's prayers.

One deed of charity I may not omit, one memorable act, to shut up his devotion with. In anno 1575 a great famine followed the pestilence of the better sort of people. The towns, streets, and ways swarmed with rogues, idle beggars, and counterfeit cripples; no riddance could be made of them in the time of scarcity. Proclamation was made they should resort to receive the emperor's great alms upon such a day at Sloboda. Out of some thousands that came seven hundred of the most vilest and counterfeits were all knocked in the heads and cast into the great lake, for the fish to receive their dole there; the rest most feeblest were dispersed to monasteries and hospitals to be relieved. This emperor, among many other such like acts, did build in his time 155 castles in all parts of his kingdoms, planted them with ordnance and garrisons. He built three hundred towns in waste places and wildernesses, called iamy, of a mile and two in length; gave every inhabitant a proportion of land to keep so many speedy horses for his use as occasion requires.[10] He built a goodly, strong, and spacious stone wall about the Moscow, planted and placed ordnance and officers to maintain his garrisons.[11]

Thus much to conclude with this Emperor Ivan Vasil'evich. He was a goodly man of person and presence, well favored, high forehead, shrill voice; a right Scythian; full of ready wisdom, cruel, bloody, merciless; his own experience managed by direction both his state and commonwealth affairs. Was sumptuously entombed in Michael Archangel Church, where he, though guarded day and night, remains a fearful spectacle to the memory of such as pass by or hear his name spoken of, who are contented to cross and bless themselves from his resurrection again, etc.

10. In the middle of the sixteenth century, the Muscovite system of post stations underwent fundamental change. Previously the responsibility for providing carts and maintaining the stations rested on the whole population of a district. From this time, however, the stations were run by a special group of post agents (iamskie okhotniki) chosen from the population. The population as a whole still had to pay post taxes to the treasury and help in clearing the roads and maintaining the station buildings. In addition, they now had to provide support for the post agents as well. The agents usually settled in hamlets by the stations and were granted allotments of land as part of their compensation for service (Zimin, Reformy, pp. 332–33; I. Ia. Gurliand, Iamskaia gon'ba v moskovskom gosudarstve do kontsa XVII veka [Iaroslavl', 1900], pp. 83–94, 122–31).

11. Perhaps a reference to the construction of a stone wall around the Kitaigorod section of Moscow in 1535.

XIV

Ambassadors were nominated and appointed, such as Boris Fedorovich best affected to illustrate his greatness, to be sent abroad to all princes, allies to this empire. But first, preparation being made for the emperor's coronation,[1] which, for that it will take up more room here than we can well spare, I, being an eye and ear witness thereunto and receiving much grace and honor at the same, must refer the relation thereof to Mr. Hakluyt's book of voyages[2] and Dr. Fletcher's treatise, with other discourses of the state and government of this commonwealth procured at my hands long since; I, among others, was nominated and appointed to be sent unto the queen. The substance of our errands was most alike, to make known that, by the providence of God, Fedor Ivanovich was *coroberavated* (their term), crowned, and settled in the imperial kingdoms and territories which his father, late Emperor Ivan Vasil'evich, of famous memory, was possessed of. Thought good, out of the tender care and holy desire he had to peace, to intimate and make known unto their imperial qualities and wisdom how desirous he was of their allies and brotherly amity, also who embracing the same did promise all reciprocal correspondency, trade, and commerce with them and theirs.

With which letters and commissions to treat of such other matter as fell properly in question for the weal on both sides, I was dispatched with extraordinary grace, terms, and titles, especially from the prince protector, Boris Fedorovich, both in private and in public and with instructions and commissions apart. I set forth well appointed and attended, and received, guarded, and accommodated in the reputation of an ambassador wherever I came. My journey was overland from the Moscow, the 20th of August 1585,[3] six hundred miles to Pskov,[4] and

1. The coronation took place on May 31, 1584.
2. Horsey's own account of the coronation is found in Hakluyt III, 336–47.
3. In his work on the coronation, Horsey gives September 5, 1585, as the date of his departure.
4. Vobsco in the original text. The distance from Moscow to Pskov is 685 versts or about 465 miles.

thence to Dorpat in Livonia, Pernau, Wenden, Libau,[5] etc. and to Riga,
the capital city of that province, where my commission was to treat
with Queen Magnus, the next heir of the imperial crown of Muscovy,[6]
she being left in great distress and kept upon small allowance, issuing
out of the treasury of the crown of Poland, in the castle of Riga. Could
not have access but by the means and leave of the Cardinal Radziwill,
being by chance resident there, a bouncing princely prelate, loving the
company of the Livonian ladies, the fairest women of the known
world.[7] Great means I made to speak with her. The cardinal at first
showed his austere countenance as a matter of great difficulty, but
when we became better acquainted, more merry and pleasant, and
laughed upon me as he passed in procession, to the end, as it were, I
should behold his gravity.

When I was brought to Llona,[8] Queen Magnus, I found her combing
of her daughter's head and hair, a proper girl of nine years of age. She
asked me what my will was. I desired to speak with her apart; began
to look somewhat more strange upon me; told me she knew me not and
had not many withdrawing rooms nor attendance. Left her daughter
with her gentlewoman, a widow,[9] in the same room; began to put on a
more stately behavior. "Madame, I have no long time you see to discourse with you of my message unto your highness; let me entreat your
princely promise to keep secret that I shall speak unto you, tending all
for the good of you and yours." Though she used silence yet I went
forward. "The emperor, Fedor Ivanovich, your brother" (for so
cousins-german[10] call each other) "takes notice of your necessity you
and your daughter live in, desires your return into your native country
to hold your state and well being according to your royal birth and
place, and the lord protector, Boris Fedorovich, doth with due re-

5. Now Liepaja.
6. During the early years of Tsar Fedor's reign, it was uncertain who was next
in line for the crown. The person with the best claim was Dmitrii, son of Ivan IV
and Mariia Nagaia. Even he faced barriers to the succession because he was
canonically a bastard, being the child of a seventh marriage. Mariia, widow of
Magnus, had only a tangential claim to the throne.
7. Jerzy Radziwill (1556–1600) was bishop of Vilna in 1574, and was made
cardinal in 1586. He was governor of the Polish-controlled areas of Livonia
between 1582 and 1586.
8. Her name was actually Mariia.
9. *widow.* window in the original text.
10. *cousins-german.* cozen-garmans in the original text.

membrance of his service vow the performance of the same." "Sir," says she, "they neither know me nor I them. Your countenance, speech, and attire makes me to believe you more than reason can persuade me." I was interrupted, hastened away, and somewhat mistrusted by the lieutenant. She was as loth to part as I; began to shed tears, and so did her daughter and her gentlewoman to see her do so; wished me to make means for access to her again. The cardinal was told this; sends for me; asketh what merriment it was I made the queen to laugh at. I told him he was misinformed. "You know what I mean; have access, but be not too bold." I besought his warrant, and had it; she longed to hear out the rest, and so did I to deliver it. "You see, sir, I am kept as a prisoner and my allowance small, not a thousand dollars a year." "You may remedy that if please you." "Two special doubts trouble me: if I should be of that mind I have no means to escape, and hold it a thing very difficult, perceiving the king and state purpose to make use of my birth and blood like unto the Egyptian goddess; and knowing their fashions in Muscovy, I have little hope to be dealt otherwise with than they use to do with their queens widows there, to be shut up in a hellish cloister, before which I choose death." "Your case differs much from theirs, and times have altered that kind of course, none enforced thereunto that hath a child or children in being and to educate." "What assurance have I of that or know this to be from those you speak of?" "Your willingness must make trial of that; the assurance whereof may make your adventure the more prosperous, when you shall see and be persuaded of the means intended to effect the same without danger." "Then must I rely upon God and your Christian secrecy and promise; let me know your name and the time as near as you can." "Doubt not, gracious lady, but within two months your highness shall know both; by the token I leave one hundred Hungarian ducats in gold, and your grace shall receive four hundred more this day seven weeks or near that time." Her highness received them thankfully, and her daughter twenty pieces more. I took my leave, and her highness and daughter embraced my hand in hers for my farewell, and glad I had effected so much.

My servants marveled, and so did the lieutenant of the castle, at my long stay. He told the cardinal again, "Tush, suspect him not; you see he is a suing youth and fine, etc. I wish he had her, so I had the charge she hath cost me." "So would not the king nor crown of Poland for a hundred thousand dollars more." I presented the cardinal a fair golden wrought handkerchief and humbly thanked him for his favor. "I am glad you have sped so well, sir; when we meet in Poland we[11] shall reruminate our acquaintance merrily."

Passing out of the gates of the town, a gentlewomanlike maiden in her hair delivered me a curious white wrought handkerchief, in the corner whereof a little hoop ring with rubies of small value, but told me not from whom. I guessed aright and hied me out of the cardinal's jurisdiction, through Courland, Prussia, Königsberg,[12] Elbing,[13] and Danzig, where I did a little repose and sent back one of my servants, a Danziger born, by sea to the Narva with my letters, handkerchief, and relation to the emperor and Boris Fedorovich what I had done, all sewed up in his quilt doublet. He passed so speedily and safely that this queen and daughter was sent for, stolen away very cunningly, and posted with through Livonia before she was missing. The lieutenant sent divers horsemen after her, but too late; he put by his place in displeasure and a more trustier chosen.[14] At my return out of England, to make an end of this matter, I perceived she was much esteemed of, had her officers, lands, and allowance according to her estate, but not long after she and her daughter were disposed of into maids' monastery among the rest of the queens, whereat she exclaimed woe be unto the time she was betrayed and that ever she gave faith to me, but could not be permitted sight of me nor I of her. This piece of service was very acceptable, whereof I much repent me. From Danzig I passed through Kassubia, Pomerania, Stettin, Mecklenburg, Rostock (where I escaped miraculously death), came to that famous imperial town of Lübeck, where I was exceedingly well and honorably entertained. The burgomaster and ratsherren presented me with their presents of wines and cakes and thanksgiving for my former favors done them.

11. *we.* you in the original text.
12. Quinsburgh in the original text.
13. Melvinge in the original text.
14. D. Tsvetaev has suggested that, once Mariia Vladimirovna agreed to return to Moscow, the tsar's government brought her back not by stealth but with the formal approval of the Polish court which had no desire to keep her in custody any longer (D. Tsvetaev, *Protestantstvo i protestanty v Rossii do epokhi preobrazovanii* [Moscow, 1890], p. 429, n. 1).

XV

From Hamburg I arrived in England, came to the court at Richmond, showed myself to the lord treasurer and Sir Francis Walsingham. They brought me to the queen, whose highness received the emperor's letters and my speech most graciously and with great applaud commended me; was glad she had such a servant attained to such knowledge and trust to be employed in so weighty affairs from so great and foreign prince. Speaking to Mr. Vice-Chamberlain, Sir Thomas Heneage, "Have you and the harbinger care for his lodging; 'tis late, I will speak with you farther tomorrow."[1] Sir Jerome Bowes and his brother, Mr. Ralph Bowes, came to welcome me with no small compliments, with some temerity sounded me. Gave, as he said, great commendation of my languages, favor, and estimation I had in the emperor's court, all which I believed, for the queen told me as much. The next day it pleased her majesty to have a great deal of conference with me, and somewhat concerning Sir Jerome Bowes' misbehavior, to which I said little as yet. The letters[2] committed to the trust of my translation, the which I did sparingly for the terms used against Sir Jerome Bowes, which Mr. Secretary took ill, told me the queen would be displeased if she knew of it, whose highness bid me not to fear the face of any. After I had perfected it, Mr. Secretary read the same to the queen. Her majesty required to know my commissions, for that, besides what was contained in the emperor's letters, was referred to word of mouth. I told her highness it was so much as I feared would weary her majesty's patience, being so late. "Then will I appoint a time of purpose to give you farther audience." Turned her highness to the lords and said, "I promise you, my lords, these letters show as honorable matter as ever we received from any prince newly come to his crown to offer and intimate unto us, that in courtesy and by the law of princely common right we should first have offered and done from ourselves."

1. Heneage (d. 1595) was vice-chamberlain, member of parliament, privy councillor, and chancellor of Lancaster (*DNB*).
2. See Tolstoy, pp. 261–69.

I was well housed in London, well provided and attended on, much respected, feasted, and entertained by the company of Muscovy, Sir Rowland Heyward, Sir George Barne, Mr. Customer Smythe,[3] and of many other aldermen and grave merchants. The queen calls for me at Greenwich; I deliver as much as I was to say, and so much as pleased her highness to inquire of me; said, we have lost a fair time and a great deal of treasure that her realm might opportunely have been possessed of. I spent a good time as well in providing the emperor's and lords protector's provision according to commission, as also inquiring of the learned physicians of Oxford, Cambridge, and London their opinions and directions concerning the Empress Irina in some difficult matters [for conception and procuration of children]; had been married seven years and often [conceived],[4] with some other marriage matters wherein I was charged with secrecy, which fell out to be very dangerous unto me.

Sir Jerome Bowes, upon some displeasure of the queen towards him, practices much malice against me; incenses my lord of Leicester, now regent in the Low Countries (from whose excellency I had received great honor, countenance, and particular letters of grace, and done his lordship service; upon his letters of request sent him rich furs, white gerfalcons, white bears and their provision of good value, and paid my friends assigned for the same), that I should report at my table such a day to divers dukes and noblemen how that he had cast his wife down a pair of stairs, brake her neck, and so became the queen's minion; by which he meant to have broken my neck and the negotiation I had in hand, never having heard of any such thing before. The earl of Leicester writes to the queen thereof, prays my questioning and stay. The queen alters her countenance, swears I should answer it, commands the

3. Heyward, the son of George Heyward of Bridgnorth, Shropshire, went to London as a boy and was apprenticed to a clothworker. He was master of the Clothworkers' Company in 1559, an alderman of London from 1560 to 1593, mayor in 1570/71 and in 1591. He was a member of parliament from 1572 to 1581. He died in 1593 (Willan, *Muscovy Merchants,* pp. 102–3). George Barne: Barne was a member of the Haberdashers' Company, an alderman of London from 1542 to 1558, mayor in 1552–53, knighted in 1553. He died in 1558 (Willan, *Muscovy Merchants,* p. 78). Smythe, son of John Smythe of Corsham, Wiltshire, a yeoman, haberdasher, and clothier. He was himself a haberdasher and wealthy landowner in London and was the customs official of the Port of London. He died in 1591 (*DNB sub* Sir Thomas Smythe).

4. In the original manuscript, the words in square brackets are in English but written in the Cyrillic alphabet.

lords of her majesty's council to examine the cause. Sir Jerome Bowes
offers to prove it by one Finch, a by-hanger of his, whom he said I
would have roasted in the Moscow for a spy.[5] Yet the queen answered
openly, "I doubt not but Horsey will prove himself an honest man for
all this." The Lord Hunsdon,[6] then lord chamberlain, only took Sir Jerome Bowes his part; my lord treasurer, Sir Christopher Hatton,[7] and
especially Sir Francis Walsingham, were strong and confident in their
good opinions of me; many good friends and allies I had that stuck
firmly to me. The court and city were possessed of this heinous matter.
We were convented. Sir Jerome Bowes feigned himself sick; the lords
sent express messengers to bring him, for so was her majesty's pleasure.
He present, the parties' accusation was so faint, faltering, and fearful,
ever looking upon Sir Jerome Bowes what he should say to the lords,
that they all seemed displeased. I had four very substantial merchants
ready kneeling before them that were present at all times whiles this
Finch was in the Moscow, being but ten days at any time with me;
avowed and witnessed how favorably I dealt with him, and how
friendly I dispatched him thence in their companies, being in necessity
and danger, at my own charge; showed forth his own letters of thanks
and acknowledgment, never more bounden to any. The lords willed Sir
Jerome Bowes forth of the council chamber; bid Finch declare the
truth; he acknowledges those letters to be of his own writing and confessed Sir Jerome Bowes had lain at him very often and earnest to
maintain this accusation, which he never heard of before, saying he
was in the way to crush Mr. Horsey and his ambassage. The lords committed him to the Marshalsea,[8] with weighty irons to be laid upon
him, my lord treasurer telling him, "Though you were not roasted, sir-
rah, it was pity you had not been a little scorched." The lord chamber-

---

5. John Finch was a servant of Horsey. Finch's father was a long time "secret
trader into Russia." (*Calendar of State Papers, Foreign, 1584–85*, p. 94). Toward
the end of 1585 he wrote to the lords of the Privy Council complaining of some of
Horsey's activities in Russia (*Calendar of State Papers, Foreign, 1585–86*, p. 268).

6. Henry Carey, first Baron Hunsdon (1524?–1596), son of Anne Boleyn's sister
and first cousin to Queen Elizabeth. He was in command of the forces at Tilbury
in 1588 (*DNB*).

7. William Cecil, Lord Burghley (1520–98), was lord high treasurer and chief
minister of Queen Elizabeth. See Conyers Read, *Mr. Secretary Cecil and Queen
Elizabeth* (London, 1956), and *Lord Burghley and Queen Elizabeth* (London, 1960).
Hatton (1540–91), was a member of parliament from 1571–86, and lord chancellor
from 1587–91 (*DNB*).

8. A prison in Southwark, long used as a debtor's prison.

lain hied him from the lords to the queen; Mr. Secretary got another
way before him, told her majesty what had passed. She blamed my
Lord Hunsden, who laid the fault upon Bowes, whom the lords told he
had discredited himself more than his worth could repair. "Let him, my
lords, that made the false information smart for it." The queen forbade
him her presence. I have been tedious, and yet can say no less out of
the malignity of this man's ill spirit towards me, that hath deserved as
much as his life is worth.

When time was, my discontentment was perceived; fair weather was
made; and I, notwithstanding, in the interim, with much help of my
good friends, Sir Francis Walsingham and Sir George Barne, etc., had
made my provision of lions, bulls, dogs, gilt halberds, pistols, pieces,
armor, wines, store of drugs of all sorts, organs, virginals, musicians,
scarlets, pearl chains, plate of curious making, and of other costly
things of great value, according to my commissions. Taking my leave
of the queen received her highness' letters[9] to the emperor and prince
protector and letters patents for my passage, with many good words
and gracious promises, and also remembrances and instructions from
the lords and from the company worth the reading, with some recompense for favors and services already done for them in the emperor's
court.

XVI

I departed well accommodated in company of nine good merchants
ships; arrived at St. Nicholas; posted up to the Moscow 1,200
miles; came to the lord protector, now prince of the province of Vaga,
who received me joyfully and after much discourse brought me to the
emperor a back way, who seemed glad of my return, pochivated[1]
and made me merry, and so dismissed me for that time. The prince
protector sends for me the next day; tells me of many strange accidents
and alterations and matters passed since I went thence, such as I was
sorry to hear of, practices between the empress' mother to Tsarevich

9. Horsey returned to Russia in early 1586 with a letter from Elizabeth to
Fedor and one to his wife Irina (Tolstoy, pp. 270–88).
1. *potchevat'*. To show honor, to entertain.

Dmitrii her kindred and some other the princes joined with him in commission by the old emperor's will, which he, knowing now better his own strength and power, could not accept for competitors. "You shall hear much; believe little more than I tell you." On the other side I heard much and of many the nobility their discontentments, both dissembling wrought upon the advantage of their intemperancies with great causation, providence, and policy, which could produce no good end to neither. Asked, "When comes your presents and my provision?" I thought it near at hand.

I was called for before the emperor and most of his council sitting in state. With some preamble of speech, illustration of his titles, and magnanimity of his imperial monarchy, I delivered over in writing the account of my employment, as other his ambassadors did, and those letters recommended for answer to his highness from the majesty of England, which being received, I was willed to withdraw. I was asked for such presents as was sent unto his majesty. I answered, they were such in nature as did require some longer time for transportation. Commandment was given presently for a gentleman and fifty huntsmen to be sent and attend with all allowances the speedy bringing up the river Dvina of the same. For that time I had commendation for the good service done and performance of the emperor's pleasure and commission given concerning Queen Magnus' safe arrival.

Bogdan Bel'skii, the chief favorite and minion to the old emperor, was now sent to a castle and town remote, Kazan', in displeasure, as a man feared to be a conspirator and sower of sedition between the nobility and this time of discontentment. Petr Golovin, chief treasurer to the old emperor, a man of great birth and courage, became bold and peremptory against Boris Fedorovich; was likewise sent away in displeasure under the conduction of Ivan Voeikov, a favorite to the prince protector;[2] was dispatched of his life upon the way. Kniaz' Ivan Vasil'evich Shuiskii, prime prince of the blood royal, of great esteem, power, and command, chief competitor in commission for the government, his discontentment and greatness was much feared;[3] some color of offense conceived; the emperor's displeasure cast upon him; was

2. See Fletcher, above, p. 141, for Golovin. Voeikov was listed in the service records as holder of the court rank of stol'nik in 1575/76 and as a minor commander in the Livonian War in 1576/77 and 1580/81 (RK, pp. 261, 277, 312). He took part in the reception of Sir Jerome Bowes in 1583 (Sbornik IRIO, XXXVIII, 80).

3. Ivan Petrovich Shuiskii, the hero of the siege of Pskov, was murdered in prison in 1587.

suddenly commanded to depart the Moscow to his own repose; surprised with a colonel's guard, and not far off was smothered in a cottage with wet hay and stubble set on fire, lamented of all men. Here was the chief stumbling block of fear removed away from that house and family of the Godunovs, yet many more suspected were also quarreled with and by degrees had the like measure. I was sorry to see in what hatred the prince protector grew in the hearts and opinion of most men to whom his cruel dissimulation appeared too grossly. He took me out with him one day at the postern gates with small attendance, besides his falconers, to see his gerfalcons to fly at the crane, heron, and wild swan, princely pastime with their hardy hawks, not caring for spoiling and killing them, having such infinite choice ready made at hand. A beggarly friar met him, wished he would hie him home speedily; all were not his friends that were coming to see his pastime. Some five hundred horse, young noblemen and waiters at court, were coming to meet him for honor, as was said, to attend him into the city. He meant none should know of his going nor follow him; followed the friar's advice, and after a slight falcon that stopped at a foul t'other side of the river, he ventured the ford a nearer way, was at the castle gate before that company could come about. I saw him perplexed and glad he was safely come to the palace, where bishops, dukes, and gentlemen and other suitors attended him with their petitions and could not come near him sometimes in two or three days, he passing in the entry more out of sight towards the emperor's lodgings. I prayed him to look back and show himself upon the terrace; he cast a fierce countenance upon me, as though I counseled him not well, yet bethought himself, went towards them, saluted many, and took their petitions with great applaud and cry "God save Boris Fedorovich his health!" Told them he would present their petitions to the emperor. "Thou most noble Boris Fedorovich art king; say thou the word and it is done." Which words I perceived disliked him not, for he aims at the crown.

My presents and all other things were now come safe to the Moscow. The day appointed, I must now repair and come before the emperor again from her majesty, accompanied with Petr Pivov, a pensioner of good esteem.[4] I was as well mounted as he, attended with twenty men with fair liveries and garments after their fashion, best

4. A member of the oprichnina (Kobrin, p. 57). In 1587 he went with Rodion Birkin to Georgia as ambassador (E. N. Kusheva, *Narody severnogo Kavkaza i ikh sviazi s Rossiei* [Moscow, 1963], p. 61).

liked of, each of them carrying one piece or other of my present. Stayed the king's pleasure in a withdrawing chamber until the emperor and empress had viewed out of the palace windows the bulldogs and lions brought by the *biriuch* and his company, which was above five thousand people that followed the sight of them; a goodly fair white bull, all spotted over with black natural dapple, his crop or gorge hanging down to his knees before him, gilt false horns, collar of green velvet studded and red rope; made kneel down before the emperor and empress, stands up and looks gazing and fiercely on every side, appearing to the people to be some other strange beast called *buivol;* twelve goodly large mastiff dogs led with twelve men, decked with roses, collars, etc, in like fashion; two lions brought forth of their cages (drawn upon sleds) by a little Tatar boy with a wand in his hand, standing in awe of no other. These were left before the palace to the lookers on.

The emperor was set in his chair of majesty. Now come we to more serious matter and compliments. I was sent for in, my men with their presents put at one side. "Most noble, most mighty, and most renowned Emperor Fedor Ivanovich, emperor of all Russia, Vladimir, Moscow, Kazan', Astrakhan', Tver', Novgorod Velikii, Perm', Viatka, Siberia, Kondinskaia [Zemlia],[5] Iaroslavl', Nizhnii-Novgorod,[6] emperor, lord, and great duke, etc., of many other provinces, Queen Elizabeth, by the grace and mercy of God, queen of England, France, and Ireland, and queen of many other territories and principalities, defender of the most Christian catholic faith, her most high, most mighty, far and most renowned majesty doth in all loving and sisterly manner salute your imperial majesty, her dear and most beloved brother, and hath sent your imperial majesty her highness letters gratulatory, wishing unto your imperial majesty all perfect health and safety, that you may govern and reign in all happiness, peace, and tranquillity. Her highness commandeth me, her servant and vassal, to say unto your most excellent majesty that your late letters sent unto her majesty are most thankfully received and most acceptable unto her majesty. The contents and intimation of your brotherly amity therein contained, her imperial majesty doth most willingly embrace, and maketh protestation and promise inviolable to hold the like sisterly amity and correspondency with your imperial majesty, as she hath done heretofore with Ivan Vasil'evich, late emperor, your majesty's father, of most famous and most renowned

5. Condonscoie in the original text.
6. Nezna in the original text.

memory, to the mutual comfort and commodity of both your imperial realms, loyal and loving subjects, most high, most mighty, and most renowned emperor." And therewith my low obeisance sat down at one side upon a little form covered with a carpet. The emperor said little, showed good countenance. But the chancellor whispered him in his ear; stood up, put off his cap, said he was glad to hear his loving sister Queen Elizabeth to be in such good health, and therewith dismissed and conducted in manner as I was brought. The particular of the presents delivered in a schedule with the letters. There followed me Ivan Chemodanov,[7] a kinsman of the lord protector's, with a hundred and fifty dishes of all sorts of meats for my dinner from the emperor, drinks, bread, and spice, sent by a hundred-fifty gentlemen through the streets to my lodging. I presented the chief gentleman a garment cloth of scarlet; pochivated, drank, and made merry, and gave each of the rest a reward.

The next day divers gentlemen, officers, priests, and merchants, my friends and acquaintances, came to congratulate with me, as the manner is, of the emperor's favor; drank, ate, and made merry upon the emperor's good cheer as long as it lasted. The protector, Boris Fedorovich, having spent a whole day in perusing the jewels, chains, pearl, plate, gilt armour, halberds, pistols and pieces, white and red scarlet velvets, and other curious and costly things provided for him, which he exceedingly well liked of; and the empress his sister, invited to behold the same, admired especially at the organs and virginals, all gilt and enameled, never seeing nor hearing the like before, wondered and delighted at the loud and musical sound thereof. Thousands of people resorted and stayed about the palace to hear the same. My men that played upon them much made of and admitted into such presence often where myself could not come. So well liked was all things, and my own picture also taken away, that the protector sent me all the cost thereof, which was above £4,000, three Persian jennets with rich sad-

---

7. During the reign of Boris Godunov, Ivan Ivanovich Chemodanov (d. 1630) was an important figure at court. When the tsar led his armies to Serpukhov in 1598 to defend against the Crimean Tatars, Chemodanov was entrusted with the care of Boris' son, Fedor (*RK*, p. 543). In 1610 he was made one of the military governors of the Perm' area and subsequently played an important role in the national movement that restored the Russian government at the end of the Time of Troubles. Mikhail Romanov named him to the court office of *striapchii s kliuchom,* that is, assistant to the gentleman of the bedchamber (*RBS; Dvortsovye razriady,* I [St. Petersburg, 1850], 132).

dles, furnitures, and scimitars, with the master of his horse, Ivan Volkov,[8] to make choice of which I pleased to ride upon, which I did, esteemed worth £200; and by one other of his chief gentlemen, Mikhail Kosov,[9] his highness sent me three thousands pounds of fine silver coin for a remembrance and earnest of his farther favor and love. All which being received, I dismissed the bringers well rewarded. The sight of these rarities, bulldogs, lions, organs, music, and other delights, made me continually to be thought upon with gold wrought handkerchiefs, towels, shirts, canopies, carpets, diets, and such dainties as the lord protector's and his friends' good will and favor did afford, which was in such bountiful measure as many towns, monasteries, offices and officers, natural and stranger merchants procured by my means freedoms and exemptions of many taxations and impositions, privileges and pardons, not without good acknowledgment and recompense. And although the truth hereof be more larger set forth and more memorable in their histories, yet not so much pertinent to our discourse of the state of Russia.

XVII

The emperor, I may say the prince protector, being now possessed of so infinite a treasure, and daily increasing, knew not well how to employ, dispose, or make use of it to illustrate his fame. The king of Persia being greatly oppressed by the mighty armies and yearly inroads of the Turk,[1] who having won from him all Media, Derbent, She-

8. Volkov took part in the negotiations with the Swedes at the Pliussa River in 1586. On October 7, 1593, he met Niklas Warkotsch, the ambassador of the Empire, during negotiations conducted at Boris Godunov's palace (PDS, I, 1276).

9. A courtier attached to Boris Godunov who assisted in receiving Hapsburg ambassadors in 1597 and 1599 (PDS, II, 518, 621).

1. War between Turkey and Persia broke out in 1578 and lasted until 1590. In reaction to Turkish conquests in Transcaucasia, both the shah of Persia, Muhammad Khudibandih, and Alexander, ruler of the Georgian principality of Kakhetia, tried to win Muscovite support for an anti-Turkish alliance. In 1587 a Persian ambassador came to Moscow and proposed a treaty of alliance by which the Muscovite government would provide detachments of cavalry and artillery and would receive in return the districts of Baku and Derbent should these be recaptured from the Turks. Negotiations continued with the embassy of Grigorii Vasil'chikov to Persia in 1588–89 and a second Persian embassy to Moscow in 1589–90. Before the negotiations were completed, however, the new shah, Abbas, made peace with

makha, Bilbill, Ardebil,[2] and other his most richest, best, and fruitful provinces, driving him to the Alps, as it were, or high countries of Persia, Kashan, Tabriz,[3] Persepolis, Kazvin, etc., and also invading and annoying that maiden and unconquered kingdom of the Georgians by reason of their situation, Christians environed in the midst of all those Mohammedan and heathen countries;[4] they[5] both issuing and sending unto the emperor and prince protector their several ambassadors for aid and succor, who, not being so well able to transport an army so remote over the Mare Caspian Sea, was contented to lend and transfer unto the king of Persia, upon good hostages, two hundred thousand rubles marks sterling for five years *gratis,* and to the king of the Georgians one hundred thousand marks sterling more upon the pawn and resignation of the title of his kingdom, by an authentical instrumental manner agreed upon, paid, and perfected by commissioners on both sides. But hereupon grew a quarrel between the Turk and the emperor.

Boris Fedorovich,[6] having aim to a more absolute and greater title, sent ambassadors to have some more nearer alliance and correspondency with the king of Denmark, Frederick, Kniaz' Fedor Khvorostinin,[7] but it was so young an age yet between Herzog Hans,[8]

---

the Turks and gave up plans for an alliance with Muscovy.

Prince Alexander, who had previously recognized Persian suzerainty over his domains, transferred his allegiance to Moscow in 1587 in hopes of gaining protection against the Turks. At about the same time, the Muscovite government rebuilt its military outpost in the delta of the Terek River (Kusheva, *Narody severnogo Kavkaza,* pp. 268–69, 273–75). The Muscovite government soon discovered that it could not muster strong enough forces to extend its control over the northern Caucasus: the Shamkhal of Tarki defeated Russian expeditions against him in 1594 and 1604–5. After these setbacks, the Muscovite commanders pulled back to their base on the Terek and the government abandoned its commitment to support Kakhetia.

2. Ardoll in the original text.

3. Tauris in the original text.

4. At the conclusion of the first phase of the Turkish-Persian war in 1590, the Turks gained the districts of Shirvan, Tabriz, Luristan, and Georgia (Sir Percy Sykes, *A History of Persia,* 3rd ed., II [London, 1930], 173–74).

5. *they.* the in the original text.

6. The chronology of the following passages is very confused. Consequently it is not always possible to decide to which negotiations Horsey alludes. His version of the issues discussed is vague enough to refer to any one of several embassies during the reign of Fedor.

7. See Fletcher, above, p. 154.

8. Son of Frederick II of Denmark. He was betrothed to Godunov's daughter Kseniia in 1601 and travelled to Moscow in the following year, but died there before the wedding.

his third son, and Maria, his daughter,[9] as little could be resolved upon. Also, to show and make known his greatness there was an ambassador sent, one Alphonasse Masolove,[10] an approved wise secretary of estate, well set forth with men and presents, to Maximilian, the German emperor; passed Dvina; took shipping at St. Nicholas in an English ship to Hamburg and Lübeck, where he was well entertained and feasted; came to the emperor at Prague; delivered his letters and presents, white gerfalcons, two fair Persian carpets, two pieces of whole cloth of gold, four timber of rich black sables, four black foxes, a curious wrought scepter of gold, a rich Persian armor of bullat. With these were desired affinity with the imperial crown prince and house of Austria, a firm and everlasting league and amity, ready to take arms with them against the Turk, mortal enemy to Christ and Christendom, that had now invaded Hungary and other parts of the empire, and thereupon offered to furnish him with fifty thousand horse, gallant and expert soldiers at three months warning, he only procuring of Stephen Bathory king of Poland, free passage and safe conduct for his said army through his countries. This ambassador was much made of, his message well liked, sightly entertained, and with a great acceptance dismissed. But the emperor, not obtaining leave of the king of Poland, who would not trust his enemy the Muscovite to come into his king-

9. Horsey refers to Kseniia Godunova.

10. Probably Afanasii Ivanovich Vlas'ev, a state secretary and member of the duma, who was a leading Russian diplomat in the last years of the sixteenth century. In 1595 and 1599 he conducted negotiations at the court of the Holy Roman Emperor. Later, he was a representative at negotiations with Poland (1600) and Denmark (1602). Because of his close connection with the False Dmitrii, he was sent from court to be military governor of Ufa when Vasilii Shuiskii came to the throne.

The passage seems to refer to the mission of Vlas'ev to the Hapsburg court in Prague in 1599. Like "Masolove" in Horsey's account, Vlas'ev traveled to central Europe via the northern sea route and the ports of northern Germany, a rather unusual procedure. Moreover, although the official record of his mission does not indicate that he sailed in an English ship, the ambassador was clearly under the protection of English agents during his departure and on his arrival in Germany. Once he reached Prague, the core of his message was Boris Godunov's offer to send the emperor 10,000 strel'tsy for use against the Turks (PDS, II, 656–68, 692–95). There are, to be sure, several inconsistencies in Horsey's story. The emperor at the time was Rudolf II (1576–1612); Horsey apparently confused him with the Archduke Maximilian, his younger brother. The king of Poland was Sigismund Vasa, not Bathory who died in 1586. Likewise Christian IV reigned in Denmark following the death of Frederick II in 1588.

dom with such an army, sent his ambassador with like presents of goodly horse, German clocks, etc., to make trial and some use of this his so proffered friendship; would borrow of him three hundred thousand rubles, which is nine hundred thousand dollars. But the emperor and Boris demanding such hostages, and Frederick the king of Denmark his assurance, that nothing came of this great offer but deridings,[11] ill will both of the Turk and Krym Tatar, whom the Turk set on the Muscovites' back with such an huge army as cost the emperor of the Muscovites infinite charge and loss of men.[12] And the Poles and Swedes combined and plotted how each of them might invade each other's territories and ancient bounds; took good opportunity to recover all back again which the old emperor Ivan had gotten from them before, especially in this time of division.[13] And the Russe, being otherways employed with an army to conquer Siberia, enlarged his domi-

11. Perhaps a reference to Michael Schiele's mission to Moscow in 1601. Although the fragmentary official records of his visit in the Muscovite capital do not mention that he conveyed the emperor's request for a subsidy to aid his war effort against the Turks, Hapsburg emissaries made such requests on several occasions at the end of the sixteenth century. When the emperor began to make plans to send an envoy to Moscow to reply to Vlas'ev's proposals, for example, he chose as his ambassador Abraham zu Dohna and instructed him to obtain a subsidy from the tsar. When Dohna tried to carry out his order, however, the Polish government turned him back at the border. Then Schiele was sent by another route to maintain the emperor's ties with the Russian court (*PDS*, II, 753–87; H. Uebersberger, *Österreich und Russland seit dem Ende des 15. Jahrhunderts* [Vienna and Leipzig, 1906], I, 573–75).

12. The last great Tatar raids of the century took place in 1591 and 1592. See A. A. Novosel'skii, *Bor'ba moskovskogo gosudarstva s tatarami v pervoi polovine XVII veka* (Moscow-Leningrad, 1948), p. 41.

13. Perhaps this passage refers to the conflict between Poland and Sweden arising from the claims of Sigismund Vasa to both thrones. Sigismund was chosen king of Poland in 1587 and then in 1592 succeeded his father Johan III to the Swedish crown. After his second coronation, he returned to Poland and left his uncle to rule Sweden in his absence. Sigismund's devotion to Roman Catholicism antagonized his Protestant Swedish subjects who looked to the regent rather than the king as their ruler. In 1598 Sigismund returned to Sweden in an attempt to restore his authority but met increased hostility that finally led in 1600 to the outbreak of a war between the two countries that ushered in six decades of almost continuous conflict. In 1604 the regent of Sweden was crowned king as Karl IX, and thereafter the Catholic branch of the House of Vasa was excluded from the succession to the Swedish throne.

War broke out between Muscovy and Sweden in 1590. In the peace settlement of 1595, the Muscovite government regained some of the territory lost during the Livonian War, including Ivangorod and Korela.

nions much and brought away the emperor of Siberia, Chiglicke Alothe,[14] with his mother and his best nobles and *mirza*, as they term them, to the Moscow, where I saw him do many strange feats at arms, on horseback and on foot, after their fashion, and heard him tell he had some Englishmen in his country, at least way such men of countenance as I was, taken with a ship, ordnance, powder, and other riches but two year before, that would have passed the river Ob to seek Cathay by the northeast.[15] Some Swedish soldiers escaped thence and came to the Moscow to serve the emperor, among whom was one Gabriel Elphingstone, a valiant Scottish captain by the report of the letters he brought to me from Colonel Steward, that served the king of Denmark, in commendation of him and six other Scots, soldiers in his company, but all very bare of money and furniture. Desired me to grace place and supply their necessities. I disbursed to him and them three hundred dollars, put them in apparel, and bought them pistols and swords, and when they were marched were better liked of than the[16] Swedish soldiers that came in their company. I got Captain Elphingstone the charge over them all, begone of money, horse, and allowance for meat and drink. Behaved themselves well for a time, yet could not repay nor recompense me to this day, as by their letters appeareth. At this time there was some secret practice by the discontented nobility to supplant the protector and all his designs and greatness, which he durst not take open notice of; strengthened himself with good guard. A practice was discovered to poison and make away the young prince, the old emperor's third son, Dmitrii, his mother, and all his alliances, friends, and families narrowly guarded in a remote place at Uglich.[17] Also Nikita Romanovich, this emperor's uncle, the third nobleman trusted in the old emperor's will with Boris Fedorovich, who could endure no competitor now to govern, two of the other prime princes being made away, as before you have heard. This Nikita Romanovich, a stout, valiant prince, honored and beloved of all men, was now bewitched, his speech and sense taken suddenly from him, yet lived awhile. But the protector told me it should not be long.[18] His eldest son, a gallant

---

14. Probably Muhammad Kul (see Fletcher, above, p. 190).

15. This passage probably refers to one of the ships of the Jackman expedition of 1580–81 that was lost near the mouth of the Ob River.

16. *the.* they in the original text.

17. Fletcher relates a similar incident (above, p. 128). Both stories are examples of the rumors which circulated at the time about threats against the life of Dmitrii.

18. Nikita Romanovich Romanov-Iur'ev died in 1586.

young prince, first cousin to the emperor, Fedor Nikitich, of great hope and expectancy (for whom I made a Latin grammar as well as I could in the Slavonian character, in which he took great delight), was now enforced to marry his sister's Kniaz' Boris Cherkasskii's wife her waiting woman, by whom he had a son, of whom you shall hear more hereafter; and not long after, his favor and greatness in the popular opinion being feared, was, not long after his father's death, shorn a friar and made a young archbishop of Rostov.[19] His next brother, being of no less a generous spirit, named Aleksandr Nikitich, out of his great discontentment could not contain nor dissemble longer; took opportunity to stab the prince protector, not so dangerous as meant; escaped into Poland, where he and Bogdan Bel'skii, the old emperor's great minion and favorite, wonderful rich, and others there and at home, practiced not only the utter ruin of Boris Fedorovich and all his family, but also the ruin and subversion of the whole kingdom, as you may hear and read hereafter.[20] In the mean, it is time to return unto our own business and negotiation committed to my charge.

19. In his youth, Fedor Nikitich, son of Nikita Romanovich, was one of the outstanding figures of the court of Tsar Fedor. He was already a boiar in 1586 and in the same year was named governor of Nizhnii-Novgorod. On several occasions during the 1590's he held important military commands. In Boris Godunov's purge of the Romanov family in 1601, Fedor Nikitich was forced to enter the Antoniev-Siiskii Monastery and was given the religious name of Filaret. After the collapse of Godunov's regime, the first False Dmitrii raised him to the dignity of metropolitan of Rostov. Filaret was one of the members of the delegation that went to Smolensk in 1610 to discuss with King Sigismund the conditions under which his son, Wladyslaw, would become tsar. When the negotiations broke down, Sigismund imprisoned Filaret and sent him to Poland where he remained until 1619. In the meantime his son Mikhail was chosen tsar in 1613. When Filaret returned to Moscow after his imprisonment, he was elevated to the patriarchal throne that had been kept vacant until his return. From that time until his death in 1633 he was honored as co-ruler with his son and, in practice, ruled the Muscovite state. His wife was the former Kseniia Ivanovna Shestova, the daughter of a poor service noble.

Boris Kanbulatovich Cherkasskii was a Kabardinian prince who entered Muscovite service about 1580. From the beginning he held very important military posts; he served as commander-in-chief of the defense forces on the southern border in 1585/86 and in the winter of 1591/92 and commanded the forces in the Novgorod area in 1582/83 and 1588/89. He was married to Marfa, sister of Fedor Nikitich Romanov-Iur'ev, and consequently fell into disgrace with the rest of the Romanovs during the reign of Boris. He was arrested in 1599 and died in exile in 1601 (RBS; RK, pp. 332, 352, 368–69, 407, 462).

20. On Aleksandr Nikitich Romanov-Iur'ev, see Fletcher, above, p. 240, n. 5. No other source states that Bogdan Bel'skii fled to Poland.

And yet not idle, I procured unto the company of merchants the freedom of all their houses in Moscow, Iaroslavl', Vologda, Kholmogory, and St. Nicholas, seized upon for great impositions laid on them in displeasure upon Sir Jerome Bowes his ill behavior; the release of a thousand rubles laid upon the company towards the building of the great new wall about the Moscow, which all other strangers and merchants did pay.[21] I obtained the free release of a suit between the merchants of Moscow and the company for the debts of thirty thousand rubles, owing by a factor of theirs, one Anthony Marsh, backed by some great counselors and officers.[22] There was recovered an old debt owing by the emperor for copper, lead, and other commodities, two thousand rubles, as desperate. The release of John Chappell and the goods he had of the company's in his charge, £3,000, taken in displeasure from him as a merchant of Lübeck to color the same. Borrowed of the emperor four thousand rubles for the use of the merchants sending to Pskov to provide flax before they had made sale of their merchandises. Borrowed of the prince protector likewise for their use, and for nothing, five thousand rubles, who offered ten thousand pounds more *gratis* out of his treasury, when it should be required. All interloping merchants trading in those countries without leave of the company, being twenty-nine, were delivered into my hands to transport into England. This year's custom due unto the emperor, being two thousand rubles for all their merchandises, was freely forgiven them. I obtained a free privilege from the emperor for the company to trade and traffic through his countries by the river Volga and the Mare Caspian Sea into Persia, free of all customs and tolls. I obtained and procured under the imperial seal a free privilege granted unto the company of English merchants from the emperor to trade and traffic through all his dominions free from paying any manner of customs and tolls whatsoever

21. In this and the following passages Horsey takes credit for concessions that were in fact made to Fletcher in 1589. In 1587 Horsey received a grant of privileges in which the members of the Russia Company were exempted from all customs duties (Hakluyt II, 348; Bond, p. 282). Before long the Muscovite government refused to recognize this stipulation. It was Fletcher, however, who in 1589 negotiated the compromise on the issue of Marsh's debts. Fletcher also won an agreement that the Company should be compensated for goods impounded by the tsar's officials and secured renewed recognition of the Company's right to trade with Persia. The Muscovite government undertook to trade only with the company and not with independent English traders (Berry, pp. 373–75).

22. Marsh was an agent of the Russia Company in Moscow. He embezzled company funds and borrowed from the Russians themselves to carry on private trade. See Willan, *Early History*, pp. 196–97.

upon their merchandises, either transported or imported, in as ample and large a manner as I could devise and set down myself. Never the like obtained by any ambassador heretofore, though thousands expended to procure the like; ratified, confirmed, and delivered by the prince protector in magnificent manner before all the lords and officers present, and proclaimed accordingly throughout the kingdoms. The protector sends treasure to Solovetskii monastery, standing upon the seaside near the confines both of the Danes and Swedes on the north coast. His intent is to have it there ready to be transported into England, holding it the surest refuge and safest receptacle in case of necessity he should be inforced there unto; it is all his own treasure, nothing appertaining to the crown, and of infinite value, if it be England's happiness to have the custody thereof. But he is yet wavering, as desirous to enter into league and alliance with Denmark to back him with their friendship and power. He and his cannot keep nor contrive this purpose so secret but that some hath betrayed it, and the ancient nobility grow suspicious of me; and they and the bishops are so jealous of his inward favor that they show not that familiar and favorable countenance they were wont to do towards me. Therefore I speed my business with as much celerity as I can, and having dispatched and compassed as much and more than is required of me or expected at my hands by the commissions and instructions given me, as well from the council as the company of merchants trading into those countries, at time appointed I receive the emperor's letters,[23] honorable dispatch, and leave.

XVIII

A gentleman, one Afanasii Saburov,[1] with seventy carts or *telegi*, was appointed me to conduct and convey such carriages I had from the Moscow with forty post-horse, besides my own geldings, for me and my company, to Vologda, five hundred miles by land. Rich

---

23. See *Sbornik IRIO*, XXXVIII, 179–84.

1. The only Afanasii Saburov who appears in the service lists of the sixteenth century is an Afanasii Iur'evich who was a commander in Vasil'gorod in 1551/52 (*RK*, p. 133). It is most unlikely that he was still active in service in the period to which Horsey refers. We cannot be sure which of the multitude of other Saburovs Horsey had in mind.

presents from the emperor, especially from Boris Fedorovich, to the queen were delivered me, with his large commissions for providing many costly things and doing some secret messages. He sent me a very curious rare robe or garment of cloth of silver, wrought and made in Persia without seam, valued at much more than I esteemed it; a fair pavilion or tent embroidered; wrought handkerchiefs, shirts, and towels; with beaten gold and silver brought unto me by Semen Chemodanov his near kinsman,[2] from and in the name of Mariia[3] Fedorovna; a timber of excellent good sables; store of very choice hawks of all sorts, and men to convey and carry them to the seaside. At my taking leave I entreated two favors for my farewell, which were granted, the freedom and release of all the Livonians,[4] men, women, widows, and children, with their families, sent in displeasure to Nizhnii-Novgorod, five hundred miles[5] in a desert place remote from the city of Moscow, whose case and misery was very lamentable, as by many of their letters and petitions doth appear. A roll and catalogue of all their names were taken. Mikhail Konsov was presently sent by commission and the emperor's letters to the voevoda for their delivery.[6] Their hearts rejoicing for this their redemption, letters, tears, and prayers of thanksgiving were sent after me, yet extant and worth the reading. The other was the release and freedom of a nobleman's son of Gelderland, Herr Zacharius Glisenberght, chief lieutenant of all the emperor's horse, stranger soldiers, who died there, and this his son and heir of ten years of age could not be redeemed by mediation and letters both from the states and king of Denmark. He was delivered into my hands and sent to his mother, Margareta de Feoglers, by a servant of mine, Hans Frees. Giles Hooftman and Antony van Zelman, that were engaged, sent me a thousand rix-dollars and well rewarded my man.[7]

2. Semen Ivanovich Chemodanov (d. 1630) attended the zemskii sobor that elected Boris Godunov tsar in 1598 and remained loyal to the Godunov regime until Boris's son Fedor was overthrown in 1605. He served as a military governor in the Viatka area between 1625 and 1627 (RBS).

3. Should read Irina.

4. Liefflanders in the original text.

5. Actually about 250 miles.

6. No one of the name "Konsov" appears in the court lists of the sixteenth and seventeenth centuries. This is perhaps a reference to the "Kosov" mentioned earlier, p. 326.

7. Charles Sisson gives a similar version of the story from a case in the Court of Chancery in 1597. He gives the name of the boy as Goddard von Glyssenberg ("Englishmen in Shakespeare's Muscovy or the Victims of Jerome Horsey," *Mélanges en l'honneur de Jules Legras* [Paris, 1939], p. 245).

I departed the city of Moscow very honorably attended, went easy journeys and pitched my tents, dinner and supper, provision of all things prepared upon the way. At Vologda, Kniaz' Mikhail Dolgorukii, the voevoda, came to me well attended to welcome me with the emperor's goodness. Prepared two great barks or doshchaniki with pilots and fifty men to row me down the river Dvina a thousand miles. My gentleman attendant, with one of my servants to see he did not bribe nor misuse the country, still passing before me in a light boat to make provision of meat, drink, and men at every town I came at, till I arrived at the monastery and castle Archangel, where the duke Kniaz' Mikhail Zvenigo-rodskii met me at the castle gate with three hundred gunners;[8] shot off their calivers and all the ordnance he had in the castle for honor of my welcome; all the Dutch and French ships in that road shot off also their ordnance by the duke's appointment before I came. He feasted me the next day, brought me to my barge, had appointed fifty men to row and one hundred gunners in small boats to guard me to Rose Island; did me all the honor he could in his golden coat, told me he was commanded by the king's letters so to do, took leave and prayed me to signify his service to Boris Fedorovich, came with me few hours to Rose Island, being but thirty miles, where all the English masters, agent, and merchants met me. The gunners landed before me, stood in ranks, and shot off all their calivers, which the ships hearing, shot off also some of their ordnance. The gunners and bargemen made drink at the cellar door and dispatched that night back again to the castle. The next day friars of St. Nicholas brought me a present, fresh salmons, rye loaves, cups, and painted platters. The third day after my arrival there was sent a gentleman, Sablock Savora,[9] a captain, from the duke; delivered me a copy of his commission of the emperor's and Boris Fedorovich their grace and goodness towards me; presented for my provision seventy live sheep, twenty live oxen and bullocks, six hundred hens, forty flesh of bacon, two milk kine, two goats, ten fresh salmons, forty gallons of aqua-vitæ, one hundred gallons of mead, two hundred gal-

8. Horsey probably refers to Vasilii Andreevich Zvenigorodskii, who held a variety of military commands between 1579 and 1584. He was one of the commanders in the defense of the southern frontier against the Crimean attack in 1591. Then in 1595 he was made responsible for strengthening the fortifications of Smolensk and remained there as commander-in-chief until at least 1598. He served as military governor of the Dvina area from 1585 to 1587 and later was governor of Nizhnii-Novgorod (1612–13) and Kolomna (1615–16) (*RBS; RK,* pp. 459–61, 536; *PDS,* II, 630 ff.).

9. Probably Saburov.

lons of beer, a thousand loaves of white bread, three score bushels of meal, two thousand eggs, garlic and onions store. There was four great lighters and many watermen and other that came with this provision, which were all orderly dismissed; and I contented a little to repose myself and peruse the queen's most gracious letter wherewith she did me that honor, the lords of her majesty's most honorable Privy Council their general and particulars letters, the company's general letters, and other my good friends their remembrances, which remain extant to this day to my comfort and for my posterity to read after me. I took some time to make merry with the masters and merchants, having some pastimes that followed me, players, dancing bears, and pipes and drums and trumpets; feasted them and divided my provision in liberal proportion. In the mean, I sent a discreet servant, Sameiten, post up to the court to Boris Fedorovich with my letters of humble[10] thanks for all these favors, and to other lords and high officers, from whom I received most gracious letters and new presents again by Mr. Francis Cherry,[11] a whole piece of cloth of gold for to wear in a garment, for Boris Fedorovich his sake, with a fair timber of sables to line it withal. These letters are worth the showing and reading, both for manner and phrase, to whom it shall please to have a sight thereof.

After all this, being well fitted and ready, I and my company were shipped in a tall ship named the "Centurion" the next day after St. Bartholomew, and I, with them, arrived in safety that day five weeks at Tynemouth in Northumberland; posted up with four men to York and so to London in four days; came to the court at Richmond.

10. *humble*. Humbly in the original text.
11. Cherry (1553–1605) was born at North Kilworth, Leicestershire. He became a member of the Vintners' Company, but he spent most of his life in Russia where for a time he traded independently of the Russia Company. He became, nevertheless, one of the most powerful members of the Company in the late 1580's and was allowed by the Company to undertake a large private venture in Russia in the 1590's (Willan, *Early History,* pp. 260–69).

XIX

By my lord treasurer's and Mr. Secretary's means, which was then Sir Francis Walsingham, I was brought to the queen; had audience, delivered the emperor's letters[1] and his free privileges granted unto her majesty's subjects as a token and present of his brotherly love unto her highness, with golden spread eagle seals at them. After an account of my employments given (which it pleased her majesty very exactly to inquire with good words and gracious countenance), her highness commended my good usage and entertainment to Mr. Secretary Walsingham, and so dismissed me for that time. Some week after, the letters and privileges being translated and read to the queen, she said, "Indeed, my lords, this is a princely present from the emperor of Muscovy, and such as the merchants do not deserve," against whom she was much incensed by the complaints of Sir Jerome Bowes, by reason of the suits[2] and differences between them, "but I hope they will give better usage and recompense to this my servant, Jerome Horsey, and I pray you see it be so," speaking to my lord treasurer and Mr. Secretary. Made me kneel by her; perused the limning and characters of the privilege, having some affinity with the Greek; asked if such and such letters and asseverations had not this signification; said she, "I could quickly learn it." Prayed my lord of Essex[3] to learn the famous and most copious language in the world, after which commendation his honor did much affect and delight it, if he might attain thereunto without painstaking and spending more time than he had to spare.

The ships were well arrived at London; had my presents and necessaries all ready. I made means for a new audience; at Greenwich I was called for. I had twelve servants and attendants well attired carrying my presents, which her majesty would have brought up a back way against my will, conducted by Mr. Henry Sackfield;[4] came into a withdrawing chamber where her majesty sat, accompanied with the earl of Essex,

1. See Tolstoy, pp. 346–53, for the letter.
2. *suits.* shuts in the original text.
3. Robert Devereux, the second earl of Essex, 1566–1601 (*DNB*).
4. Henry Sackfield (also spelled Seckford and Sackford) was groom of the privy chamber and keeper of the privy purse.

the lord treasurer, Sir Christopher Hatton, Sir Francis Walsingham, Sir Thomas Heneage, Sir Walter Raleigh, and other, the Lady Marquess, the Lady Warwick, and other ladies.[5] I delivered my letters from the prince Boris Fedorovich,[6] with his style, love, and most humble salutations of service, and to make known unto her highness that, above all the princes and potentates of the world, he most desired to adore and serve her most imperial and sacred majesty. "If this prince be so illustrious in words, what will his letters declare? Pray open them; let them be read, Mr. Secretary." Who said, "It requires some time, and please your majesty, to translate; I will trust him with them that brought them." Then her majesty asked for the presents. They were attending in the gallery. Commanded some to forbear and withdraw, fearing belike some would be begging. I delivered to her highness, she touching every parcel with her hand, first four pieces of Persian cloth of gold and two whole pieces of cloth of silver of curious works; a large rich cloth of state of white arras, the representation of the sun shining in his full splendancy, gold and silver beams interwrought with most orient colors, silks, silver and gold, the thread slicked flat, to illustrate the beauty thereof; a fair large Turkey carpet; four black very rich timbers of sables; six white well grown spotted lucerns; two shuby or gowns of white ermines. The queen did even sweat by taking pains to handle the canopy cloth of gold, especially the rich sables and furs; commanded Mrs. Skidmore and Mrs. Ratcliff,[7] both of her majesty's bedchamber, and Mr. John Stanhope,[8] to help them to lay these things into her majesty's closet. Two white gerfalcons, a last of jerkins, and a last of slight falcons and two goshawks she looked upon out of the windows, commanded my lord of Cumberland and Sir Henry Lee to take charge and give good account of them.[9] Her majesty held up her hand

5. Lady Warwick was Anne (d. February 9, 1604), daughter of Francis Russell, earl of Bedford. She married Ambrose Dudley, earl of Warwick, on November 11, 1565.

6. See Tolstoy, pp. 354–64, for the letter.

7. A Mrs. Mary Ratcliffe is mentioned in a list of the queen's jewels in 1587 as being of the queen's bedchamber. See Thomas Wright, *Queen Elizabeth and Her Times* (London, 1838), I, 80a.

8. Possibly John Stanhope, first baron of Harrington (1545?–1621), a member of parliament in 1572, 1586, and 1588. He was appointed Master of the Posts in 1590 and Treasurer of the Chamber and knighted in 1596 (*DNB*).

9. George Clifford, third earl of Cumberland (1558–1605), was a naval commander and a favorite at court (*DNB*); Henry Lee (1533–1611), a great sheep

and said this was a rare and a royal present indeed, gave me thanks, and dismissed me.

I prayed Mr. Vice-Chamberlain to be a means that the artisans of London might be called for to make estimate of the furs, the mercers of the cloth of gold, my lord of Cumberland and Sir Henry Lee to value the worth of the hawks. The letters were translated and the privileges. Sir Rowland Heyward, Sir George Barne, Sir John Hart,[10] and Mr. Customer Smythe, and some other grave aldermen and merchants were to receive their privileges with a sharp and yet a gracious admonition, by whom I was much made of and friendly entertained. Among whom I perceived faction and such underhand dealings that private respects and commodities was more preferred and sought for than the general good, so that their disagreeing and ill handling of their trade both at home and abroad did not produce, much less preserve, the freedom and benefit of so great and gracious a privilege.[11]

I was weary with the holy water of the courts, as my honored good friend Sir Francis Walsingham termed good words and applauding commendations; was willing to retire myself to a more safer, private, and quieter life than I had spent this seventeen years past; still in dangerous passages, fearful actions, and turbulent, troublesome state of living, expending what I got and much more than a frugal wise man remembering future times would have done, desirous now to settle and gather my poor estate together and my stock and adventures and profits thereof out of the company's hands. It pleased her majesty and her council to command my service yet farther in a more difficult and dangerous employment than ever I have been exposed heretofore, in regard only of the languages and experience those seventeen years had taught me, which my lord treasurer and Mr. Secretary Walsingham desired to have set down, to hear and perceive the pronunciation and difference each had with the other; some exactly and familiarly attained unto, other some by conversing with the ambassadors, noblemen, and merchants, but in part, as Persian, Grecian, Polish, and the German, viz.,

---

farmer and builder, was Master of the Ordnance, and personal champion to Queen Elizabeth, 1559–90 (*DNB*).

10. Governor of the Russia Company in 1583, 1591–92, 1596–98, and 1600.

11. The Russia Company, in answer, claimed that the privileges of 1587 for which Horsey took so much credit were of no significance, since they were quickly withdrawn because of the fast dealing of several Englishmen in Russia, notably Horsey and his associate Marsh (Bond, p. 333).

Sclava.—Iasik slavonskomu khospod is v[?]za khrista sina bozhia.
Polish.—Bozia da vashinins Coopovia malascova mōia pāna.
German.—Der hemmell ys hoth und de erde doep averst der h°.
Persian.—Sollum alica. Barracalla. Shonam cardash. alica so' [sollum?].
Livonian.—Cusha casha keil sop sull yu umaluma dobrofta.[12]

A smack there is in other things, but small purpose.

At a time it pleased the queen to fall into some serious talk of Boris Fedorovich the prince protector, of his greatness and government, and of the empress and his lady wife; questioned many things and wished she had some of their stateliest attire, which cost my purse more than I made benefit of, and what drift of encouragement by way of some good policy might be used for that prince to continue his purpose, sithence he was so well persuaded and affect to trust her realms with the safety of his treasure, etc. To the which I answered and wished all secrecy might be used, for that some other privacies committed to my charge had been so whispered out, not of myself, as not long after it came to the prince and empress' ears, whereat grew no small jealousy and displeasure; as divers messengers were prepared, as Beckman at one time, Crow and Garland at another,[13] to come and learn not only how the same was taken, who and what the report was, which made diversely, so as great displeasure came thereof and brought exceeding great disaster both to myself and other greater personages, not fit almost to be spoken of, much less published. God forgive Sir Jerome Bowes for one. "Well!" says the queen, "we will have the truth better examined and known." "No, for the passion of God! If your majesty expect any good success by my farther employment, let it not be farther spoken of nor stirred in."[14] Now Frederick, king of Denmark, had made

12. Horsey's performance raises grave doubts about his gifts as a linguist. None of the samples makes sense.

13. Beckman was probably Reynold Beckman, Tsar Fedor's interpreter. He was sent to England in 1584 and returned to Russia in 1585. He made a second trip to England in 1588, escorting Anthony Marsh who had been expelled from Russia (*Sbornik IRIO*, XXXVIII, 198). The consultations mentioned in this passage could have taken place during his second visit.

Giles Crow was Pisemskii's English interpreter; but we cannot identify Garland, unless he is the Edward Garland mentioned in the *Calendar of State Papers, Domestic*, 1581–90, pp. 354–55, who instructed Thomas Sinkirson to go to Dr. John Dee and inform him that the "emperor of Russia was desirous he should take up his abode in that court." However, exactly what was the relationship of Horsey to Beckman, Crow, and Garland, is unknown.

14. Horsey's account of his mission of 1590–91 is a complicated mixture of fact

a great embargement and stay of the English merchants' ships and goods within his sound at Copenhagen, for false entering in his custom house of their clothes and merchandises, whereby all was confiscated to his mercy. They sued unto the queen for letters of redress, and so did the Eastern merchants also to the king of Poland for remedy of divers doléances and wrongs sustained by them from his subjects. Mr. Secretary wishing my advancement and good, I, being appointed to take Cologne in my way, where the Diet was to be now kept, and to accompany Sir Horatio Palavicino and Monsieur de Fresne,[15] the French king's ambassador, into Germany, thought these business might be performed all in one way to the emperor of Muscovy. I prepared accordingly and was ready in good fashion; forty shillings a day allowed me; received my letters and patents commendatory for passing so many kingdoms and countries, with my commissions and instructions of all sorts. The queen gave me a little glass of wholesome balsam, part of that Sir Francis Drake had given to be very precious and sovereign against poison and hurts. Her highness gave me also for divers Muscovy handkerchiefs, cushion cloths, towels, etc., wrought curiously in gold, silver, and Persian silks, all of good worth, her majesty's picture cut in a fair blue sapphire, which she wished me to wear in remembrance of her grace. Kissing her hands I took my leave.

XX

One of her majesty's ships was appointed for Sir Horatio Palavicino and the French ambassador and another, named the "Charles," for me and my company. Came to King's[1] Lynn; the council

and fiction. In general, he gives an accurate description of the international situation but exaggerates or even invents outright his own role in it.

15. Palavicino (d. 1600) was an extraordinary merchant and political agent. Born in Genoa, knighted by Elizabeth in 1587, he amassed an enormous fortune and lent money to Elizabeth, Henry of Navarre, and the Low Countries. See Lawrence Stone, An Elizabethan: Sir Horatio Palavicino (Oxford, 1956). Philippe de Canaye, sieur de Fresne (1551–1610), was a French diplomat and Protestant. He travelled to Germany, Italy, and Constantinople in 1577. He was sent to England in 1586 as ambassador of Henry IV (La Grande Encyclopédie).

1. King's. omitted in the original text.

was advertised from thence that was a dangerous haven for the queen's ships to come into. Then were we appointed to take shipping at Yarmouth; took Cambridge at the desire of the French ambassador on our way, much against Sir Horatio his will, where he and we were very academically entertained; passed to Norwich and to Yarmouth, where being sometime wind-bound, the townsmen and gentlemen near thereabouts used our company with good humanity. Some dislike there was between these two ambassadors; I sought a reconciliation; the one over-haughty, the other takes advantage by policy; I fear me will be some obstacle to the effecting of the affairs they go both about. Time serves for our embarking, they to their charge and I to mine; were both endangered of casting away by storm upon the Emden coast to Stade, where at last we did arrive. The queen's ships known by their ordnance and ensigns, we were well received, both of the townsmen and English merchants, each of us well placed and accommodated with wines, fresh victuals, and orations for our welcome. Sir Horatio and the French ambassador hardly escaping the malcontents, a troop of them laying wait for them near a nunnery by Buxtehude,[2] and valued their ransoms. They towards the duke of Saxony and other the imperial princes, the queen's best allies, and I towards Cologne. When I came to Hamburg I caused my man, John Frees, to prefix early in the morning upon the townhouse door an edict, both in Latin and Dutch, a prohibition from the queen's majesty of England to that and all other Hanse and maritime towns to transport through the narrow seas into Spain any victuals, corn, munition, powder, cables, or any other tackle and provision for shipping, upon pain of confiscation, and then I hied me away towards Lübeck, ten miles off, where I delivered the like to the burgomaster, who huffed thereat, saying they would pass with their shipping in spite of the queen of England's power.[3] From thence to Lippstadt[4] and so to Cologne, where the Diet was appointed to be held, where, by reason of the inequality of the imperial princes meet-

2. *Bucktohow* in the original text.
3. Elizabeth was eager to cut off trade between the northern German cities and Spain. When she sent Sir Horatio Palavicino to Germany in 1590, she requested him to try to convince the Free Towns that trade with Spain was against their own best interests as Protestants (*Calendar of State Papers, Foreign*, 1589–90, pp. 409–10). There is no evidence that Horsey delivered any warning from Elizabeth although he did visit Hamburg and Lübeck and sent back reports on the Spanish trade (*Calendar of State Papers, Foreign*, 1589–90, p. 411).
4. Liepswiche in the original text.

ing, it held not. The bishop of Trier sick, the bishop of Metz, the palsgrave, Saxony, and dukes of Brandenburg failing, and other princes wanting, I sent an express messenger, Mr. Parvis, according to my commission, to advertise the queen and council the Diet was adjourned for three years to Regensburg; whereupon Sir Edward Dyer, her majesty's ambassador appointed, was stayed.[5] And yet, to behold the rest of the princes, cardinals, ambassadors, and the trains, people, and provision there assembled was worth the sight.

Sir Horatio Palavicino, her majesty's ambassador, and Monsieur de Fresne for the king of Navarre, were now a negotiating and soliciting the dukes of Saxony, Brandenburg, and some other the imperial princes for eight thousand Switzers to aid the French king and set that crown on his head now in combustion with his subjects.[6] They would take no notice of the French king nor of his ambassador, but for the love and honor they bore to the majesty of England, and upon her word of assurance and pay, they would provide and furnish the king of Navarre with eight thousand ancient soldiers, whereof four thousand were prepared and sent away within fourteen days through the industry and credit of Sir Horatio Palavicino, taking up upon bills of exchange at Frankfurt, Stade, and Hamburg, eighty thousand pounds sterling, by the means of Giles Hooftman (whose daughter he married there),[7] Antonio Anselman, and other great merchants in those parts, the which was paid in press for setting forth of those Switzers. Letters came from the French king to his ambassador to tell the imperial princes that would not trust him he held himself most beholding unto his loving sis-

5. Dyer (d. 1607) was a poet and courtier, introduced at court by the earl of Leicester. He was sent on a diplomatic mission to Denmark in 1589. He was Chancellor of the Order of the Garter and was knighted in 1596.

6. Palavicino was sent on two missions to the continent in 1590 and 1591 to raise a German army to invade France and support Henry of Navarre against his enemies. The final agreement specified an army of 5,000 cavalry and 8,000 infantry in return for an English subsidy of 15,000 pounds. The German army finally began operations in 1591 but after initial success, fell apart in early 1592. Meanwhile, the English had supported Henry by dispatching 4,000 troops to Dieppe in 1589 and 5,000 to Rouen in 1591 (Stone, *An Elizabethan: Sir Horatio Palavicino,* pp. 156–76).

7. Hooftman, or Gielis van Eychelberg, was a wealthy burger of Antwerp. With his brother Henry, he created a business and banking house of European reputation. Denounced as a Calvinist heretic in 1566, he proved too valuable and too popular to fall a victim to the duke of Alva's persecution. His daughter Anna married Sir Horatio Palavicino on April 27, 1591.

ter the majesty of England. The four thousand Switzers were at hand, and seven thousand voluntary soldiers more sent him by the queen of England under the conduct of a noble chieftain,[8] with which, and the infinite numbers his friends and allies that did daily adhere unto his aid and army, he should be able not only to conquer peace over his enemies at home, but also ready to sack the walls of Rome or long be. He should lose the press money and dismiss the other four thousand Switzers. Well! I must leave these affairs to them that have charge of them and return to my tedious journeys and journals.

Came back to Weimar and Rostock in Mecklenburg, and so crossed over to Helsingor and Copenhagen, where, by means of Ramel, the Dutch chancellor, I was brought to Frederick, king of Denmark.[9] De-

8. There is a marginal note in the manuscript identifying this person as Lord Willoughby, which is correct. Peregrine Bertie, Lord Willoughby de Eresby (1555–1601) was a military commander and succeeded the earl of Leicester as commander of the English forces in the Low Countries in 1587 (*DNB*).

9. Horsey's story about his mission to Denmark is one of the most perplexing passages of his account. In all probability, he did not visit Denmark in 1590 and certainly had no official commission to do so. Moreover, there are outright errors of fact in the narrative. King Frederick died in 1588 and the visits of Sir Andrew Keith both took place in the summer of 1589. The simplest conclusion would be to dismiss the whole episode as a fabrication. Yet Horsey knew a good deal about Denmark and the issues involved in its relations with England. Ramel (see below) was "Dutch chancellor" or head of the Tyske Kancelli. Horsey also knew of Frederick Leiel and was aware of the purposes of the Keith missions. His version of the negotiations at the Danish court mentions the main issues of Anglo-Danish relations of the time—the seizure of English ships by the Danes, English use of the northern route around Norway, and German trade with Spain. In fact, his narrative is very similar to Christopher Perkins' reports of his negotiations in Denmark in 1590 (*Calendar of State Papers, Foreign*, 1589–90, pp. 433–35). The contradiction can be resolved by suggesting that Horsey visited Denmark early in 1588 after his flight from England. Reports of his movements trace his path across northern Germany toward Denmark. He had no official commission to negotiate and therefore probably did not have an audience with Frederick. He may well have ingratiated himself with courtiers like Ramel and have discussed the state of Anglo-Danish relations with them. (We are deeply indebted to Mr. Harold Ilsøe of the Royal Library, Copenhagen, for his comments on Horsey's visit to Denmark. For Mr. Ilsøe's own views on the question, see his *Udlaendinges rejser i Danmark indtil år 1700* [Copenhagen, 1963].)

Heinrich Ramel (d. 1610) was a German from Pomerania who entered Danish service and rose rapidly to a position of great power. In the late 1580's, he was *hofmester* (majordomo) and head of the German chancellery (foreign ministry). His opponents at court forced his resignation as hofmester in 1590 although he remained director of foreign policy. For the next few years, he sought to advance his position by exploiting the differences between the young Christian IV and his mother and their respective supporters. When the two parties were reconciled in

livered the queen's letters and speech unto the king; he saluted me. I laid my hand on his ankle. Asked how the queen his loving sister did. "Her majesty was well in health at my departure, wishing the like unto his highness." Dismissed and conducted to my lodging at Frederick Leiel's house.[10] Fritz van Ward, one of the masters of request, or king's referendaries, was sent to me from the king to know if I had any more to say than was contained in the queen's letters. I told him "Yea, if it pleased his majesty to admit the audience thereof." There was a gallant gentleman, one Sir Andrew Keith,[11] the king of Scots his ambassador, well attended, that became acquainted with me, lodged at the next house, of whom I was in some jealousy at first; showed me kindness; told me my answer was resolved upon already, that the king was moved against the queen for not giving her consent so freely as it was expected for the match between the king and his daughter. I was sent for, gave his majesty the best style and title I could devise to please him. "Our sister, the majesty of England, requires at our hands too great a loss. We are possessed of thirty thousand pounds forfeiture to our crown by the treachery and falsehood of her subjects, who have not only upon our princely trust deceived us in our customs of many more thousands forgiven them heretofore, for the love and true correspondency we ever held towards her majesty, but also thereby they have encouraged other nations to do the like, to our exceeding great indemnity. Not only be her admiral and treasurer weary, and insult upon our willingness and desire of the continuance of our ancient treaty and amity, but they[12] have of late seized upon divers ships and goods belonging to our subjects for passing only in traffic through the narrow seas, and they[13] can receive no reason nor restitution thereof. For the other point, yearly pay of one hundred rose nobles, it is but acknowledgment of our right, an homage ever due and payable by her majesty's ancestors unto our predecessors, lords and kings of Norway, and of all the said ocean seas adjacent, so lately confirmed and ratified

1596, Ramel was made a member of the *Rigsraad* (state council). In the last years of his career, he devoted most of his attention to foreign policy, arranging Christian's marriage with Anne Catherine of Brandenburg in 1597 (*Dansk Biografisk Leksikon*).

10. Leiel (d. 1601) was tax collector on the Oresund from 1583 and in 1591 was mayor of Copenhagen.

11. Keith was for eighteen years in the service of the king of Scotland, and in 1584 was created Lord Dingwall. He was one of the ambassadors sent to Denmark in the summer of 1589 to settle the marriage of James VI.

12. *but they* omitted in the original text.

13. *they* omitted in the original text.

by the deliberate contemplation and commission of her majesty's ambassador Herbert, the which we purpose to enjoy and not to forego. These are the points and terms we stand upon for answer unto the majesty our loving sister her letters.[14] You see time is spent and will not permit reply. If you desire it I will appoint commissioners to receive the same, but I hold them unanswerable." It was past twelve a clock. "I will not press your princely patience for a present reply, since it stands with your majesty's pleasure, though to a great disadvantage, to appoint commissaries to receive the same. I only pray your majesty's letters for answer to her highness." He made a slight *congé* and so turned away, and my dinner called me home with no great appetite or stomach to digest some words.

The next day I was sent for. The Dutch chancellor, two masters of request, and a secretary were ready to receive me in a large chamber, fairly hanged, as seemed to me, with arras. I was attended only with a gentleman, my servants, and four or five merchants, who gave me instructions. "My lords, since it is his majesty's pleasure not to hear me, yet, seeing I am addressed to treat of matter and not to stand upon ceremony, his majesty's verbal answer to those two points contained within her majesty's letters, as I remember, are these"—which my memory served punctually to recite. "A third, by way of inference, wherein it pleased his wisdom to use much art of elocution, I may not reply unto but by way of discourse with your lordships, for the truth inserted in her majesty's letters doth sufficiently maintain and serve both for answer and reply. The merchants' faults, which is termed treachery and falsehood, I may not defend. If it be so, they are here ready to answer and approve their allegations, that it is no other than ever hath been used, known, and tolerated by his majesty's customers since this coacted tax hath been imposed upon them. Their entry for their number and sorts of cloths were just, only the wrappers of every pack excepted; however, now upon misprision or some displeasure conceived,

14. At the end of the 1570's, the Danish government, fearful of a loss of revenue from the Sound tolls, took steps to make good its claims that Denmark had the right to charge duty on all ships sailing north around the coast of Norway. Queen Elizabeth vigorously protested in the name of freedom of the seas. Finally, in 1583, she sent John Herbert as ambassador to Denmark. He negotiated a compromise solution by which the Danes agreed not to charge duty on English ships using the northern route and accepted instead an annual payment of one hundred rose nobles from the English merchants for the right to sail around Norway without further interference.

questioned. If other nations have offended, they might presume upon
so firm amity and league professed, subjects to so mighty a prince as
doth retribute the like to fare no worse than they, not questioned at
all the stay of their ships and of no other nations. Their charge and loss
of their mart and hindrance in traffic, which is free to all other, is not
only an inevitable loss, but more than sufficient punished if they had
offended, the necessity whereof may enforce their innocency to some
other course of remedy. But that the queen's majesty requires in their
behalf is but the common justice which his majesty affordeth to all
other without suit. To the other point, I am commanded to let you
know her majesty's late ambassador, Mr. Herbert, had no commission
to assent to any such exaction or yearly payment of one hundred rose
nobles by her majesty's subjects trading into the northern ocean seas;
neither can any such due or right be acknowledged, never paid by her
majesty's ancestors to his highness' predecessors; no record, history, nor
chronicle doth make mention of any such thing. If her majesty's subjects be[15] employed in fishing or trade in any of his majesty's towns,
Norbergrav, Trondheim, or Vardo,[16] upon those coasts, they pay their
usual customs as other nations do, from whom no such taxation is required, much less any homage, which term I fear will be distasted, and
therefore resolutely not be expected nor enforced. Concerning stay of
ships and goods of his majesty's subjects by the lord treasurer and lord
admiral of England, it is no dependent of the other occasions; but in
discourse, as I said to you, my lords, be it spoken, the royal majesty of
England is and ever hath been very curious and careful not to suffer
any such cause of offense to be given to the majesty of Denmark. His
highness may be misincensed. Those ships so stayed, though coming
out of his sound, are Esterlings of Lübeck, Stettin, Danzig,
Königsberg,[17] remote from the territories of Denmark, laden with munition, powder, cables, and victuals to serve her majesty's common
enemy, forbidden to pass her highness' narrow seas; as his majesty
would no doubt of have,[18] as in like case hath, prohibited her majesty's
subjects and other nations to transport or pass through the sound and
Baltic seas to his common enemy the king of Sweden, they two ever
being in hostility, as England and Scotland, though perhaps colored by

15. *be* omitted in the original text.
16. Wardhowse in the original text. Norbergrav is perhaps Bergen.
17. Quinsborrowgh in the original text.
18. *have* omitted in the original text.

some of his subjects for some private commodity, by reason of the so firm league and amity between both. Let it be, otherwise, truly proved, either by their charters, policies, or bills of lading, and no doubt justice and restoration will be made accordingly. O! let not the apprehension of these suggestions from those firebrands sever and part the ancient league and treaties between these two great monarchies, or cause to be called in memory the unkind interruption of her majesty's subjects passing the ocean seas, the majesty of England known to be the only proprietor thereof as well as of the narrow seas, Great Britain's revenues; the buffeting and misusing of her majesty's subjects by your admiral, Johan Wolf,[19] trading for fish and oil upon those northern coasts, taking by violence their victuals, sails, cables, anchors, exposing them to death and the mercies of the seas, for he showed none; they rest unsatisfied to this day; the enticing away her majesty's servants and shipwrights to fashion your navy after the same molds; the carrying away out of her majesty's kingdom much ordnance, both brass and iron, pieces, and other munition, in the time of your greatest wars with the Swede. How often and many times the strength of her highness' merchants' navy have been instigated, not only to pass the eastern seas without acknowledgment, but also to compass through the Norway and Finland seas to trade and traffic into Sweden, Stockholm, Narva, Riga, Reval, Danzig, Königsberg, and all other the maritime towns of trade, leaving the passage through the Sound, which now they are enforced to do for peace, precedent, and amity sake, against the like and wills of such other princes as affect neither, rather pleased with the effusion of blood it may be upon such light occasions of small moment practiced to be spilled; the which I doubt not but you, such principal lords of state, will in your grave and great wisdoms seek to prevent." They began to reply. I prayed them to pardon my weariness for want of repose, and so was attended by some gentlemen to my lodging. The king sent to know whether I had commission to conclude and determine of anything. "No, I was to propound, intimate, and observe her majesty's letters; the contents granted and answered was all I attended for." "Soft, sir, there goes two words to such a bargain." I dined with the king, but could not drink so well, only her majesty's, his highness', and the Queen Sophia's, their healths, etc.

I received his majesty's letters, a chain of gold worth some £40, sa-

19. An error. The admiral of the Danish fleet between 1576 and 1593 was Peder Munk.

luted, and so dismissed. Came again to Lübeck; dispatched there my letters and notes on what was done and sent them by a worthy merchant, Mr. Daniel Bond. It seems this treatise wrought some good effect. The merchants that offered composition did now refuse; procured Mr. Doctor Perkins to come with the queen's letters; had quick dispatch and release of the merchants' ships and goods, not without some good charge, but to me for my pains little or none. Yet I must go forward to such or like other business.[20] When I came to Danzig, five hundred miles from Lübeck, the deputy and assistants of the English merchants, Mr. Barker, etc., understanding of my arrival, invited my way by Elbing,[21] where they had their residency, towards the king's court of Poland. There was I to receive their instructions. Therefore I went by Thorn and through Podolia, a fruitful region, and so to Warsaw, where the King Sigismund was, and where the said deputy, Mr. Barker,[22] and his company met me, very well prepared to enter into such another labyrinth, though somewhat more differing and difficult. The great chancellor Zamoyski[23] was ten miles of the court, at his own town, built and called after his own name, to whom I would first have had access, being the prime voevoda, lieutenant-general, and statesman of that kingdom. But, lest then I should be noted by other lords and officers of

20. It is clear that Horsey went through Poland on his way to Russia in 1590. There is, however, no other record of any negotiations about the position of English merchants in Poland and no trace of any royal decree on the subject. Sir Christopher Perkins (1543?–1622), B.A. Oxford, 1565, joined the Jesuits in 1566. He was employed by the queen from 1590, when he became a Protestant, as a diplomatic agent. He became Master of Requests in 1617 (*DNB*).

21. Melvin in the original text.

22. Possibly William Barker who was also deputy at Elbing (British Museum, Cottonian MS, Nero B. II, fol. 202b).

23. Zamoyski (1541–1605) received a thorough classical education at Padua. When he returned to Poland, he soon established himself as the chief spokesman for the broad mass of the nobility against the pretensions of the magnates. During the succession crisis following the death of Sigismund II in 1572, Zamoyski was an outspoken opponent of the pro-Hapsburg party and it was he who in 1575 proposed Stephen Bathory of Transylvania as a candidate. When Bathory became king, Zamoyski was made vice-chancellor and in 1581 was raised to the offices of chancellor and grand hetman. In 1587 he supported Sigismund Vasa as Bathory's successor. Although he did not get along with the new king, he remained a powerful political figure until his death. The highlights of his distinguished military career were his campaigns against the Russians in 1580 and 1581 and against the Swedes in Livonia in 1601–2. He was an enthusiastic patron of learning and culminated his activity by founding an academy in Zamosc in 1594. In religion a staunch Roman Catholic, he was a strong supporter of the Union of Brest of 1596 which created the Uniate Church.

state and prejudice my negotiation, I addressed myself to the principal secretary and under chancellor, who procured a time for my access and delivery of my letters to the king. But stay was made of any proceedings till the great chancellor came to the court, to whom I made means to have access, but could not. Pan Jan Chlebowicz, palatine of Kaunas,[24] a great favorite of his, was of my acquaintance, to whose allies and friends, captives sometimes to the old emperor Ivan Vasil'evich, I had done some favors unto. He mediated some countenance from the chancellor towards me, received me with honor, but with some note of dislike that I did not attend his pleasure.

XXI

Two commissioners were appointed, the secretary Stannislave and *referendarius* Obroskie,[1] to confer with me about the queen's majesty's complaint on the behalf of her merchants trading those countries, who had trusted the merchants and subjects of that crown and kingdom with cloth and other merchandises, to the value of four score thousand pounds sterling, and became insolvent, altering their dwellings and purchasing with these monies, houses and land goods upon which they did inhabit, having gotten and procured the king's letter of protection for their exemptions from justice to the exceeding great prejudice and undoing of many her said majesty's merchants. They told me it was a new complaint which they had not heard of; therefore thought it was not so current true as the queen's majesty of England was informed. Here did the merchants attend, ready to approve and attest the same before their lordships, with a catalogue of their names and their bills of debt, which did show how long they had forborne the same. "So it may be, and yet much thereof paid and discharged; this requires some larger time of examination. They ought to be heard also." Both myself and many of the said merchants did attend his majesty's answer, remedy, and pleasure therein. "His majesty and the rest

24. Chlebowicz (1544–91) was made voevoda of Troki in 1586. He was known as a military commander, a defender of Lithuanian autonomy within the Polish-Lithuanian union and a patron of Protestant scholarship. *Kaunas:* Cowen in the original text.
1. Probably Oborski.

of the lords should be forthwith made acquainted with the cause, and you accordingly shall hear farther with what expedition may be." I made my good friend, the palatine, the means again to pray the great chancellor his favor and furtherance for[2] my dispatch, whose frowning and slighting seemed to be overpassed; sent sometimes congratulatory messages and presents to me, and called for me before himself and other lords of the council, who told me the king's majesty marveled much the queen of England would write such peremptory letters to so high a majesty in the behalf of a sort of peasants that might complain without just case. "And please your excellency, with the rest of your lordships, the queen's high majesty of England writes unto the majesty of Poland in the same style and manner as her highness doth to all other imperial kings, her loving allies and friends, placing and esteeming his brotherly amity and greatness in the forerank of many others, and no exception can justly be taken for truth and matter contained in her highness' letters, complaints upon due inquiry and examination made unto her majesty by her highness' worthy subjects and royal merchants, reckoned in her majesty's esteem far above the rank of peasants, who require in all humble manner but justice, which his imperial seat affordeth all men." "Prove your assertions and justice shall be ministered accordingly; but know this, I pray you, your queen cannot limit nor let his majesty's princely pleasure and preeminence royal to grant his kingly protections to whom and to such subjects as his royal wisdom shall think worthy of." "Far be it from the meaning of that strain, noble sirs, or restraint; all that is required is but your way to justice of this kingdom for recovery of her majesty's subjects' goods and wealth, gotten into the hands of such as have perhaps abusively procured such protections, and thereby do detain the same. The policy and providence of this state is so well known to the world to maintain trade and commerce with all nations by their well usage, as well to transport such superfluous commodities as originally groweth within these kingdoms, and to import such foreign commodities as the necessity thereof requires, whereby the crown customs are advanced, noblemen's revenues employed to the best advantage, merchants', and all other sorts of artisans' turns served, which maketh this commonwealth and people to live in such flourishing estate above many other foreign nations. All which I must leave to your lordships' better knowledge and wisdoms,

2. *for*. from in the original text.

and crave pardon for anything you conceive amiss." We parted with some more familiar countenance than we met, and the next morning the chancellor sent to know how I had rested and prayed me to send him, by one of the merchants, the catalogue of the creditors' names, their bills of debt, and dwelling places. Which I did, and, by one of my own servants, a fair and curious cutwork handkerchief, a pair of perfumed gloves, and a chain of ambergris, which the chancellor received thankfully with good reward to the messenger. In the mean we made merry with hope, went abroad and saw many monuments and recreations, expecting the good day that the chancellor and the same lords sent for me; told me the king's majesty had granted the queen's[3] majesty's request and desired to live in amity with her, and her merchants should be well entertained and receive no wrong. There were twelve proclamations imprinted, which should presently be sent forth, published, and proclaimed by an herald in Elbing,[4] Danzig, Königsberg, and such other great towns of traffic and places where the merchants should advise, to this effect: "That all such his subjects, merchants or other, that were indebted for any goods, merchandises, monies, or contract unto any of the English merchants trading into his kingdoms should presently repair unto them and make satisfaction, payment, or agreement with them and either of them within the space of three months after the date hereof, upon his majesty's high displeasure, sale, and confiscation of all their livelihoods, lands, goods, houses, and chattels whatsoever, notwithstanding any protection, privilege, or letter whatsoever to the contrary. Dated at our imperial town of Warsaw, this last of July, the second year of our reign, *anno Domini* 1589, *stilo veteri*."

I dined with the king; had few words of him, his majesty's letters and patents; kissed his highness' hand and dismissed. I was feasted by the lord high chamberlain Pan Lucas Obrovscoie, his only favorite. I dispatch the merchants with my letters unto Mr. Secretary Walsingham of all what had past. They presented me some good reward and promised their company should farther recompense me; Mr. John Herbert, before me, could not prevail.[5]

---

3. *queen's* omitted in the original text.
4. Melvin in the original text.
5. Obrovscoie could not be identified. John Herbert was an Englishman who spent about two years in Poland between 1583 and 1585 negotiating rights for English traders in the port of Elbing. Once he had made an agreement with the

I was willing to see Queen Anna,[6] King Sigismund the third his daughter, King Stephen Bathory his late widow and wife. Let me, after our business done, a little digress, though to a matter of small pertinency. I put on one of my men's liveries, passed to her palace, before the windows whereof were placed pots and ranks of great carnations, gillyflowers, province roses, sweet lilies, and other sweet herbs and strange flowers, giving most fragrant, sweet smells. Came into the chamber she sat and supped in; stood among the rest of many other gentlemen. Her majesty sat under a white silk canopy, upon a great Turkey carpet in a chair of estate, a hard-favored queen, her maids of honor and ladies attendants at supper in the same room, a great traverse drawn between; saw her service and behavior and attendance. At last one spied me that had taken notice of me before; told the lord steward standing by her chair; he casting his eye upon me made other to behold me. I shifted back; he told the queen, "Call him hither, though not in state." Sayeth the old lord, "Will you anything with her majesty?" "No, sir, I came but to see her majesty's princely state and presence,[7] for which I crave pardon if it be offense." "Her majesty will have speech with you." I was discovered by my curious ruffs. The ladies hasted from their table, came about the queen. The queen, after I had done my obeisance, asked if I were the gentleman of England that had lately negotiated with the king, and by her interpreter would know the queen's name. "Elizaveta is too blessed a name for such a scourge of the Catholic Church; her sister's name was Maria, a blessed saint in heaven." I desired to speak without her interpreter, who did not well. "Pray do." "Queen Elizabeth's name is most renowned and better accounted of by the best and most puissant, greatest imperial kings and princes of this world, the defendress of the true and ancient catholic church and faith, so reverenced and styled, as her due, both by foes and friends." "Nay! nay! sir, if she be so, why doth she so cruelly put to death so many holy Catholics, Story, Campion, and other

city fathers of Elbing, he worked to win the Polish king's official sanction of the conditions. He was successful in March, 1585 (Neva Ruth Deardorff, "English Trade in the Baltic During the Reign of Elizabeth," *Studies in the History of English Commerce in the Tudor Period* [New York, 1912], pp. 305–25).

6. Anna (1523–96) was the daughter of Sigismund I. When her brother, the last male descendent of the Jagellonian line, died, she agreed to marry whomever would be chosen to succeed him. Thus, in 1576 she married Stephen Bathory and remained a powerful influence at court even after his death.

7. *presence.* presents in the original text.

godly martyrs."[8] "They were traitors to God and her crown, practiced her subversion and ruin of her kingdom." "Yea! but how could she spill the blood of the Lord's anointed, a queen more magnificent than herself, without the trial, judgment, and consent of her peers, the holy father the Pope, and all the Christian princes of Europe." "Her subjects and parliament thought it so requisite, without her royal consent, for her more safety and quiet of her realm daily endangered." She shook her head with dislike of my answer. Her majesty's ghostly father Possevino, the great Jesuit, came in;[9] took displeasure at my presence, one whose skirts I had sat before in the city of Moscow when he was nuncio there and rejected. Her majesty called for a glass of Hungarian wine with two slices of cheer[10] bread upon it. Willed the lord steward to give it me, which I refused till her highness had taken it into her own hands to give it me, and so dismissed. I was glad when I came home to put off my livery, but my hostess, a comely gentlewoman well known to the queen, was presently sent for. Her majesty was desirous to see the pearl chain I wore a Sunday when I took my leave of the king, the rather because a bold Jew, the king's chief customer, took it in his hand and told the king, as the queen said, that they were counterfeit pearl, fish eyes dried; and to know how my ruffs were starched, handsomely made with silver wire and starched in England. My chain was returned and no honor lost by the queen's sight thereof. It is time to leave troubling of you for reading any more unless more serious.

The evening I parted from Warsaw I passed over a river upon the side whereof lay a crocodile serpent dead, which my men broke with boar spears. I was suddenly so poisoned with the stench thereof as I was forced to lie many days sick in the next village, where I found such Christian favor for my attendance and help from divers that came to visit me, being a stranger, as I miraculously recovered. When I came to Vilna, the chief city in Lithuania, I presented myself and letters patents from the queen that declared my titles and what I was unto the

8. John Story (1510?–71), B.C.L. Hincksey Hall, Oxford, D.C.L., 1538, was the first Regius Professor, 1544. He was imprisoned in 1560 but escaped to Flanders. Pensioned by Philip II, he was kidnapped for the English government in 1570. He was executed at Tyburn and was beatified in 1886 (DNB). Edmund Campion (1540–81), Jesuit martyr, was arrested at Lyford, Berkshire, sent to the Tower, and executed on December 1, 1581.

9. Possevino was not in Poland at the time of Horsey's visit. He left that country for the last time in 1587 and taught theology in Padua between 1587 and 1591.

10. cheer. chea in the original text.

great duke voevoda Radziwill, a prince of great excellency, prowess, and power, and religious Protestant.[11] Gave me great respect and good entertainment; told me, though I had nothing to say to him from the queen of England, yet he did so much honor and admire her excellent virtues and graces he would also hold me in the reputation of her majesty's ambassador, which was some policy that his subjects should think I was to negotiate with him. Took me with him to his church; heard divine service, psalms, songs, a sermon, and the sacraments ministered according to the reformed churches, whereat his brother, Cardinal Radziwill, did murmur. His highness did invite me to dinner, honored with fifty halberdiers through the city; placed gunners and his guard of five hundred gentlemen to bring me to his palace; himself, accompanied with many young noblemen, received me upon the terrace; brought me into a very large room where organs and singing was, a long table set with palatines, lords and ladies, himself under a cloth of estate. I was placed before him in the midst of the table; trumpets sound and kettle drums roared. The first service brought in, jesters and poets discourse merrily, loud instruments and soft played very musically; a set of dwarfs, men and women finely attired, came in with sweet harmony, still and mournful pipes and songs of art, David's timbrels and Aaron's sweet sounding bells, as they[12] termed them. The variety made the time pleasing and short. His highness drank for the majesty the angelical queen of England her health, illustrated her greatness and graces. The great princes and ladies every one their glass of sweet wines pledged, and I did the like for his health. Strange portraitures, lions, unicorns, spread eagles, swans, and other made of sugar paste, some wines and spigots in their bellies to taste of, every one with his silver fork. To tell of all the order and particular services and rarities were tedious; well feasted, honored, and much made of, I was conducted to my lodging in manner as I was brought. Had my letters patents and a gentleman to conduct me through his country, with which I took my leave. Some pastimes with lions, bulls, and bears, strange to behold, I omit to recite.

11. Krysztof Radziwill "Piorun" (1549–1603) was one of the leading Polish commanders in the Livonian War. In 1584 he was made voevoda of Vilna. When war broke out with Sweden in 1600, he was chief Polish commander in Livonia and rallied the battered forces of the commonwealth by defeating the Swedes at Kokenhausen. Radziwill and his second son after him were outstanding defenders of the rights of religious dissenters in the Polish-Lithuanian state.

12. *they*. the in the original text.

XXII

A s I passed through Lithuania, I received good entertainment and came to Smolensk, a great town of trade and the first bordered town in Russia. My old acquaintance and next neighbor in Moscow, Kniaz' Ivan Golitsyn,[1] now voevoda and chief governor there, looked sad and somewhat strange upon me. He, the emperor, and prince protector, having heard of my coming, being, and entertainment with Sigismund king of Poland and the great prince of Lithuania, would make my welcome worse than I did expect; suffered me to pass, but sent word and news before me of my coming, so that I was met some ten miles from the Moscow by a syn boiarskii who brought and placed me in the bishop's house of Suzdal', where I was narrowly looked unto, not usual, because I should have no conference with the king of Poland's ambassador,[2] who came with an unpleasing errand to demand restitution of a great part of those southern countries sometimes belonging to the crown of Poland, and carried himself very peremptory; his negotiation goes onward and mine at a stay. Some of my ancient friends send me secret messages, by poor women, there was an alteration; I should look well to myself. I was sent for, delivered the queen's letters to the emperor; he delivers them to Andrei Shchelkalov, chief officer of ambassages, no friend of mine for Sir Jerome Bowes' sake. The emperor began to cry, silly prince, crossing himself, saying he never gave me cause of offense; something troubled him. I was hasted out of his sight. The prince protector was not there, nor could I hear from him until one evening, passing by my lodging, he sent a gentleman to will me to come a-horseback unto him under the inside of the Moscow walls in a private place. Commanded all apart; kissed me, as the man-

1. Perhaps Ivan Ivanovich Golitsyn who served as commander on the southern frontier in 1588 and 1592. In 1590 and 1591 he was commander of the troops in Smolensk (*Sinbirskii sbornik,* p. 100; *RK,* pp. 434, 458, 463).

2. On October 10, 1590, a Polish embassy, led by Stanislaw Radominski and Gabrjel Vojna, arrived in Moscow. After lengthy discussions about the prospects for transforming the existing truce between the two parties into a permanent peace treaty, the envoys and their hosts agreed simply to extend the truce for twelve years (N. N. Bantysh-Kamenskii, *Obzor vneshnikh snoshenii Rossii po 1800 god* [Moscow, 1894–1902], III, 109; S. M. Solov'ev, *Istoriia Rossii s drevneishikh vremen,* Book IV [Moscow, 1960], 234–36).

ner is; told me he could not, for divers great causes, show himself towards me so friendly and favorably as he had done, with tears. I told him I was the more sorry, my conscience bore me witness I had given him no cause of offense, but had been ever faithful, honest, and true to him. "Then let those souls suffer that are the occasioners of thy disalter[3] and mine." Spake some things not fit to commit to paper, took leave, and bid me be assured he would not suffer a hair to fall from my head—a phrase. Yet many warnings I had from my good friends, though many were gone and made away in my absence; many articles laid to my charge: exception against the queen's letters, style, and seal, not as in former times, by which the emperor was slighted, the empress slandered; combination with the king and prince of Poland; carrying great treasure out of the kingdom. All which I answered both fully and pithily, so as they left farther questioning, and beyond their wills was so divulged as I gained both love and like of many thereby. My water to dress my meat withal was poisoned, my drink and herbs and muskmelons sent poisoned, my laundress hired to poison me, which she confessed by whom, when, and how; still I had good intelligence. My cook, my butler died both of poison. I had a servant, a lord's son of Danzig, Agacius Dusker, burst out with twenty blains and boils, and escaped narrowly. There were too many strange ambassadors for jealousy to stay me in Moscow. Boris sends me word I should not fear. The emperor and council would have me remove for a while to Iaroslavl', 250 miles thence.[4] Many other things passed not worth the writing, sometimes cheerful messages, sometimes fearful. God did miraculously preserve me. But one night I commended my soul to God above other, thinking verily the time of my end was come. One rapped at my gate at midnight. I was well furnished with pistols and weapons. I and my servants, some fifteen, went with these weapons to the gate. "O my good friend, Jerome, ennobled, let me speak with you." I saw by moonshine the empress' brother, Afanasii Nagoi,[5] the late widow empress,

3. Alter or change for the worse.

4. Actually a distance of 240 versts or about 159 miles (Petrov, "Geograficheskie spravochniki XVII v.," *Istoricheskii arkhiv*, V [1950], 104).

5. Horsey probably had in mind Andrei Fedorovich Nagoi, since Afanasii Fedorovich had already died in 1585 (A. B. Lobanov-Rostovskii [ed.], *Russkaia rodoslovnaia kniga* [St. Petersburg, 1895], II, 2). Andrei held a number of important military commands in the latter part of the Livonian War. When his sister, Mariia, married Ivan IV in 1581, he occupied a place of honor at the marriage ceremonies. After Ivan's death he was exiled to Uglich. He returned to the court only in 1605 during the reign of the first False Dmitrii, his supposed nephew (*RBS*).

mother to the young prince Dmitrii, who were placed but twenty-five miles thence at Uglich.[6] "The Tsarevich Dmitrii is dead; his throat was cut about the sixth hour by the d'iaki;[7] some one of his pages confessed upon the rack by Boris his setting on; and the empress poisoned and upon point of death, her hair and nails and skin falls off; help and give some good thing for the passion of Christ his sake." "Alas! I have nothing worth the sending." I durst not open my gates. I ran up, fetched a little bottle of pure salad[8] oil (that little vial of balsam that the queen gave me) and a box of Venice treacle. "Here is what I have! I pray God it may do her good." Gave it over the wall, who hied him post away. Immediately the watchmen in the streets raised the town and told how the Prince Dmitrii was slain. Some four days before, the suburbs of the Moscow was set on fire and twelve thousand houses burned. Boris his guard had the spoil, and four or five soldiers suborned, desperate fellows hired to endure the rack, confessed, and so was published that the Tsarevich Dmitrii, his mother the empress, and the Nagois their family, had hired them to kill the emperor and Boris Fedorovich and set the Moscow on fire. This was so published to move the peoples' hearts to hatred against the prince, his mother, and family.[9] But it was too gross a falsehood and abhorred of all men in general, as God did not long after recompense and revenge with as fearful and palpable an example, to show that he is just in all his doings and turns the wicked devices and devilish practices of men to

6. The distance from Iaroslavl' to Uglich was 90 versts or about 60 miles (Petrov, "Geograficheskie spravochniki," p. 104).

7. Most of Horsey's contemporaries, Russian and foreign alike, believed that Dmitrii was murdered on Godunov's orders and many nineteenth-century historians accepted their judgment. Since the end of the last century, however, a number of scholars, notably Platonov, have defended the story recorded by the official commission appointed by Boris to investigate the incident. In their view, Dmitrii, who was an epileptic, suffered a seizure while playing a game of knives and fatally stabbed himself. In the ensuing confusion, the boy's mother and her kinsmen spread the story that Dmitrii had been murdered. See George Vernadsky, "The Death of the Tsarevich Dimitry: A Reconsideration of The Case," *Oxford Slavonic Papers*, V (1954), 1–19.

8. *salad*. sallet in the original text.

9. A considerable number of sources, both Russian and foreign, also mention a major fire in Moscow at the time of Dmitrii's death. See, for example, K. M. Obolenskii [ed.], *Novyi letopisets* (Moscow, 1853), p. 36; "Povest' kniaz'ia Ivana Mikhailovicha Katyreva-Rostovskago," *Russkaia istoricheskaia biblioteka*, XIII, 565; Jacques Margeret, *Estat de l'Empire et Grand Duché de Moscovie* (Paris, 1946), p. 30; Konrad Bussov, *Moskovskaia khronika 1584–1613* (Moscow-Leningrad, 1961), p. 204.

open shame and confusion. The bishop of Krutitsa[10] was sent, accompanied with five hundred gunners and divers noblemen and gentlemen, to bury this Prince Dmitrii under the high altar in St. John's, I take it, in Uglich.[11] Little did they think at that time that this Dmitrii's ghost should in so short a time be stirred up to the dissolution of Boris Fedorovich and all his family. The sick, poisoned empress was presently to be shorn a nun to save her soul by sequestering her life, made dead to the world, all her allies, brothers, uncles, and friends, officers and servants, dispersed in displeasure to divers secret dens not to see light again.

Time comes I must away; some letters they say shall be sent after me from the emperor and Boris Fedorovich. Many odd ends, debts, and furniture I had, lying desperate, which I would be glad to have with me, and good sums of money in Boris his hands. Writes his letters, yet extant. He could not do as he would by me; would work me grace and favor in as ample manner as ever it was, but there were stumbling blocks to be removed first. In the mean, if I were impaired of money he would send me out of his own treasure. A pensioner was sent to attend me down Dvina, and so aboard the ships, where I was as glad to be as Sir Jerome Bowes was when he escaped thence, and many noblemen wished me their service and in no worse case.

XXIII

I arrived in England, thanks be to God, in health and safe. Came to the queen, delivered my letters, and found them a great deal more better and friendlier than expected for. The company and I made even of all things ever passed between us, by compromise of four wor-

---

10. The see of Krutitsa (also known as Sarskii and Podonskii) was administered from the Novo-Spasskii Monastery in Moscow. In 1589 when the patriarch of Constantinople created the Moscow patriarchate, the see became a metropolitanate. At that time the occupant of the see was Gelasii (d. 1601) (P. Stroev, *Spiski ierarkhov i nastoiatelei monastyrei rossiskoi tserkvi* [St. Petersburg, 1877], p. 1035).

11. In 1606, on the orders of the new tsar, Vasilii Shuiskii, Dmitrii's remains were brought to Moscow for reburial and the prince was canonized. The ceremonies were designed to emphasize that the first False Dmitrii, Shuiskii's predecessor on the throne, had been an impostor since the real Dmitrii had been martyred in 1591.

thy personages. They paid me for my stock and goods found due in their hands £1,845. A general release,[1] discharge, and acquitances passed each other hands and seals very authentical by their governors, Sir George Barne and Sir John Hart, who in the name of their fellowship presented me, for a final and friendly parting, a goodly gilt bowl with cover, all which, with their commissions and instructions, letters, privileges, and matters of great consequence that had passed between us, are extant; and also the copies of the queen's letters, commissions, and instructions, and the like for all foreign negotiations and employments that hath passed from time to time, very memorable and worth the sight and reading, some passages whereof are set down long since by Mr. Hakluyt in his book of voyages, some by Mr. Camden,[2] and most by Doctor Fletcher, more scholastically: the original nature and disposition of the Russe people, the laws, languages, government, discipline for their church and commonwealth, revenues, commodities, climate and situation, whereof it most consist, and with whom they have most league and commerce—with all which I did furnish him—in a treatise of itself. For the other two treatises I promised of Poland, Lithuania, Livonia, Hungary, Transylvania, Germany, the Higher Cantons and the Lower, the seventeen United Provinces, Denmark, Norway, and Sweden, according to my collections, knowledge, and instructions, I have also severally discoursed of, to the end it may appear to my friends I have spent my time with great desire of inquiry to attain to perfection and knowledge, and ready to give an account to them, in love, of anything they shall farther require.

XXIV

A nd yet I may not leave this story so bereaved of some more discourse that necessarily dependeth to the former, though perpetrated and done after my time, the consequence being so very material

---

1. There is a marginal note in the original text that dates this "anno 1589." The note is in a later hand, and the year 1589 is not in keeping with the progress of the narrative at this point.

2. William Camden (1551–1623), antiquary and historian. The work alluded to is probably the *Britannia*.

to the end God's most just judgments may be also made known to follow those foul and wicked demerits, which the innocent blood spilled
in that smothering time of tyranny did call for, from his most almighty
power, whose examples never faileth to the comfort of his elect, the
just punishments of such as for want of grace do give themselves over
to a reprobate sense to follow the devil's enticements and their own
wicked wills and ambitious desires. For the verity and truth thereof I
would not have the reader to doubt.

You have heard, and but some part neither, of the cruel, barbarous,
and tyrannical reign of the Emperor Ivan Vasil'evich, how he lived,
what infinite innocent blood he spilled, and what horrible sins did not
he commit and delight in, what his end and his eldest son's was, and
how he left a silly son, the true proverb of Solomon,[1] of more than
weak capacity, to govern so great a monarchy, by which the effusion of
so much more blood also followed; he made away and his third son,
ten years of age, a sharp witted and hopeful prince, his throat cut; and
the race of that bloody generation, continuing above three hundred
years, cut off and now utterly rooted out, extinguished, and end in
blood. Come now to the usurper, called in their language [smothering
tyrant],[2] Boris Fedorovich Godunov. I pray look a little back and remember how I left him. I received letters from my ancient and very
worthy friends, and other good advertisements thence, extant to show,
and have since had conference with two several ambassadors and a
friar of good intelligence how the state of that kingdom and government stood. Boris and his family, as you have heard, a-growing mighty
and very powerful, suppressing and oppressing by degrees, and making
away most of the chief and ancient nobility, whom he had wonderfully
dispensed, long tormented with all impunity to make himself redoubt-
able and fearful, removes also now the emperor himself, Fedor Ivanovich,[3] and his sister the empress into a monastery,[4] though himself was
emperor in effect before, causeth the patriarch, metropolitans, bishops
and friars, and other the new upsprung nobility, his officers, merchants,
and all other his own creatures, to petition unto him to take the crown
upon him. Their fear and time appointed, he was solemnly inaugurated

1. "The house of the wicked shall be overthrown" (Proverbs 14:11).
2. The words in square brackets are in English, written with Cyrillic letters.
3. Tsar Fedor died in 1598, apparently of natural causes.
4. Tsar Fedor's widow Irina entered the Novodevichii convent at her own insistence before the succession to the throne was finally settled.

and crowned, and styled from a gentleman with open acclamation, Boris Fedorovich, emperor and great duke of Vladimir, Moscow, and of all Russia, king of Kazan', king of Astrakhan', king of Siberia, and the rest described. He is of comely person, well favored, affable, easy and apt to ill counsel, but dangerous in the end to the giver, of good capacity, about forty-five years of age, affected much to necromancy, not learned but of sudden apprehension, and a natural good orator to deliver his mind with an audible voice, subtle, very precipitate, revengeful, not given much to luxury, temperate of diet, heroical in outward show; gave great entertainment to foreign ambassadors, sent rich presents to foreign princes. The more to illustrate and set forth his fame desired, above all other kings and princes, amity and firm league with the emperor of Almaine and the king of Denmark, the Scythian khan, the king of Poland and the king of Sweden his enemies, and to them did adhere all those that did not love him, which became his ruin. He continued the same kind and course of government he held before, only made show to give more general applaud, security, and liberty to his subjects. Still fearing his own continuance and safety, desired to match his daughter, for more strength, with the king of Denmark's third son, Herzog Hans; conditions and terms and all agreed upon, contract, apparel, state, and time appointed for solemnizing the marriage; a valorous, wise, and hopeful young prince, by whom and by whose allies and means the emperor thought to work wonders. But God upon a sudden sickness took away his life; died in the Moscow. The marriage, his hope and purpose, all prevented.[5] Not long after he was put to extreme exigencies by the Krym, the Pole, and the Swede, all invading and warring upon each their borders and confines.[6]

But, to omit many other strange passages and practices between him, his nobility, and people, and to come nearer to his dismal time and strange catastrophe that befell him, his partakers, and all his designs, you have formerly heard of one Bogdan Bel'skii, the great favorite and minion to that great Emperor Ivan Vasil'evich, with whom he served this emperor his trusty turn and time in making way to that was aimed at. None so familiar nor inward, none so powerful nor better able to achieve or bring to pass the subversion of his greatest enemies, the nobility and others that favored him not. But he was rewarded

5. See p. 327, n. 8, for the death of Herzog Hans.
6. Between 1602 and 1604 Muscovy was at peace with all of her traditional European enemies.

with such a recompense as commonly followeth such treacherous instruments. This emperor himself, his sister the empress, and all their family and friends stood in fear of his subtle working will; found means and many feigned occasions to be rid of his presence; placed him and his confederates far off and safe enough, as they thought, in displeasure to work or practice any more mischief in that state. Yet the infinite treasure and mass of monies which he had gotten and conveyed away in the time of his greatness and fear of continuance served him in such good stead for his purpose of revenge, now escaped, joining with many other discontented nobles and men of might, not only to supply but also to stir up the king of Poland and greatest palatines and princes of power in Lithuania. Who, with but a mean army, assured of all sufficient power upon their arrival in Russia, gave out that they had brought the pleasing tidings unto them for their redemption, the right and true heir to the crown and kingdom, Dmitrii emperor, Ivan Vasil'evich his slain son by the practice of this usurped Emperor Boris Fedorovich, who miraculously by the divine will of God and mercy of his distressed people was preserved alive and present in this army approaching the city of Moscow for their comfort and delivery.[7] Boris emperor prepares, as time would permit, arms with all his trustiest friends and nobles; had men, munition, artillery, and all other provision abundantly, but wanted courage and hearts to fight, which killed his heart; nothing availed against the time that was come. The prince palatine that had the leading of the army, Dmitrii newly revived, and many other of name, besieges and blocks up the Moscow round, no hope of escaping. The Emperor Boris Fedorovich, the empress his wife, son, and daughter took all their potions and poison,[8] laid their heads all together lying upon one floor;[9] three of them burst and presently died; and the son, languishing, was, by some of the greatest of that

7. Bel'skii was apparently not one of the original sponsors of the False Dmitrii. In the last years of Godunov's reign he was in exile and reappeared on the political stage immediately after the death of Boris in 1605. He quickly grasped the realities of the situation and instigated a revolt in Moscow on June 1, 1605, that completed the victory of the False Dmitrii. The new regime rewarded him for his service by raising him to the rank of boiar (S. F. Platonov, *Ocherki po istorii smuty v moskovskom gosudarstve XVI–XVII vv.* [St. Petersburg, 1910], pp. 271, 275).

8. As the False Dmitrii advanced toward Moscow, Boris died on April 13, 1605. While it is generally assumed that he died of natural causes, some contemporary commentators, notably Horsey and Conrad Bussov, believed that he committed suicide (Bussov, p. 230).

9. *floor.* flower in the original text.

family, to prove, pacify, and settle the minds of the distracted people, proclaimed Ivan Borisovich emperor of all Russia, etc., but soon after departed this life.[10] Then the people longed the more for this innovation and to see their slain Dmitrii. The gates of the Moscow were made open; Dmitrii with his army enters.

The city possessed, he placed in the palace and inner castle, all prelates and people come and swear obedience; proclaimed and crowned emperor and great duke of all Russia, being but an impostor[11] and counterfeit, son to a priest that carried aqua-vitæ to sell about the country. The people murmuring at this change and mightily discontented for the boldness and incursion of the Poles, having now mastery of the city, proclamation was made to stop and stay the people's outrages, tongues, and furies. Which to pacify, the palatine, chief voevoda, he that had countenance and grace of leading this Polish army and bringing in this counterfeit Dmitrii, was enforced for his safety and hold there to marry his daughter to this emperor Dmitrii, and so she became empress.[12] The Poles, a haughty nation and a very insulting people upon advantage, began so to domineer over the Russe nobility and to interrupt their religion, pervert their justice; began to tyrannize, oppress, ransack, and make havoc of the treasure; roots out Boris his faction and posterity, puts many of them to shameful deaths and ransoms, and carries themselves as conquerors; so that the Russe nobility, metropolitans, bishops, friars, and all sorts of people, much repining and murmuring at this new kind of government and alteration, take opportunity and head to vanquish and suppress the Poles' insolencies; put aside their faction, a hundred soldiers for one, so that there became a wonderful confused estate between them. The king and princes of Poland, always enemies to the Muscovites, takes now opportunity of that advantage, prepares an army to keep possession of this crown and country. In the mean the Russe sets upon this counterfeit Emperor Dmitrii one day, kills his guard, takes him from his wife's bed, the empress, drags him out upon the terrace. The gunners and soldiers thrust their knives in him, hacks, hews, and mangles his head, legs, and body, carries it into the marketplace, shows it for three days space about the city, the people flocking and cursing him and the traitors that brought him; dispatches this palatine and his daughter the empress and the Pol-

10. Godunov's son was named Fedor.
11. *impostor.* apostur in the original text.
12. Marina Mniszek.

ish soldiers with more humanity than they deserved; proceed to the election and nominating of a new emperor of their own tribe.[13] Two were spoken of, Kniaz' Ivan Fedorovich Mstislavskii[14] and Kniaz' Vasilii Shuiskii,[15] they both made in this turbulent time very timorous to take it, between the Pole and them fractions, and factions among themselves, all out of joint, not likely to be reduced a long time to any good form of peaceable government. Yet a crown and kingdom did most tempt the more willinger thereunto, which was Kniaz' Vasilii Petrovich Shuiskii, a valiant and most generous prince, third brother to that noble duke Kniaz' Ivan Shuiskii made away and smothered, as you have heard. This duke was crowned and inaugurated with general applaud and great solemnity, after their ancient manner and custom;[16] named Kniaz' Vasilii Petrovich, emperor and great duke of all Russia, with the rest of all his style and titles. He and his people betakes to arm, not only to free their thralldoms but also to expel the Poles and prepare against a new invasion threatened.

This new emperor, Kniaz' Vasilii, was summoned as a vassal by a herald at arms to yield obedience to the crown of Poland,[17] who had now gotten and styled as a conquered addition the monarchy and great dukedom of all Russia, and would not so soon nor slightly leave it, and had many Dmitriis in store to maintain the same title; no reasons, capitulations, nor fair defensive answers should prevail. The Pole strikes the iron whiles it was hot, had gotten good footing and interest among the tired nobles and wearied people of Russia, who were now marvelously well pleased and contented with their Emperor Kniaz' Vasilii and

13. Taking advantage of popular demonstrations against the Poles who had flocked into Moscow in the wake of the pretender, noble conspirators broke into the tsar's palace on May 17, 1606, and murdered the False Dmitrii. Marina and her father, however, were not killed in 1606. Jerzy Mniszek died in 1613 and his daughter soon after her capture by the troops of Mikhail Romanov's regime in 1614.

14. Actually Fedor Ivanovich Mstislavskii. See Fletcher, above, p. 153.

15. Shuiskii was a member of one of the most distinguished princely families of Muscovy. He became a boiar in 1584. In 1591 he was head of the commission sent to Uglich to investigate the circumstances of the death of Dmitrii. Soon after the first False Dmitrii reached Moscow, Shuiskii was arrested for plotting against the new government. He was condemned to death but was pardoned at the last minute. He remained in Moscow and resumed his intrigues which culminated in the *coup d'etat* that overthrew the pretender on May 17, 1606. His patronymic was actually Ivanovich.

16. The coronation took place on June 1, 1606.

17. There is no evidence that Shuiskii was ordered to recognize the suzerainty of the king of Poland.

his kingly government, praising God for the continuance of the same.[18] But God denies their desires, hath yet a farther plague and scourge at hand for this perfidious and unhallowed generation. The Pole comes with his courageous and now fleshed army, assaults the fainthearted armies and towns of the Muscovites; many captains and gallant soldiers are slain on both sides. The Poles have the victory and conquest and possession of the Moscow again, many put to the sword. The Emperor Kniaz' Vasilii taken prisoner and divers nobles carried with him captives, kept straight and strongly in the castle of Vilna, the capital city of Lithuania.[19] They[20] now begin to insult and tyrannize more over the Russe than before; seizes of their goods, money, treasure, and wealth; many conveys great booties and treasure into Poland and Lithuania. But those hidden by the old Emperor Ivan Vasil'evich and Emperor Boris Fedorovich in such unknown secret places no doubt of remains yet much undiscovered by reason the parties trusted and employed therein were always made away. The Russe submits and becomes vassals and acknowledges the king of Poland their emperor and lord, and desire by a very authentical instrument and solemn manner, remaining forever in record of their crown, his son to come and be crowned their emperor and king and to live among them in the famous city of Moscow. Which the king would not hearken unto nor trust them with the person of his son;[21] neither would their nobles, being voluntary lords, do that crown that wrong to dispossess it of so hopeful a succession, nor the enemy so much honor, but to give them by their precedents from time to time such laws and rules as may subdue and govern at their wills until a farther settled resolution should be determined of. They put on patience and endured with much heart burning until they found a remedy for their more freedom. The inroads and invasions of the Tatar Krym troubled the Pole much; but the insurrections and in-

18. Horsey's contention has no basis in fact. Shuiskii's regime never exerted effective control over more than a fraction of the country. Its four-year existence was marked by continuous court intrigues and massive popular revolts.

19. Shuiskii was overthrown on July 7, 1610, by a popular demonstration stirred up by Zakharii Liapunov, not by the Polish invasion.

20. *They.* The in the original text.

21. The treaty outlining the conditions on which Wladyslaw was recognized as tsar was signed on August 17, 1610. The prince was to accept Orthodoxy and undertake to rule in cooperation with the boiar duma and the zemskii sobor. These conditions were unacceptable to Sigismund III who consequently would not allow his son to go to Moscow and take up his office.

cursions of the Lugovoi,[22] Nogai, and Mordvinian Tatars and Circassians and their princes and rulers, being good and hardy soldiers, all horsemen, as subjects long settled in the obedience of the Russe emperors and best used of all other nations by them, being now oppressed and straightened of their wonted good usage, hated the Pole and his usurped government, stood the Russe and themselves now in most opportune stead. They took head and arms in great numbers, beset the Poles, and so endangered their safeties, robbing, spoiling, and killing so many of them, as they were forced to hasten and pack them with their treasure and booties with as much expedition as they could. They freed the country of them.[23]

The nobility left, the clergy and all sorts of people took good courage and heart again; began to frame a settled estate and government among themselves; discharged the Poles and other strangers and disclaimed their subjection, not without some good cautions and conditions neither. Though loosening the bit, yet left some hold of the reins upon their bordered towns and territories of ancient belonging to the crown of Poland. Their last emperor, Kniaz' Vasilii Shuiskii,[24] much lamented, cannot be ransomed, kept still in a miserable prison. They bethink them of another emperor; so great a people and monarchy cannot subsist without a head and great governor. You have heard in the beginning of Boris Fedorovich his protectorship, loth to have any competitor greater than himself, the emperor's uncle, Nikita Romanovich, was bewitched, his tongue and speech, and after his life, taken away upon magic or ill imagination or by both. His eldest son, Fedor Nikitich, of a valiant and hopeful prince was shorn a friar and made a young bishop of Rostov, and now they say patriarch of Moscow,[25] who had a son before he was exposed to that monastery life. This his son is now placed and crowned Mikhail Fedorovich,[26] emperor and great duke of all Russia, in the succession of his ancestors, with the general applaud, like, and consent of all estates of the kingdom. God send him

22. A branch of the Cheremiss. See Fletcher, above, p. 200.

23. Russia was freed of Polish occupation by revolts which originated in the towns of northern and eastern Russia and in the south-central region of the country.

24. After his fall from power, Shuiskii was imprisoned and taken to Poland where he died on September 12, 1612.

25. On his return from Poland, Filaret (Fedor Nikitich Romanov) was consecrated patriarch on June 24, 1619.

26. He was chosen tsar by a zemskii sobor on February 21, 1613, and crowned on July 11 of the same year.

long to reign with much more safety, happiness, peace, and better success than his predecessors hath done. For he cometh upon great disadvantage of all other, for want of treasure, all being confiscated, and other royal means to uphold and maintain his crown and government, and yet goes on and makes it as feasible with as much dexterity as the grave advice of his holy father's great experience and time will permit. Whose pleasure was, out of his love, in his young years, to have me make in the Slavonian character, in Latin words and phrases, a kind of grammar, wherein he took great delight; and as I hear say, which I cannot omit to repeat so worthy a part and report, the famous company of English merchants that trade those countries hath offered him, the said emperor, of late, the loan of a hundred thousand pounds towards the supply of his majesty's great occasions, a remembrance of their thankfulness very commendable for the love and favor his ancestors hath always showed towards them.

How the estate of things since and now stands in those countries I must refer you to the relation of Sir Thomas Smythe,[27] sometime employed there, and especially to Sir John Meyrick his knowledge, a man of great employment and long experience in those parts.[28] Some ampassages hath interpassed of late years more abusively than commodious, only to serve private ends, as the common report goes.

XXV

Thus, fearing I have wearied your patience with the tediousness of these collections, though much more might be said and amplified, have forborne to insert and add some proper inferences for explanation of such names, parentheses, and terms[1] as you have not been

27. Smythe (1558?–1625) was governor of the Russia Company and the first governor of the East India Company. He served as governor of the latter company from its inception to 1621, except for the periods of 1600–3 and 1606–7. His mission to Russia was in 1604–5. His account, *Sir Thomas Smith's Voiage and Entertainment in Rushia,* was published in 1604 (*DNB*).

28. Meyrick (d. 1638) was successively agent, member, and governor of the Russia Company. He was ambassador in the early seventeenth century and was knighted in 1614 (*DNB*).

1. *terms:* the manuscript is torn; the only letter present is the "t."

used to read, especially in so scribbled a hand, leaving it to your more mature deliberation to conceive, not without admiration, in regard no history makes mention of the like, of the strange passages which God, in his divine pleasure, doth permit for the sins of the world to be perpetrated in the inequity and influence of wicked man's so short a time.

Since changing another course, I have lived for above thirty years' space in that fruitful region of Buckinghamshire, serving in all commissions with my best endeavors and painstaking to discharge the duty of an honest justice of peace, high sheriff of the same, wherein I have found much favor and love both from judges and justices and gentlemen and of all other sorts, giving the magistrates but their due, who[2] govern religiously with great humanity, good discretion, and judgment, through God's blessing the influence and extraordinary painstaking and preaching of the Gospel through the whole country, by most worthy, learned, godly, and holy divines, planted and placed among them. God prosper them, and long may it so continue!

Having also served above thirty years' continuance in parliament, the experience of this wicked world, both at home and abroad, makes me now the more willing to live in a better. In the mean I must be contented, as an old ship that hath done good service, to be laid up in the dock unrigged, and to say truly that all the known nations and kingdoms of the world are not comparable for happiness to this thrice blessed nation and angelical kingdom of Canaan, our England. And so I take leave of all other experience and knowledge in this life, and hold of this true *adagium: Si Christum sis, nihil est si cetera non sis.*

2. *who* omitted in the original text.

Reference Matter

Reference Matter

Glossary and Index of Russian Terms

Altyn (pl. *altyny*): a monetary unit equal to 6 *den'gi* (200 *den'gi* = 1 ruble), 117, 162

Arbuz: watermelon, 117

Armiak: a cloth tunic, 81

Beluga: white sturgeon, 120, 122

Beschest'e: dishonor, 145

Beza: perhaps *oboz,* a portable fortification, 185

Biriuch: herald, 324

Blagoslovi, Vladyka: "Bless me, Lord," 220, 221

Blaveshina Collicalits: perhaps the Bell Tower of Ivan the Great in the Moscow Kremlin, 312

Boarstva duma (or *boiarskaia duma*): Boiar Council, 153

Boiar. *See Boiarin*

Boiare vladychnye: noble servitors of members of the church hierarchy, 212

Boiarin (pl. *boiare*): boiar, member of the highest rank of the Boiar Council; any member of the highest court nobility, 143, 145, 153, 168, 170, 190, 212

Boiarin koniushii. See Koniushii

Boiarskii: pertaining to a boiar, 243

Bol'shie dvoriane. See Dvorianin

Bol'shoi prikhod: literally, "great income"; state revenue chancellery, 158, 160, 161, 162, 163

Bol'shoi voevoda. See Voevoda

Bozhii dom: cemetery building in which corpses were gathered before burial, 235

Buivol: bison, 324

Bulat: Damascus steel, 198, 328?

Bulatnyi: of fine Damascus steel, 183

Charka: cup, 231, 241

Chernye popy: "black priests"; priests who have taken monastic vows, 216

Chetvert' (pl. *chetverti*): (1) a dry measure which, in the late sixteenth century, was equal to about 4 puds or 144 pounds of rye, 117, 158, 159;

373

Kolymaga: a heavy carriage, 230

Kon' (pl. *koni*): horse, 197

Koniushennye slobody: villages which were assigned to the master of the horse to provide provisions for the tsar's stables and revenue for the master himself, 144

Koniushii: master of the horse, 144, 239

Konnik: literally, a cavalryman. *See Koniushii*

Korchma: tavern, 57

Kreshchenie: Epiphany, 175

Krest'ianin (pl. *krest'iane*): peasant, 146, 245

Krestnoe tselovanie: "kissing the cross," a form of oath-taking, 174

Krestnyi d'iak: literally, "clerk of the cross"; in Fletcher's usage, a clergyman attached to the tsar's chapel, 236

Krym: the Crimea, 111, 113, 115, 116, 124, 140, 150, 179, 191, 192, 193, 195, 196, 199, 200, 223, 264, 265, 270, 271, 272, 283, 287, 288, 289, 290, 311, 329, 362, 366

Kvas: a fermented drink, made from water and rye or rye bread, 75, 225, 242

Letach vechshe (perhaps *letuchaia veksha*): flying squirrel, 122

Letnik: a woman's light outer garment with long wide sleeves, 244

Levyi polk: regiment forming the left wing, 181

Liakhi: Poles (archaic), 191

Los': elk, 119, 121, 202

Luchina: wood splinter used for lighting purposes, 119

Lugovoi (pl. *lugovye*): pertaining to meadows; used of the Cheremiss who lived on the low or east bank of the Volga, 200, 367

Micholsea crest: probably the Cathedral of the Archangel Michael in the Moscow Kremlin, 276

Mirza: literally, "prince's son"; a Tatar noble, 193, 196, 200, 273, 330. *See also Divei-mirza.*

Molitva: prayer, 215

Molodaia kniaginia: young princess, 231

Molodoi kniaz': young prince, 231. *See also kniaz'*

Morzh: walrus, 33, 57, 121

Muzhik (pl. *muzhiki*): peasant; common man (often pejorative), 75, 76, 78, 79, 120, 146, 168, 169, 171, 172, 177, 178, 244

Nagoi: naked, 168

Nagornyi (pl. *nagornye*): pertaining to mountains; used of the Cheremiss who lived on the hilly or west bank of the Volga, 200

Nariadnyi voevoda. See Voevoda

Nasady: river boats with raised sides, 51

Nemets (pl. *nemtsy*): German; foreigner in general, 180

Nerukotvornyi: "not made with hands" (used of icons), 234

Novremanskoy *Lopari:* according to Fletcher, Norwegian (*Norvezhskie*) Lapps, 204

Obednia: Mass, 221, 237

Obrok (pl. *obroki*): quitrent paid in money or kind, 158

Odnoriadka: long tunic without a collar, 81, 243, 244

Okhaben': long outer garment with slits under the sleeves and a folding rectangular collar, 243

Olen': reindeer, 121, 202, 205

Opashen': man's long outer garment with short wide sleeves, worn in summer, 244

Oprichnik (pl. *oprichniki*): member of the *oprichnina*, 139

Oprichnina: that part of the Muscovite state that Ivan IV set aside as his private principality in the years 1565–72; the military units that formed the army of that principality, 275

Osetrina: sturgeon, 122

Otets dukhovnyi: "spiritual father," confessor, 236

Ozero (pl. *ozera*): lake, 115, 122, 267

Palach (pl. *palachi*): executioner, 165, 278

Pech' (pl. *pechi*): stove, 242

Piatidesiatskie: commanders of units of 50 soldiers, 182

Pochivated: from *potchevat'*, to show

honor or to entertain, 321, 325

Podat': a general term for direct taxes (see p. 159, n. 4), 159, 160

Po grekham: according to one's sins, 219

Polk (pl. *polki*): regiment, 183, 185

Pomest'e: an estate, held on condition of service to the crown, 140, 144

Pomestnaia chetvert' (or *Pomestnyi prikaz*): the chancellery responsible for the distribution of lands held on service tenure, 147

Pop (pl. *popy*): priest, 203, 206, 214, 215, 216

Portki: pants, 81

Posol'skaia chetvert' (or *Posol'skii prikaz*): chancellery of foreign affairs, 144, 146

Postel'nichii: lord chamberlain, 240

Pozhalovat': to grant or favor, 218

Pravezh: the practice of publicly whipping a defaulting debtor on each of a specified number of days in order to force him to meet his obligation, 164, 175

Pravyi polk: regiment forming the right wing, 181

Prechase, shisivoy nemshoy: presumably *Inozemnyi* (or *Inozemskii*) *prikaz*, the chancellery that registered and paid the salaries of the foreign soldiers in Muscovite service, 162

Precheste. *See Prechistaia*

Prechista. *See Prechistaia*

Prechistaia: "most pure" (in reference to the Virgin Mary), 129, 209, 226, 233, 236, 312

Pristav (pl. *pristavy*): (1) an official sent to welcome foreign ambassadors, 68; (2) a bailiff, 174

Protopop (pl. *protopopy*): archpriest, dean of a cathedral, 206, 216

Pshenitsa: wheat, 117

Pud:= 36 pounds, 118, 119

Pushkarskii: pertaining to cannon (refers to the *Pushkarskii prikaz*, artillery chancellery), 162

Pytka: torture, 150, 151, 176, 292

Raspop: former priest, 215

Razboinyi prikaz: the government department responsible for bringing brigands to justice, 162

Razriad: used by Fletcher to designate the director of the *Razriadnyi prikaz*; also used of the chancellery itself, 147, 157, 162, 178, 183

Razriadnaia chetvert' (or *Razriadnyi prikaz*): the chancellery that kept records of the servitors of the state and their duties and directed the organization and supply of the army, 147

Reka: river, 50

Riasa: cassock, 213

Ribazuba: walrus tusk, 121

Rosomakha: wolverine, 23

Rubashka: shirt, 81

Rusnoy polyskoy: refers perhaps to the *peredovoi polk* or advance regiment of an army, 181

Ryba belaia: white salmon, 122

Rynda (pl. *ryndy*): a member of the ceremonial bodyguard that accompanied the tsar on great occasions of state, 303

Sbornoe voskresen'e: the first Sunday in Lent, 175

Ser'gi: earrings, 243

Sevriuga: a kind of sturgeon, 120, 122

Shapka: cap, 243

Shestoper: a mace or scepter, 184

Shliapa: hat, 244

Shuba (pl. *shuby*): fur coat, 81, 244, 338

Skoryi pomoshchnik: speedy helper, 226

Slava: glory, 172

Sliuda: mica, 79, 121

Sloboda: settlement (used in reference to the Aleksandrovskaia Sloboda, the headquarters of the oprichnina), 70, 278, 283, 313

Sobor: council or assembly, 135, 136, 137, 169

Sotskii: commander of a unit of 100 soldiers; a city official, 151

Sotskii starets. See Sotskii starosta

Sotskii starosta: elected local official, one rank below the *gubnoi starosta*, 149, 173

Srednie dvoriane. See Dvorianin

Starosta (pl. *starosty*): elder; alderman, 151

Stoianie (pl. *stoianiia*): probably refers

to the *Andreevo stoianie*, the service celebrated on the Thursday before Palm Sunday, 235

Stollie: probably Stolovaia Palata, 136

Storozhevoi polk: rearguard regiment, 182

Streletskii (pl. *streletskie*): pertaining to *strel'tsy* or musketeers, 162

Strel'tsy: musketeers, 162, 180, 184

Stremiannye strel'tsy: mounted musketeers, 180

Striapchii (pl. *striapchie*): a member of the fifth rank of court servitors, 240

Sud'ia: judge, 149

Sukhar': dry crust of bread, 184

Sviataia voda: holy water, 237

Sviatoi: holy, 268

Syn boiarskii (pl. *syny,* or more commonly, *deti boiarskie*). See *Deti boiarskie*

Taf'ia: skullcap, 242, 243

Telega (pl. *telegi*): cart, 333

Tiaglo: a general word meaning the sum total of fiscal obligations and labor and services imposed by the government on tax-paying citizens, 159, 160

Tolokno: oat flour, 184

Troitsa: the Trinity; in this case, a reference to the Holy Trinity-St. Sergius Monastery north of Moscow, 217, 272, 284

Tsar, 132, 175

Tsarevich: tsar's son, 277, 280, 286, 292, 293, 294, 300, 321, 358

Tsarskiia Dveri: the "Royal Doors," the doors in the center of the iconostasis, separating the Sancta Sanctorum from the main part of a Russian church, 220, 222

Ubrus: kerchief, shawl, 243

Udel'nyi kniaz' (pl. *udel'nye kniaz'ia*): appanage prince, 138, 140, 143, 145

Vaghnoy: according to Fletcher, a kind of root, 117

Vechernia: vespers, 221, 238

Velikii kniaz': grand prince, 166, 264

Verii: according to Fletcher, "praise," 222

Verst: two-thirds of a mile, 112, 113, 115, 116, 121, 144, 171, 203

Vladyka (pl. *vladyki*): lord; the form of address used for a member of the church hierarchy, 206, 211

Voevoda (pl. *voevody*): military commander, 145, 181, 182, 186, 270, 273, 278, 334, 335, 349, 355, 356, 364

bol'shoi voevoda: commander of the great or central corps of an army and commander-in-chief of the whole force, 181, 182

nariadnyi voevoda: artillery commander, 182

voevoda gulavoy: according to Fletcher, the commander of a guliai-gorod, 182, 185

Votchina: estate held in absolute ownership; in this case, the tsar's own estates, 148, 158

Vypis': a document, especially an extract from a longer document, 174

Vyt': a tax assessment unit of land, equal to between 65 and 81 acres (Fletcher uses the word to describe a dry measure of grain), 159

Zautrenia: matins, 220, 237

Zemshchina: that part of Muscovite territory that was not incorporated into the oprichnina, 275

Zemskii (fem. *zemskaia;* pl. *zemskie*): pertaining to land (1) used by Fletcher to refer to the residents of the zemshchina, 139; (2) *zemskii* house or *zemskii dvor:* the chancellery that administered the city of Moscow, 151, 168; (3) used also of women's apparel, probably instead of *zhenskii,* "woman's" 243, 244

Zhalovan'e: grant; salary, 158

Zhena boiarskaia: boiar's wife; noblewoman, 243

Zhilets (pl. *zhil'tsy*): a member of the lowest rank of Moscow service personnel, 237, 240

Zhil'tsy, striapchie. See *Zhilets; Striapchii*

Zipun: an outer garment similar to a kaftan, 243

Zlata Baba: legendary rock formation on the lower Ob River, supposed to represent an old woman, 202

General Index

Abramov, Sapun, 147, 156

Adams, Clement: contribution of, to Chancellor's account, 4

Adashev, Aleksei Fedorovich: adviser to Ivan IV, 25

Alfer'ev, Roman Vasil'evich: member of duma, 156

Andreevich, Vladimir, prince of Staritsa: daughter of, marries Prince Magnus, 276, 277; poisoned, 276; mentioned, 54

Andrew I, king of Hungary, 126

Anna, wife of Stephen Bathory: Horsey's interview with, 353–54

Barker, William, 349

Barne, Sir George, 319, 321, 339, 360

Bathory, Stephen: repulsed in the siege of Pskov, 141, 186; military ability of, 187–88; defeats Ivan IV, 276, 277, 287; threatens to invade Moscow, 290; mentioned, 328, 353

Beckman, Reynold, 340

Bekbulatovich, Simeon: tsar of Russia, 166–67, 275; marries daughter of Ivan Mstislavskii, 275

Bela I, king of Hungary, 126

Bela II, king of Hungary, 126

Belozerskaia, N. A.: translates Horsey's *Travels*, 260–61

Bel'skii, Bogdan: favorite of Ivan IV, 304, 306; confined to Kazan', 322; flees to Poland, 331; conspires to aid the False Dmitrii, 362–63

Bel'skii, Ivan Dmitrievich (Dmitrii Fedorovich): stratagem of, against the Crimean Tatars, 192–93

Berkh, V. N.: translates Jenkinson's account, 45

Berosus: cited by Fletcher, 123

Berry, Lloyd E.: cited, xx, xxi; edits Fletcher's *Russe Commonwealth*, 108

Bertie, Peregrine, Lord Willoughby de Eresby: sent to aid Henry of Navarre, 344

Bezobrazov, Istoma Osipovich: chamberlain, 240

Birkin, Rodion: attends Ivan IV, 306